The Complete Book of
Pregnancy and Childbirth

SHEILA KITZINGER

The Complete Book of
Pregnancy and Childbirth

NEW EDITION

Black-and-white photography
by Marcia May

Alfred A. Knopf • New York • 1999

Library of Congress Cataloging-in-Publication Data
Kitzinger, Sheila
    The complete book of pregnancy and childbirth/Sheila Kitzinger.
    —Rev. and expanded ed.
    p.   cm.
    Includes index
    ISBN 0-679-45028-9
    1. Pregnancy—Popular works.   2. Childbirth—Popular works.
I. Title.
RG525.K518   1996   96-17649
618.2—dc20   CIP

Manufactured in the United States of America
First Published in 1980
Revised Edition 1989
This revised and expanded edition 1996
Reprinted Twice
Fourth Printing, June 1999

The Complete Book of Pregnancy and Childbirth
was conceived, edited, and designed by
Dorling Kindersley Limited, 9 Henrietta Street,
London WC2E 8PS

FOR THE REVISED AND EXPANDED EDITION
Project Editors **Charyn Jones** and **Heather Jones**
Senior Art Editor **Cathy Shilling**
Design Assistant **Nathalie Hennequin**
Production Controller **Meryl Silbert**
Managing Editor **Gwen Edmonds**
Senior Managing Art Editor **Lynne Brown**
Editorial Director **Jackie Douglas**
Art Director **Peter Luff**

Additional color photography **Andy Crawford**
Illustrations **Joanne Acty**, **Karen Cochrane**, and **Halli Verrinder**

FOR THE REVISED AND EXPANDED U.S. EDITION
Editor **Jennifer Bernstein**
Consultant **Penny Simkin**

Reproduction by Colourscan, Singapore
Printed by R. R. Donnelly & Sons, Crawfordsville, Indiana

Contents

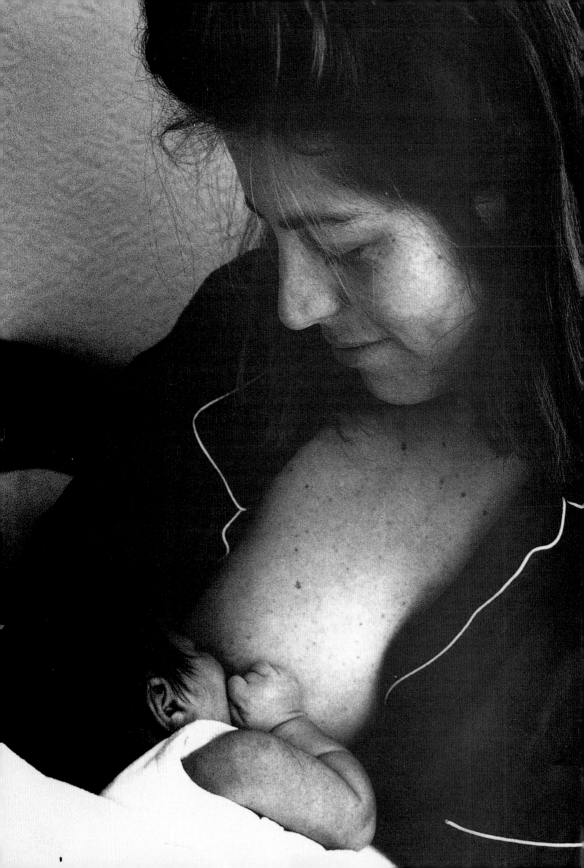

Introduction

When I first started to teach and counsel pregnant women in the sixties, there was little birth education around. For a small minority of women there were breathing and relaxation exercises taught by physiotherapists (who then had no training for helping women in childbirth) and talks by midwives about "what to expect."

There was a handful of books written by the pioneers: Grantly Dick-Read, Kathleen Vaughan, Minnie Randall, Helen Heardman, Velvovsk, and Lamaze. Though some discussed the fear of childbirth, there was nothing about the socially inculcated lack of confidence we felt in our bodies and in ourselves, nor about the pressure on women by a powerful medical system to surrender themselves to it as passive patients. It seemed that all we could hope for was to put on as good a performance as possible and to be told "well done."

After the birth of my first child, when I started teaching for what is now the National Childbirth Trust, I remember talking to obstetricians from the USSR who had introduced psychoprophylaxis (a system of training for labor based on breathing techniques) into some of their bigger hospitals and were actually proud because "there is now no noise in the labor ward." It was supposed to be a great achievement – to silence women!

When psychoprophylaxis was first introduced in Britain from France, one woman told me that the day after a grueling labor involving drugs and the use of forceps her childbirth teacher had shown up at her bedside and commented: "You didn't do too well!" In those days, if you needed painkilling drugs or help with the birth, you were made to feel that you had failed. The choice was between having doctors take over completely and putting on a solo performance without support or encouragement from professionals.

Remarkable changes have now taken place – largely due to women in the childbirth movement who have joined together across continents. It is now acknowledged that women have a right to full and accurate information about their bodies and to participate in all decisions made about them. *Pregnancy and Childbirth* reflects the many changes that have come about because we refuse to remain ignorant of what doctors are doing to us. It is an expression of women's courage and growing self-confidence, and of the ways in which we have reached out to each other to explore and understand those experiences which we share in our lives.

In order to take an active part in giving birth rather than submit passively to delivery, it helps to prepare yourself well in advance, understanding how to adapt to the work being done by your uterus, using breathing, relaxation techniques, change of position, massage, and focused concentration to "get in tune with" contractions. So there is a good deal of practical material in the book on the various

Opposite
The birth of a baby is a normal biological process. Yet it is more than that. Giving birth and caring for a baby is an act of love.

methods to do this. It is not just a matter of learning exercises. There is a harmony and rhythm about a natural labor: with the wave of each contraction you are swept on toward the birth of the baby in a pattern that transforms birth into a process greater than all its separate parts, one in which all the techniques you have practiced are submerged by the total amazing experience.

The book describes the choices which are available so that you can decide how you would like to have your baby, the kind of setting and care you prefer, and how you wish your baby to be welcomed into the world. I include suggestions on talking with your doctor, how to ask about all the things that worry you, and how you can share in the decisions about yourself and your baby. The book also sets out to give a map of the route through pregnancy and labor and out the other side, explaining who does what to you and why, and what happens when things are not straightforward. In doing this I have used some of the words and phrases that you may see written on your medical chart or hear used by doctors or midwives, so that you will understand them when you meet them, but the main focus is on experiential aspects of birth – how it feels.

The book is threaded through with recognition of the father's importance for his partner and baby and suggestions as to how he can help most effectively during pregnancy, labor, and the time after the birth. A baby is bound to change a couple's way of life, their feelings about each other, and the kind of partnership they have. The man, as well as the woman, often faces emotional challenges, and this is rarely acknowledged in our society. So another thing that I have done is to focus on the experience of childbirth for him.

Most new parents gain confidence and find it easiest to have "conversations" with their baby when there are no rules to be obeyed and no standards to live up to, when they can take the baby into bed with them and stroke, hold, and cuddle their newborn as much as they wish. In this book I hope to show how a couple, or a woman alone, can create the kind of setting and atmosphere for birth, whether at home or in the hospital, that nurtures relationships.

Pregnancy and childbirth are normal life processes, not illnesses. You feel the incredible surge of life moving inside you, the ripening of your body heavy with fruit deep inside it, and then at last the flood of vitality as labor starts and your uterus contracts in wave after wave, bringing your baby into your arms. It is exciting, awe-inspiring, and deeply satisfying. At the same time, you grow up a bit, learn more about yourself and your partner, and develop understanding. I hope this book will help readers savor the intense reality of the experience of childbearing and enjoy it to the fullest.

NOTES TO THE READER

It is always difficult when writing about babies to know whether to use "he" or "she." I have mainly used a mixture of "he" and "she," since babies are people with their own budding personalities right from the start. I hope that the reader will not find this too awkward, and if there is a bias toward "she" in the text, note that my five babies were all girls, so it comes naturally to me.

Throughout the text all references to research findings are marked with an asterisk (*); this indicates that the works in which the research findings have been published are listed in Appendix 2, in order, under the appropriate page number.

AUTHOR'S ACKNOWLEDGMENTS

A number of people have contributed to this book, bringing their knowledge and special skills. I want to thank particularly Penny Simkin in Seattle, who read every word of the typescript, commenting on it for the benefit of American readers, and made many helpful suggestions. If there are any mistakes, they are not Penny's! She is meticulous and utterly committed to the cause of making birth better for women everywhere.

Kay Millar, Active Birth teacher in Oxford, has been superb, too. She oversaw all the exercise sequences taken in the photographic studio, ensuring they were not only accurate but clear. Marcia May took the wonderful photographs of birth. It is lovely to have a photographer who is so in tune with my beliefs. Vreni Booth, who teaches movement classes based on the Feldenkrais method, has helped me rethink postnatal exercises in a constructive way.

Nicky Leap, the midwife in some of the birth photographs here, is one of the most innovative thinkers and courageous practitioners in midwifery today. I value my discussions with Dr. Michel Odent. They always stimulate lateral thinking, as he raises important questions that need to be answered. I am also grateful to Professor Lesley Page of Queen Charlotte's Hospital, London, for the many times that we share our thoughts about the future of midwifery, and its meaning for women and families.

In addition, I should like to thank Dr. Iain Chalmers, former Director of the British National Perinatal Epidemiology Unit, now Director of the Cochrane Institute, for all the work he has done to base obstetric practice on scientific evidence rather than medical "hunches," and to present the benefits and risks of different practices, so that women can make up their own minds about what they want. I have drawn heavily on the *Cochrane Pregnancy and Childbirth Database* for the new material in the book.

My birth activist colleagues, Beverley Lawrence Beech of the Association for Improvements in the Maternity Services, and Janet Balaskas, who created the Active Birth Movement, both contribute to my own vitality by their strength and energy.

In the writing of this book, I owe a great deal to my daughter, Tess, for her clarity of thinking, her understanding, and her skills with the computer. As I write this we have her three-day-old baby, Josh, who was born at home, under water, as were her other two children, in an atmosphere of love and celebration.

Pregnancy week by week

This is a week-by-week guide to what may be happening to you and your baby throughout pregnancy. As different women's pregnancies develop at different rates, do not expect to be at exactly the same stage for the week described. Read the information for the two weeks either side, too. Since pregnancy is dated medically from the first day of your last period, the record begins with what is termed the third week of a 40-week pregnancy, the week of conception.

WEEK 3

You have ovulated and an egg is traveling along one of the two fallopian tubes toward your uterus. During intercourse one of the millions of sperm your partner has ejaculated has fertilized the egg while still in the fallopian tube.

Your baby is a cluster of cells which multiply rapidly as they continue the journey along the fallopian tube.

WEEK 4

You have probably not noticed anything different, though some women have a strange, metallic taste in their mouths.

The fertilized egg has arrived in your uterus and, after floating in the uterine cavity for about three days, has embedded itself in the uterine lining. It is nourished from blood vessels in the lining of your uterus, and the placenta begins to form around it.

WEEK 5

You are beginning to think that you may be pregnant. Your period is late, but you can't be sure, because you may feel as though it is about to start at any time. Your breasts are slightly enlarged and tender and you may find you need to pass urine more often than usual.

The embryo is about ⅒ in (2 mm) long and would be visible to the naked eye by now. Its spine is beginning to form and the brain has two lobes.

WEEK 6

You may be feeling nauseous first thing in the morning or when you are cooking a meal. Your vagina has become a bluish or violet color. From the 6th day after your period was

due it should be possible to find out by a urine test whether or not you are pregnant. Your uterus is now the size of a tangerine.

The baby has developed a head and trunk, and a rudimentary brain has formed. Tiny limb buds are starting to appear. By the end of this week its circulation is beginning to function. The jaw and mouth are developing and 10 dental buds are growing in each jaw.

WEEK 7

You may sometimes feel dizzy or faint when you stand for a long time. Your breasts are noticeably larger and small nodules called Montgomery's tubercles may appear on the areolae, while your nipples may become more prominent. Pregnancy can be confirmed by a vaginal examination.

The limb buds have developed rapidly and now look like tiny arms and legs. At the end of these limbs are small indentations which will later become fingers and toes. The spinal cord and brain are now almost complete and the head is assuming a human shape. The baby is now about ½ in (1.3 cm) long.

WEEK 8

You may find that you have "gone off" certain foods and that you particularly fancy others which were not your favorite foods before. Many pregnant women can no longer drink alcohol, even if they previously enjoyed it, and a dislike of cigarettes or tobacco smoke is common. Your hair may seem less manageable than usual. You may also have a slight vaginal discharge. This is quite normal as long as it is not irritating or painful.

The baby now has all its main organs in a rudimentary form. The eyes and ears are growing. The face is taking on a human shape, and the baby is just under an inch (2.5 cm) long.

WEEK 9

You may notice changes in your skin because of pregnancy hormones in your system. Any wrinkles you have may be less obvious. Your gums may be softening because of these hormones, and you need to be careful about dental hygiene now and through the rest of the pregnancy. The thyroid gland in your neck may be more prominent.

The baby's limbs are developing very rapidly, and fingers and toes are beginning to be defined on the hands and feet. The baby is moving about gently to exercise its muscles, although you cannot feel it. At this point the baby weighs only about as much as a grape.

WEEK 10

Your uterus has expanded to the size of an orange, but is still hidden away within your pelvis. You should be wearing a bra with good support by now. If you buy a bra that fits your breasts but is adjustable to allow for later chest expansion, you may not need to get another size during the rest of your pregnancy.

The placenta, to which the baby is attached, begins to produce progesterone in a process which is completed by the end of the 14th week, when the progesterone produced is sufficient for the placenta to take over the function of the corpus luteum. The baby's ankles and wrists are formed, and fingers and toes are clearly visible. The baby has grown to about 1¾ in (4.5 cm) long.

WEEK 11

If you have been nauseous during the last weeks, the sickness may gradually lessen from now onward. The amount of blood circulating through your body has started to increase, and will go on increasing until about the 30th week. You should be thinking about arranging childbirth classes, as they often get booked up early.

Your baby's testicles or ovaries have formed, as have all of its major organs. These organs will not develop much further, but will continue to grow in the uterus. The baby is relatively safe from the risk of congenital abnormalities from the end of this week.

WEEK 12

You will probably have your first prenatal visit this week. The doctor or midwife will be able to feel the uterus by external examination, as it has risen above your pelvis. Arrangements are made for future appointments, probably once a month until you are 32 weeks pregnant. At each visit ask about anything that is bothering you.

The baby's head is becoming more rounded and it has eyelids. Its muscles are developing and it is moving about inside the uterus much more. It is now about 2 in (6.5 cm) long but still weighs only ½ oz (18 g).

WEEK 13

If you have had early-morning sickness this may have gone by the end of this week. From now on your uterus will be enlarging at a regular and noticeable rate.

The bag of water cushions the baby from bumps, keeps it at a constant warm temperature, and enables it to move freely, turn its head, stretch, and bounce around.

WEEK 14

You are less tired than you were at the beginning of pregnancy and probably feel fit and active. You may notice a dark line (the linea nigra) down the center of your abdomen. This will begin to fade after the baby is born. Your nipples and the area around them are also starting to darken. Your uterus is the size of a large grapefruit.

The baby has eyebrows and a small amount of hair has appeared on its head. Its heart can be heard by ultrasound. The baby drinks some of the amniotic fluid and can pass urine. It is now receiving all of its nourishment from the placenta and measures about 3¾ in (8–9 cm) in length.

WEEK 15

Your clothes will now be getting too tight for you. It is best not to try to cram yourself into tight jeans. To cope with the increased amount of blood circulating in your body and the baby's need for oxygen, your enlarged heart has increased its output by 20 percent.

The hair on your baby's head and brows is becoming coarser. If it has a gene for dark hair, the pigment cells of the hair follicles are beginning to produce black pigment.

WEEK 16

You feel butterflies in your stomach that might be the baby moving. Your waistline will be starting to disappear. If you have not already done so, book childbirth education classes. An "early-bird" class might be available to discuss diet, exercise, posture, emotions, and health.

The baby is now completely formed. From now on its time in the uterus will be spent growing and maturing until it is able to survive independently. Lanugo (fine down) is starting to form all over the baby, following the whorled pattern of the skin. The baby is 6¾ in (16 cm) long and weighs nearly 5 oz (135 g).

WEEK 17

You may find you are sweating more than usual (due to the extra blood in your system) and also that your nose feels congested. This is common in pregnancy and will cease after the birth. Vaginal secretions may also increase.

The growing baby has pushed the top of the uterus to halfway between your pubic bone and your navel. From now on the baby weighs more than its placenta. It is probably aware of – and may be startled by – loud sounds outside your body.

WEEK 18

If this is your first baby, you may feel the first prods, which are definitely nothing to do with indigestion! At last you know that there really is a baby in there! Trouble with sleeping at night will be helped by increasing the number of pillows you use to support yourself.

Measuring about 8 in (20 cm) long, your baby is now testing its reflexes. Babies often move especially energetically in the evening

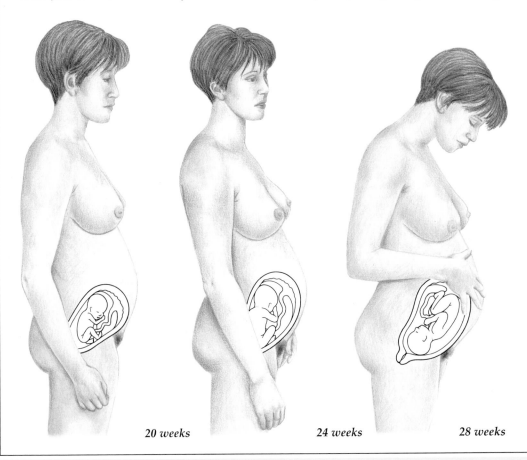

20 weeks   *24 weeks*   *28 weeks*

and bounce around like a cork in water. As well as kicking, the baby is grasping and sucking. Some babies find their thumbs and are confirmed thumb-suckers even before they are born.

WEEK 19

Now is not too early to start practicing deep relaxation and steady, rhythmic breathing. Set aside some time each day for this. You may notice that you are putting weight on your buttocks as well as your abdomen.

Buds for permanent teeth are forming behind those for the baby's milk teeth that have already formed.

WEEK 20

You will notice your baby being more and more active (often in the evenings), and you may even be able to see some of its movements. The growing uterus is pushing

up against your lungs and pressing your tummy outwards. Your navel may suddenly pop out and stay that way until after the birth. Your chest (rather than breasts) has expanded and if you do not already have an adjustable bra now is the time to buy one.

The baby is now about 10 in (25 cm) long. Sebum from the sebaceous glands mixes with skin cells and begins to form the protective vernix, which clings to the lanugo all over the baby's skin, especially on the hairier parts and in the creases.

WEEK 21

You may start having heartburn (a form of indigestion which is felt as a burning sensation in the lower part of the chest). You may also bring up small amounts of acid fluid. Ask your doctor to recommend some antacid tablets for you to take.

The baby weighs just under 1 lb (450 g). It is still moving about freely in the amniotic

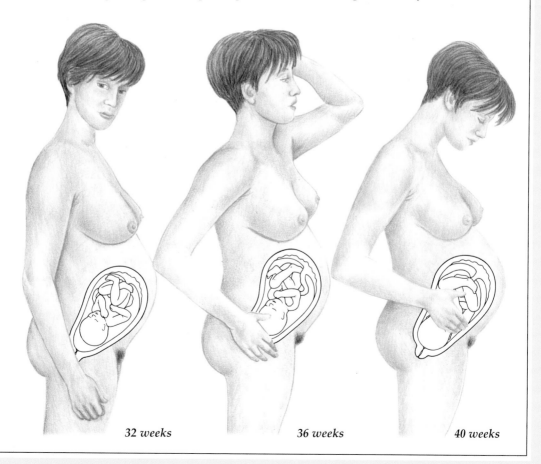

32 weeks   *36 weeks*   *40 weeks*

fluid and can be felt kicking, sometimes high in your tummy, at other times low down near your pubis.

WEEK 22

Your gums may be swelling because of the pregnancy hormones in your system.

The baby's fingernails are forming. It is settling into a pattern of activity and sleep. It is most active while you are resting, and you may feel you have a jumping bean inside you.

WEEK 23

The different parts of the baby can be felt (palpated) through your abdominal wall. You may feel a stitchlike pain at times down the side of your tummy; this is the uterine muscle stretching and the pain will probably go away after you have had a rest.

Braxton Hicks "rehearsal" contractions may be more noticeable, gripping and massaging the baby regularly. The baby's fingernails are almost fully formed.

WEEK 24

Another visit to the doctor or midwife – by now the baby's heart can be heard through a stethoscope or a special fetal trumpet. The top of your uterus (the fundus) now reaches to just above your navel.

The baby is growing rapidly – it is now about 13 in (32 cm) long and weighs over 1 lb (0.5 kg). Although its vital organs are maturing, its lungs are unlikely to be sufficiently developed for survival outside the uterus.

WEEK 25

You may get cramps now and later. Avoid pointing your toes down. The baby may also be pressing against your bladder, causing you to want to pass urine.

The baby's bone centers are beginning to harden. Tiny veins are visible through the skin.

WEEK 26

You may notice streaks in your skin where it has been stretched from underneath. These fade after birth.

When you speak your voice goes down into your body, and your baby can hear you. The baby's body is covered with fine downy hairs and the skin is beginning to change: instead of being paper-thin and transparent, it is gradually becoming opaque.

WEEK 27

You will be putting on weight fairly regularly now until about the 36th week. It may be a good idea to start thinking about what to get for the baby before you become so big that shopping becomes an unpleasant chore.

The baby's skin is very wrinkled, but it is protected and nourished by a layer of vernix.

WEEK 28

Colostrum may leak from your breasts. From now on you will probably be visiting the doctor every two weeks. If you are Rhesus negative, an antibody check is done.

Your baby's heartbeat speeds up when you speak and he or she can recognize your voice after birth. The baby is about 14 in (38 cm) long and weighs around 2 lb (0.9 kg).

WEEK 29

You probably feel as if all your internal organs are being crowded out by the baby. There is pressure on your diaphragm, liver, stomach, and intestines.

By now the baby's head is more or less in proportion with the rest of its body.

WEEK 30

It is important to remember to maintain good posture when you are standing or sitting, even though the weight of the baby seems to be dragging you off balance.

The baby is probably very aware of the Braxton Hicks contractions, coming at regular intervals, even when you do not notice them.

WEEK 31

You may get very breathless when you climb stairs or exert yourself.

However breathless you feel, the baby is getting enough oxygen through the placenta. It now weighs 4 lb (1.8 kg). If the weather is hot or you have eaten a heavy meal the baby may be drowsy.

WEEK 32

At each visit the doctor or midwife feels the baby's position. He or she will also assess the baby's rate of growth and check its heart.

The baby is 16 in (42 cm) long. It is perfectly formed but the fat reserves beneath its skin are only gradually laid down. If the baby were to be born at this time, it would still need to be cared for in an incubator.

WEEK 33

You may be able to distinguish the baby's bottom from a foot or knee. You feel its movements more as prods and kicks – it may be too big now to swoop around in the amniotic fluid.

Your baby has probably adopted the most usual head-down ("vertex" or "cephalic") position, in which it will now stay until the birth. From now on, lying flat on your back may make you dizzy.

WEEK 34

The baby can differentiate between dark and light, and is bathed in a red glow when sunlight is on your tummy.

WEEK 35

You may have backache. This is because ligaments and muscles supporting the joints in the small of your back relax.

The baby's bottom presses against your diaphragm. The baby measures approximately 18 in (44 cm) and weighs around 5 lb (2.5 kg).

WEEK 36

Doctor visits may be every week from now on. If this is your first baby, it will probably engage some time this week or soon after,

Pelvic engagement
A baby may engage in your pelvis at any time from six weeks before the birth. When you lie flat on your back the baby may not appear to be engaged, but as you sit up the baby's presenting part slips down into your pelvis.

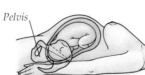

Pelvis

Not yet engaged

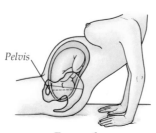

Pelvis

Engaged

and may have done so already. Your lump will settle lower down and you find that breathing becomes easier, though you may also need to pass urine more often, and your sleep is interrupted.

The baby is almost fully mature and any time now the presenting part may drop into your pelvis ready for birth. It is about 18 in (49 cm) long.

WEEK 37

You may have a chance to make a tour of the birthrooms of the hospital in which you are planning to have your baby.

The baby is rehearsing breathing movements, though there is no air in its lungs. In this way amniotic fluid passes into the baby's trachea, sometimes giving it hiccups!

WEEK 38

You may notice that the baby moves less now and that, instead of whole body movements, there are only jabs from the feet and knees, and the strange buzzing sensation inside your vagina as the baby's head moves against your pelvic floor muscles.

The baby may be putting on as much as 1 oz (28 g) a day at this stage.

WEEK 39

Your cervix is ripening in preparation for labor. You may feel heavy and weary and have strong Braxton Hicks contractions. The amniotic fluid is renewed every three hours.

The baby's bowels are filled with greenish-black meconium, excretions from the baby's alimentary glands mixed with bile pigment, lanugo, and cells from the bowel wall – its first motion after birth.

WEEK 40

The long-awaited day is near, and you probably feel fed up with being pregnant. You may have slight diarrhea.

The baby is about 20 in (55 cm) long. You feel sharp kicks under your ribs at one side or the other. The presenting part is pressing through the softened, partially opened, cervix. You will soon hold your child in your arms and at last be able to see each other face-to-face.

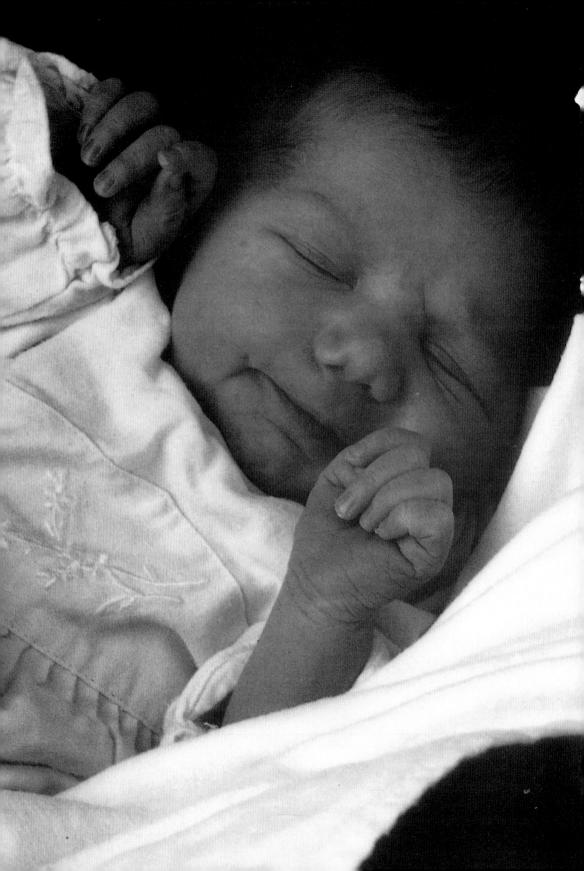

PREGNANCY

The early weeks

Finding out you are pregnant

Some women are convinced that they are pregnant from the moment of conception; others have such irregular periods that a long gap in between does not alert them to the possibility of pregnancy. But for most women the first sign of pregnancy is a missed period.

Perhaps it is five days since the day when you expected it, but then you start wondering if your dates were wrong. Perhaps you usually make a note in your diary, but last time you forgot. You lie in bed, unable to sleep, trying to fix the dates firmly in your mind by finding some useful landmark, like your mother's visit or the end of a particular work assignment. Still another three days go by and the reality gradually dawns: you might be pregnant. You might not be, but it does seem quite possible that you are. When is it sensible to go to the doctor and how early can you know for certain?

WHEN TO DIAGNOSE

Until recently it was usual to visit the doctor after missing two periods. Nowadays there is a strong case for finding out if you are pregnant before two periods have been missed. It is during these few weeks, while the embryo is still no larger than a hazelnut, that the major organs of the body and the brain itself are being formed; the sooner you know that you are pregnant the sooner you can start caring for yourself and for the baby.

An early confirmation of pregnancy is also important if you take any medicines. You will want to avoid taking drugs which could harm the developing baby (see page 100). It can also be useful to know early for social reasons – you may be planning to go abroad or to move at the time the baby is due.

If there is any possibility at all that you may want to terminate the pregnancy, it is essential to diagnose pregnancy in the early weeks: a termination (abortion) at eight weeks is much safer and less up-setting than one after ten weeks.

HOW TO DIAGNOSE

Pregnancy can now be diagnosed about two weeks after conception, on the day your period should have started if you have a regular monthly cycle, though you are likely to get more accurate results if you wait at least another four days – which can be difficult if you are feeling anxious or excited. When you are pregnant, the embryo releases the hormone called human chorionic gonadotrophin (HCG) into your bloodstream. Minute traces of HCG will be present in your urine about six days after conception, but then the level builds up rapidly, doubling every two or three days until it reaches a peak about 60 days after conception – approximately 74 days after your last period started – when it begins to decrease. It is possible to detect the presence of this hormone in your urine or blood. You can have your doctor or midwife take a urine or blood sample for analysis in the office or at a laboratory.

Many women's centers will do a free urine test for you or you can use one of the do-it-yourself kits that are widely available. Whichever method you choose, if at all possible test urine passed first thing in the morning, when you have not drunk anything during the night, since it is at this time that urine contains the highest concentration of pregnancy hormone.

Do-it-yourself tests There are a number of different kits on the market, and most involve mixing a drop or two of urine with the chemicals provided. If you are pregnant, the presence of HCG in your urine will, depending on the test, either prevent the mixture from coagulating (ring test) or change the color of the chemical in the test tube or on the dipstick (color test). Depending on the kit, you can use these tests when your period is between one and four days late, but you do need to be sure of when your period was due.

Occasionally a woman notices a little spotting (light bleeding) 10–12 days after fertilization. This is not really a period and the dating of pregnancy can start from your last actual period.

If the result is negative, but your period still has not arrived a few days later, do the test again. It is possible that you conceived later than you thought likely and that at the time of the first test there was not enough HCG in your urine to indicate that you were pregnant. If your periods are irregular or far apart, the chances of a false result are increased. After perhaps one conception in every ten, the fertilized egg does not manage to embed itself in the lining of the uterus. In this case, a pregnancy test will give a positive result, but a second test a few days later will produce a negative result. For this reason, some packs carry the recommendation that you always wait three to five days and then re-test, and they include two tests in each pack in order for you to be able to do this.

"I wanted to find out myself, not get the news from the doctor. I wasn't sure I wanted this baby and didn't know how I'd react."

Going to the doctor or midwife A doctor or midwife will perform a blood or urine test and you will also be given an internal examination. He or she introduces two gloved fingers into your vagina as far as they will go, while pressing with the other hand into your abdomen where the top of the uterus lies. If it is more than six weeks since the first day of your last period the doctor can feel the already softened lower part of the uterus, which is also slightly enlarged. The neck of the uterus, or cervix, which protrudes into the vagina, is felt as firmer than the lower part of the uterus, and it is about the same consistency as the tip of your nose. This internal change is known as "Hegar's sign." The examination may be uncomfortable but will not be painful. As the examining fingers are introduced, give a long, slow breath out through your mouth and continue breathing as slowly as you can.

DATING YOUR PREGNANCY

Once the pregnancy is confirmed by your doctor it will be dated from the first day of your last menstrual period (LMP). If you cannot recollect this date with accuracy the doctor will probably ask you to make a guess at it. This means that from then on the length of your pregnancy is reckoned in terms of so many weeks, including the weeks from the beginning of your last period to the time when conception occurred. Since ovulation is most common midway between two periods, the usual medical way of dating pregnancy adds an extra two weeks to its length. The length of the average pregnancy is some 266 days from the date of conception: your doctor will therefore arrive at your expected date of delivery (EDD) by adding 280 days, or 40 weeks, to the first day of your last period. You may find that you pay your first visit to the doctor knowing that it is ten weeks since you conceived, but emerge from the consultation three months pregnant!

But since not all women ovulate halfway between two periods, the medical convention of adding on an extra two weeks is an artificial one, and an inaccurate method of working out when a baby is due. It is wise to think of the EDD as an approximate date rather than the day when you expect to go into labor.

If you have just stopped taking the birth control pill your dates may be completely wrong. The period which immediately follows your last pill may not be followed by ovulation or you may have a slight spotting of blood which is not really a period. It may take several months to re-establish your natural cycle, and until then you cannot predict with any certainty when, or whether, you are going to ovulate. You might be a month or more off in your dates. This is obviously very important in estimating when the baby is due, especially since it could lead to labor's being induced unnecessarily (see page 324). It is advisable to wait for a clear three months after stopping the pill before trying to conceive; during this time you should use some other method of contraception.

CONCEIVING WHILE USING CONTRACEPTION

If you conceive with an IUD (intrauterine device or coil) still inside you, your chances of miscarrying are increased. It is therefore important to see your doctor quickly, as the IUD should be removed without delay if possible and this can only be done early in pregnancy. Sometimes doctors advise termination. This is certainly not necessary if you want the baby: even if it is by now too late to remove the IUD, many women deliver the IUD with the placenta after an uneventful pregnancy and birth.

WHEN IS YOUR BABY DUE?

This chart will help you to estimate the date your baby is due. Look along the columns at the figures set in bold type, to find the first day of your last period. The date below it is 280 days later and is your estimated date of delivery (EDD). It is perfectly normal for a baby to arrive two weeks before or two weeks after this date.

January
Oct/Nov

1	2	3	4	5	6	7	8	9	10	11	12	13	14	15	16	17	18	19	20	21	22	23	24	25	26	27	28	29	30	31
8	9	10	11	12	13	14	15	16	17	18	19	20	21	22	23	24	25	26	27	28	29	30	31	1	2	3	4	5	6	7

February
Nov/Dec

1	2	3	4	5	6	7	8	9	10	11	12	13	14	15	16	17	18	19	20	21	22	23	24	25	26	27	28
8	9	10	11	12	13	14	15	16	17	18	19	20	21	22	23	24	25	26	27	28	29	30	1	2	3	4	5

March
Dec/Jan

1	2	3	4	5	6	7	8	9	10	11	12	13	14	15	16	17	18	19	20	21	22	23	24	25	26	27	28	29	30	31
6	7	8	9	10	11	12	13	14	15	16	17	18	19	20	21	22	23	24	25	26	27	28	29	30	31	1	2	3	4	5

April
Jan/Feb

1	2	3	4	5	6	7	8	9	10	11	12	13	14	15	16	17	18	19	20	21	22	23	24	25	26	27	28	29	30
6	7	8	9	10	11	12	13	14	15	16	17	18	19	20	21	22	23	24	25	26	27	28	29	30	31	1	2	3	4

May
Feb/March

1	2	3	4	5	6	7	8	9	10	11	12	13	14	15	16	17	18	19	20	21	22	23	24	25	26	27	28	29	30	31
5	6	7	8	9	10	11	12	13	14	15	16	17	18	19	20	21	22	23	24	25	26	27	28	1	2	3	4	5	6	7

June
March/April

1	2	3	4	5	6	7	8	9	10	11	12	13	14	15	16	17	18	19	20	21	22	23	24	25	26	27	28	29	30
8	9	10	11	12	13	14	15	16	17	18	19	20	21	22	23	24	25	26	27	28	29	30	31	1	2	3	4	5	6

July
April/May

1	2	3	4	5	6	7	8	9	10	11	12	13	14	15	16	17	18	19	20	21	22	23	24	25	26	27	28	29	30	31
7	8	9	10	11	12	13	14	15	16	17	18	19	20	21	22	23	24	25	26	27	28	29	30	1	2	3	4	5	6	7

August
May/June

1	2	3	4	5	6	7	8	9	10	11	12	13	14	15	16	17	18	19	20	21	22	23	24	25	26	27	28	29	30	31
8	9	10	11	12	13	14	15	16	17	18	19	20	21	22	23	24	25	26	27	28	29	30	31	1	2	3	4	5	6	7

September
June/July

1	2	3	4	5	6	7	8	9	10	11	12	13	14	15	16	17	18	19	20	21	22	23	24	25	26	27	28	29	30
8	9	10	11	12	13	14	15	16	17	18	19	20	21	22	23	24	25	26	27	28	29	30	1	2	3	4	5	6	7

October
July/Aug

1	2	3	4	5	6	7	8	9	10	11	12	13	14	15	16	17	18	19	20	21	22	23	24	25	26	27	28	29	30	31
8	9	10	11	12	13	14	15	16	17	18	19	20	21	22	23	24	25	26	27	28	29	30	31	1	2	3	4	5	6	7

November
Aug/Sept

1	2	3	4	5	6	7	8	9	10	11	12	13	14	15	16	17	18	19	20	21	22	23	24	25	26	27	28	29	30
8	9	10	11	12	13	14	15	16	17	18	19	20	21	22	23	24	25	26	27	28	29	30	31	1	2	3	4	5	6

December
Sept/Oct

1	2	3	4	5	6	7	8	9	10	11	12	13	14	15	16	17	18	19	20	21	22	23	24	25	26	27	28	29	30	31
7	8	9	10	11	12	13	14	15	16	17	18	19	20	21	22	23	24	25	26	27	28	29	30	1	2	3	4	5	6	7

It is possible to conceive while taking the pill if you miss one or more days when you should have been taking it, or if you have an upset stomach with vomiting so that you fail to absorb the hormones, or if you have been on antibiotics. If you do conceive but continue to take the pill for several months while pregnant, there is a slightly increased risk to the baby of congenital abnormalities. But the vast majority of women who have taken the pill while pregnant give birth to babies who are healthy and normal.

Sometimes a doctor prescribes pills containing the hormones estrogen and progestogen in order to discover whether or not a woman is pregnant, the idea being that you take them and if you are not pregnant then your period starts. These types of hormone pill carry the same slight risk to the baby as the pill does: other diagnostic methods are therefore preferable.

Pregnancy and HIV infection

If you are anxious that you or your partner has been exposed to the virus that causes AIDS (acquired immune deficiency syndrome), you may decide before you get pregnant, or in very early pregnancy, that you should be screened for it. The test does not identify the virus (the human immunodeficiency virus, or HIV) itself, but reveals whether antibodies to it are in the bloodstream. If someone has been infected, antibodies will be present. Even though that person may show no symptoms of infection, he or she can transmit the virus to someone else. A pregnant woman can infect her unborn baby, though 85 percent of babies of HIV-positive mothers are born healthy. Most infections occur as the baby passes down the birth canal. cesarean section seems to halve the risk of infection. But further research is taking place and your doctor may give you up-to-date information. Even if a baby has HIV infection at birth there is a slight chance that symptoms will not develop, and 6 percent of babies born HIV-positive still have no symptoms at five years.

Before being tested you will have thought through the implications – social, emotional, and physical – of getting a positive result. As one woman carrying the virus said: "The only difference between now and before is this piece of knowledge. And it's such depressing, unhappy knowledge, I find it quite paralyzing."* According to current research, anyone who is antibody-positive has a 10 to 30 percent chance of developing AIDS within four years. Pregnancy affects the immune system, so it may trigger AIDS in a woman who is antibody-positive but who has had no previous symptoms. It is possible that she may develop the disease during pregnancy or soon after the baby is born.

Babies born to HIV-positive mothers always have antibodies. Some types of antibody, however, can enter the baby's blood without the child's becoming infected with the virus, and if an HIV-positive woman is healthy during pregnancy, there is a good chance that her baby will lose inherited antibodies within 6 to 18 months. It may take more than a year, with tests every few months, to know for sure whether a baby is carrying the virus. Only about 22 percent of antibody-positive newborn babies develop AIDS. If a woman has already given birth to an infected baby, there is a 66 percent chance that her next baby will be infected, too. If she herself has AIDS the risk is still greater. A baby may have birth defects or a characteristic facial appearance with a very small head, box-shaped forehead, flat nose, blue eyeballs, widely spaced eyes, and full lips.

Antibody tests may show up negative for three months following infection. It makes sense to have a second test 12 weeks after the first if you or your partner are at high risk of contracting the virus and if you are in very early pregnancy and are sure that you would want a termination if you were antibody-positive. No test is 100 percent free from error. The "Western blot" – which is the most widely used test in North America and Britain – is 96 percent accurate.

EARLY SIGNS OF PREGNANCY

Breast changes Even before your pregnancy is confirmed there may be early indications other than a missed period. Breast changes, in preparation for milk production, occur in the first weeks. The brownish circles round the nipples (the areolae) become darker and the little bumps on them (Montgomery's tubercles) more prominent.

If you are pink-skinned you may notice that the lacy network of blood vessels in your breasts has become much more obvious. Blue veins run over the breasts like rivers on a map. Your breasts may also feel tender and heavy. Women with small breasts may note an obvious increase in size very early on. If you have large breasts already you may not notice any size change at this stage.

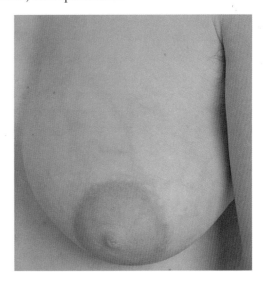

Tiredness Enormous metabolic changes take place in pregnancy and your whole body has to adjust to the process of growing a baby. It is not surprising that you may feel tired and that you cannot carry on just as you did before. Many women complain of extreme tiredness during the first eight or ten weeks. But as your body adjusts to the pregnancy the fatigue vanishes and the middle months are often easy. If you are feeling tired it is only sensible to take the message from your body and go to bed early, have a rest at midday if you can, or an early evening rest when you get home from work.

If it is your second (or third) pregnancy, you may find that you are constantly tired. Women who thoroughly enjoyed their first pregnancy say that the second one is much harder to cope with because they are exhausted by the non-stop pace of their first child's

Above
The first physical changes of which you become aware may occur in your breasts. Veins may become more prominent and the areolae darker.

daily life. The only solution is to try to have at least a short time every day when you are free from domestic responsibilities. Even half an hour every evening when your partner attends to the child and the dishes can be relaxing if you are able to enjoy it to the fullest. (See pages 170–173 for more about second and later pregnancies.)

Nausea Another common sign of pregnancy is nausea. These waves of sickness often happen early in the morning, when your blood sugar level is low, but they may also occur in the early evening, or even at other times of the day. Some women just feel very sick, others actually vomit. Tiredness contributes to nausea, but so does an empty stomach: small frequent snacks of bland foods like crackers or a banana may relieve the feeling. If you suffer from morning sickness, a cup of tea and a few crackers or dry toast immediately on waking may prevent it, or crackers alone may be better. A late-night snack may help, too. As a general rule, cut out all greasy fried foods, tobacco, and alcohol. Avoid strong odors, especially cooking smells, exhaust fumes, and perfume, and if nausea and vomiting is still bad, ask your doctor to prescribe an antihistamine, which is the drug most likely to be effective.*

Some women become really ill with vomiting (see page 135), although most stop feeling sick during the fourth month. Women who experience pregnancy nausea are less likely than others to have miscarriages. This can be a cheering thought. But nausea does not exist in all cultures; many societies have other illnesses and disabilities or special dreams which they connect with pregnancy. Margaret Mead points out that in some societies of New Guinea boils are considered a typical symptom of pregnancy. Some Jamaicans do not acknowledge pregnancy until they have had a special fertility dream of ripe fruit bursting with seed. Dreams of this kind are characteristic of early pregnancy. It is as if all women need definite signs to link with pregnancy so that they can say, "I feel this, therefore I must be expecting a baby."

You may suffer from nausea for the first time in your second or third pregnancy. This is almost certainly the result of tiredness, and you may not relieve the nausea within three months unless you can somehow arrange to have more rest.

EMOTIONAL REACTIONS TO PREGNANCY
However much you want a baby, finding out that you really are pregnant can produce a flood of conflicting emotions: triumph ("We've done it!"), a sense of being trapped ("There's no going back – now what?"), fear ("Mom had an awful time having me – will I be able to stand the pain?"), apprehension ("Will we still love each other in the same way?"), and doubt ("Will he still want me once my waist starts getting thicker?"). It is surprising how many women respond to their first pregnancy with shock and feel that it has happened "too soon," even though they very much want a baby and

have considered the matter carefully before stopping contraception. Confronted with the reality and the physical changes of pregnancy, they want to say: "Stop! I haven't prepared myself for this. Let's go back and start again."

If you discover that you are pregnant when you did not plan to be, you may also feel unfairly trapped. Yet, perversely, many women (for whom pregnancy is not a disaster) are aware of an odd pleasure that their fertility has triumphed over their conscious wish. Your partner may suspect that you wanted a baby all along and have not been "playing fair." Starting a baby under such circumstances can lead to conflict between you, because he may feel that you have not been open with him. Talk about it together: you need to understand each other.

Feelings about motherhood When you find out that you are pregnant you may actually have a crisis of self-confidence, feeling that you will be no good as a mother and have no maternal instincts. But mothering is a learned activity and little of it is purely instinctive. Moreover, for the first-time mother, who may never have handled a newborn baby, most of the learning goes on after the baby is born. The teacher is the baby. Even though you may not start as an expert, your baby will turn you into one.

Feelings about being on show You may feel suddenly that your most intimate relationship with the man you love is being publicly displayed, not just because you are pregnant and everybody knows, but because of the physical examinations and exposure at the prenatal clinic and the advice that people keep giving you. This sense of becoming public property may also be intensified by the obvious pleasure of your parents who may have long been wanting for you to become pregnant.

Yet your body holds life. The wonder of that cannot really be understood by anyone else. You stand naked in front of the mirror and look for changes. You rest your hand on your tummy and wonder if you can feel the tiny seed of a baby beginning to grow inside you. You think back to when you made love and wonder which time it was that you conceived.

Feelings about your body If you feel on bad terms with your body as it starts out on the work of early pregnancy, arrange to attend some pregnancy exercise or dance classes if these are available in your area. A list of organizations which can help you is on page 413. If these classes are not specially for pregnant women, let your teacher know that you are pregnant. Get out in the fresh air and walk. Buy a maternity swimsuit and swim regularly. Start doing the movements suggested on pages 124–125 a few times each day to pep up your circulation and increase vitality. In some countries massage is an anticipated and very pleasant part of being pregnant, so you

could go to a massage therapist or your partner could learn how to massage you (see pages 186–194). This can be particularly useful if you are tense and find it difficult to release your muscles at will.

Your partner's feelings You are not the only person who has to adjust in pregnancy. Your partner does not have to cope with physical changes, but the emotional impact of a first pregnancy is no less real than your own, and the passage into fatherhood constitutes a major transition in his life. For a man this process is often delayed until several things have happened: the pregnancy has been officially confirmed; your figure has obviously changed; the baby has moved and he has felt it fluttering.

Emotions of joy, pride, and wonder may be in conflict with other emotions of a more disturbing nature. There may be financial problems which can cause a man to feel a sense of deep and burdensome responsibility for the new life that is coming.

A man, too, may feel trapped by pregnancy. Perhaps he felt that his relationship with the woman was intended to remain free and untrammeled by babies (especially if the couple have not discussed pregnancy and planned it together). His job may now assume importance not only in its own right, but because he feels an urgent need to be successful before the baby comes, as if it threatens his own powers of achievement. A man, too, may be frightened of birth and even of his partner's pregnant body, which can seem dangerous and not to be touched in case the baby is dislodged. He may feel that his own sexual desire is a terrible threat to the baby.

DISCUSSING YOUR EMOTIONS TOGETHER

It does not help to bottle up these emotions. If you pretend they are not there they become destructive. Anxiety has a positive function. It prods you to examine options, develop coping strategies, plan ahead, prepare yourselves emotionally and practically for the future. For example, you could avoid certain relatives until you feel you can cope with them. You may be able to arrange prenatal appointments together, so that your partner can meet the doctor or midwife and be present during the physical examination. Reading together about pregnancy and birth helps to replace ignorance with knowledge about the role a man can actively play in childbirth. Lying together in bed, cuddling, and exploring each other's bodies is a way of communicating through loving touch and tenderness.

Pregnancy is not merely a waiting time. It is a time for working out together what you value in your relationship and what kind of world you both want to create for your child. This is not a question of making a nursery and buying things for the baby, but of helping each other to change from people who are responsible just for themselves into a mother and a father, with the new responsibility that parenthood brings. A man and a woman need to grow into parents. Then not only a baby, but a new family is born.

Opposite
The realization that you are responsible for creating a new person may be awesome and sometimes overwhelming.

THE WOMAN ALONE

Pregnancy and childbirth are not easy when you have no partner to give you love and care. It is even more difficult once the baby is born to take complete responsibility for a new life. Yet many women have done this successfully and have reared happy, healthy children.

Talking about the single mother and the challenges she faces is in a way misleading, because women on their own bearing babies do not fall into one category any more than women with partners do. The reasons single women embark on pregnancy, and decide to go on with it, vary widely. Some continue with a pregnancy because they are unwilling or unable to face up to it, and drift on hoping that it may go away. Others are bearing a much-wanted child "before it is too late." Others again loved the father of the child and hoped that the relationship would continue, but then found themselves rejected and bearing a child alone. There are also women whose men die while they are pregnant. And there are lesbian mothers who may have strong support from a female partner. Whatever your reasons for having a child on your own, financial problems may loom large. Trying to combine a job with rearing a child, knowing that there is no one else to take over in time of need, can be difficult. It is important to anticipate and share the problems you will be coping with, and to seek counseling from people who understand them and who can put you in touch with other sources of help. Contact the organizations listed on page 413 before you have your baby and see what they have to offer. These organizations are designed to help you cope with the practical difficulties such as housing, finding day care for the baby and sorting out to which benefits you are entitled. Register for childbirth education classes (see page 176) as early as the first trimester. Many women delay until the last minute and find that the classes are full. The International Childbirth Education Association and the American Society for Psychoprophylaxis in Obstetrics (addresses on page 413) can tell you about the different kinds of classes, postnatal support, and breastfeeding counseling available in your area.

Sometimes a man who is not a permanent partner is still willing to accept some of the responsibilities of fatherhood. It is quite common in a prenatal class to have couples who do not plan to marry or even stay together. Be frank with your childbirth educator so that she has a chance to get to know you. It may be possible for you to arrange to see her privately for a session.

"The doula made all the difference. She's had three children herself and understood exactly what I was feeling. She made suggestions, like thinking of my cervix opening up during contractions, and helped by massaging the back of my neck with lavender oil and breathed with me when the going got difficult."

EMOTIONAL SUPPORT IN LABOR

Think ahead to the birth and decide whether you would like to have a companion with you. Childbirth can feel very solitary if you do not have someone with you to encourage you and provide continuous emotional support. This person could be a good woman friend, a childbirth educator, a doula (who is trained and experienced in supporting laboring women), your sister or mother, or a man friend who knows what birth is about and can give the right kind of help. Most hospitals allow companions in labor, though some restrict you to one person. Discuss the matter with your doctor and your childbirth educator, and if necessary state your request in writing to the Chair of the Obstetrical Department or in person to the Director of Nursing. Doula organizations are listed on page 413.

If there is no one who can be with you, discuss the subject in advance with your obstetrician or midwife. Say that you want someone with you throughout labor, and that you do not know anyone who can come with you; ask whether there is anyone in the hospital – preferably someone you could meet beforehand – who could be with you. Ask if there are doulas in your area. The doctor may say that you will have the nurses and will not be left alone. But a birth companion is different and is simply there as a friend to give you emotional support and to remind you of your relaxation and breathing. If you are in a teaching hospital there may be a student nurse who can do this for you. If it is a midwifery training school there is usually a student midwife who can fill the same role.

But suppose that you have to be without a companion in labor. Make the nurse your friend and ask her for help. Unfortunately there is not much continuity of care in hospitals, and you may have to get to know two or three nurses, one after another – a lot to ask of someone in labor. On the other hand, sometimes one will stay on duty so that she can be with you until after the delivery.

Managing alone

If a man has been unwilling to accept responsibility or perhaps even acknowledge your pregnancy, you probably feel angry and resentful. One woman, who had been told she could never have a baby but who found herself pregnant, said, "I hadn't realized just how much his marriage was a going concern. Just when I most needed him I had to come to terms with the fact that he didn't want to break up his marriage and was devoted to his kids. My pregnancy was terribly embarrassing for him! I felt dreadfully on my own. I didn't hear from him through a large part of the pregnancy because it was the summer holidays and he went abroad with his family."

Another woman's husband left her when she was four months pregnant because he said he could not stand the idea of a third child. He had left her before for short periods and the baby was conceived during a reconciliation. Her great fear was that she would find him on the doorstep again, since she had been through so much emotional turmoil that she did not feel she could cope mentally with any more scenes. This led to a strained and difficult pregnancy followed by a prolonged labor and forceps delivery. A university lecturer who had decided in advance that she wanted a baby but not a man said that her colleagues accepted this but that she found it difficult to tell her family: "Mother thought I was mad and said how could she ever let her friends know. I thought about them all at their coffee mornings and thought, 'Oh my God, I don't suppose she can.' I thought it would be hardest explaining to my 80-year-old grandmother but she was the one who understood best." In fact, her parents adjusted to the idea of her single motherhood after the baby was born and they became proud grandparents.

Some women are rejected by parents, but one woman said: "In a way I rejected them and their values, by going ahead and having the baby." Even so, however "free" of your parents you may feel and however you delight in being independent of them, cutting roots like this can be extremely painful. You may feel guilty, even if you do not accept the social conventions which thrust feelings of guilt upon you. You may worry about imposing your views on your child, who will learn that in friends' houses there is a father as well as a mother.

Yet single mothers all stress that you do need help and must have the grace to accept it, for your child's sake as well as your own. There are the all-important questions of where you are going to live, what you are going to live on, whether you should and can go back to work, and if so, when. You must also then consider how you are going to retain any sort of mobility with a baby, how you will deal with the relationships between sex, motherhood, and the other things you want to do, and how you are going to feel when things are difficult or impossible because of the baby. Many difficulties confronted by single women are the same as those faced by those with partners, but intensified because they are alone and unsupported. As one woman said, in order to go through with having a baby on your own, "you need to really want that child!"

Planning & preparation

Throughout history most babies were born at home. Maternity hospitals were first started for homeless women and were really extensions of the poor-houses. Many of the babies born in these hospitals were often then put in foundling institutions. The first maternity hospitals were convenient centers for medical students to learn and practice obstetrics, but infection was rampant, as doctors conveyed bacteria on their hands from one patient to another, and many babies and mothers died. They were the most dangerous places in which women could possibly give birth.

Today, modern hospitals are no longer dangerous places to have a baby. Yet, despite very rapid advances and the tendency for most doctors to recommend a hospital birth, many women still feel a home birth would be the most appropriate for them.

WHERE WOULD YOU LIKE TO HAVE YOUR BABY?

Even before you are pregnant, or as early in pregnancy as you can, it is worth thinking about whether you would like to have your baby at home, in a birth center, or a hospital and finding out which of those options are available in your area. You may have decided, for example, that you want to have your baby at home, yet discover that there is no doctor or midwife willing or able to attend you, so home birth is not an option for you. This is the case in many parts of North America. Or partway through your pregnancy you may

"I'm considering the options open to me and am finding out about home birth because I'd like it to be as natural as possible."

discover a midwife or doctor who does attend home births. If there are no specific medical reasons against your planning a home birth, you will probably want to switch to their care. You can do this at any stage of pregnancy, but it is sometimes difficult to make different arrangements once wheels have been set in motion. It is a good idea to make a list of things that are really important to you about the birth and the time right after and to decide which environment best meets your requirements: home, hospital, or birth center.

Hospital birth

Most women who decide to have their babies in the hospital do so primarily because they are convinced it is the safest place. They want to be sure that all the skills and equipment of modern obstetrics are at hand for their babies' sake. For some women, especially those having their first child, giving birth is a frightening experience, a step in the dark, and they feel more secure in the knowledge that they are in the hands of a team who have been specially trained to cope with any possible emergencies that might arise. Often a woman who fears that her labor will be painful opts for a hospital delivery, knowing that there are certain painkillers that are available only in a hospital and not wanting to take the chance of finding herself in labor at home without any relief from pain when it is far too late to do anything about it.

Sometimes a woman may know and trust a particular obstetrician and want to be cared for by this person, while another woman wants to go to a hospital because she feels she would probably benefit from a short period of release from the pressures of home and family. Occasionally a woman's partner wants her to go to a hospital because he is very worried about birth at home. He may just be frightened of being involved, but more often he is afraid that he might have to deliver the baby himself.

MEDICAL REASONS FOR HOSPITAL BIRTH

As well as those women who would prefer the security of a hospital birth, there are those for whom it is advisable to give birth in a hospital whatever their personal preferences. It is wise to consider hospital care if you have diabetes or a heart or kidney condition. Your doctor or midwife will have you admitted to a hospital if you get preeclampsia (see page 139) or if you go into labor three weeks or more before your baby is due; you will probably be advised against home delivery if your baby is breech, since the baby may need some help with breathing immediately after birth (see page 366). There are really no absolutes, but there are certain things which tend to make childbirth a little more risky.

If you are over 40 and a first-time mother, for instance, labor may be longer than if you were younger, and many doctors would advise you to be in a hospital so that you can have labor speeded up or get help with the delivery. Some doctors believe that all first-time mothers (primigravida) should give birth in a hospital because, they say, a labor is only normal in retrospect and there is always a small chance that even after a perfectly normal pregnancy you may have complications which will entail your being moved to the hospital at the last minute for specialist care.

If you have had a hemorrhage with a previous labor, either before or after the delivery, you might want to choose a hospital birth because you may need a quick blood transfusion if it happens again. (On the other hand, did you bleed because of aggressive intervention, and are you less likely to bleed if the labor progresses naturally?) The same goes for a retained placenta in a previous labor. Sometimes hospital interventions themselves contribute to the likelihood of birth complications.

Opposite

For some women a one-to-one relationship with a midwife is an important element in choosing a home birth.

If you are very short, under 5 ft 2 in (1.55 m), your pelvis may be a tight fit for the baby to get through, though many short women can and do give birth easily. Any other indications of disproportion, because of the way the baby is lying, for example, could also lead you to consider a hospital birth. Three or more miscarriages are

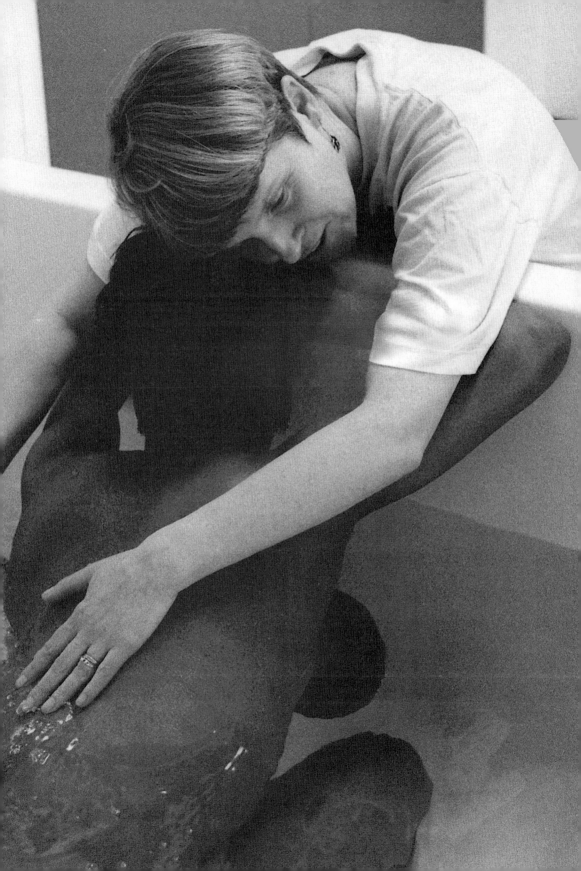

another reason for having the baby in a hospital, because previous problems of this kind may mean that labor will present problems (though often everything is straightforward). If you have lost a baby because of a previous difficult birth, you will want to know that, if the baby should need it, intensive care is available at the hospital where you are giving birth. Doctors also advise mothers of twins to give birth in a hospital, partly because they may come early and be of low birthweight and partly because the second twin sometimes gets stuck. But if both bodies are head down and full term, you may decide that home is the best place for the birth because you want to avoid any unnecessary intervention and know that you have experienced and skilled midwives.

CHOICES IN HOSPITAL CARE

There are two main kinds of hospital obstetrical care: private and public (or clinic). In addition, many hospitals are beginning to offer a certified nurse midwife program. If you have decided that a hospital birth is the best one for you, you will need to think about the alternatives available to you within the hospital system.

The private obstetrician or family physician Most women choose a private obstetrician although some prefer a family physician, some of whom provide maternity care as part of their practice. It is convenient if the doctor is affiliated with a hospital near your home, but it is more important to find a doctor whom you like and who understands the kind of birth you desire and who is prepared to help you have it. Finding a private obstetrician or family physician with whom you have a good relationship can be difficult. Most in the United States are men and may not see your point of view about birth. They also work in groups, and the various members of the group do not necessarily manage your care in the same way. Go to the first visit with a list of questions such as the following so that you can make your decision on a practical basis.

"The obstetrician was very pleasant. He told me they'd just had a baby three months ago. That made a lot of difference."

• What is your policy on induction?
• When do you recommend induction?
• What percentage of your patients had a natural unmedicated birth last year?
• Do you usually order medications, intravenous drips (IVs), enemas, and monitors, or do you judge each situation individually?
• What position do most of the women you deliver adopt for the second stage?
• Are they encouraged to try different positions?
• Do these include kneeling, being on all fours, and squatting?
• Do you usually perform an episiotomy?
• Do you usually hand the naked baby straight to the mother?
• Can the mother lift the baby out herself if she wishes?

• Are you willing to wait until the cord has stopped pulsating before clamping it?

• How much time do the mother and baby normally have skin contact following delivery?

• Can the baby be put to the breast on the delivery table?

• Are you willing to dim the lights when the baby is born?

• Do you routinely suction the baby at delivery?

• If the baby is breathing well would you be willing to wait and see whether this is needed?

• If the baby requires special care can both parents visit the intensive care unit and touch and hold their baby if it is well enough?

• Can the mother breastfeed the baby in the intensive care unit if it is well enough?

• What percentage of your patients breastfed last year?

• Would your colleagues differ from you in the way they would answer these questions?

Obviously, the higher the proportion of women in this doctor's care who have had the type of birth experience you are hoping for, the greater the probability that the doctor will help you realize your hopes. Remember that the private doctor can write orders for anything you agree on together, regardless of whether or not it is routine practice in that particular hospital.

The obstetrical clinic Most obstetrical clinics are located within large metropolitan teaching hospitals. As the name suggests, in exchange for low cost or free care the patient serves as "teaching material" for the medical students and resident physicians. Thus there is a higher risk of having unnecessary procedures performed on your body. Teaching hospitals tend to have a great deal of technologically advanced machinery and may be justified for the mother and baby "at risk," when there is a higher than average chance of something going wrong during the labor. These hospitals often have neonatal intensive care units where sophisticated technology and a specially skilled staff will be available to treat the high-risk baby immediately after birth. Those teaching hospitals with family practice residency or nurse-midwifery training programs may provide lower intervention care.

Certified nurse midwife care This type of maternity care is now becoming much more available throughout the United States. For information on the availability in your area, contact the American College of Nurse Midwives (see page 413).

The typical hospital nurse midwife practices in a group, backed by one or more obstetricians. The certified nurse midwife has been specifically trained to deal with normal pregnancy, normal birth, and normal postpartum. She cares for the well woman at all stages but if any abnormality develops will refer the patient to an obstetrician. Even if this happens, the nurse midwife usually stays with her client, offering her emotional support. No matter what type of hospital care you choose, be sure to tour the hospital before you make a definite decision. If this is not the usual practice in the hospital, contact the Head Nurse of Obstetrics and ask for the name of the childbirth educator. Another source of information about the hospital, obstetricians, midwives, and clinics is your local childbirth education association (see page 413 for a list of organizations to contact). If there is no childbirth education association anywhere near you, then try contacting your local women's organization. They should be able to tell you exactly what you need to know to make hospital birth a rewarding experience.

The birth room

Until recently birth rooms were organized exclusively for the comfort and convenience of doctors and midwives, instead of the woman having the baby. In many hospitals that has changed and there are birth beds and other equipment which enables the woman to sit upright, kneel, squat, and stand with something solid to grip onto. But obstetric practice often limits women's opportunities to move about and get into different positions. If you have had an epidural or are harpooned to an intravenous drip or electronic fetal monitor – or both – it may be almost impossible to move at all. In the United States and Canada most hospitals have no policy against women moving around in childbirth. In effect, however, almost all women are in a reclining position through much of labor and the birth. This is often because of staff expectations and obstetric interventions, such as having an IV set up and being tethered to an electronic fetal monitor, which keep women in bed and leave them with little or no choice of position.

"I got stuck flat on my back last time I was in labor and felt trapped. This time I was much better as I was able to move about; I felt in control, and it was so much easier to handle the pain."

Women who can remain upright in the first stage of labor have less pain, so need fewer pain-relieving drugs, and dilate faster than those women who are lying down. Their babies' heart rates are also more likely to fall within the normal range.*

In the second stage being upright also results in less pain, fewer drugs, easier pushing, fewer tears, more normal vaginal births, and a more positive birth experience.* When you look round the hospital take special note of how you could use ledges at different heights and furniture in the birth room to give you support and move your pelvis. Ask for a bean bag to flop over or lean against, or take one into the hospital, if it is not already provided.

Hospitals may now also offer a rocking chair for the first stage and a birth stool and squatting bar to grasp in the second stage. Many have elaborate birth beds or chairs which can be switched to almost any position. These may look impressive, but the important thing is to have the equipment under your own control, not someone else's, and to be free to move your pelvis. If there is no birth bed take a floor exercise mat into the hospital on which to kneel or sit.

Whatever happens, the equipment is less important than you. It should not be allowed to dominate or restrict what you do during birth. So look critically at whatever is on offer and think how you may want to use it, if at all. A beautiful sculptural design is not helpful if it limits your movements. One problem with sitting on a rigid chair or stool for a long time, especially one with back support which limits the pelvic movements you can make, is that you may develop some swelling around your vulva and the circulation of blood may be impeded there, with the result that you bleed more heavily with the birth.* When it comes down to it, the best physical support may come from other human beings who will hold you while you do whatever you want to do at the time.

Another item of equipment that may be available is a birth pool or whirlpool bath. Seize the opportunity to use it, if only during the first stage of labor. It gives extraordinary relief from pain and because the pool is often in a small room separate from the birth room it gives a more private, personal environment for labor. In larger pools or tubs you can move freely, and there is plenty of room for you to give birth in the water (which is an option in a limited number of hospitals, but in many out-of-hospital birth settings).

In the United States and Canada tubs or Jacuzzis are often used which were not designed as birth pools but are intended for very elderly people and those with physical handicaps. They are designed for easy entry, easy cleaning, and water conservation. The tub is raised off the floor and is molded to put the bather in a semi-sitting position. The woman seats herself in the tub much as she would on a chair, and the entire tub then reclines, allowing the water to cover her body.

This design does not allow freedom of movement, and although most women experience profound relief from pain, some with severe back pain do not because of the back reclining position. These tubs are not practical for birth in the water, and are used only to relieve discomfort during labor.

If tubs are not available in your hospital or birth center, or if you wish to have a larger tub in which you could give birth, you may be able to rent a portable tub and have it temporarily installed when in the hospital. Discuss this with your caregiver. Ask your childbirth education or midwives' organization about local tub rentals.

Home birth

While hospital birth remains the standard way to have a baby, there is a small but steady increase in the number of women who decide to have their babies at home. Most women who have a baby at home

Right
A midwife gets to know her client during the pregnancy and routine checks are part of an ongoing relationship.

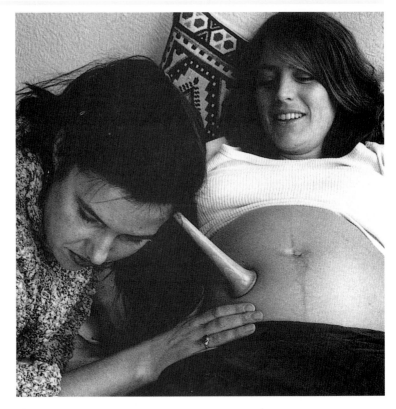

Below
Your blood pressure is less likely to be raised when you are happy and relaxed.

after a previous hospital birth say that they enjoyed it much more and feel that it must have been much pleasanter for the baby. Some opt for home births because they want to give birth in a familiar, comfortable, nonmedical environment, surrounded by their own possessions, in the home they have created with their partner. They want to be able to make their own decisions, to give birth in their own way and behave spontaneously, without being forced into the role of patient and having to conform to hospital rules and regulations. They also want to avoid having to change rooms and move from a bed to a delivery room, and to be able to adopt any position they find comfortable. In your own home you are in charge and the midwife or doctor and his or her assistant are familiar and welcome guests in your home. For some women, this continuous relationship and cooperation with just a few helpers is important.

Some women say that since birth is an act of love, personal and intimate, it should take place in one's own environment, without unnecessary observers, among friends in a loving atmosphere. They want to know that the father of the baby or a close friend can be present throughout, can take an active part, and can give emotional support through the labor. Some would like the father to "catch" the baby himself. Most hospitals allow fathers to be present for labor and delivery nowadays, but they are sometimes sent out for some procedures, just when the laboring woman feels she needs her partner most. Often a woman would like to ensure that her baby has a "gentle birth" and is welcomed into the world with tenderness, without the machinery and bright lights that are nearly always inevitable in hospitals.

"BONDING" OCCURS NATURALLY

Evidence of research on "bonding" between mother, father, and baby points to the importance of the time immediately following birth for the couple to get to know their baby and feel it belongs to them and that they belong to it. In many hospitals separation immediately after the child is born is still arbitrarily imposed on new parents, time for cuddling is either restricted or denied and routines take precedence over the emotional unfolding which heralds the birth of a family. Many women also suspect that medical intervention is often unnecessary and that they will have a better chance of giving birth naturally and without drugs at home. They believe that full awareness of what is happening to them is a valuable experience and that drugs can harm their unborn babies. After a previous difficult hospital birth, one pregnant woman said: "I was determined to have a natural birth this time. Last time I had the whole works, and finished up with an epidural and a forceps delivery. I can't help thinking that if I let things take their own time and keep walking around and can relax and use my breathing and feel comfortable in my own home, with the people I love around me, my body will know what to do."

UNDERSTANDING YOUR MEDICAL RECORD

It can be very confusing to try to decipher your medical records, and some of the abbreviations may suggest alarming abnormalities. Here are some of the abbreviations most likely to be used. You can ask your doctor or midwife to explain any that you do not understand. Two-way communication is vital in a working partnership.

Abbr/term	Full title/Name	Meaning of abbreviation
Para 0		The mother has had no previous birth.
Para 1 (or 2)		The mother has had one (or two) previous births.
Para 2 + 1		The mother has had two previous births plus a miscarriage (or termination) before 28 weeks.
LMP	Last menstrual period	Date of first day of last menstrual period.
EDD/EDC	Expected date of delivery	Expected date of delivery or expected date of confinement.
Alb	Albumin in urine	Your urine is analyzed for the presence of sugar, which is a sign of diabetes, and albumin (protein) which can be a sign of preeclampsia. When sugar is present, it is noted as a percentage. Two percent is a large amount. Ideally albumin should not be present at all. There are occasional traces of sugar and albumin in a normal pregnancy.
MTLP	Metabolic toxemia of later pregnancy	An alternative name for preeclampsia.
Hb	Hemoglobin	Hemoglobin is an oxygen-carrying substance present in red blood cells. If your hemoglobin level is lower than 10.5 percent, or your hematocrit (see below) is below 32 percent, you may be considered to be anemic and be prescribed iron. Because of the greater quantity of circulating blood, most healthy pregnant women have reduced hemoglobin.
Hct	Hematocrit	Hematocrit is the percentage of red blood cells in the blood.
Fe	Iron	This means that you have been prescribed iron.
BP	Blood pressure	This is the pressure inside the arteries as the blood is pumped from the heart. The pressure that is built up every time the heart beats is called systolic pressure. Between beats the heart muscle relaxes and the pressure drops. This lower level is called diastolic pressure. Systolic pressure is the upper figure on your card, diastolic pressure the lower. The lower figure is more significant than the upper one. A woman is considered to have moderately high blood pressure, hypertension, if it exceeds 140/90 when measured on more than one occasion.
FHT	Fetal heart tones	The number of fetal heartbeats per minute.

Abbr/term	Full title/Name	Meaning of abbreviation
H/NH	Heard/not heard	This usually refers to the fetal heart. In the last weeks of pregnancy the actual heart rate is often written in.
Edema	Swelling	Part of your weight gain is due to water retention, causing puffiness in the feet and ankles, hands, and vulva. A great deal of fluid retention may be a sign of preeclampsia, but it can be perfectly normal.
Fundus	The top of the uterus	As the baby grows, the fundus is pushed up to just above your navel at 22 weeks and under your ribs at 36 weeks. But when the baby drops down into the bony pelvis ready for birth the fundus is lower again. You can find your own fundus and chart its position week by week through your pregnancy. Lie on your back with your tummy bare and, with the sides and palms of your hands, feel around the hard top of your uterus, pressing against what feels like a wall of muscle.
Cx	Cervix	The neck of the uterus, which softens, shortens, and opens during birth.
PP	The presenting part of the baby	This is the part which is down at the bottom of the uterus and likely to be the first to press through the opening cervix if you are at the end of pregnancy. In the last few weeks the doctor or midwife may note the presentation precisely, so that you can get an idea of exactly what part of the baby is in the cervix.
Vx/Vtx	Vertex	This indicates the baby's position is head down, as it should be.
Ceph	Cephalic	This also indicates that the baby's position is head down.
Brim		The inlet of your pelvis.
Long L	Longitudinal lie	The baby is lying parallel to your spine.
LOA LOP ROA ROP	Left Occipito Anterior Left Occipito Posterior Right Occipito Anterior Right Occipito Posterior	These terms all refer to the position (anterior or posterior) of the crown of the baby's head (occiput) in relation to your body (right or left). Therefore ROP means that the baby's head is to your right and back.
RSA	Right sacrum anterior	This is the most common breech presentation.
Eng/E	Engaged	This is written on your card when the baby's head has dropped down into your pelvis, which can happen any time from about six weeks before you go into labor until after you have actually started.
T	Term	The doctor or midwife writes this on your card when it is estimated that you are right at the end of your pregnancy and the baby is ready to be born.

If you already have other children, you may be concerned that they should see birth as a normal, happy part of life and not, as a surgical operation that entails your going off to a hospital. Birth is a family affair and the baby should belong to the whole family. Some women hope that the other child or children can be involved in the labor, and some would like them present at the birth. This is difficult or impossible to arrange in most hospitals. Some mothers who have never left their toddlers worry that separation from them will lead to emotional and behavioral problems in the older child, and this just at a time when the new baby puts in an appearance. And there are those mothers who just find it impossible to get someone to look after their family while they are away in the hospital. It is sometimes stated that women having their fourth or subsequent babies should always give birth in a hospital, but if all your previous pregnancies and labors have been straightforward, there is no additional risk with a fourth or fifth birth and some definite advantage in giving birth at home where the other children can also be involved.

"My eight-year-old daughter made a birthday cake for the baby while I was in the first stage of labor and we celebrated afterwards with the cake, champagne, and lemonade."

ISSUES FOR PARENTS CHOOSING HOME BIRTHS

Since home birth is not the standard in the United States, a pregnant woman has additional responsibilities when she chooses to deliver at home. It is useful to think about how you are going to take on these responsibilities. They include:

Selection of a competent birth attendant This may be a physician, certified nurse midwife, a professional direct-entry (non-nurse) midwife, or well-trained and experienced lay midwife.

Understanding of nutrition There is a significant relationship between the mother's diet in pregnancy and the health of her baby at birth and after.

Preparation for childbirth Mothers planning a home birth benefit from having an especially clear understanding of how their bodies function in labor and delivery.

Understanding the third stage Breastfeeding after birth helps the uterus contract, making use of oxytoxic drugs less necessary.

Attendance at home birth classes, if available.

Obtaining supplies, as requested by the birth attendant.

Preparing for postpartum needs of mother and baby Planning ahead for the household simplifies life after birth.

BIRTH CENTERS

A third option is the freestanding birth center. A birth center provides midwifery care in a pleasant, homelike setting in which couples and families participate fully in their own prenatal care, attend preparation-for-birth classes, and give birth and have uninterrupted time together afterward in the same setting. Birth centers tend to be staffed by certified nurse midwives, or direct-entry midwives, backed up by obstetricians. Women are carefully screened to assure they are low risk and can return to their own homes within twenty-four hours of giving birth. But some birth centers do have high transfer rates to hospital, and it is worth asking what the transfer rate during labor is. You can contact the National Association of Childbearing Centers for a list of those near you.

Prenatal care

One ingredient of a happy birth is good prenatal care, so that you are confident that you are healthy and the baby starts life under the best possible conditions. But the care you give yourself is probably more important than the care you receive from professionals. It also includes learning how to cope with stress in everyday life, and understanding how to work with your body. You do not need to attend classes until you are five or more months pregnant, but it is worth thinking about the different classes available and perhaps beginning a few exercises earlier than this.

Prenatal care has progressed piecemeal since the nineteenth century and we do not really know which elements in the package are valuable for all women, which are best kept for those at special risk, and which might be discarded altogether. It is common for confusion to occur about whether a baby is growing well inside the uterus, for example, and many women are told that there is intra-uterine growth retardation when, in fact, it turns out that everything is fine. In spite of this, good medical care during pregnancy can every now and then make all the difference between life and death for the baby – and even, very occasionally, for you, too.*

Unfortunately, whether you have private or clinic care, waiting for appointments is usually a fact of life. Take a good book or needlework or make friends with another expectant mother going to the same doctor or clinic and you can keep each other company.

Some couples come together (many doctors and clinics and most midwives actually encourage fathers to be there) but usually this is not expected and fathers may be asked to remain in the waiting room. If, however, it is important to you that you both talk to the doctor and that your partner be involved in the pregnancy, not only the birth, it is worthwhile being quietly but firmly persistent to get what you want. Think through beforehand any questions or worries you may have. Many women find it easier to write down their questions so that they will not forget to ask in the rush. If there is anything you particularly hope for about the way in which you have your baby, ask the obstetrician or nurse midwife if it can be noted on your record.

Many tests in pregnancy, the value of which has been taken for granted in the past, are now being questioned. Multi-center research is taking place to determine whether they do what they are assumed to do or even if they do more harm than good. This is the only way to discover which are useful and which should be discarded. If there is justifiable uncertainty about a screening procedure or other intervention and you are invited to take part in a randomized controlled trial, consider all the implications seriously. You have the right to be fully informed about any research in which you are taking part; you can consent or refuse, and can leave the study if and when you wish.

ROUTINE TESTS

Most women see their doctor or midwife once a month until they are 32 weeks pregnant. At this stage you will be seen every two weeks and in your final month will be given weekly appointments.

During a typical visit you may be weighed before you see the doctor. While your baby is growing, you will probably be putting on weight fairly steadily (see page 94).

At the first prenatal visit the doctor may listen to your heart. Heart sounds change during pregnancy, and a heart murmur may be detected. This is usually perfectly normal.

Your blood group is determined at your first visit and a test is done to check whether the baby might develop Rhesus disease (see page 113). Your blood is automatically tested for syphilis, and you may be offered amniocentesis (see page 227). At each visit your

Having a vaginal examination
You may be examined vaginally early on in your pregnancy. If you are more than six weeks pregnant the doctor will be able to detect a slight enlargement and softening of the uterus. The developing embryo is well protected and cannot be dislodged by the examination.

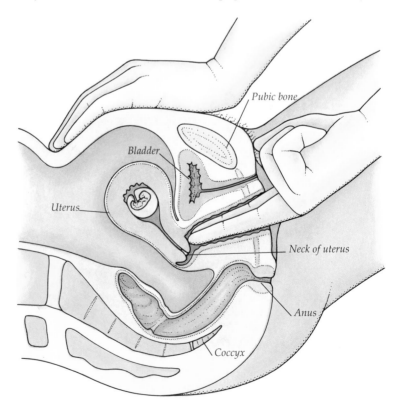

Pubic bone

Bladder

Uterus

Neck of uterus

Anus

Coccyx

blood pressure, complete blood count, and urine will be tested and your weight, the height of the fundus, and the fetal heart beat (as soon as it is audible) will also be checked. You may be offered screening for spina bifida and Down's syndrome (see pages 220–223). Regular blood tests are done for anemia (see page 143). However, what was once treated in pregnancy as "anemia" is usually a normal drop in hemoglobin due to plasma volume expansion. A pregnant woman has about 40 percent more blood flowing in her body. It used to be thought that women's hemoglobin levels must be kept high during pregnancy by iron supplementation. But women whose hemoglobin concentration *does* fall are more likely to go to full term and to have babies of good birth weight. If hemoglobin concentration fails to fall there is a marked increase in the incidence of low birth weight and preterm birth.*

In fact, a woman who is pregnant is better able to absorb iron from food. If you drink orange juice instead of tea or coffee, both of which inhibit absorption of iron, your body will make good use of the iron which is naturally present in the food you eat.*

An ultrasound scan (see page 223) may be indicated at any time during the pregnancy. The use of ultrasound is routine in most practices. In late pregnancy a single scan can show the size of the baby's head in relation to your pelvic outlet. If you have a series of scans at different sessions, an estimate can be made of the baby's rate of growth and expected date of delivery.

At the first prenatal visit you may have a vaginal examination. At most subsequent visits the uterus and baby will be felt by abdominal palpation, not by a pelvic examination. As this is done, you should give a long breath out and release your tummy completely, then go on breathing slowly, releasing more on each breath out. This makes it easier to feel how the baby is lying and is much more comfortable for you than if you are tense.

The examining hands feel first for the distance between your pubic bone and the baby and then the top of the uterus. This process is called fundal palpation. The hands move down the sides of the baby so that by late pregnancy the back and limbs can be felt. The part of the baby that is positioned over the cervix is said to be "presenting." The doctor or midwife turns to face your feet and presses his or her hands downward and from side to side to determine whether the baby's head, buttocks, or any other part, is presenting. The next maneuver tends to be uncomfortable but is quickly performed. Facing you again, the doctor spreads one hand wide and presses in above your pubic bone to feel the exact position of the presenting part in relation to the pelvis.

In late pregnancy, take the opportunity to find out from the doctor or midwife how your baby is lying and discuss anything that may be worrying you. Become aware of fetal movements and tell your caregivers about any pronounced change in their frequency or how they feel.

Talking to doctors and midwives

Some people have doctors or midwives with whom they quickly feel at ease and experience little difficulty in finding out the medical alternatives open to them in pregnancy and discussing their own requirements. However, the expectant mother and her doctor or nurse-midwife are likely to meet in a system in which time is at a premium and sometimes one or both of them finds it difficult to break out from a formal relationship with all that this implies of authority and subordination.

Being pregnant is a physiological process. It also involves a kind of emotional journey into being a patient. And as if all this were not enough, it propels you into new kinds of social relationships. Some of these are with the professionals you encounter during your pregnancy. So, as well as having to understand the changes taking place in your own body and your emotions, you may have to develop new social skills to create a satisfactory dialogue with those who care for you and your baby. This is especially the case when you meet different doctors and nurses at each visit and others again when in labor. The lack of continuity in care is one of the main criticisms that women make about childbirth in a hospital today.*

Some women feel very vulnerable emotionally when they are pregnant, and cannot help crying under pressure, even though (or perhaps because) it is the last thing they *want* to do. You are not abnormal if you feel intense surges of emotion which are difficult or impossible to control, but you may feel at a disadvantage in an interview with a doctor or nurse when you want to ask for something or talk about the kind of birth you are hoping for.

This possibility is a good reason for having your partner or a close friend or relative with you on such occasions. It is important, of course, that you discuss your wishes thoroughly with this person first. You may find it useful for him or her to play "the devil's advocate" and act out an imagined encounter so that you have some practice in discussing the subject and can develop a strategy. Do not make the mistake of anticipating opposition from the hospital staff; you will probably be pleasantly surprised. But do be prepared to give carefully thought-out reasons for what you want.

See that you are well briefed about the matters you want to discuss. Today there is a good deal of published research on emotional and sociological aspects of maternity care, for example, and many papers on the technology of modern obstetrics and the active management of labor (see page 329) are published in medical journals. It will help if you have a clear idea of some of the most important statements. If you are attending childbirth education classes, you can ask your teacher to help. The International Childbirth Education Association produces booklets and sells relevant books,* and there are other organizations which may be willing to give advice (see page 413).

Opposite
In childbirth classes you learn different positions and movements to help you give birth actively.

PREPARING YOUR QUESTIONS

Since questions may go out of your head when you have a chance to ask them (pregnancy amnesia is a well-known phenomenon), and because some doctors seem to concentrate on the lower end of your body to the exclusion of interest in you as a person, it is a good idea to jot down subjects you want to discuss. Different treatments are done routinely in different hospitals. You may not want some or all of these, and it is best to state your preferences as early as possible. On the other hand, you may want a treatment which would not usually be given but is probably available if you make a special request. Your list could include questions concerning the use of ultrasound in pregnancy. You can find more about that on page 223. You may also want to explore your doctor's attitude toward induction and augmentation of labor, routine enemas or suppositories, the use of intravenous drips, electronic fetal monitoring, episiotomy, and the use of forceps (see page 34). You could also ask about the availability of epidurals (see page 309) and whether you will be able to keep your baby with you day and night. It may also be important for you to know whether there will be a special midwife or lactation specialist to help with breastfeeding, and to know her name in advance. Be specific in your requests, to avoid misunderstandings later on.

Sometimes the office or clinic is so crowded that you feel reluctant to take up anybody's time with your questions. Even so, it is probably worth saying that you have made a note of things you would like to discuss and ask whether it is convenient that day, or, if not, whether you can arrange to have some time to talk at the next visit. There is no need to be apologetic about wanting further information or asking for help to achieve the kind of birth you would like. After all, you are not just a baby-producing machine!

During the interview make sure you sit in a relaxed way, check that fingers and toes are unclenched, and breathe out just before speaking for the first time. Make eye contact and address the doctor by name or ask his or her name if you do not know it.

When a woman is feeling nervous, she tends to pitch her voice too high. Modulate it so that it does not sound too demanding. You might also smile nervously without realizing it. This can be confusing for the doctor, who then thinks that you are happy about something when you are not. Or it may be that the doctor unconsciously smiles because he or she is concerned to get you to accept another point of view and is sugaring the pill; your spontaneous reaction may then be to smile back, giving the doctor the idea that you are content when in fact you are not.

Avoid aggression and state your requests clearly and concisely. If you lose your temper, you may be classified as difficult or neurotic. If you encounter opposition or are made to feel that you cannot know what is in your best interests, restate your wishes firmly and give the reasons for them. It is a good idea to include requests that are not top priority, so that there is a possibility of compromise on some matters. Belligerence provokes further opposition. Tell your doctor instead how happy or disappointed you are. Always try to give "I" messages rather than "you" messages. Say "I prefer...." or "I'm unhappy about...." Be assertive in a pleasant way. You may not have any medical knowledge about your body, but you know a great deal about it all the same, since it is you who lives in it. If a woman acts as if she expects to be bossed around, the more likely it is that she will be. Some doctors think it is enough to have a chat with you when you are lying flat on your back with your panties off. You can say that you would like to talk clothed and face-to-face. If a test or intervention is proposed that you do not want, either now or during childbirth, simply say, "No, thank you," and repeat it if

"I'm not used to being assertive but my doctor was OK about it and we've had some lively discussions."

necessary. If this seems too difficult, practice speaking out in less threatening situations, perhaps with your colleagues at work or with members of your family, for instance. Complain in a shop that has sold you shoddy goods, tell guests who are still hanging around your home at midnight that it is time you went to bed, or send back bad food in a restaurant.

You may want to take notes of the conversation you have with your doctor, and can always say: "I'd like to think more about that; may I just make a note of it?" However, you should be careful not to imply that you are cross-examining the doctor and writing down any answers in preparation for a later attack. Make it clear that you are listening closely by "playing back" the important statements: "Do you mean...?" "So you are saying that...?" and rephrase whatever has been said as accurately as you can. You can sometimes add to your remark the implications that you think such a statement entails. By clarifying a point in this way you may be working toward modifying it. For example, if the doctor says, "I never allow husbands to remain if I have to give the patient a vaginal examination or do a forceps delivery because they only get in the way," you might ask: "Are you saying that it is dangerous for a husband to stay because he might affect your judgment?" Few experienced obstetricians would say that the presence of a husband could affect their professional judgment, and the doctor might reply by telling you a story about men who have fainted. You might then say: "I take it you feel happier about a man who stays calm and who gives emotional support to his wife?"

If your interview has gone badly, you can consider changing your doctor or, if there is more than one in your area, the hospital where you are to give birth. But it is best to give yourself a few days to simmer down and think it over calmly before making a final decision. You can write a letter explaining your reasons for seeking other care; it is a good idea to send copies to the Medical Director and the Chair of the Obstetrical Department if it concerns a hospital.

Making your birth plan

Here are some of the questions you might like to consider in constructing your birth plan. Some may not be relevant to you and you may wish to include others, but this list should get you off to a good start.

Q Who would you like to have with you during labor and at the birth? Do you want to place a limit on the number of people caring for you?

Q What is your top priority while in labor? Is there anything that matters to you apart from the safety of your baby and yourself?

Q Do you want to put yourself unreservedly in your caregivers' hands and leave them to get on with it, or do you want to be kept fully informed of all developments and to share in any discussions and decisions made?

Q How do you plan to cope with the pain you are likely to experience during labor?

Q Are there any things you would like to have in the birth room with you, e.g., pictures, familiar objects, candles, aromatherapy essences, music, or equipment to give you physical support and enable you to get into comfortable positions?

Q Have you any special requests about the birth itself, such as having the lights in the birth room dimmed, receiving or avoiding an episiotomy, and the way in which the baby is delivered?

Q Is there anything that is important for you to be able to do during labor, such as using a shower, tub, or birth pool, being able to adopt upright positions and move your pelvis, using alternative methods of pain relief, or being free to make a lot of noise?

Q What are your thoughts about common medical procedures that may be used during labor, such as artificial rupture of the membranes, hormone stimulation of the uterus, electronic fetal monitoring, IVs, the administration of pain-relieving drugs, restriction of positions and movements, and the active management of labor?

Q Do you want the third stage of labor to be speeded up with a hormone injection and controlled cord traction immediately after the birth, or would you prefer the afterbirth to be delivered physiologically?

Q Have you any special requests about the hour following birth, e.g., keeping your baby in bed with you and in skin-to-skin contact, or being left alone with your partner and your baby to enjoy a little privacy? Would you like the pediatrician to examine the baby in your presence?

Q In the 24 hours after birth how much time would you like to spend with your baby, e.g., would you like to keep your baby in bed with you, in a crib beside your bed, or in the nursery for some or most of the time? Are you happy to be woken up at night in order to feed your baby or would you rather be left to sleep?

Q How do you intend to feed your baby? If you plan to breastfeed, are you willing for your baby to be given supplementary formula, dextrose, or water, or do you want him or her to be given breast milk only?

Q What other things are important to you after the birth, e.g., if you have a boy baby do you want him to be circumcised or not, and would you like your partner to be able to stay with you both overnight?

But such drastic measures are often unnecessary, and you will find that you can open up the possibility of getting the kind of childbirth you want with other means. There is always a price to pay for being submissive. A woman avoids conflict but afterwards frequently feels that birth was something done *to* her, not something she did herself. Women who have suffered a sense of complete powerlessness in birth may go on feeling this long after the baby is born. It often leads to their feeling incompetent with the baby, too.

Good communication means that, if for medical reasons you do not get all you had hoped for in terms of care and advice, you can at least take an active part in the decision-making. And it may well be that you will improve conditions in childbirth for other women, too.

MAKING A BIRTH PLAN

A birth plan is a list of your priorities and wishes for the birth and the time immediately afterwards. It is best constructed after you have met your caregivers and discussed your options with them, but early enough for you to negotiate any modifications in hospital protocols or an obstetrician's standard practice. One copy is clipped to the doctor's notes and you keep another copy yourself.

If you have had a baby before you will be pretty clear what is most important to you about the care you receive. If you work in the health services yourself, or have listened to other women's accounts of birth with the same caregivers or in the same hospital, you may also know exactly what you want and do not want. This includes the kind of setting in which you wish to give birth, and the general style of birth you prefer – high-tech, epidural- or drug-free, and mobile, for instance.

Some people think the idea of a birth plan is ridiculous because no one knows in advance how birth is going to be. That is true. But if you were setting off on safari, or even on a picnic when you were not sure how the weather would turn out, you would plan for alternatives. It is the same with birth. You know what you want, and you also know what you want if things do not turn out exactly as expected.

Doctors and midwives do not have to be burdened with patients' trusting reverence, and many nowadays prefer women to think through what they want and to make choices. There still are caregivers who feel threatened by birth plans and see them as undermining their authority and expertise, like the obstetrician who said he could not stand "backseat drivers." Yet when women get utterly dependent on those caring for them it can be more threatening than open confrontation, for if things go wrong and a baby is damaged or dies, total faith then often turns to litigation. It is almost invariably those who put their unquestioning trust in an obstetrician who sue for malpractice – not women who accept responsibility, weigh the pros and cons of different kinds of care, and make decisions for themselves.

It is also sometimes suggested that making a birth plan shows lack of trust in the doctor or midwife. But at best it is something you do *together*. It enables your caregiver to learn about you at the same time that you learn about him or her. It can be a positive part of your developing relationship, and can contribute a lot to it. Those who oppose the idea of birth plans often urge women to be nice to their doctors in order to get what they want. But being nice is often not enough. The kind of doctor who brushes aside a request for "natural childbirth" by saying, "Of course you can give birth naturally. All birth is natural," or who tells you, "You can hang from a chandelier as far as I'm concerned," is likely to want you harpooned to a fetal monitor, and may be knife-happy, too. Stating your wishes in writing and confidently affirming expectations gives you a greater chance of having what you want than playing the part of the obedient patient. Birth plans are a vital part of an active approach to labor as a spontaneous process in which a woman's body knows how to act without anyone's having to "manage" it. Yet they can equally well be used if a woman is certain that she wants an epidural or is convinced that induction is a good thing if she goes a week "overdue."

"Working on a birth plan helped me and my partner sort out what was most important and discuss it with the midwife."

What to include in your birth plan Some things will be simple and straightforward: for example, points such as "I should like to hold the baby immediately, skin to skin"..."I would like to be helped to lift the baby out of my own body." These may well already be standard practices for your midwife or doctor. Other choices may be more complicated and entail further discussion. As an example, if the early stages of labor are long and drawn out, what, if any, interventions might be proposed and which would you prefer? With the method of active management of labor, which is increasingly popular with obstetricians in hospitals all over the world, every woman whose cervix fails to dilate one centimeter every hour has her uterus stimulated artificially by hormones which are introduced through an intravenous drip into her bloodstream. The principle behind this treatment is that no labor should be allowed to exceed 12 hours. The Irish obstetricians who devised this system of management say this is what women want, that women like to know that the baby will be born by eleven a.m., or six p.m., or whatever. They also say that it reduces the need for cesarean section.

In the hospital in Dublin where this method was first introduced, each woman also has her own special midwife who stays with her. Meta-analysis of clinical data and randomized control of trials of active management show that it is not hormone stimulation but the presence of someone who gives one-to-one care and stays with the mother throughout labor and birth, that makes cesarean section less likely for women who have this treatment.* You may welcome the whole package of active management if it is available. Or you may want only specific elements, such as a nurse or midwife who does not disappear at the end of a shift, but stays with you until you have given birth. And you may want to add that you would like to get to know the nurse-midwives before you go into labor, so that you have a chance to talk to whoever your personal care-giver might be. In North American hospitals most doctors, midwives, and nurses do not remain with women continuously throughout labor. For that reason, "doulas" have become a popular addition to many women's support teams. A doula is a woman who is trained and experienced in providing necessary encouragement, reassurance, non-medical advice, and physical comfort throughout labor and birth. She also gives support to the father or partner. Doulas are available in most states and provinces in North America. See page 413 for ways to locate one.

There may be certain interventions you want to avoid entirely if possible, too. For many women episiotomy, the cut to enlarge the vaginal opening as the baby is being born, is one of these. There is ample research now to show that a woman is most comfortable afterwards when she has been helped to give birth gently without a cut or tear. So you may want to find out the episiotomy rate and to ask specifically for help from someone who is good at delivering without damage to the perineum. Research also shows that most tears are small – first or second degree – and that they heal better than episiotomies. So you can state in your birth plan that you would like to avoid an episiotomy, would prefer a tear if an intact perineum proves impossible, and that, whatever happens, you do not wish an episiotomy to be performed without giving your consent first. On the other hand, you may have no preferences and just want the doctor to get on with it.

Keep your birth plan concise, not longer than two pages. Retain one copy yourself and have it ready with the other things you need to take when labor starts. Make sure that whoever is going to be your birth companion also knows what is in it. Birth plans are not set in tablets of stone. Think of your plan as an expression of your individuality and a way of describing the sort of person you are, so that a doctor or midwife meeting you for the first time in labor will get a good idea of how you want to be treated and the things that matter most to you. Use your birth plan as part of a developing dialogue with the people caring for you.

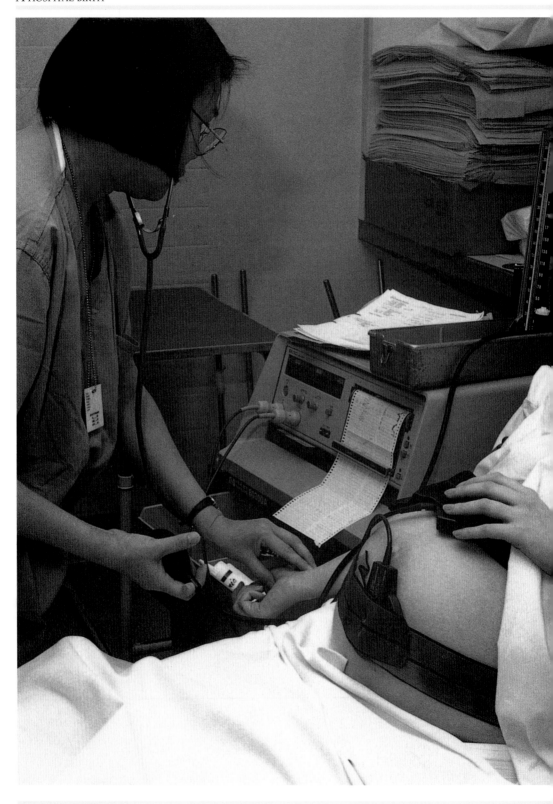

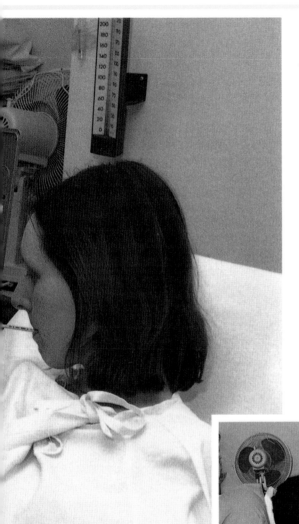

A hospital birth

Louise's first labor was long and she was worried that her second labor would be long, too. But it is usually quicker the second time around, if the baby is in a good position.

This labor lasts four and a half hours, and Louise needs no drugs for pain relief. She is wired to an electronic fetal monitor. Electrodes strapped to her abdomen record the strength of uterine contractions and her baby's heart rate, and this is registered on the chart emerging from the monitor.

There has been a shift change and another midwife is caring for her now (below). She has started to push, sitting well supported by foam rubber wedges, and is getting hot, so her midwife turns on an electric fan.

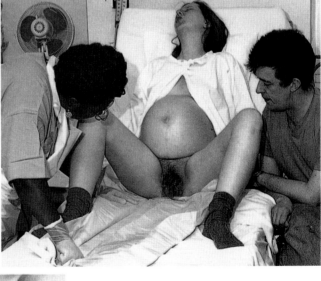

After a while she finds it difficult to push sitting on her coccyx and feels she needs to get into a forward leaning position. She decides to turn onto her hands and knees, which she finds more comfortable. Her perineal tissues fan out easily as the baby's head presses through. The midwife supports the head, then holds the baby under the shoulders as she lifts her out.

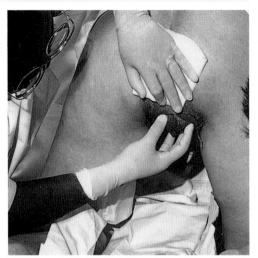

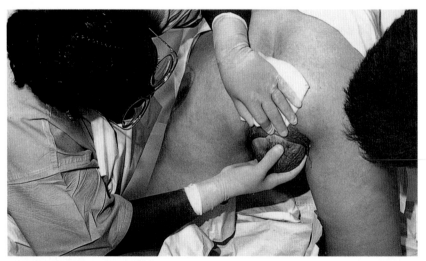

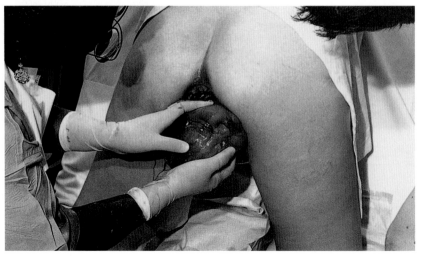

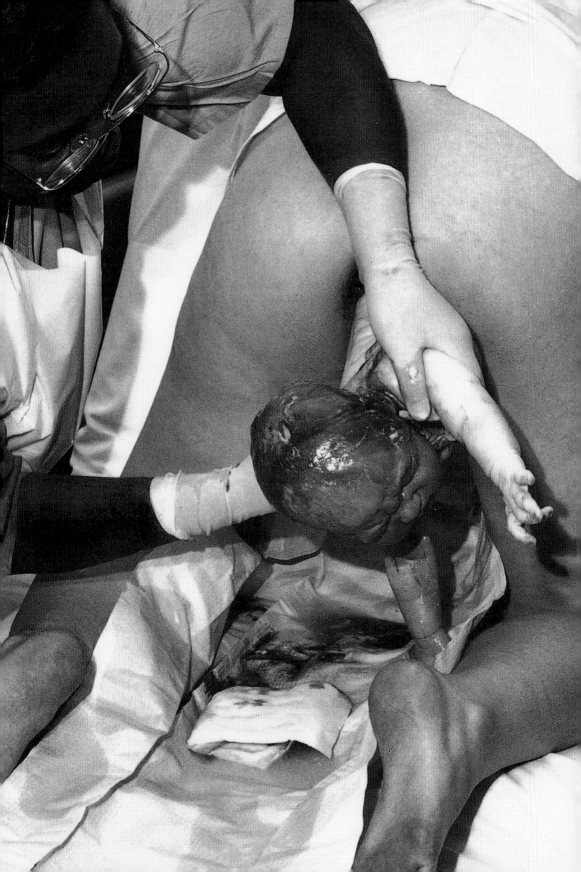

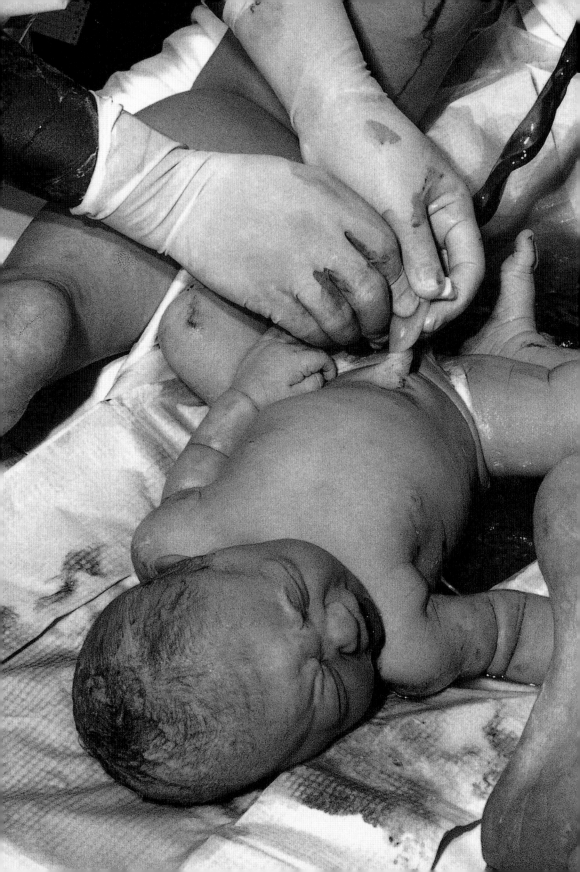

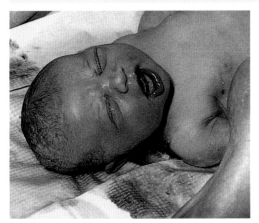

The baby is delivered between her mother's legs. The midwife clamps and cuts the cord, and then places the baby in her mother's arms. She had no episiotomy, and only a small labial tear, which her midwife sutures immediately. Her baby weighed over 9 lbs – much heavier than the first. Afterward her midwife said, "She coped brilliantly with her breathing. Her partner rubbed her back and encouraged her and she chose different positions, including kneeling, in order to help the baby's descent."

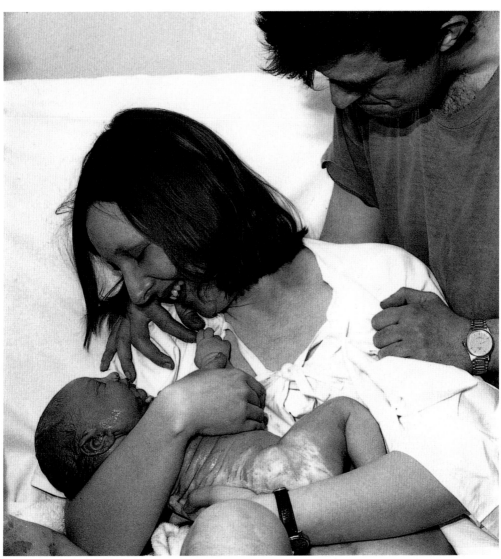

PREGNANCY

Physical and emotional changes

Life in the uterus

In the first days of pregnancy life is budding in cells far smaller than a pinhead. Because everything is happening on such a minute scale, it can be difficult to accept the reality of a baby growing deep inside you. Even when you begin to believe in your pregnancy, other people remain unaware of it. It can seem as if an explosion has taken place without anybody noticing, or as if all the colors have become more brilliant but everyone else is carrying on as usual. The chance meeting of one out of four hundred million sperm with a ripe and vibrant egg has resulted in a dramatic series of events, conducted on a scale so miniature that you cannot feel the astonishing life process unfolding inside you, even though you know it is happening.

FERTILIZATION

At birth the ovaries of every baby girl contain almost 500,000 potential single-cell eggs, but they do not ripen until the menstrual periods begin. Each cell that ripens into an egg is nourished by

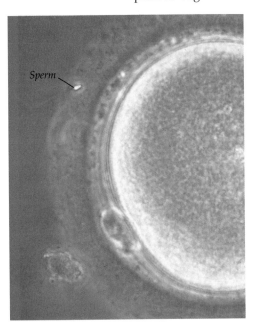

Sperm

nearly 5,000 other eggs that will never themselves ripen. From your first period until the menopause, when your periods stop, you may carry up to 4,000 ripe eggs; each month between 100 and 150 begin to ripen, but usually only one a month reaches maturity and is capable of being fertilized. The frequency with which eggs are produced and released is determined by hormones, which interact regularly in the menstrual cycle.

This cycle lasts for about a month, and begins when a hormone released by the pituitary gland stimulates an ovary to start ripening an egg. As the egg matures, the ovary releases estrogen into the bloodstream. The estrogen stops the pituitary gland's production of hormone, so no more eggs are stimulated into ripening. It also makes the uterine lining change and thicken in anticipation of the egg, which bursts out of the follicle (a capsule bulging on the surface

Above
A sperm fertilizes the ovum, penetrating the outer membrane.

of the ovary) about midway through each menstrual cycle. It is then drawn by the fingered tentacles of the fallopian tube into its long canal, which is about the thickness of a ballpoint refill.

The egg itself is a minute speck. It is barely visible to the naked eye, yet when it meets with a still more minuscule sperm it has the potential to develop into a human being. The follicle (also known as the corpus luteum) that held the egg begins to produce

Ovulation cycle

New follicle

Egg released

Ovary
An external view of the ovary of a fully grown woman.

Inside the ovary
A section through an ovary showing the stages of development of the follicle during a menstrual cycle.

The menstrual cycle
While a follicle is developing in the ovary, the uterus is building up a lining of coiled arteries and glands. If the ripe egg released from the ovary is not fertilized, the uterus sheds the lining (menstruation) and the process begins again.

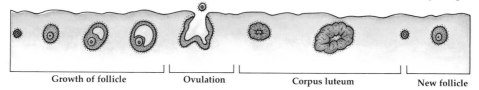

| Growth of follicle | Ovulation | Corpus luteum | New follicle |

Days

Uterine cycle

In pregnancy the lining continues to thicken

5
4
3
2
1
0
mm

| Menstruation | Lining of the uterus thickens | Menstruation |

progesterone, which carries on the work that the estrogen has been doing. If the egg is not fertilized within a few days, the follicle dries up and the progesterone level falls dramatically. As a result of this drop in progesterone level, the uterine lining decomposes, and a menstrual period occurs.

Even while bleeding is going on, the menstrual cycle renews itself: the pituitary gland is stimulating the ovary into ripening a new egg. But if the egg is fertilized, the follicle does not shrivel up, the progesterone level does not drop, and the uterine lining continues to thicken, so that you do not have a period.

The usual pattern is that the ovary on one side releases an egg one month, the one on the other side the next. Sometimes one ovary becomes especially active for a few months. Occasionally only one ovary is functioning. If part of a fallopian tube or an ovary has been surgically removed the other one usually takes on the work of both.

Sperm are so tiny that 30,000 of them placed side by side would just stretch across a bottle top. A man ejaculates hundreds of millions of sperm every time he has an orgasm. After intercourse, a mere 2,000 of these survive the journey up the vagina to the fallopian tubes, and only one can fertilize a ripe egg, which immediately puts up a chemical barrier to keep all others out. Each sperm is shaped like a tadpole with a long, lashing tail; a healthy sperm is highly mobile. The head is rounded and holds the gene-carrying nucleus.

The female reproductive organs

When a woman ovulates, the released egg from one of the two ovaries is immediately drawn into a fallopian tube, where, if intercourse has taken place, it may be fertilized by a sperm. The fertilized egg embeds itself in the lining of the uterus. If the egg is not fertilized, it is shed, along with the lining of the uterus, down through the opening in the cervix and out of the vagina: this is menstruation.

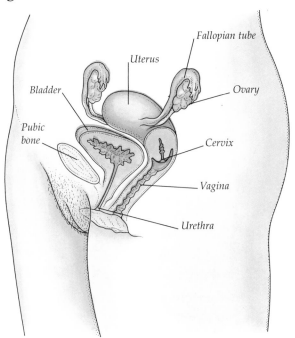

The male reproductive organs

Sperm mature in both testes, which are enclosed within the scrotum. They travel up through each vas deferens, where they are stored temporarily. When a man is sexually aroused, his penis becomes erect and the outlet from the bladder into the ejaculatory duct is closed, leaving it free for the sperm. The sperm entering the ejaculatory duct are accompanied by secretions from the seminal vesicles, Cowper's glands, and the prostate gland. About a teaspoon of the fluid (semen), containing millions of sperm, is ejaculated from the urethra at orgasm.

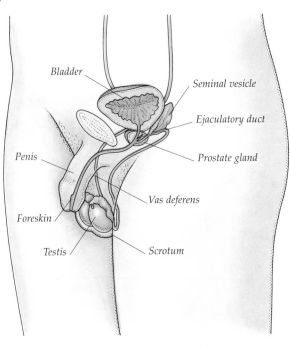

When a sperm meets the egg it burrows its way deep into it and its nucleus fuses with the nucleus of the egg. It is at this moment that the parents' genes, or units of inheritance, first meet.

Genetics

Inside the nucleus of every body cell – with two exceptions – there are 46 chromosomes, making 23 pairs. The two exceptions are the egg cell and the sperm cell, which have 23 chromosomes each instead of 46. Chromosomes are rodlike structures shaped like Egyptian hieroglyphs, each containing thousands of genes.

When the nucleus of the sperm cell fuses with the nucleus of the egg, each chromosome – and each gene inside each chromosome – unites with its opposite number. The newly fertilized cell now contains 46 chromosomes, like every other human cell. The physical characteristics of the future person are determined, and the cell can start to develop into a human being.

BOY OR GIRL?

Out of the 23 pairs of chromosomes in every human cell, one pair determines the person's sex. The two sex chromosomes in a female cell are known as XX, and the two in a male cell as XY. Since the egg and the sperm cell contain half the usual number of chromosomes, every egg cell contains 22 chromosomes plus one sex chromosome, which is an X. Every sperm cell contains 22 chromosomes plus one sex chromosome, which can be either an X or a Y.

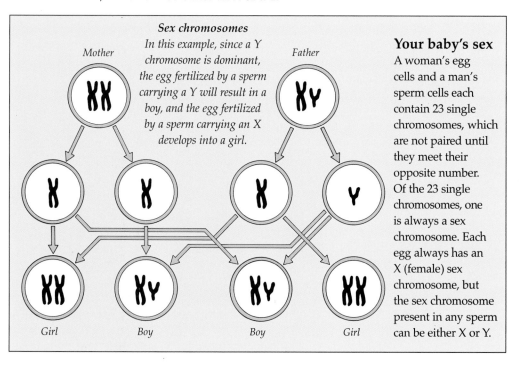

Sex chromosomes
In this example, since a Y chromosome is dominant, the egg fertilized by a sperm carrying a Y will result in a boy, and the egg fertilized by a sperm carrying an X develops into a girl.

Mother

Father

Girl   Boy   Boy   Girl

Your baby's sex
A woman's egg cells and a man's sperm cells each contain 23 single chromosomes, which are not paired until they meet their opposite number. Of the 23 single chromosomes, one is always a sex chromosome. Each egg always has an X (female) sex chromosome, but the sex chromosome present in any sperm can be either X or Y.

The sex of the baby depends on these differences between sperm cells. If the egg is fertilized by a sperm with an X chromosome, the union of the two sex chromosomes will result in XX, a girl. If the egg is fertilized by a sperm with a Y chromosome, the union of the two sex chromosomes will result in XY, a boy. There is usually a 50/50 chance that a boy or a girl will be conceived; statistically it appears that as women grow older and also as they bear more children, the chance of having a girl is slightly increased.

Although the baby's sex is determined by the sex chromosome carried by the sperm, it is also partly a consequence of the environment into which that sperm is received. Natural alkalinity or acidity of the secretions in your reproductive tract makes it easier for some sperm to survive their long journey than for others. Traditionally an acid medium has been thought to increase the chances of having a male child, and an alkaline medium a female child; because of this people have douched with acid or alkaline solutions before intercourse, but there is little evidence that this significantly affects your chances of producing one sex or the other.

DOMINANT AND RECESSIVE GENES

When a Y chromosome meets an X chromosome, the Y chromosome dominates to produce a boy. Similarly, when a gene encounters its opposite number one always takes precedence. A baby receives half of its genes from each parent. If a gene for brown eyes from one parent meets a gene for blue eyes from the other, the gene for brown eyes will always prevail. This does not mean that a child of one brown-eyed and one blue-eyed parent will always have brown eyes. But the gene for brown eyes is known as *dominant*, the one for blue eyes as *recessive*. So someone with brown eyes who has received a gene for blue eyes from one parent retains the blue-eye gene as a recessive gene. If he or she should have a child by another brown-eyed person also with a recessive gene for blue eyes, there is a one in four chance that both parents will pass on their recessive genes for blue eyes to produce a blue-eyed child.

This ability of two brown-eyed parents to have a blue-eyed child is a simple example of the way in which heredity introduces diversification with each generation.

DEFECTIVE GENES

Occasionally genes are defective, but since healthy genes are usually dominant over faulty ones, your baby's normal development is almost always assured. Some defective genes are carried by the sex chromosomes, and then the children of one sex only are affected. Color-blindness, for instance, is carried by some women in one of their two X chromosomes; since the normal gene in their other X chromosome is dominant over the faulty one they do not suffer from color-blindness. But if a boy inherits an X chromosome with a faulty gene he has no other X chromosome with a healthy gene to

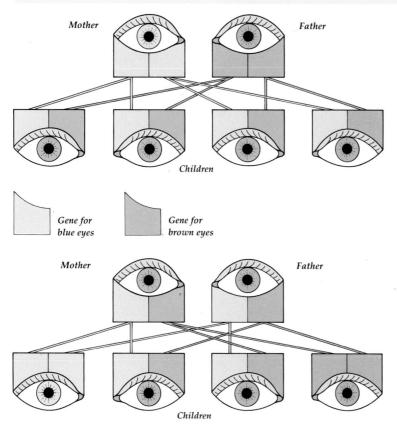

Mother   Father

Children

Gene for blue eyes

Gene for brown eyes

Mother   Father

Children

Dominant and recessive genes
When several different genes are found on a pair of chromosomes, the cell takes instructions from only one, the dominant gene. This masks those of the other, the recessive gene. For a recessive gene to succeed, a child must inherit from its parents two copies of the recessive gene.

Blue or brown eyes?
If both parents have one gene for brown eyes and one for blue, each child has a three in four chance of having brown eyes.

dominate it, so he is color-blind. This is how color-blindness is transmitted through alternating generations of affected boys and carrier mothers. Hemophilia is passed on in the same way.

If you are anxious about the possibility of your children inheriting any diseases or handicaps from your family or your partner's, tell your doctor before you become pregnant, if possible. Failing that, as soon as your pregnancy is confirmed ask to talk to a genetic counselor. There is a genetic counselor in every teaching hospital who can tell you the mathematical chances of bearing a child with a disability and tests that can be carried out (see pages 220–230). If it is discovered that you are carrying an abnormal child, your pregnancy can be terminated *if you wish*. Nobody has to agree to termination of pregnancy even under these circumstances.

The beginning of pregnancy

The genetic make-up of the future child is decided at the moment of fertilization. But conception is a process, not a split-second event. Immediately after it has been penetrated, the egg starts to divide. It divides repeatedly as it is swept along the fallopian tube to the uterus, which it reaches seven days after leaving the ovary. By then it is a ball of cells, called a blastocyst, like a tiny blackberry but hollow in the center. The blastocyst floats in the cavity of the uterus until about the tenth day, when it embeds itself into the uterine lining. Some blastocysts do not manage to root themselves into the wall of the uterus, and are swept out with the next menstrual period. Conception is complete only when the blastocyst has successfully nested into the wall of the uterus. You have not yet missed a period.

IMPLANTATION

The cells now number hundreds. The blastocyst releases enzymes which penetrate the lining of the uterus, causing the tissues to break down and the blood and cells – on which the blastocyst can feed – to seep out. It is a kind of nourishing soup. The quality depends on the state of the lining. Sometimes this is not rich enough to maintain the pregnancy and there is a miscarriage, which resembles a late and heavy period, without your ever realizing you have been pregnant. An inadequately nourishing uterine lining is one cause of infertility.

EARLY DEVELOPMENT

During the second week of the fertilized egg's life, the cells become differentiated. One set becomes the amniotic sac, an envelope of salty fluid in which the baby will later grow. Another cluster develops into the yolk sac out of which the embryo can make blood corpuscles. Yet another group becomes the placenta (see page 70). In between these structures are other rapidly developing cells which will form the baby. These cells are at first just an embryonic disk, but

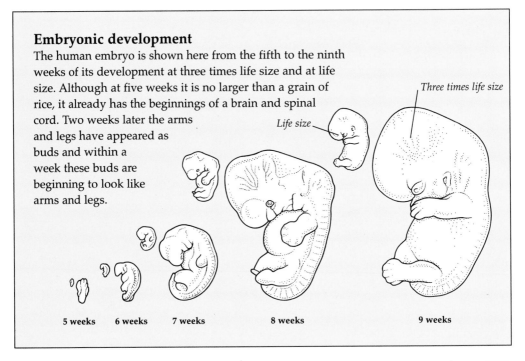

Embryonic development
The human embryo is shown here from the fifth to the ninth weeks of its development at three times life size and at life size. Although at five weeks it is no larger than a grain of rice, it already has the beginnings of a brain and spinal cord. Two weeks later the arms and legs have appeared as buds and within a week these buds are beginning to look like arms and legs.

Three times life size

Life size

5 weeks   6 weeks   7 weeks   8 weeks   9 weeks

they grow lengthways in the third week until there is a head and a tail end, with a yolk sac attached by a stalk to the middle of the disk. At this point you are about one week past the date when you expected your period to come. Although you are not sure, perhaps you suspect that you might be pregnant.

Six weeks pregnant It is three or four weeks after the meeting of sperm and egg, and about two weeks since you missed your period. According to the medical method of dating pregnancy (see page 20), you are about five or six weeks pregnant. The cluster of living cells has now developed into an embryo: there is a neck and a head with rudimentary eyes and ears, a brain, and a heart which is already beating, although it has only two chambers instead of the four which will develop shortly. There are a bloodstream and a digestive system, kidneys and a liver, and tiny buds which will become arms and legs.

A rod of cells develops – the notochord – which later becomes the spine. The embryo develops from the head end down, so that at this stage the lower part of its back is as yet barely formed and looks more like a tail. In fact, while now the size of a coffee bean, the embryo closely resembles a miniature sea horse.

Seven weeks pregnant A week later the embryo is about the size of a baby lima bean. Its body has plumped out into a baby shape, though the head is at a strange angle in relation to the body. It has nostrils, lips, and tongue, and even the buds of its first teeth. Four chambers have developed in the heart. The limb buds have grown into arms and legs, although the hands and feet are just ridges.

Eight weeks pregnant The baby is still smaller than your little toe. It floats in the amniotic sac like an astronaut in space, attached to its life-support system. The heart has started the vigorous pumping of blood which will continue for a lifetime. The brain already shows through skin as thin as waxed paper, revealing every tiny branching blood vessel beneath. The jaw is not yet fully formed and the ears are slung low and have not yet been molded into their correct position. The eyes are covered by an intact skin, which will eventually split to become the eyelids. The head of the embryo is huge in relation to its body. The limbs elongate; elbows and knees begin to appear. Even now the baby is trying out some gentle kicking, though you cannot feel any movement inside you.

All the organs and features of the embryo are completed in the course of the next month. The face grows from the top, and then as the lower parts form the neck is elongated and a chin develops. The nose and outer ears are completely constructed. Fingers and toes are visible, though webbing stretches between them.

By the time you are 12 weeks pregnant the basic physical equipment of the embryo is in working order. The head is still big for the body

Hands and feet
These develop at a slightly different rate, the feet being about a week behind the hands until the 13th week.

Hands

7 weeks

8 weeks

13 weeks

Feet

7 weeks

8 weeks

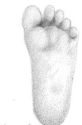

13 weeks

69

and the limbs small; few muscles are working yet. All the internal organs have formed and some of them are functioning. The genitals have developed, but it is not yet easy to tell what sex the baby is. The umbilical cord has started to circulate blood between the embryo and the group of membranes attached to the wall of the uterus. It is at this stage that the embryo begins to rely on these membranes for nourishment and the placenta starts to function. From now on the baby is known as a fetus, and the rest of its time in the uterus is spent on growth and maturation.

The placenta

In the early weeks of pregnancy one cluster of cells begins to develop into the placenta, which is an organ grown especially to nourish the baby and to excrete its waste products. The outside layer of this cell cluster develops into a membrane with hundreds of tiny roots which penetrate the uterine tissues.

Your blood does not flow directly into the baby at any stage of pregnancy. It passes across the tissues on the maternal side of the placenta and the baby's blood passes back across the tissues on the other side. The two bloodstreams are separated by the membrane; chemical substances can be diffused from one bloodstream to the other through the membrane, but the bloodstreams themselves normally never mix. (Some fetal blood cells do cross the placenta, but usually without any significant effect.) The baby can thus have a different blood group from yours, while still taking its nourishment from your blood. In just the same way the baby's waste products are passed back through the placenta into your bloodstream, to be filtered and excreted by your kidneys.

Although the baby makes breathing movements, it does not really breathe inside you: it takes its oxygen from your blood and passes back carbon dioxide. The oxygen diffuses through the membrane into its blood in the same way that oxygen from the air passes through the lining of your lungs. The placenta therefore works rather like a coffee filter: the coffee grains never enter the pot, but substances from them filter into it.

Changes in the constituents of your blood as a result of stress, illness, or any toxic substances that you might absorb will affect the quality of the substances which flow through the membrane. Blood takes only half a minute to flow from the baby's heart to the placenta and back again to the baby's heart. The flow of blood through the placenta in the fourth month of pregnancy is about 8 gallons (27.5 liters) a day, and by the end of pregnancy 100 gallons (330 liters) of blood are passing through the placenta each day.

As the placenta starts to function, it gradually takes over responsibility for production of a range of hormones, including estrogen and progesterone, from the glands which normally secrete these hormones. Estrogen and progesterone control most of the changes in your body during pregnancy. The estrogen stimulates the growth of the uterus and the development of new uterine blood vessels, and also causes the milk glands in your breasts to develop so that you can feed the baby. The progesterone prevents the uterus from contracting strongly and endangering the baby during pregnancy, and thus holds off the start of labor until term. When the baby is ready to be born, the progesterone level drops. By this time the uterus has become exquisitely sensitive to the level of estrogen in the blood, so that when the placenta reduces its output of progesterone, the estrogen takes over, initiates labor, and ensures that the uterus contracts strongly right through to the end of the third stage.

The growing baby

At 12 weeks The fetus has a large head and small, rounded rump; the sex organs are distinguishable though as yet incomplete; the eyes are closed, the retina showing dark and round through translucent skin. Toes and fingers are formed; the arms are the right length in

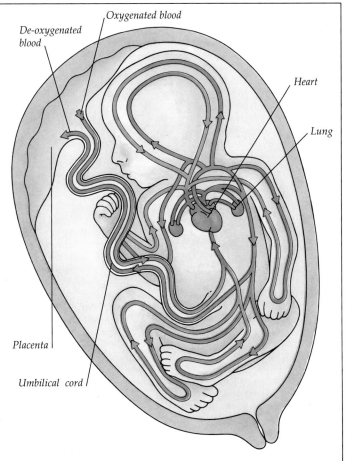

Fetal circulation
This simplified diagram shows how blood that travels along the umbilical cord toward the fetus has received oxygen from its mother through the placenta. Before reaching the fetal heart, it mixes with some of the de-oxygenated blood that has already circulated through the fetus. This mixture travels through the heart and is pumped up into the head and around the body, becoming, as it does so, less oxygenated. To obtain more oxygen, it returns to the placenta via the heart again, most of it bypassing the lungs. At birth the blood vessels around the baby's navel are automatically sealed off and the baby's circulation rapidly adapts to self-survival, with the lungs taking over the function of oxygenating the blood.

Oxygenated blood

De-oxygenated blood

Heart

Lung

Placenta

Umbilical cord

proportion to the body and the nails are beginning to grow. The ribs and spine are just starting to harden into bone and the baby is moving vigorously. You cannot yet feel these movements, but it is kicking, curling its toes up and down, rotating its ankles and wrists, clenching and unclenching its fists, pressing its lips together, frowning and making other facial expressions. The baby is also swallowing the amniotic fluid, gurgling it from its mouth or passing it out through its bladder. There is still plenty of room in the uterus, so the fetus can swoop and undulate in its own enclosed sea.

At 16 weeks Although the baby is growing rapidly, it could still nestle easily into a teacup. Its face is developing specifically human features, though the chin is still small and the mouth wide in comparison. The eyes are huge, closed, and spaced far apart. The baby is covered with a fine down, called lanugo. This is the earliest stage at which you may first become aware of movements. At first these feel like butterflies or little fish zigzagging about in bursts of activity, but soon they are unmistakably the kicking and lunging movements of a live being deep inside your body.

At 20 weeks The baby is half as long as it will be at delivery and about as heavy as a medium-sized Spanish onion (8 oz or 250 g). You could still hold it in the palm of your hand. The closed eyes are bulbous, because the face has not yet plumped out. Hair on the head is starting to grow and there are delicate eyebrows. The baby's movements are becoming more complex and it may be sucking its thumb.

You will probably notice that there are times when your baby is asleep and times when it moves very actively (often when you have just settled down to go to sleep yourself). This seems to be partly because when you lie down it is easier for the baby to move. When moving around you also automatically rock the baby in your pelvis, so when you are busiest the baby is often asleep.

At 24 weeks The baby is considered viable and has been since the 21st week. About the length of a telephone receiver (13 in or 32 cm), it is covered with vernix, a creamy substance which protects its skin and prevents it from becoming waterlogged. This sticks to hairy parts and many babies are born still coated with it. You may notice that your baby responds to loud noises and to music, especially to the brass section of an orchestra, and leaps around. The sound wave patterns of babies' cries and of adult speech can both be recorded by spectographs. The spectograph of a baby's first cry can be matched with that of its mother's speech. This is so even if the baby is born in the seventh month of pregnancy. The baby has been listening to its mother's voice and has learned her speech characteristics.

At 28 weeks The fetus weighs about 3 lbs (1.3 kg) now and is approximately 16 in (40 cm) long. The skin is red and wrinkled. If a

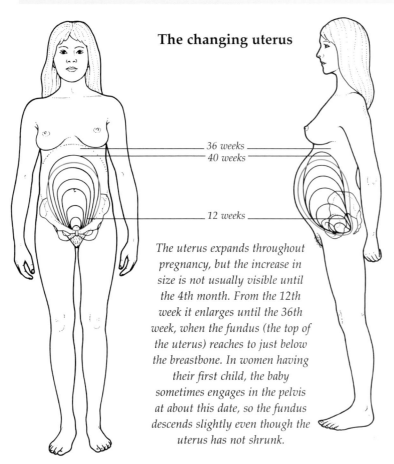

The changing uterus

36 weeks
40 weeks

12 weeks

The uterus expands throughout pregnancy, but the increase in size is not usually visible until the 4th month. From the 12th week it enlarges until the 36th week, when the fundus (the top of the uterus) reaches to just below the breastbone. In women having their first child, the baby sometimes engages in the pelvis at about this date, so the fundus descends slightly even though the uterus has not shrunk.

baby is born now, with the benefits of modern intensive care, he or she has a 60 to 70 percent chance of survival and it can even be higher in some hospitals. The main problem encountered is usually that the baby's lungs have not yet developed bubbles of surfactant, the substance which prevents the complete collapse of the lungs between each breath. Another problem is that there is still very little fat under the baby's skin, and so its temperature control mechanisms cannot yet work efficiently.

The baby has virtually filled all the available space in the uterus. Most babies turn upside down at some point during the seventh month and then seem to fit more comfortably.

By now you may be able to distinguish the baby's bottom from a foot or a knee. When you lie in the bath you can enjoy watching the baby swivel from one side of your abdomen to the other. Foot and knee movements are more jerky than whole-body movements and hands produce soft flutters like sea anemones moving. Other people may now be able to feel the baby kicking when they place a hand on your abdomen. Throughout later pregnancy you can often anticipate the periods of most hectic movement; many babies are at their most energetic between eight and eleven in the evening.

At 32 weeks By the eighth month the baby lacks only some lung surfactant and a good layer of insulating fat before it is ready to be born. Movements are vigorous: the prods coming from the feet are so energetic that they may make you catch your breath. Every now and again the baby may jerk spasmodically in what can be a rather alarming manner; some women worry that their babies are having seizures. But it is usually an attack of hiccups, brought on perhaps because the baby has been gulping amniotic fluid.

At 36 weeks At some point between 36 weeks and term (which is around 40 weeks from the first day of your last period) the baby will probably descend into the pelvis with its head firmly fixed like an egg in an egg cup. It is then said to be "engaged"; this is a good sign and one indication that the baby can pass through the pelvic cavity without difficulty. Once your baby has engaged you can often feel the head like a coconut hanging between your legs. It is not comfortable to sit down suddenly on a hard chair and you may also feel sensations in your vagina like mild electric shocks (see page 231).

When you are examined lying flat on your back, the baby's head may not seem to be engaged. But if you sit up, the head engages.

After the baby has engaged, its larger body movements tend to be limited; you will probably feel only the kicking of legs and feet, the action of the head as it uses the pelvic floor as a trampoline, and the fainter movements of the arms. But although the movements change in type no day should pass without some lively indications from the baby of its presence (see page 237).

The last weeks may be tiring and involve tedious inaction. The baby is three times heavier at birth than it was at 28 weeks, weighing anything from 5½ to 11 lbs (2.5–5 kg), and is between 18 and 22 in long (44–55 cm). It is now ready for its extraordinary journey to life.

PATTERNS OF GROWTH

Babies do not all grow at exactly the same rate. And one baby may weigh nearly twice as much as another, yet both be normal. A steady increase in your weight during pregnancy is reassuring because it suggests that the baby is growing well. But many women experience a plateau in weight gain at some stage of their pregnancy, only to put on more weight again at the next medical check-up. It can be terribly worrying when intrauterine growth retardation is suspected (IUGR). Ways of detecting IUGR are notoriously inaccurate, and it is overdiagnosed. One study revealed 2.5 false positives (that is, it was recorded that the babies were not growing well enough) for each one correctly diagnosed.*

THE QUICKENING

The moment when a woman first becomes aware of her baby's movements used to be very important. It even had a special name – the quickening. Italian paintings celebrated the meeting between

Elizabeth, who was pregnant with John, and her sister Mary, pregnant with Jesus. When the two women reached out to each other Mary's baby "leapt within her."

For centuries pregnancy had little social acknowledgment before quickening occurred and abortion was exclusively a matter for women. Only after quickening was the baby considered to be a "life." Only a woman knew when it had taken place. It was her personal experience. Neither medicine, church, nor state controlled that.

Today doctors claim "bonding" can be achieved via ultrasound, and after the scan at 16 to 18 weeks many women are handed a photograph of a spotted image of the baby. There are no studies to show whether women "bond" better if they have a scan. There have been studies of the effect on pregnant smokers who see their babies on the ultrasound screen, and it has been found that they do not reduce their smoking after a scan. So it cannot be said with certainty that ultrasound promotes bonding.* Whether this happens probably depends on the quality of communication during the scan. A woman should have a chance to discuss what she sees with the obstetrician or radiologist, and what the baby looks like and what it is doing.

You may treasure a photograph of the ultrasound image. It is proof that there really is a baby, that it has tiny limbs, feet, and hands, and is even sucking its thumb. On the other hand, it may not feel quite right. It may seem like an intrusion. Women somehow bonded with their unborn babies long before ultrasound was invented. They did not need the external image because they cherished the internal reality – the bumps, twists, turns, and kicks that assured the mother that she cradled life within her, and which were part of the continuing communication between her and her unborn baby.

It is thrilling when you first feel your baby move. But it is more than that. It is the start of a journey shared by a pregnant woman and her unborn child in which they are – quite literally – in touch with each other. You carry on an intimate conversation. Sometimes you press your hand firmly over the baby's back and the rapid movements are stilled. You have soothed your baby. You massage round where the baby lies and it is as if you are playing together – the baby rolls, dips and dances in response. You exercise on all fours and the baby drops away from your spine, cradled by the muscles of your abdominal wall. It seems that it is joining in the exercises. As the weeks pass your baby can hear the rumblings of your digestive system, the steady beat of your heart, and loud noises from the outside world – the vacuum cleaner, the bark of a dog and the zoom of a plane engine, music, TV and radio programs, the chattering of children, and your voice with its modulations of mood and intensity, changing rhythms and pitch, speaking, singing, whispering, calling and humming. By the 24th week the baby is starting to listen to and learn the sounds of language. A woman who listens to her baby, knowing that her baby is listening to her, too, is already "bonding" with her child months before she holds her newborn in her arms.

Forty weeks of life

The next ten pages show different stages of the development of a baby from the moment of conception to its last week in the uterus. The illustration below shows the five-day journey of the egg along the fallopian tube, where it is fertilized, to the uterus.

The growth of the cell cluster

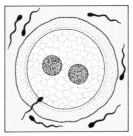

1 One of the sperm that has arrived in the fallopian tube penetrates the ripe egg.

2 The head of the sperm separates from the tail and approaches the egg's nucleus.

3 The chromosomes of the two nuclei pair off to create a two-celled egg.

The uterus and fallopian tubes

Nestling deep inside the pelvis between the bladder in front and the intestines at the back, the uterus is cupped by springy pelvic floor muscles (see page 118). The fallopian tubes branch out at either side, ending in fronds – like those of a sea anemone – which hold the ovaries.

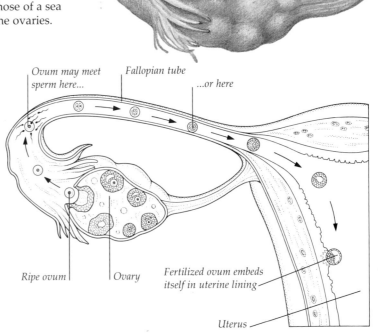

Ovum may meet sperm here...

Fallopian tube

...or here

A ripe egg is released from the ovary

The egg is ready for fertilization for only 12–24 hours. A sperm burrows its head into the egg. The sperm's tail drops off. The egg absorbs the sperm. In three days there is already a cluster of 32 cells, and in five days a cluster of 90 cells.

Ripe ovum

Ovary

Fertilized ovum embeds itself in uterine lining

Uterus

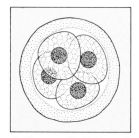

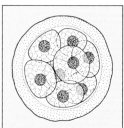

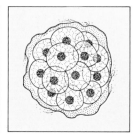

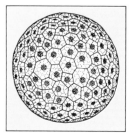

4 *The two cells divide as the egg continues its journey along the fallopian tube.*

5 *As the cells continue to divide they gradually get smaller and smaller.*

6 *On about the fifth day the egg reaches the uterus and loses its jellylike coating.*

7 *Six or seven days after fertilization the egg embeds itself in the uterine lining.*

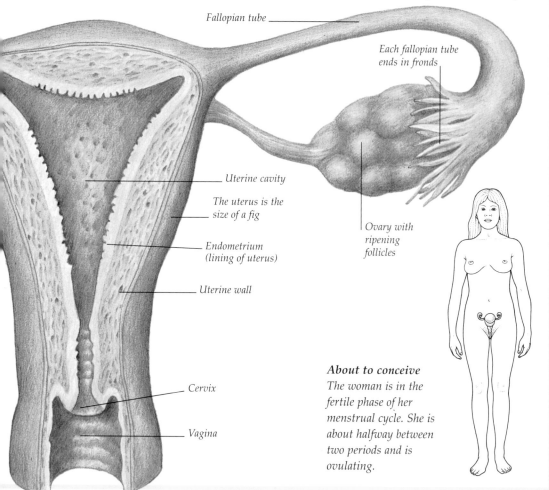

Fallopian tube

Each fallopian tube ends in fronds

Uterine cavity

The uterus is the size of a fig

Endometrium (lining of uterus)

Uterine wall

Ovary with ripening follicles

Cervix

Vagina

About to conceive
The woman is in the fertile phase of her menstrual cycle. She is about halfway between two periods and is ovulating.

Eight weeks pregnant

The baby is just under 1 in (2.5 cm) long. The bones of its arms and legs start to harden and the baby makes slight movements, still too feather-light for the mother to notice. The baby's face is developing. Some time during this week the baby starts to open its mouth and the upper palate forms. The lower jaw is taking shape, with muscles which will enable the baby to suck and chew. The sound-perceiving mechanism of the ear has now developed.

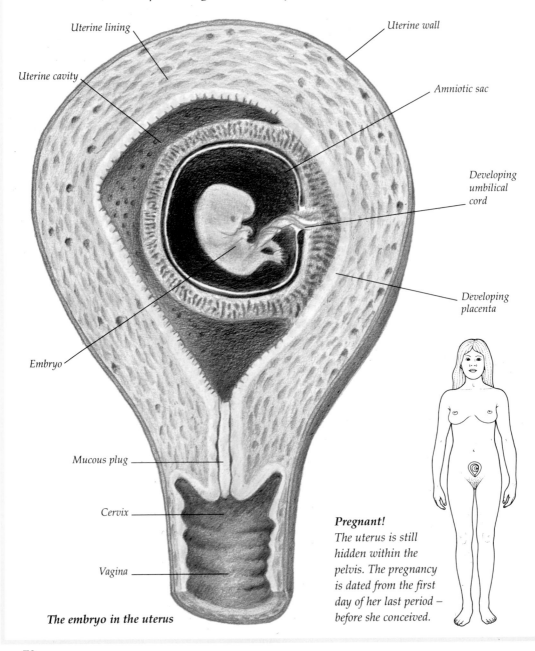

Uterine lining

Uterine wall

Uterine cavity

Amniotic sac

Developing umbilical cord

Developing placenta

Embryo

Mucous plug

Cervix

Vagina

The embryo in the uterus

Pregnant!
The uterus is still hidden within the pelvis. The pregnancy is dated from the first day of her last period – before she conceived.

Twelve weeks pregnant

The baby is now just over 2 in (5 cm) long. It has developed sexual organs that later will show whether it is male or female. Its head is more rounded and it is no longer so top-heavy: it is about two-thirds the size of the body. The eyes are widely separated in a broad face. The jaws have 32 permanent tooth buds and the baby is starting to suck. It is already exercising the muscles that will be used in breathing after birth.

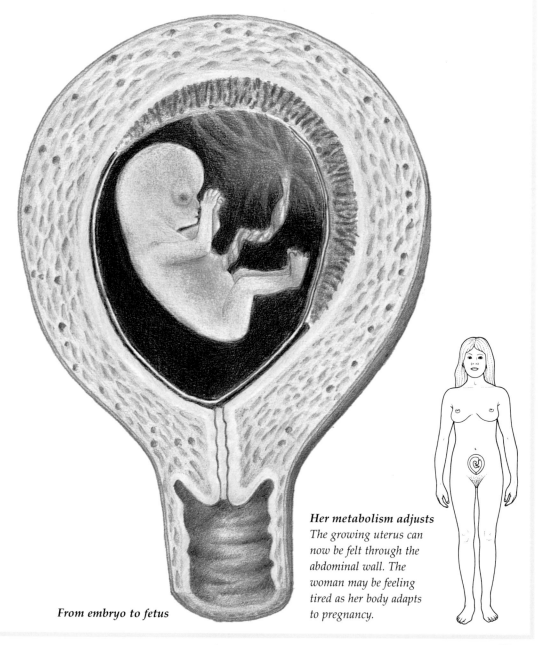

From embryo to fetus

Her metabolism adjusts
The growing uterus can now be felt through the abdominal wall. The woman may be feeling tired as her body adapts to pregnancy.

Twenty weeks pregnant

The baby's rapid rate of growth slows down a little at this stage. It is about 10 in (25 cm) long from head to toe. Legs are the right length in proportion to the body and there are miniature toenails and fingernails. The baby kicks, twists, jumps, and somersaults. Hair on the baby's head and delicately etched eyebrows have appeared and there is fine downy hair called lanugo over much of the body.

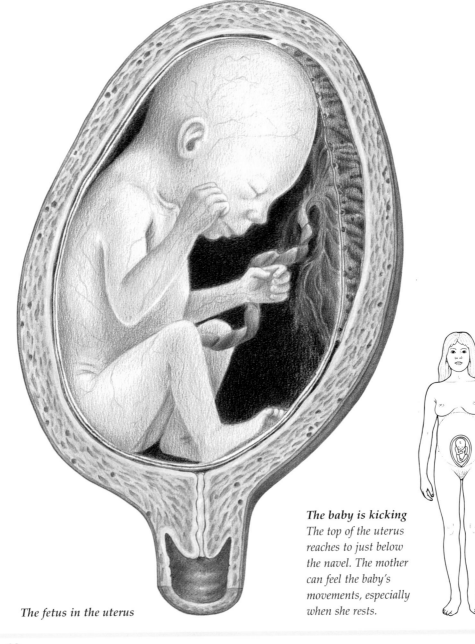

The fetus in the uterus

The baby is kicking
The top of the uterus reaches to just below the navel. The mother can feel the baby's movements, especially when she rests.

Twenty-four weeks pregnant

The baby is thin and the skin is wrinkled. A network of veins and arteries shows through the translucent skin. The face is now fully formed and the eyes are rather prominent because fat pads have not yet built up in the cheeks.

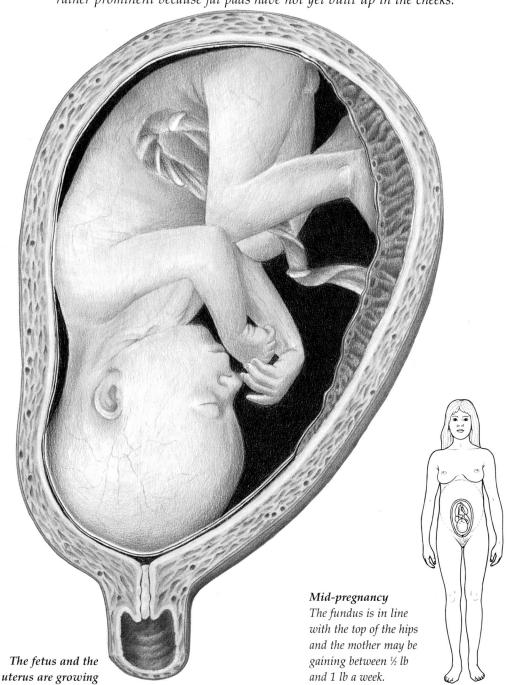

The fetus and the uterus are growing

Mid-pregnancy
The fundus is in line with the top of the hips and the mother may be gaining between ½ lb and 1 lb a week.

81

Thirty-six weeks pregnant

*There is no longer enough room in the uterus for the baby to move about freely.
It has settled into one position and the main movements the mother feels are
jabs from the arms and legs. By now the skin is smooth and peachlike and the
body has plumped out. When the baby is awake, the eyes are open and it is
aware of strong light flowing through the tissues of its mother's abdominal wall.
If it is born at this time, the baby has an excellent chance of survival.*

The baby turns head down in the uterus

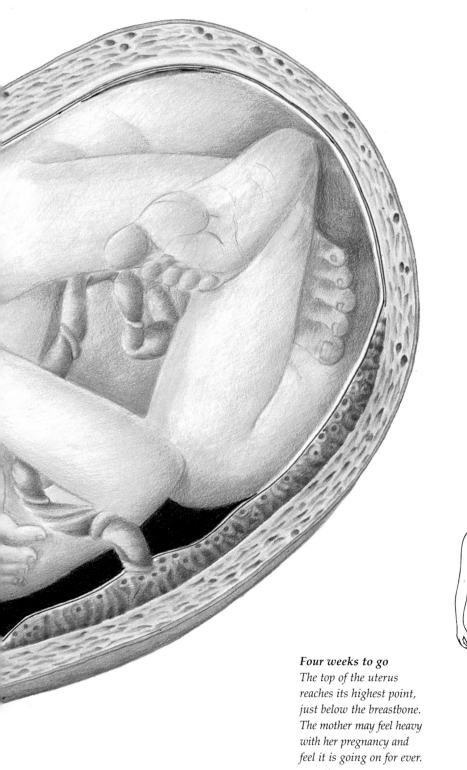

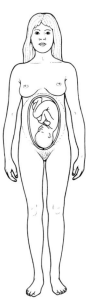

Four weeks to go
The top of the uterus reaches its highest point, just below the breastbone. The mother may feel heavy with her pregnancy and feel it is going on for ever.

Forty weeks pregnant

The baby is now about eight times bigger than it was at three months, when all its vital organs were formed, and has increased in weight approximately 600 times. Most of the lanugo has dropped off, though there may still be some down in the center of the back, in front of the ears, and low on the forehead. The fingernails extend beyond the fingers and may need cutting at birth so that the baby does not scratch his face.

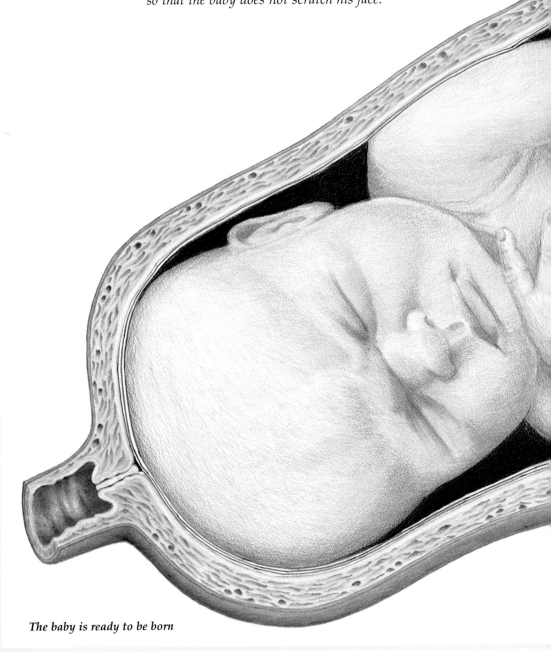

The baby is ready to be born

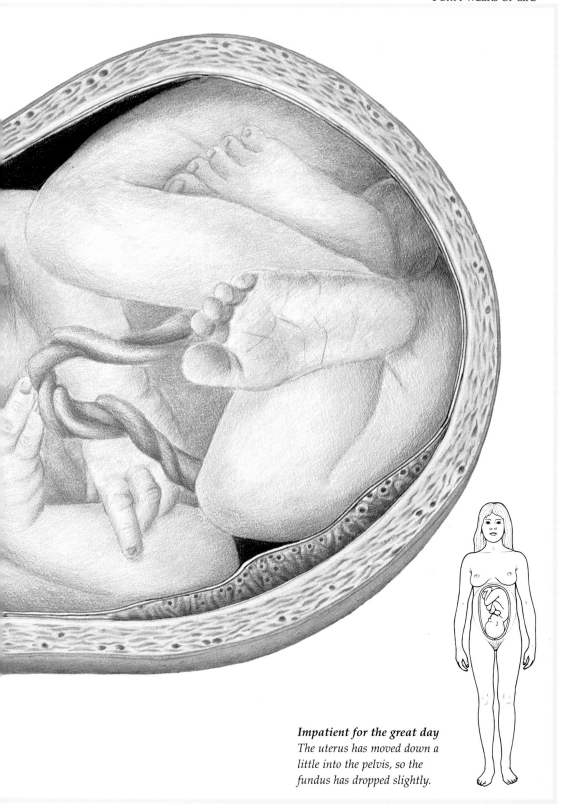

Impatient for the great day
The uterus has moved down a
little into the pelvis, so the
fundus has dropped slightly.

Expecting twins

Finding out that you are going to have twins usually comes as a shock. Some women suspect quite early in their pregnancy that this will be the case, especially if they have had a singleton pregnancy with which they can compare this one. If you are a fraternal twin (see below), you are about twice as likely to give birth to twins yourself as are other women. The chances of having fraternal twins depend on heredity, age, race, and the number of children you have already had. Although fraternal twins often skip a generation, the chances of their occurring in successive generations are high. The frequency of identical twins seems independent of these variables.

MIXED FEELINGS

However, if nothing has led you to suspect that you are carrying more than one baby, it can be very upsetting to be told, after an ultrasound scan or a prenatal visit (see page 43), that suddenly all

---

How twins are conceived

Normally conception occurs when one egg that is released from a woman's ovary is fertilized by one sperm from a man's testes. Seven out of ten pairs of twins are the result of the woman releasing two eggs, which are then fertilized independently by two different sperm (fraternal twins).

Usually the two eggs then implant and develop separately in the uterus. Less commonly, one egg fertilized by one sperm divides, resulting in two developing babies with the same inherited characteristics (identical twins). Often this division occurs after implantation in the uterus.

Identical twins
Identical twinning occurs after, rather than at, fertilization, and it often occurs after implantation in the uterus. As a result the twins almost always share a placenta although each has its own cord and bag of water.

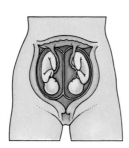

Fraternal twins
Fraternal twins have separate water bags and cords, and separate placentas. Occasionally the two eggs implant close together in the uterus, so that the placentas become fused and it looks as if there is only one.

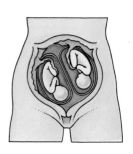

Monozygotic (one-egg) or identical twins   *Dizygotic (two-egg) or fraternal twins*

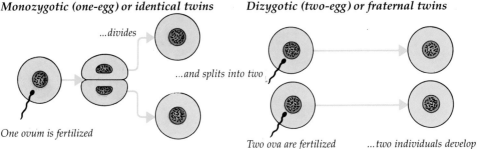

...divides

...and splits into two

One ovum is fertilized

Two ova are fertilized   *...two individuals develop*

your expectations of birth and the time afterward need readjusting. If you are to be a mother for the first time, the natural apprehension you originally felt about the labor and how you would cope with a new baby is greatly increased. Added to this you wonder how you will manage two babies at the same time in all their noisy reality – two mouths to feed, two diapers to change each time, two babies to bathe, two loads of clothes to wash, two budding personalities who will need your love and attention.

One woman, who was dismayed on hearing that she was expecting twins, said that she never really veered from this attitude throughout her pregnancy. During a hospital stay in her eighth month of pregnancy, she took the opportunity of watching mothers who had just given birth to twins, and felt that all her worries were justified, since they seemed to have such trouble in managing two babies. However, shortly after her twins were born, she was able to comment on the "totally unexpected delight of being able to breast-feed both, often simultaneously." She did admit, though, that it was hard work at first and that "the intense joy and delight the babies now give has only come as we have got to know them."

Positions of twins in the uterus

Twins fill the available space in the uterus more quickly than a single baby, so they may adopt the positions in which they will be born at an earlier stage.

The pictures below show fraternal twins (with two placentas), but the same positions apply to identical twins (with a single placenta).

This presentation with both twins in the cephalic or head down position is the most common. It is also the most straightforward: birth should present no special complication.

When one twin is head down and the other head up the breech baby is often born second. The first baby opens up the birth canal so that the breech baby can usually be born vaginally without difficulty.

If both babies are breech the risk of complications will be evaluated in advance. A cesarean section may be performed in preference to a vaginal delivery.

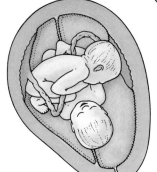

When one baby is lying transversely and the babies are large, a cesarean section will be carried out. If the babies are not large, it is usually possible to turn the second baby after delivery of the first.

Sometimes a woman is unhappy to discover that she is expecting twins because she has been planning for a home birth and this may no longer be possible. Doctors and midwives usually advise hospital birth for twins, since the chances of a complicated delivery, especially for the second twin, are increased and it is possible that the babies will be premature and underweight. If you are going to term, however, and both babies have grown well and are head down, you may decide on a home birth after all.

Alternatively a woman may be overjoyed to find that she is going to have twins. Perhaps she had wanted more than one child, but was not particularly enjoying her pregnancy and certainly not looking forward to another. Suddenly she discovers that she can have two children for the price of one pregnancy and labor!

GETTING ADEQUATE REST

The first thing to accept is that a pregnancy with two babies tumbling about inside can be more of a strain than an ordinary pregnancy. The risk of developing preeclampsia (see page 139) is higher; the babies are more likely to be born prematurely, and they may not be very strong. Because they have to share the space in the uterus and the nutrition available through the placenta, twins are often of low birthweight. You will feel better if you have regular rest times and frequently go to bed early. You need help with housework and cooking and someone who will, at least occasionally, bring a delicious meal to your bed. If you already have other children, it is worth making an effort to find some motherly (or fatherly) person who can look after them for an hour or so each day so that you can relax without feeling that you will be needed in a minute. Many obstetricians require women pregnant with twins to get more rest. However, there is no evidence to support the value of total bed rest in twin pregnancies.* If you are able to plan ahead for your pregnancy you may be able to reorganize your life well enough to allow you to take an adequate amount of rest at home.

There is no need to be an invalid. Plan ahead things you can do in bed: read, write, sew, learn a language, take up a craft you have always wanted to try your hand at. If you think about the extra demands made on your body by a multiple pregnancy you will realize that your whole system has to adjust to the babies' needs. Such an adjustment involves widespread metabolic changes; there is also extra pressure put on your digestive organs and on your diaphragm and lungs, as well as stress on bones (on your lower ribs, which tend to splay out, and on your spine, for example). Your muscles, too, will have to cope with much of the stress of a twin pregnancy, especially your tummy muscles, your pelvic floor, and the muscles of legs, feet, arms, shoulders and back, which have to support the extra weight and do the work of lifting and coping with your body mechanics. Above all there is a general crowding out that may well make you feel very full and heavy.

Opposite

They may look like two peas in a pod but they have distinct personalities.

So rest will help your body adjust to the increased demands made on it by a multiple pregnancy. And the rest that helps most is rest taken before you become exhausted and irritable and *before* you feel that you cannot carry on a minute longer.

LYING COMFORTABLY

You may find it very uncomfortable to lie flat. Your heavy uterus is pressing on major blood vessels in that position, too, so, both for your own comfort and for the blood supply to the babies, lie either well propped up or in the "three-quarters-over" position. Prop your breasts with one pillow and put two under your upper knee if this feels good. Even more so than with a singleton pregnancy, special back supports may be needed in the last few weeks. A large bean bag may feel comfortable; and so might a contour pillow used with other pillows, two firm foam wedges, or the kind of cushion that is sold for making it more comfortable to read in bed. Whatever you choose, try to get something solid which will support the exaggerated curve of your lower spine.

POSTURE AND EXERCISE

Sensible body mechanics are also more important when you are expecting more than one baby (see pages 120–122). Learn how to counteract the effect of the enlarged and heavy uterus by standing straight and tall, with tail tucked in. Aim to balance on the balls of your feet rather than going flatfooted and waddling like a duck, which is only too easy to do when you are overtired. Above all, learn how to get up from a lying-down position by rolling over, if necessary kicking off with your foot and hand against solid objects, and then rising on to all fours.

Pelvic-floor toning activity (see pages 118–119) is very important throughout, whether you are carrying one baby or two; with twins it will be especially vital after the birth, as the muscles around the vagina have been stretched by the extra weight of two babies. It is a good idea in any case to do these movements from early pregnancy, before there is any appreciable change in weight, as muscle tone is really best built up before there is any particular stress on the muscles.

"I've never been keen on exercises, but I like the idea of keeping muscles toned by activity, having a body that's alive."

If your pelvic-floor muscles are under a great deal of strain, you can do these movements while lying on the floor with your lower legs raised on a chair. In this position weight is not pressing on the pelvic muscles, and it is easier to feel what is happening there. In advanced pregnancy, however, when the babies are low down, it may be impossible to use this position. Try letting your pelvic muscles 'dance' when sitting propped up with pillows.

You will probably be aware of the babies moving a great deal inside you. Your abdomen feels like a basket full of puppies. It can be difficult to sleep, and you are often awakened by all the internal activity. Practicing release from tension and letting muscles relax all over your body can help enormously. Some mothers worry that with all this movement the babies are in danger of harming each other. They can certainly shuffle each other up a bit, but each one is sealed off in its own bag of waters, and this also means that each baby bobs around like a cork in a glass of water. The water cushions them from shock and allows free movement until the very last weeks of pregnancy when the pelvic girdle cradles the babies so closely that you may feel only small movements.

DIET AND NUTRITION

For a detailed discussion of diet in pregnancy see pages 93–100. The demands made on your body by a twin pregnancy require an even more careful attention to diet than is necessary in a singleton pregnancy. Aim for a nutritious diet with plenty of salads and fruit and only those foods which are of positive value to yourself and the babies. Cut out ice creams, sickly doughnuts, and cookies. The easiest way to do this is to convince yourself how awful these foods really are and to think instead of rich golden hunks of cheese, glowing fruit salad, a peach that melts in the mouth, jade-green watercress, rosy apples, and a luscious, long glass of milk.

To save laboring over a hot stove have at least one raw food meal a day, which will give you a good supply of vitamins. You may like to buy some new cookbooks that concentrate on salads and fruit and stimulate your imagination. If you normally eat white bread and cereals, now is the time to switch to whole wheat bread and flour, brown rice, and whole grains. Eating like this will help you after the babies come, too, as you cannot feel full of vitality if you are poorly nourished and weighed down with "junk" foods.

The more tired you become the more you may feel that you cannot be bothered about preparing nutritious meals and shopping for food. But your health depends on your having a good diet and not skimping on protein, vitamins, and minerals. Is there any chance of getting help with groceries? Could someone else shop for you? Or could you and your partner or a friend do it together in bulk, loading up a car? (But do not lift boxes and bags into the trunk yourself or attempt to unload them!) If you have to shop unaided, use a wheeled shopping cart and avoid carrying bags. There is probably a store in your area which will deliver to your home provided that you order enough at one time. If you live in the country, a village store may do this when they know you are expecting twins. Or could your partner take a neighbor who has no car to the supermarket, so that she can help do your shopping?

Your baby's wellbeing

Looking after yourself in pregnancy, from the very first weeks, is probably more important for the welfare of your baby than anything else you can do. It ensures that you provide the best possible environment for the developing baby – and, equally important, it gives you the best chance of being healthy and full of vitality, ready for the birthday and the first stages of motherhood.

Nutrition

Your baby depends on what you eat and drink for adequate nourishment in the uterus. It used to be thought that provided the expectant mother had a "sensible" diet there was no need to give her any advice about what she should eat, because the fetus would always take what it needed. There were certain "do nots," the most important of which was "do not eat for two." However, such a vague instruction led to the unfortunate result of large numbers of women going through pregnancy on inadequate diets.

Then research revealed that when pregnant women have an inadequate diet, their babies may die or be born in poor health, and women may have difficult pregnancies and labors, as well as subsequent illness after delivery.* If a woman is nutritionally deprived, her baby is deprived, too; she is more likely to have a miscarriage and, if the pregnancy is maintained, her baby is more likely either to be born prematurely or to be of low birthweight because it has not received sufficient nourishment in the uterus. The research also revealed that poor nutrition in the later part of pregnancy can affect a child's brain development.*

However, recent research has shown that sometimes too much emphasis has been placed on having huge quantities of food and a great deal of animal protein. Metabolic changes in pregnancy mean that most women can make better use of the food they eat, and this increased efficiency extends into the period of breastfeeding, too.* So there is no need to worry about whether you are having the right diet, to take vitamin pills and mineral supplements routinely, or to feel you ought to be eating foods you dislike just because you are told that they are good for the baby.

Women often develop food intolerances in the first weeks of pregnancy. They cannot digest food they liked before. The modern emphasis on good nutrition in pregnancy can make women who are suffering from nausea and vomiting feel very anxious about depriving their baby of essential foods. In many traditional cultures it is believed that the baby asks for the food it wants and rejects others, and that it is important to give a pregnant woman exactly what food she fancies because it is her baby speaking through her.

Opposite
Take time to enjoy your food during pregnancy and eat plenty of fresh fruit and vegetables.

93

Vomiting is one way in which your body refuses food with which it cannot cope. If you are experiencing nausea it is best to trust your feelings and eat only what you fancy. Do not worry that you are not having a "balanced diet." In a few weeks you are likely to enjoy a much wider range of foods again. If you have a very restricted diet take vitamin supplements to ensure that you supply the nutritional elements necessary for your baby's development.

WEIGHT GAIN

It is quite normal to put on between 20 and 30 lbs (9–13.5 kg) during pregnancy. Some women put on more, with no ill effects. Do not assume that because your baby will weigh only 6¼ to 8½ lbs (3–4 kg) at birth, the rest of the weight you put on is fat. Consider the weight of the placenta, membranes, and amniotic fluid, the increase in size of the uterus and breasts, and the increase in volume of your blood. Fluid retention also accounts for a substantial weight gain in some women. All these things return to normal after the birth.

Since different women gain weight at different rates it is impossible to be dogmatic about how much weight you should put on. Medical opinion is that "arbitrary weight restriction is potentially harmful to both mother and baby."* If you start your pregnancy underweight you and your baby may benefit from a bigger weight gain than the woman who starts pregnancy overweight. It is most unwise for any woman to try to remain slim in pregnancy, and an attempt to keep your figure might result in the eventual loss of your baby. However, if you start pregnancy overweight, you are likely to put on more weight than a woman who is not fat at the onset of pregnancy, and also to suffer from high blood pressure and urinary tract infection.*

WEIGHT GAIN IN PREGNANCY

Since most women gain weight at different rates it is impossible to say how much weight you should put on. However, if you are seriously overweight or underweight this may lead to complications during pregnancy and labor.

Proportions of weight gain

Your total weight gain in pregnancy is made up as follows:

Weight of baby	38%
Weight of placenta	9%
Weight of amniotic fluid	11%
Increase in weight of uterus and breast	20%
Increase in weight of blood	22%
Total weight gain	100%

Timing of weight gain

0–12 weeks	0%
12–20 weeks	25%
20–30 weeks	50%
30–36 weeks	25%
36–40 weeks	0%

So you can assume that if, for instance, you are 30 weeks pregnant, the weight you have gained in pregnancy will be about 75% of your total weight gain.

One way of checking to see whether you are putting on superfluous fat during pregnancy, which you will then be left with after the birth, is to measure your upper thighs each week, keeping an accurate record of the measurement. This is an excellent way of recording any increase in your own body fat as distinct from the weight you are gaining as a result of the pregnancy. The upper thigh measurement should stay about the same, although fluid retention may increase it slightly in the last weeks of pregnancy.

PROTEIN

Women who are not pregnant are recommended to have 1½ oz (46 g) of pure protein a day for optimum health. When you are pregnant you may need about twice as much protein as this. The foods that are rich in protein are lean meat, fish, beans, nuts, brewer's yeast, milk, yogurt, cheeses and other dairy products.

All proteins are made up of chemical substances – called amino acids – in different combinations. Animal or "first-class" proteins contain all the amino acids necessary for the protein to do its body-building work; vegetable proteins, which used to be called "second-class," contain only some of these amino acids, and therefore they should be eaten either with a small quantity of animal protein or in different combinations. If you are a vegetarian who eats no animal products, combine beans with a wheat product at the same meal – say, beans with wholegrain flour pastry, chickpeas with pasta, or lentils with whole wheat bread.*

You will obtain adequate protein if every day you have one dish from each of the following categories: (a) one helping of meat or fish, two eggs, a cup of peanuts or cashew nuts; (b) 4 oz (100 g) of hard cheese, 8 oz (200 g) cottage cheese or 1 quart of milk (substitute soy, or tofu); (c) four slices of whole wheat bread, a helping of brown rice or wholegrain pasta, or one large potato that has been baked in its jacket. If you are a vegan and do not eat any animal products, you will obviously not want cheese and milk, and should have a good helping of pulses instead.

CARBOHYDRATES

You need carbohydrates for energy. They are found in foods you eat in bulk, such as bread, flour, cereals, and root vegetables. Most foods containing carbohydrates have other valuable nutrients, too; potatoes – especially if you eat them in their jackets – can contribute protein and vitamin C as well as carbohydrates, and whole wheat bread provides B vitamins, iron, and the fiber which helps to prevent constipation. If you eat small quantities of these foods daily, you should need no other carbohydrates.

If you are already overweight before starting pregnancy, or if you are putting on a lot of superfluous fat during pregnancy (see above for a method of checking this), it is a good idea to try to cut out all white flour and sugar, as well as all the products containing them.

A balanced diet

Presenting food so that it looks attractive enhances the pleasure in eating and will help you digest it better, too. Even for a solo meal, arrange each plate of food so that it is a vibrant mixture of colors and textures. Below are suggestions for breakfast, lunch, and supper dishes.

A bowl of granola
A breakfast of cereal with fresh fruit and wholegrain toast.

A grapefruit snack
Citrus fruits such as grapefruit are a valuable source of vitamin C.

Fruit salad
Top a colorful mixed fruit salad with a large spoonful of thick yogurt.

Bean salad
Mixed beans, chick peas with vinaigrette and chopped herbs.

Carrot and artichoke soup
Serve this soup hot or cold, finished with a swirl of crème fraîche.

Salad sandwich
Use a mixture of young salad greens on wholegrain bread.

A fish dish
Serve with pilaf of rice, green vegetables, and lemon.

Stir-fry
Arrange stir-fried baby vegetables in the center of a decorative rice ring.

Pasta
Mix with tomatoes, red peppers, olives, and olive oil.

Cakes, desserts, and cookies do not do much to help your unborn baby's health. If you like sugar in tea and coffee, train yourself to enjoy both of these drinks without it.

FATS
Your body's need for fat is minimal. You can reduce your intake by trimming fat off meat, using less butter, drinking low-fat milk, boiling or steaming foods rather than frying or sautéing them, and cutting out rich sauces. You will find that cottage or ricotta cheese and yogurt are both useful ingredients of low-fat sauces, and that you can make fat-free sauces with puréed vegetables.

MILK AND DAIRY PRODUCTS
Milk is usually recommended for the pregnant woman, but unless your diet is grossly inadequate in protein you do not need more than one pint a day. Consumed in large quantities whole milk is fattening, and if you fill yourself up with drinks of milk you are likely to dampen your appetite for other foods you and your baby need. Some women do not like milk or are allergic to it. You can have fat-free milk or take cheese or yogurt instead; if it is simply a matter of taste, disguise milk in sauces or dishes where you are not aware of it.

VITAMINS
It is important that most of your vitamin intake should come from food rather than supplements. Trying to get the right dosage of vitamins, and the right balance between different vitamins, from supplements is unwise. A well-balanced and varied diet including vitamin-rich foods such as vegetables, fruits, and nuts will supply all the vitamins necessary for you and your developing baby.

FOLIC ACID
There is one exception to this. Folic acid supplementation in the first 12 weeks of pregnancy cuts down the risk of having a baby with spina bifida or other neural tube defects by up to 70 percent, and also reduces the risk of cleft palate.

When women who had previously given birth to a baby with a neural tube defect (spina bifida or anencephaly) were given folic acid supplementation for one month before their conception and then up to the second missed period they were much less likely to have another handicapped baby.*

From the time of conception and through these crucial early stages the baby's spinal cord is being formed. If the spine does not close up then the baby has spina bifida, which can result in paralysis of the legs and incontinence. If the brain and skull do not develop properly the baby is anencephalic and is severely mentally handicapped.

A healthy diet does much to help to prevent neural tube defects. Even before you get pregnant, eat plenty of broccoli, spinach, and other dark green leafy vegetables.

MINERALS

Minerals and trace elements are a vital part of your diet, but if you are eating plenty of food that is rich in protein and vitamins you are unlikely to suffer from any mineral deficiency. Iron, calcium, magnesium, and zinc are probably the only minerals about which you need to be concerned during pregnancy.

Iron is necessary for the formation of red blood cells. Red blood cells contain a substance known as hemoglobin; if blood contains insufficient hemoglobin, not enough oxygen is carried to your baby and you become very tired. Vitamin C helps your body to absorb iron, whereas antacid medicines stop you from benefiting fully from it. Good sources of iron include dark molasses, egg yolk, whole grains, legumes, all dark green leafy vegetables such as watercress, raisins, prunes, brewer's yeast, and nuts.

Extra iron is often prescribed in pregnancy. If you eat foods rich in iron, you should have good reserves stored in your liver, and not need to take iron supplements. The fetus draws on these reserves, so that it can store enough in its liver to last for several months after birth. If you are iron-deficient (anemic) before embarking on pregnancy (and some women are without realizing it), a supplement may be advisable. Iron supplementation is not necessary for the normal drop in hemoglobin from mid-pregnancy. This reduced hemoglobin is a sign that plasma volume is rising and that the placenta is providing good nutrition for the baby (see page 70).

Calcium is necessary for the formation of strong bones and teeth. It enables blood to clot and your muscles to work smoothly. The oxalic acid in spinach and cocoa reduces the absorption of calcium: do not depend on chocolate milk for your calcium intake.

Your baby's teeth start to bud very early on in pregnancy, so your calcium intake in the first four months matters a great deal. Milk is a useful source, as are other dairy foods. Calcium is also present in leafy vegetables, sea vegetables, whole grains, legumes, carrot juice, and nuts. You need almost twice as much when you are pregnant.

Magnesium levels in pregnant women are often low. This may be one cause of muscle cramps. Good sources of magnesium are cereals, nuts, soy beans, milk, fish, and meat.

Zinc deficiency may result in miscarriage, growth retardation in the uterus, stillbirth, or congenital handicap.* There is also some evidence that zinc is necessary for muscles to contract well and, though it is difficult to measure accurately the concentration of zinc in human tissues, that shortage of zinc is one cause of long labor.* Taking an iron supplement can interfere with the absorption of zinc. High fiber foods – especially bran – contain zinc, as do brazil nuts, Parmesan and other hard cheeses, seeds, herring, and meat.

WOMEN AT RISK

Certain women are at "nutritional risk" and need to pay special attention to diet; for them vitamin and mineral supplements may be useful. The ones who may be at risk are those pregnant during adolescence (while they are still growing themselves), women who are underweight when they become pregnant, women who are overweight because of excess consumption of carbohydrates and fats, those living on a very restricted range of foods as with a macrobiotic diet, women who have lost a baby from miscarriage or stillbirth before, and women who have had three pregnancies within two years. Also included in this category are women suffering from some chronic diseases involving the regular use of drugs, women who smoke, heavy drinkers, and those with multiple pregnancies.

SALT AND FLUID RETENTION

It used to be thought that salt was dangerous in pregnancy and was one cause of preeclampsia (see page 139). It has now been established that salt is necessary for a normal pregnancy. When a group of expectant mothers were given no-salt diets they had *more* preeclampsia than a control group of women who had as much salt as they wished.* Cutting out salt can also cause muscle cramps in hot weather. Since you tend to retain more fluid when you are pregnant, you will only maintain the usual level of saltiness in all your body fluids by having as much salt as your appetite dictates.*

Occasionally special diets are prescribed for pregnant women in order to reduce fluid retention, which used to be thought dangerous in itself. But these special diets can harm the unborn baby. Women with mild fluid retention (edema) usually produce babies in just as good a condition as those who have no signs of it at all. Ankle, foot, and leg swelling on very hot days, when you have been on a plane trip, or after you have been standing for a long time is therefore nothing to worry about. If your skin is looking very puffy,

"My feet swelled uncomfortably in the heat while I was pregnant, so I showered my legs with cold water and rested with my feet up."

take more rest and look carefully at your diet to see if you should increase your protein intake (see page 95); if your fingers and face become swollen you should be sure to mention it to the doctor or midwife, as it is a sign that your kidneys are not coping well with the excretion of waste products from your body. This in turn may mean that your placenta is not working efficiently.

You cannot prevent edema by cutting down on fluid intake, so drink as much liquid as you want. Four or five glasses of water a day helps your kidneys to function well throughout your pregnancy.

EATING A BALANCED DIET

Bear in mind that you are providing nutrition for three distinct but interdependent biological entities: your own body, the developing baby, and the placenta.* This triple nutritional task demands a good, high-protein diet rich in vitamins and minerals. A salad a day is a must, but remember that you can use finely chopped cabbage and other greens to make a change. Experiment with salads and try mixing fruit and vegetables. Apples go with most savory things. A baked potato with cheese and a cabbage-based salad are a good source of protein, vitamin C, and calcium. If you can spare time to bake your own wholegrain bread, add extra wheat germ or soy flour and you have thereby added to your diet another valuable source of protein, iron, B vitamins, and fiber.

Eating well does not always mean eating expensively. Some women save money by avoiding unnecessary foods such as carbonated drinks, coffee, packaged desserts and soups, bakery and candy store items, and starchy sugary puddings. Milk and cheese are relatively cheap, and a delicious main course can be made from a selection of vegetables in season covered with a white sauce and topped with a layer of grated cheese browned under the broiler.

Drugs

Around 25 percent of all the birth defects that occur are genetic in their origin. Around 65 percent of birth defects have an unknown cause. Only 2 to 3 percent are caused by drugs. This is partly because the total amount of water in a woman's body goes up by 14 pints (8 liters) in pregnancy, so drugs are more diluted.* On the other hand, the range of substances to which the embryo may be vulnerable is not yet known. For this reason it is wise to take the fewest possible medicines during pregnancy, especially in the first few weeks when the embryo is forming and when the placenta is only just starting to be active. (You should therefore take care during the second half of the menstrual cycle if there is any chance that you might be pregnant.) It used to be thought that the placenta acted as an effective barrier to all poisons that might be present in the maternal bloodstream. But it is now known that drugs can cross the placenta and may affect the baby.*

"At the restaurant I ordered a glass of wine. The waiter said, 'Have apple juice!' I felt so angry – I had no rights, no choices."

If you think of how the fertilized egg has to segment, travel along the fallopian tube, embed itself into the lining of the uterus, and develop into a baby, you can imagine how such delicate and complex processes can be interfered with by chemicals which have been introduced into your bloodstream.

The liver and the kidneys are the organs of your body which deal with drugs and turn them into material which can be excreted in the urine. In an unborn – and even a newborn – baby these organs are still immature. The fetus is therefore not able to excrete many of the drugs which may reach it through the placenta. Instead, such drugs can accumulate in its body in toxic quantities. It is vital to remember, when taking any drug, that a dosage which may be right for you is far in excess of that which is suitable for your tiny baby. There was , for example, the thalidomide disaster,* when a sedative which was thought to be mild and safe was prescribed for women in early pregnancy. As a result of this sedative more than five thousand babies were born with badly deformed limbs, or none at all. Thalidomide is an extreme example of the effect that a drug can have on the development of an unborn baby. But all drugs, including prescribed drugs, medicines bought over the counter such as laxatives and painkillers, and nicotine and alcohol, are potentially harmful if misused. You should think carefully before taking any drug when pregnant, especially in the early weeks.

Drugs that are known to cause abnormalities of any kind are said to be "teratogenic." In the first few days of a pregnancy, any toxic or teratogenic drugs would probably prevent the egg from ever settling firmly in the uterus, so that you would not even realize that you were pregnant but would just have a delayed period; if you were to take the same drug slightly later, you would probably miscarry. At a later stage still, the pregnancy might continue, but there would then be a risk of the baby's being damaged by the drug.

If the cell cluster is damaged sometime between conception and 17 days it either dies and there is a very early miscarriage, it is reabsorbed into the mother's tissues, or the embryo survives intact because cells multiply to replace those which have been lost. Organogenesis, the development of the different parts of the baby's body, takes place during the period 18 to 55 days from conception. After 56 days drugs do not cause major handicaps, though they may reduce growth and cause loss of function.

Weighing the different risks

Some pregnant women need drugs, and may be very ill without them. Illness in the mother can also affect the developing baby. For instance, running a very high temperature (see page 111) seems to be teratogenic at certain phases of pregnancy, so it may be safer to take aspirin to get your temperature down than to try and cope without taking any medicines. It is always a question of balancing the risks to the baby against your need and the stress which may be caused to you by not having drug treatment.

Since the thalidomide disaster there has been acute awareness of the need to screen all new drugs before they are prescribed to pregnant women, and doctors are being increasingly careful. But drugs which have been in use a long time remain on the market without being tested. And it is difficult to be certain about any drug, because animal experiments may produce damage in one species, yet not in another. This can work either way: rats may be affected, but not human babies, or babies may be affected when rats are not.

People are often ignorant about the chemical substances they introduce into their bodies. Antacids for the relief of indigestion, cough medicines, sleeping pills (barbiturates), antihistamines used in the treatment of hay fever, and antibiotics are just some commonly used drugs which alter the body's chemical balance. A great many pregnant women take over-the-counter as well as prescribed drugs of one kind or another in the first weeks of pregnancy, and no one has much idea of the possible risks. There are other substances which you may perhaps not think of as being drugs, including cigarettes and alcohol. Even tea and coffee have been researched for possible harmful effects, though normal use (up to half a dozen cups a day) seems to be fine.*

SMOKING

There are positive steps you can take to give your baby the best start in life and other things which you should avoid since they are known to be detrimental to your baby's health. First and foremost among the various dangers is smoking. Whether or not you inhale, nicotine passes into your bloodstream and from there into the baby's

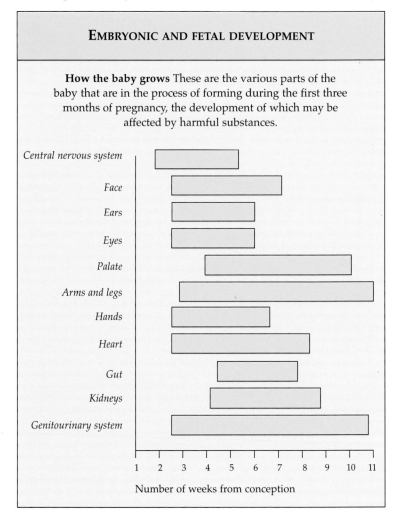

EMBRYONIC AND FETAL DEVELOPMENT

How the baby grows These are the various parts of the baby that are in the process of forming during the first three months of pregnancy, the development of which may be affected by harmful substances.

Number of weeks from conception

bloodstream. It makes the fetal heart speed up and interrupts the baby's respiratory movements which are the baby's rehearsal for breathing. In effect, the unborn baby actually coughs and splutters. Smoking also interferes with the efficiency of the placenta and is the most widespread and efficient way of pumping a powerful poison into an unborn baby's bloodstream. Nicotine makes the blood vessels in the mother's placenta constrict so that less oxygen and fewer nutritional substances can reach the baby.

Mothers who smoke bear babies who weigh less than babies of mothers who do not smoke and the baby's weight drops in relation to the number of cigarettes consumed.* This does not mean that some smokers do not have good-sized babies but that statistically babies of smokers are deprived of the best possible nutrition. It is not just that a woman who smokes tends to eat less food. Cigarettes have a direct effect on the growth and development of the baby.* It could be that some women make the mistake of thinking that labor will be easier if their babies are lighter in weight. Labor with a tiny, underweight baby is no easier or shorter than labor with a good-sized baby, and your baby is much more likely to be healthy and easy to care for if you have not smoked during your pregnancy. When a woman does not smoke herself, but her partner does, she and the baby are exposed to secondhand smoke, and fetal growth may well be affected as a result.*

Smoking after the fourth month of pregnancy is a major cause of prematurity and the birth of underweight babies who are stunted in development and may have to be cared for in a special care baby unit. Smoking also increases the chances of bleeding, miscarriage (women who smoke are twice as likely to miscarry as those who do not), premature rupture of the membranes, premature separation of the placenta, hemorrhage before or early in labor, hemorrhage after delivery, congenital abnormality, stillbirth, and death of the baby in the week following delivery.* The more a woman smokes, the more likely these things are to happen.

How to give it up If you are a heavy smoker and dependent on cigarettes to get through the day it may be very difficult to give them up, even for the sake of your baby. Fortunately, the nausea of early pregnancy or just a sudden dislike of cigarettes prompts many women to cut them out. Even if this does not happen spontaneously you can use the techniques of aversion therapy to condition yourself to break the habit. Every time you feel queasy or vomit make yourself think "cigarette" and use the association between vividly picturing the act of smoking and the overwhelming sensations of nausea to train yourself to develop a dislike of cigarettes.

How to cut down If you are past the nauseous stage of pregnancy or feel perfectly fit throughout, as many women do, you can still try to reduce your cigarettes to at least half the usual number. Ask your partner to help by cutting down his consumption in the same way; if the two of you are in the process of making the same effort, your determination is strengthened. Also, cutting down on smoking is a concrete way in which your partner can contribute to your baby's health, by reducing the amount of passive smoking to which you are subjected. The more you can both cut down on your general consumption of cigarettes the better.

You may be feeling terribly guilty about smoking while still being unable to give it up. You may feel like a murderer, but the guiltier you become the more you want a cigarette in order to help you calm down. It is certain that guilt and emotional stress can also affect your metabolism adversely, including your heart rate, blood pressure, breathing, muscle tone, and the adrenaline in your bloodstream. The question then arises as to how much stress you should tolerate in trying to give up smoking. If you know how to release tension you may be able to cope by smoking each cigarette only halfway down and still find that it helps you enough to be able to "unwind."

"Actually, it was very easy to give up smoking because I couldn't stand the taste or smell of cigarettes in the first couple of months. I cut out coffee for the same reason."

This is where your own judgment of the relative importance to you of smoking or not smoking in pregnancy is essential. Every pregnant woman has the right to be fully informed of the risks of smoking and to make her own decision on the subject of smoking during pregnancy. No one can *make* you stop smoking, however many dire warnings they give: you decide.

On the other hand, your baby cannot choose whether or not to smoke. A mother chooses for her child.

ALCOHOL

Because alcohol is socially accepted it is easy to forget that its use in pregnancy should be restricted. Fortunately, many women develop an aversion to it during pregnancy.

Alcohol crosses the placenta, and the baby's blood levels are about the same as the mother's. The risk the baby incurs from alcohol depends on how often the mother drinks, how much she drinks, and the baby's stage of growth. Alcohol in early pregnancy is more likely to have a bad effect, and even a single "binge" then can cause damage to the developing baby.

It depends on the mother's metabolism, too. Some women cannot break alcohol down into harmless substances, so alcohol passes through the placenta in its poisonous form. Heavy chronic alcohol use can cause Fetal Alcohol Syndrome (FAS). The baby has distinctive facial features and may be mentally and developmentally retarded.

However, most women can drink in moderation during pregnancy and have a perfect baby. Limit your intake to 10 units of alcohol a week and do spread them out over the week. One unit is a small glass of wine, a single measure of spirits, or a half pint of beer.

BEING CAREFUL ABOUT DRUGS

Think about any drugs you may be taking when you intend to conceive, and ask your doctor's advice. Do not wait until your first prenatal visit or even – if possible – until you are sure you are pregnant. If there is any chance that you might be pregnant, to be on the safe side it is best to avoid taking any drugs which are not essential to your health.

If a doctor other than your obstetrician is treating you, especially in the early months of pregnancy before it is obvious that you are having a baby, make sure that he or she realizes that you are pregnant before prescribing. This may be particularly relevant if you are ill when away from home and have to consult a different doctor.

Go through your medicine chest carefully when you stop using contraception. Make a list of the contents and ask your doctor whether there are any which are likely to be unsafe during pregnancy. Throw away, by flushing down the toilet, any drugs which were not prescribed for you or which are out of date, in addition to those which your doctor advises you to get rid of.

MOOD-ALTERING DRUGS

Because so little is known about the effect of mood-altering drugs it is wise to limit their use or cut them out altogether. You may feel that cannabis or Valium helps you to relax on occasion when you cannot "switch off." But explore other ways of releasing tension. The effects of disciplined relaxation (see pages 186–194) are likely to help your unborn baby more than anything you can take in through your mouth. They are some positive things you can do for yourself and your baby, ways of tuning in to your body rather than making an attempt to escape from it or deaden its sensations.

Cannabis Little is known of the effects of cannabis on the baby. Its strength varies widely, and its immediate effects on the user vary with expectation, the company in which it is taken, and previous experience of it. Claims have been made that it can be teratogenic, but this is still being investigated.

Cocaine Whether the drug is taken by inhaling a powder (snorting), smoking it (crack), or injecting it (shooting up), a woman using cocaine is very likely to have a baby who is small for dates or premature, and who is addicted to the drug. These babies tend to be irritable and jumpy, and it is difficult to calm them down enough so that they will take a satisfying feed.*

Mild tranquilizers are often prescribed during pregnancy and do not seem to be harmful. Diazepam (Valium) is sometimes used in treating preeclampsia (see page 139) to bring blood pressure down. But it is best to stop taking even a mild tranquilizer as you approach the time when you expect to go into labor. Valium taken just before labor starts or during the course of labor can result in the baby having a low Apgar score (see pages 358–360) at birth as well as breathing difficulties. The baby may also take a long time to start feeding properly, as well as becoming chilled more easily than usual.*

Powerful tranquilizers such as chlorpromazine (Thorazine) and haloperidol (Haldol) should be avoided in pregnancy unless essential. If you think you might have conceived, talk it through with your psychiatrist and with a pediatrician. You could change to a milder tranquilizer and see if it is sufficient to control your anxiety and reduce tension. Strong tranquilizers taken in labor may make the baby lethargic or very stressed and trembling at birth.

SLEEPING PILLS

These include tranquilizers, antihistamines (see opposite), and hypnotics. Hypnotics are of two different kinds. Some are barbiturates, which are highly addictive even over a short period and now almost never prescribed: phenobarbital (Luminal), amobarbital (Amytal), pentobarbital (Nembutal), and secobarbital (Seconal). Others are non-barbiturates: chloral hydrate, flurazepam (Dalmane), and glutethimide (Doriden). Non-barbiturates also seem to be addictive if taken over a long period. Not enough is known about the effect of hypnotics on the unborn baby, but they are certainly cumulative. The drug concentrates in the mother's fatty tissues; the baby is doped along with the mother. Large doses of barbiturates can cause respiratory depression at birth and feeding difficulties. Over-the-counter sleeping pills have not been tested for safety in pregnancy. The best solution is to do without sleeping pills; try to overcome insomnia by making time for relaxation and exercise in the open air, and perhaps an aromatherapy bath at bedtime and lavender essential oils sprinkled on your pillow.

PAINKILLERS

Aspirin The most widely used painkiller is aspirin (salicylate) and its derivatives. If you have a headache or other pain, try to get rid of it by resting in a quiet, darkened room. If rest is not effective, a few aspirin are unlikely to be harmful. But never dose yourself repeatedly: a recurring headache should be discussed with your doctor. If taken regularly (say, every four to six hours) during the few days before you go into labor, aspirin can produce difficulties in blood clotting in both you and your newborn baby and neonatal jaundice.

Codeine is addictive: the baby whose mother has been taking several pills daily throughout pregnancy may be born dependent, have severe withdrawal symptoms, and even die. Use it sparingly.

Acetaminophen (Tylenol) can cause liver and kidney damage if taken in large doses. Use it with caution in pregnancy, since the baby's liver and kidneys can suffer from relatively small doses.

Ibuprofen (Advil, Nuprin, Motrin) has not been shown to be safe for the developing fetus. There is some evidence that it actually impedes the fetal and newborn circulation and may also cause cardiac malformations and delay the onset of labor.

Naproxen (Aleve, Anaprox, Naprosyn), like Ibuprofen above has not been found to be entirely safe for the developing fetus and has the same potential harmful effects.

Drugs to treat migraine can cause the uterus to contract during pregnancy, thus endangering the fetus.

ANTINAUSEA DRUGS

Drugs for for nausea and vomiting are of three different kinds: anticholinergic drugs, antihistamines, and phenothiazines.* They can all have side effects. The first category treats nausea by acting on your nervous system; it reduces secretions, including stomach acid, and relieves muscle spasm. No one can be sure whether these drugs are completely safe for the fetus. Antihistamines, which include Benadryl, Dramamine, and Chlor-Trimeton, block the action of histamine (a substance to which some people are allergic) and may cause drowsiness. They are best avoided in pregnancy as high dosage may cause fetal abnormalities. The last category, the phenothiazines, are major tranquilizers, and are therefore inadvisable in pregnancy: the fetus may suffer the same adverse effects as from Thorazine (see opposite).

It seems then that drugs to control pregnancy sickness should not be used unless specifically prescribed by a doctor who knows you are pregnant, and then only when you have weighed together the advantages and disadvantages of taking the drug. Do not take any pills for travel sickness if you think you may be pregnant.

ANTIBIOTICS

Antibiotics may be prescribed in pregnancy; obviously their use is sometimes necessary and any disadvantages to the baby are outweighed. Never use antibiotics left in a bottle which were prescribed for a previous infection, even if you have exactly the same kind of infection. Tell your doctor that you may be pregnant, or remind him or her that you are pregnant, when you ask for a prescription.

Penicillin appears to be a safe antibiotic that can be taken without risk at any time during pregnancy.

Sulfonamides (which are not really antibiotics but effective antibacterials) are used to treat urinary tract infections. If you need to have sulfonamide treatment you should stop a week or so before the baby is due to be born, to allow the drug to get thoroughly out of your system before you go into labor. Otherwise the newborn baby's kidneys may not be able to cope with excreting the drug and the baby may then develop jaundice, which can cause some amount of damage to its central nervous system.

Tetracycline, a wide-spectrum antibiotic, is actually deposited in the unborn baby's teeth and may then go on to cause an unsightly yellow mottling and staining. It can also stop the growth of the baby's bones during the period when it is being taken, so it should definitely not be used during pregnancy.

Streptomycin, another wide-spectrum antibiotic, should never be taken in pregnancy. One of the drugs used to treat tuberculosis, it can cause deafness in the baby.

DRUGS TO TREAT CONSTIPATION

Stool bulk producers, such as Colace, do no harm provided that they are used only in moderation.

Stimulant laxatives, which include senna-based laxatives such as Senokot, cascara, and Dulcolax, seem to be safe for the developing fetus, but they may cause you to lose excessive amounts of fluid. Make sure that you drink plenty of liquids if you are in the process of taking any of these preparations.

Saline laxatives, including milk of magnesia and magnesium sulfate (Epsom salts), can also cause dehydration if you do not drink plenty of fluids, but otherwise they do not appear to harm the fetus.

Various types of oil will lubricate the bowels. However, avoid liquid paraffin because it reduces the absorption of vitamins A, D, and K. Lack of vitamin K may lead to disorders of blood clotting in the baby. Extra fluids alone may cure your constipation, especially if you adjust your diet to include a regular intake of bran. (See page 134 for more advice and information about constipation.)

DRUGS TO REDUCE FLUID RETENTION

Diuretics increase the excretion of salt and water from the body, and in so doing make your kidneys work very hard. They are used in the prevention and treatment of preeclampsia (see page 139). Since there is no proof that reducing fluid retention does prevent preeclampsia, it is almost certainly best to avoid taking diuretics altogether.* Discuss the matter with your doctor.

STEROIDS AND DRUGS TO TREAT ASTHMA

Steroids are used for the treatment of asthma and hay fever, eczema and other skin disorders, and rheumatism and arthritis. Severe and prolonged asthma attacks are more likely to harm the baby than the drugs that are used to control asthma.*

ANTI-DEPRESSANTS

Little is known about the effects of anti-depressants on the development of a baby. But certainly the old tricyclate anti-depressants do not seem to be teratogenic; the risk of miscarriage or of congenital abnormalities does not appear to be greater than if a woman is not taking these drugs. Because drugs like Prozac, Zoloft, and Paxcil – which are very long-acting – have been around for a much shorter time, psychiatrists usually err on the side of caution and do not prescribe them in pregnancy, even though there are no reports of their causing harm to the baby.

Depression in pregnancy may need treating with drugs, especially if a woman is actually suicidal, and the possible risks of medication must always be properly weighed against the risks of not having it. But doctors usually decide to take women off anti-depressants once they are known to be pregnant. If you do need anti-depressants through your pregnancy the sensible thing is to taper them off gradually so that you are no longer having them about four weeks before the baby is due. Then you can, if necessary, go back on them after the birth of your baby.

ANTI-PSYCHOTIC DRUGS

Clozapine should not be taken during pregnancy, as it affects bone marrow. It makes sense to avoid using anti-psychotic drugs which have only been on the market for a short time, and to stick to what has been tried and tested, and to those drugs the side-effects of which are already known. Anti-psychotic drugs affect the newborn baby's behavior, and side effects in the mother will also appear in the baby after birth – if she is sedated, the baby will be too, for example – but these are reversible. However, in such cases a pediatrician should be standing by at the birth to ensure that the baby is stabilized. Babies who have received anti-psychotic drugs are more likely to have convulsions and diazepam causes babies to get jittery as they come off it. So these drugs should be tailed off four weeks before the birth or reduced by half. To give the baby the best chance of dealing with the stress of being born, as little as possible of any drug should be taken.

"I discussed taking the drug with my psychiatrist and she switched my medication to one least likely to affect the baby."

DRUGS TO TREAT THYROID CONDITIONS

You may need to take drugs for an under- or over-active thyroid, but be aware that such drugs can have an effect on the baby's thyroid. Propylthiouracil should be used only in low doses during pregnancy. You should stop using it four or five weeks before the expected date of delivery, to allow the baby time to produce an adequate number of its own thyroid hormones, which the drug destroys. Discuss the drugs you are taking with your doctor, if possible before embarking on a pregnancy.

ANTICOAGULANTS

These drugs are prescribed for deep vein thrombosis or for a pulmonary embolism – both serious conditions that are caused by blood clots. Taken early in pregnancy, they may cause miscarriage. Anticoagulants can also cause hemorrhage in the baby and some, such as Coumadin, should not be taken in the last three months of pregnancy. If an anticoagulant needs to be given toward the end of the pregnancy, Heparin by injection is the safest one to use. Any adverse effects on the fetus can be reversed by small doses of vitamin K given to the baby after delivery.*

DRUGS TO TREAT DIABETES

Drugs which are taken by mouth in order to reduce blood sugar should not be used during pregnancy.* They can sometimes cause miscarriage or fetal abnormalities. Injections of insulin, however, are quite safe. If you are diabetic and you want to get pregnant, let your doctor know so that you can discuss in advance exactly how the pregnancy will be best managed (see page 141).

ANTICONVULSANTS

If you normally take anticonvulsants or antiepileptic drugs, discuss with your doctor the possibility of modifying your treatment before you conceive. These drugs may possibly cause cleft palate and a range of other handicaps. Carbamazepine is probably the best anticonvulsant for pregnancy.

GENERAL ANESTHETICS

There are times when a general anesthetic may be necessary during pregnancy; but if possible such anesthetics should be avoided because the baby becomes anesthetized too. Make sure that your doctor or dentist knows that you are pregnant if he or she recommends general anesthesia for anything.

Other risks

X-RAYS

In pregnancy it is wise to cut down the use of X-rays to the minimum, because there is no safe threshold for radiation, and hence no minimum level at which you can be assured that X-rays are safe for your unborn child. So avoid X-rays during pregnancy if possible, and in the second half of the menstrual cycle if there is a chance that you might be pregnant.

Radiation can partially destroy the genetic material which acts as the blueprint for the normal development of each cell of the body. A damaged cell is called a mutation. Radiation can have the strongest effects on an embryo in the initial stages of development, and a badly affected embryo is then likely to be aborted spontaneously. But X-rays taken in pregnancy can also have an effect after birth*:

there is evidence that X-rays are associated with a higher than usual chance of developing diseases of the respiratory system, blood disorders, and infectious illnesses in childhood.

There are some cases in which diagnostic X-rays are particularly important and the only means of discovering certain disorders during pregnancy. If a doctor or a dentist advises X-rays, take professional advice, but always check first to ensure that they really are essential. Your abdomen and thyroid should always be protected during the X-ray by a lead shield.

HIGH TEMPERATURE

If you find you are running a temperature, go to bed, drink plenty of fluids and sponge yourself down with cold water, or take cool baths or showers to lower your body temperature. Do not just let your temperature rise. There is a slight chance that a very high temperature – say, over 102°F – in the first four months of pregnancy can damage a baby.* The most crucial time is during the third and fourth weeks after conception. This is a horrifying thing to learn in late pregnancy if you know you had the flu earlier on, but most babies are born whole and healthy even when the mother has run a high temperature. Nevertheless, it is sensible to

"It's like walking in a minefield – there are so many risks! In a way I think I'd actually be happier not knowing about any of them."

avoid becoming run-down, and so more susceptible to the risk of infection, if you think you may be pregnant. Keep up a high intake of vitamin C in your diet and have some protein each day to reduce the risk of contracting an infection. As far as we know, there is no longer any real risk of serious damage to the baby from a high temperature after the 16th week of pregnancy, but you could make the developing baby's heart race by getting over-heated yourself.

Saunas and long, very hot baths can also produce a temperature that is high enough to harm a developing baby, so be sure to keep these temperatures down during your pregnancy. Your own comfort is usually the best guide to safety.

FOOD POISONING

Listeriosis Soft cheeses and precooked chilled foods like ready-to-serve chicken and pâté are sometimes contaminated with listeria if they are not stored at sufficiently low temperatures. The symptoms of listeriosis are similar to those of the flu. If a pregnant woman suffers from this she may have a miscarriage, or her baby may be stillborn or have birth defects.

Salmonella Raw as well as partly cooked eggs are sometimes contaminated with salmonella which also causes food poisoning. It is wise for a pregnant woman to eat only eggs that have been thoroughly cooked, and to avoid eating mayonnaise and other dishes with raw egg as an ingredient.

Toxoplasmosis This is another disease which can harm the developing baby. It is not usually thought of as a form of food poisoning because most people associate it with contaminated cat litter. It is true that it can come from handling cat litter or soil containing cat feces, and if you have a cat you should always wear rubber gloves when emptying a dirty litter box and wash your hands afterwards. If you are a gardener be very careful to wash thoroughly after handling soil. But toxoplasmosis is also a food-borne infection. Eat only meat that has been completely cooked. Be particularly careful at barbecues, especially with kebabs. Meat should never be pink or bleeding, as it is with a rare steak. Do not eat raw cured meat such as Parma ham. Wash your hands after handling raw meat and wash down kitchen surfaces and wooden utensils. Because toxoplasmosis may be present in soil, salad vegetables and fruit should also be well washed. Goat's milk and yogurt made from it should be pasteurized. You can get further information from some of the organizations listed on page 413.

VACCINATION

Vaccinations are not recommended during the first four months of pregnancy, during which time there is a small risk of damage to the fetus. In the later months, most vaccinations (apart from rubella; see below) are considered harmless.

Rubella (German measles) is such a mild disease that many people have it in childhood without knowing it. Unfortunately, if you contract rubella when you are pregnant, the virus may cross the placenta and in the first 20 weeks of pregnancy it can have a serious effect on the baby. Even if you were vaccinated against rubella as a child, it is sensible to have a blood test before you even become pregnant: if the test shows that you have never had rubella you can be vaccinated against it. Alternatively, if you are already pregnant when you discover that you are not immune, you can be vaccinated immediately after the birth of your baby.

The protection afforded by rubella vaccination lasts at least seven years, and probably much longer. After you have been vaccinated, be very careful about contraception for the next three months, since you should not conceive until you have had time to build up immunity to the virus in your system. Never have a rubella vaccination if you think you might be pregnant.

If you did not get a rubella vaccination before you started your pregnancy and have never had the disease, avoid all contact with children who might possibly have it. If you think you have been in contact with rubella, get in touch with your doctor immediately. He or she will offer you an injection of gamma globulin, but the chances of the baby's being damaged by rubella in the first three months of pregnancy are high, especially in the first eight weeks; if you contract the disease you may want to consider an abortion.

THE RHESUS NEGATIVE WOMAN

All blood is either Rhesus positive or Rhesus negative. By far the most common type of blood group is Rhesus positive. In fact, some 86 percent of people are Rhesus positive, which means that their blood contains something known as the Rhesus factor. This factor is tested for early on in your pregnancy as part of your routine blood test. Its presence or absence is noted on your records, but is only important in one combination of circumstances: if you are Rhesus negative and the baby's father is Rhesus positive. There is no problem if the baby is Rhesus negative, but 40 percent of all Rhesus positive babies of Rhesus negative mothers become anemic, and if this goes untreated the baby may die before or after birth.

If you are Rhesus negative with a Rhesus positive baby and some of the baby's red blood cells leak into your circulation, a risk can arise with the next pregnancy. This can happen after an accidental

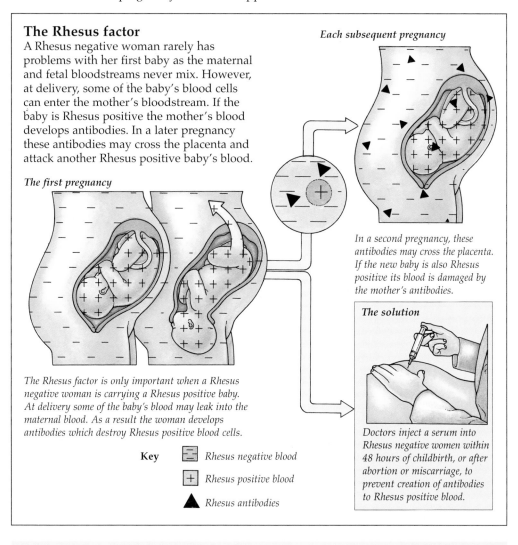

The Rhesus factor

A Rhesus negative woman rarely has problems with her first baby as the maternal and fetal bloodstreams never mix. However, at delivery, some of the baby's blood cells can enter the mother's bloodstream. If the baby is Rhesus positive the mother's blood develops antibodies. In a later pregnancy these antibodies may cross the placenta and attack another Rhesus positive baby's blood.

The first pregnancy

Each subsequent pregnancy

In a second pregnancy, these antibodies may cross the placenta. If the new baby is also Rhesus positive its blood is damaged by the mother's antibodies.

The Rhesus factor is only important when a Rhesus negative woman is carrying a Rhesus positive baby. At delivery some of the baby's blood may leak into the maternal blood. As a result the woman develops antibodies which destroy Rhesus positive blood cells.

The solution

Doctors inject a serum into Rhesus negative women within 48 hours of childbirth, or after abortion or miscarriage, to prevent creation of antibodies to Rhesus positive blood.

Key

⊟ *Rhesus negative blood*

⊞ *Rhesus positive blood*

▲ *Rhesus antibodies*

hemorrhage in late pregnancy or at delivery, or if you have miscarried or had an abortion. Your body then responds to the Rhesus factor present in the baby's cells as if to an invader, and begins to manufacture antibodies against it. If some of these antibodies leak back from your circulation into the baby's they proceed to destroy large numbers of the baby's own red blood cells.

The flow of red blood cells each way across the placenta is not usually substantial enough during a first pregnancy to cause your body to develop such antibodies. But when your first baby is born, some of its blood may flow from the placenta into your circulation. This triggers the creation of antibodies to the Rhesus factor in your blood. From then on you produce antibodies to the Rhesus factor, and the next time you are pregnant with a Rhesus positive baby your antibodies may attack the baby's blood vigorously. It may get jaundice, its brain may be damaged, severe anemia may develop and, in the worst cases, it may not even survive.

"I hadn't realized that a termination is counted as a pregnancy when considering whether to give a Rhesus negative woman anti-D immunoglobin."

There are several things that can be done about this. The first and simplest is an injection of anti-D immunoglobin at 28 weeks of pregnancy, and another immediately after the birth of a Rhesus positive baby. It consists of a serum which stops the mother's biological defense mechanisms acting against foreign Rhesus substances. A fresh injection of this serum is then given during and after each subsequent pregnancy. The same routine is followed after a miscarriage or a termination of pregnancy, since it is possible that the fetus was Rhesus positive and that some of its blood will have entered into the mother's bloodstream.

It is no good giving this serum *after* a woman's body has already produced antibodies. If a high proportion of antibodies is detected in your blood during a second or subsequent pregnancy, and your baby is known to be at risk, amniocentesis may be performed (see page 227) and the amniotic fluid analyzed for the presence of bilirubin (bile pigment). An anemic fetus excretes into the fluid large amounts of bilirubin from destroyed red blood cells.

A woman who is Rhesus negative and whose partner is Rhesus positive is tested for Rhesus antibodies every two to three weeks. If there are antibodies, a blood test is done on the baby in the uterus, using ultrasound to guide the needle into the umbilical cord. If necessary, the baby can be given one or more transfusions before birth, again using ultrasound to guide the needle. If the baby is sufficiently mature to face life outside, labor may be induced early. If necessary, the baby can be treated immediately after delivery and given a complete blood transfusion to thoroughly eradicate all the antibodies from its bloodstream.

Fortunately, as more and more Rhesus negative women are routinely immunized soon after the delivery of their babies, this situation is becomingly increasingly rare.

AN "INCOMPETENT" CERVIX

Occasionally a woman's cervix may be torn from a previous difficult labor or mid-pregnancy termination, or be damaged by a cone biopsy. She would not find this out until her next pregnancy, when she might lose her baby after the fourth month as a result of "cervical incompetence" (see page 374). The term "incompetent" is an unfortunate one and makes women feel as if they have failed to reach some standard of reproductive ability.

An obstetrician may recommend cervical cerclage – sewing the cervix closed for the duration of any subsequent pregnancy. This is a relatively simple procedure: once the pregnancy is established, a suture is inserted under anesthesia and is threaded through and around the cervix like the drawstring of a purse. The suture is removed at about the 36th week of pregnancy or later. Some obstetricians like to induce labor at this point because they say it is simpler, since contractions often start shortly after the removal of the suture anyway. You are not compelled to have labor induced, however, and should decide whether this is what you want in such circumstances. A random trial of cervical cerclage, conducted on women at high risk of giving birth prematurely, produced no evidence of its benefit.* Since twins and triplets are often born a few weeks early, some obstetricians perform cervical cerclage to try to prolong a multiple pregnancy. This does not work.*

A generation ago some pregnant women were prescribed a drug called diethystilbesterol (DES) to prevent miscarriage. The sons born to these women had a much greater incidence of genitourinary malformations and infertility. The daughters had higher rates of vaginal cancer and cervical malformations. Some of these women with malformed cervixes need cervical cerclage and some do not.

PRETERM LABOR

If you pass blood (which could be coming from the cervix), feel a sudden rush of warm liquid from your vagina (which could be the membranes rupturing), or have regular contractions like menstrual pains which get longer, stronger, and closer together over several hours, chances are that you are going into labor. If this happens before you have reached the last month of your pregnancy the baby may need special care at birth. So call your doctor or midwife, or go straight into the hospital. It is best for the baby to be born in a center which has intensive care facilities, with a neonatologist standing by in case the baby needs help with breathing.

If the baby is very premature you will be given corticosteroids to mature the fetal lungs, and this gives the baby a much better chance. There is evidence that administering ethanol, diazoxide, or progestogens in an attempt to stop labor is likely to be harmful.*

Your physical wellbeing

To make the most of the experience of being pregnant, you will probably want to get your body in good condition. Healthy activity can be pleasurable in itself as well as being an excellent preparation for labor. Sometimes books on pregnancy and even childbirth educators give the impression that childbirth is an athletic event for which you have to train like a marathon runner, a kind of examination for which you must study assiduously, or even an ordeal with which you are unlikely to cope but which will be quickly forgotten afterward. No wonder expectant mothers become anxious! No mention is made of the excitement, joy, and sheer pleasure that many women experience in childbirth.

Most women look forward to childbirth with excited anticipation. They know that there is a slight chance of something going wrong ·but that the better they have prepared themselves with body-toning movements and exercises, the more likely they are to be able to handle any problems that occur during pregnancy.

Getting to know your body

Before beginning exercises, it is useful to gain an awareness early in pregnancy of how your body works and what is taking place in your reproductive organs. One way of doing this is to have a closer look at your genitals. To get a clear view, you can kneel or squat over a mirror. A flashlight might help you to see the area better.

YOUR PERINEUM
The perineum is the tissue around your vagina and over the area between your vagina and anus. Just before delivery the perineum begins to bulge and its tissues fan out and open up as the ball of the baby's head begins to press through it.

YOUR VAGINA
Your vagina is the soft, cushioned canal which holds the penis during sexual intercourse; it is also the passage through which the baby is delivered. The outer part of the vagina is the vulva, consisting of layers of outer and inner lips (labia) constructed like the overlapping petals of a rose. During pregnancy they change in color from red to violet as the blood supply to them is increased. Pregnancy hormones also darken your nipples, and you may notice dark patches on your face and on other parts of your skin.

Insert one or two fingers gently into your vagina and feel around the stretchy folds inside. Though the sides of the vagina are normally touching each other and there is no hollow space, notice how readily they spread apart. They open like an accordion when the baby is pressing down through them to be born, and the action of hormones that are released into your bloodstream will make them become even more flexible during the last few weeks of pregnancy.

YOUR CLITORIS

Your clitoris is like a bud rising from the inner lips at the upper (front) end of your vagina. Its base and the inner lips around it are very sensitive, and pressure on or stroking of these parts produces sexual excitement. As you touch its root, you may notice that it swells up. You will feel that there is a hood or fold of skin surrounding the clitoris and that this connects up with the inner lips. So anything in your vagina which stretches the inner lips apart will also pull on this hood and will stimulate the clitoris, too.

A woman's genitals vary as much as a man's. Just as penises are different sizes, for example, the clitoris may be the size and shape of a small pea or more like the curved center of an orchid. Women's labia vary, too. Some are firm, some soft, some large and fleshy, others smaller. A woman may worry that masturbation might have changed the shape of her labia or clitoris, but these organs are so flexible that pulling, pressing, or rubbing them does not produce permanent structural changes. Doctors and midwives cannot tell anything about your sexual habits by examining your vulva, though many women harbor a secret fear that they can, especially if they have suffered previous sexual abuse.

At delivery the baby presses against this whole area that you are examining, easing forward the tissues so that they open up like elastic, and then slides out with a rush of liquid. After the baby is born these flexible tissues spring back again; at first they will not be as firm as they were before, but they will gradually gain in tone.

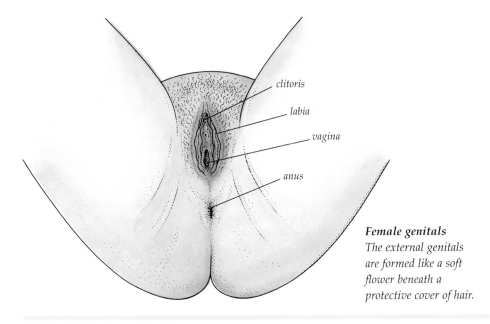

clitoris

labia

vagina

anus

Female genitals
*The external genitals
are formed like a soft
flower beneath a
protective cover of hair.*

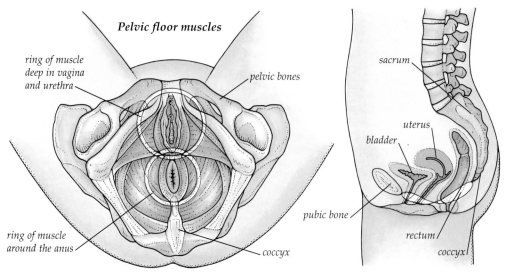

Pelvic floor muscles

ring of muscle
deep in vagina
and urethra

pelvic bones

ring of muscle
around the anus

coccyx

sacrum

uterus

bladder

pubic bone

rectum

coccyx

Pelvic cavity and lower spine

Pelvic floor

The muscles of the pelvic floor form a springy support for your uterus, bladder, and rectum.

YOUR CERVIX

Now introduce your longest finger deep inside your vagina and you meet the rounded, firm cervix (the neck of the womb), the part of the uterus that will open (dilate) when you are in labor. Early in pregnancy it will feel like the tip of your nose. You may notice a little dip in the middle, like the dimple in the center of a buttoned cushion. This is where the mucous plug is situated, and this plug, like the cork in a bottle, seals off the uterus from the outside. At the end of pregnancy the cervix will have softened and, when you touch it with your finger, it will feel more like your mouth when it is soft and relaxed than like your nose. This is one of the signs that you are ready to go into labor. The cervix is "ripe," and ready to open up.

YOUR PELVIC FLOOR

The muscles which support everything inside the pelvic cavity (including the uterus, the bladder, and the rectum) form the pelvic floor. They have special significance for your health, whatever age you are and whether or not you are pregnant. The upright position that humans have adopted in preference to the all-fours stance puts an extra stress on these muscle layers in pregnancy.

Though these muscles form a coordinated working structure, they are not really a "floor" at all. They are slanted at different angles and levels and can be held with varying degrees of firmness. The easiest way to find these muscles, of which some women are unaware, is to interrupt a stream of urine, since you bring all of the pelvic floor muscles into play when you do this. Or you can think of them as forming a figure eight around the vagina and anus. In the middle of the eight is a horizontal bar, the transverse perineal muscle. When the muscles of the pelvic floor are contracted, the circular shapes of the eight change to almond shapes and the transverse perineal muscle is pulled towards the pubic bone (the firm ridge of bone just above the clitoris) like the opening lid of an old-fashioned roll-top desk. You can feel this from both inside and outside if you put one finger inside the vagina and a thumb over the pubis.

Your pelvic floor muscles contract spontaneously during love-making, increasing your sensations of pleasure and those of your partner. Awareness and control of these muscles are important in labor, too, when you will need to be able to release them as you press the baby down the birth canal to be born.

Some people can hold their pelvic muscles contracted for much longer periods than others, and you may notice, when you first try to contract these muscles, that they tire and tremble. To exercise your pelvic floor muscles gradually, you can pretend that this area is an elevator which you are taking up to the second floor. You hold it there, then move on to the third floor, and so on until the muscles are fully contracted. Then release them gradually to the ground floor. Finally end with a toning movement by drawing the muscles up to the second floor again. If you do this 10 or 12 times a day you will be able to hold them firm for longer periods, building up to a count of eight or nine without holding your breath or tightening up your shoulders. But always remember to alternate tightening movements with resting spaces to allow the muscles to be reoxygenated in the intervals between activity.

Caring for your spine

The spine is a flexible column of vertebrae which acts as the central scaffolding of the body and, because it is sinuous and lithe, enables all the parts that are attached to it to move freely. Your spine is not rigid like a lamp post. It is both strong and elastic. Caring for it properly depends on using it well. When it is used like a crane, you run the risk of backache and back injury.

The section of the spine situated at the rear of the pelvis is the sacrum. It is the central pillar to which the pelvis is fixed. The large flaring ilia, the bones that look rather like elephant's ears, are fixed to the sacrum by the sacroiliac joints.

The spinal vertebrae are cushioned by discs, like a dynamic hydro-elastic pillow.* When you bend, these cushions soften the movement. When the vertebrae are pulled apart the discs open up. The discs contain fluid which is gradually lost during the day if you have been in an upright position, especially when you have been sitting a lot. For this reason, a person is nearly one inch shorter at the end of the day than at breakfast-time. Lying down enables the discs to fill up again, but they depend *on movement* to suck in fluid. In pregnancy the sheer weight of your body, and the extra weight of the baby and all its luggage, also sits heavily on the discs in your lower spine. The result is that all this extra weight squashes the discs even more. So to have a healthy back in pregnancy you need to use it

Posture and balance

Good posture is essential to your physical wellbeing during pregnancy. This means not only learning to stand and walk in the best way so that your baby is cradled in the pelvis in a position that is comfortable for both of you, but also performing other everyday movements, such as getting out of bed, in a way calculated to avoid unnecessary strain. These exercises will help you to achieve good posture, to improve the tone of your muscles, and to learn how to use only those muscles necessary for whatever you are doing. If you are looking good and walking with a spring in your step, you will probably also feel much better.

Standing well

Stand with your feet evenly planted, as wide apart as your hips, and parallel to each other. Keep your knees loose. Release any tension across your buttocks. Listen to your breathing. As you breathe out, feel the weight of your seat bones and sacrum pressing down through your heels and imagine a thread attached to the crown of your head, drawing you upward through your spine and neck. Let your shoulder blades drop apart and relax, and your arms hang loosely by your sides. Visualize your baby nestling toward the inside of your spine. Be aware of your breathing.

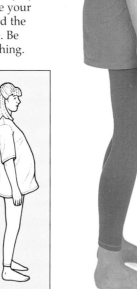

Relax shoulders

Keep knees loose

Standing badly

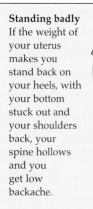

If the weight of your uterus makes you stand back on your heels, with your bottom stuck out and your shoulders back, your spine hollows and you get low backache.

Tailor sitting

This is an ideal way to release tension in the lower back. It can be one of the most comfortable sitting positions during pregnancy, as long as you make sure you do not slouch.

Drop knees toward the floor

Avoid slouching shoulders

Sit on your seat bones, cross-legged, and let your knees drop naturally toward the floor. Allow your spine to lengthen upward as in good posture for standing. Try sitting with your back against a wall for support sometimes.

The rocking-chair exercise

This encourages good posture during pregnancy by allowing you to press out the small of your back, while keeping the rest of your body aligned. For the exercise, you become like a rocking chair that rocks to and fro, and you need a partner to set you in motion. Avoid hollowing your back at any time as you do this.

1 *Stand well, as described opposite. Your partner should face you, with her hands resting firmly on your hips.*

Rest hands on hips

2 *Bend your knees very slightly and breathe easily as you rock your pelvis gently backward and forward between her hands several times.*

Rock pelvis backward and forward

Rest hand under lower tummy

3 *Now your partner stands at your side and puts one hand firmly on the small of your back and the other over your lower tummy.*

Rock pelvis backward and forward

4 *You continue rocking, pressing against her hand with the small of your back, then releasing away from it.*

Getting up from lying down

If you sit up suddenly after you have been lying on your back, you put great pressure on your tummy muscles, especially in advanced pregnancy. The method shown below helps you avoid strain on these muscles, and since it involves changing from a horizontal to an upright position in gentle stages, it also good for a healthy circulation.

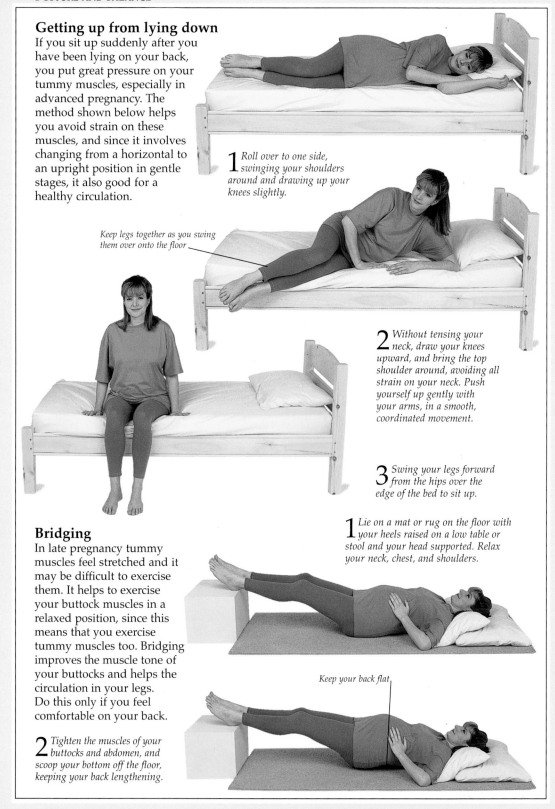

1 *Roll over to one side, swinging your shoulders around and drawing up your knees slightly.*

Keep legs together as you swing them over onto the floor

2 *Without tensing your neck, draw your knees upward, and bring the top shoulder around, avoiding all strain on your neck. Push yourself up gently with your arms, in a smooth, coordinated movement.*

3 *Swing your legs forward from the hips over the edge of the bed to sit up.*

Bridging

In late pregnancy tummy muscles feel stretched and it may be difficult to exercise them. It helps to exercise your buttock muscles in a relaxed position, since this means that you exercise tummy muscles too. Bridging improves the muscle tone of your buttocks and helps the circulation in your legs. Do this only if you feel comfortable on your back.

1 *Lie on a mat or rug on the floor with your heels raised on a low table or stool and your head supported. Relax your neck, chest, and shoulders.*

Keep your back flat

2 *Tighten the muscles of your buttocks and abdomen, and scoop your bottom off the floor, keeping your back lengthening.*

wisely. This means knowing how to lift without straining your back, for example, and how to vary your position so that you do not sit still for long periods. It is a good idea to get your weight off your spine and onto all fours now and again and to have rest times when you lie on the bed. But rest is not enough. It is important to move around as well so that you plump up the discs. Dancing, special exercises for pregnancy, and swimming are all effective ways of keeping the spine flexible and revitalizing the discs.

Because of the forward load produced by the increased size and weight of your uterus, strain is put on your spine, especially in the small of the back, and your upper spine may be pushed into the wrong position in order to compensate.

Toning your abdominal muscles

Four-legged mammals take the extra weight of pregnancy on their abdominal muscles slung evenly between the front and back limbs. Despite their upright stance, human beings also need well-toned abdominal muscles for comfortable pregnancy because, if these are flabby, the back muscles are forced to compensate by taking on too much work to support the spine. When this happens, the vertebrae of the lower spine are forced into an unnatural position and the discs between them are subjected to a great deal of pressure. They may slide and become displaced. This leads to exhausting backache. Girdles cannot help much; they just take over some of the work that healthy muscles should be doing. The best girdle is composed of your own tummy and buttock muscles, and both sets need to be toned to provide mutual support.

To understand what will benefit your abdominal muscles and what might be harmful to them, it is useful to know how this girdle of muscles is constructed and how it works.

The muscle running from top to bottom down the front of the abdomen is called the rectus muscle and it bears much of the load of late pregnancy. It is separated into two halves by a line down the center which is like a seam. When you are about halfway through your pregnancy, this may show as a dark line in your skin from your navel down to your pubic-hair line, although it does not occur in all women. You can see the same line as an indentation about the width of a pencil in photographs of Mr. Universe flexing his muscles and caving in his abdomen. The two sides of the rectus muscle can be pulled apart if the muscle is subjected to too great a stress — then the muscle "unzips." Constipation and straining on the toilet can sometimes cause this muscle to separate as well.

You can test yourself to find out if there is any separation of the rectus muscle. Lying on your back with a pillow under your head, rest your hands on your tummy and *very slowly* lift your head and shoulders with your chin tucked in. If you can feel a soft bulging area the width of a finger or more the muscle has separated, in which

Keeping fit during pregnancy

While you are pregnant it is easy to allow muscles that were previously firm and elastic to sag. You are putting on weight, your figure is changing, and you may assume that sagging muscles are an inevitable accompaniment to these changes. However, gentle toning exercises, aimed at firming up your abdominal muscles and avoiding back strain, can do you, and your body, nothing but good. Through all the movements it is important to be aware of your breathing, and never to hold your breath.

Pelvic rocking

For this exercise you should lie on a flat surface with your head and shoulders supported by pillows, and your knees bent with the feet flat. Experiment by pressing the small of your back against the floor, or the bed, and then releasing it so that you produce a gentle, rocking movement. Then roll your hips around in a slow, circular, hula-hoop movement.

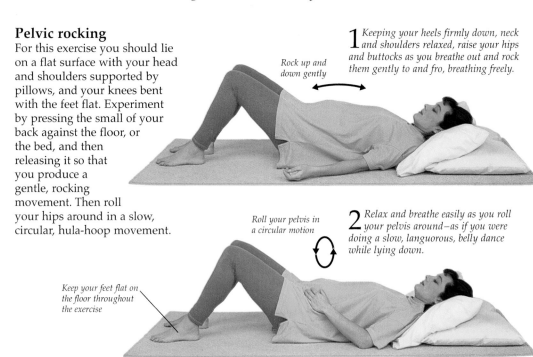

Rock up and down gently

1 *Keeping your heels firmly down, neck and shoulders relaxed, raise your hips and buttocks as you breathe out and rock them gently to and fro, breathing freely.*

Roll your pelvis in a circular motion

2 *Relax and breathe easily as you roll your pelvis around—as if you were doing a slow, languorous, belly dance while lying down.*

Keep your feet flat on the floor throughout the exercise

Exercises to avoid

Although double-leg raising and sit-ups are exercises often recommended for pregnant women, they do not in fact strengthen the abdominal muscles. These muscles do not work to lift the legs but to stabilize the lower back. If they are not strong enough to start with, they cannot cope with the effort involved when the legs or trunk are raised, and the result is back strain or torn abdominal muscles.

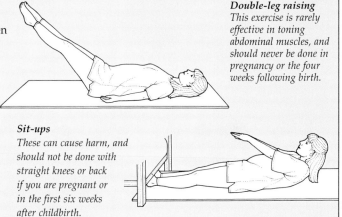

Double-leg raising
This exercise is rarely effective in toning abdominal muscles, and should never be done in pregnancy or the four weeks following birth.

Sit-ups
These can cause harm, and should not be done with straight knees or back if you are pregnant or in the first six weeks after childbirth.

Leg sliding

Leg sliding is a gentle exercise that allows you to tone up your tummy muscles both pre- and postnatally. Do it five or six times at first, and gradually build up until you can do it comfortably 10 or 15 times. If you feel your back aching, stop. Leg sliding is best done lying on your back on a firm surface with a pillow under your head. Keep your neck, shoulders, and arms relaxed. Follow your breathing rhythm, moving on an out-breath, allowing your breath to flow in between movements.

1 *Keeping the small of your back pressed down, bend your knees so that your feet are flat on the floor.*

2 *Slowly extend both legs until they are straight. Keep the rest of your body relaxed as you extend.*

Draw up each knee alternately

3 *Draw one knee back up, then the other, without lifting the small of the back off the floor.*

Testing for separation of the rectus muscle

If you are starting exercises in the last months of pregnancy, find out whether you have already damaged your rectus muscle. You will need to be careful when doing exercises for toning up your abdomen if this muscle has separated (see page 123).

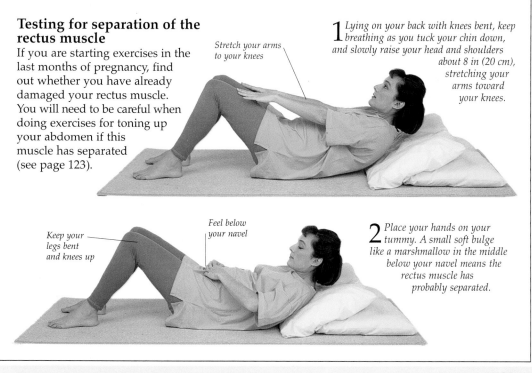

Stretch your arms to your knees

1 *Lying on your back with knees bent, keep breathing as you tuck your chin down, and slowly raise your head and shoulders about 8 in (20 cm), stretching your arms toward your knees.*

Keep your legs bent and knees up

Feel below your navel

2 *Place your hands on your tummy. A small soft bulge like a marshmallow in the middle below your navel means the rectus muscle has probably separated.*

case you can rehabilitate it with postnatal exercises after the baby is born (see pages 398–401). Meanwhile concentrate on leg sliding (see page 125). Some exercises that are intended to strengthen the abdominal muscles can cause the rectus muscle to separate. You should not try double-leg-raising exercises while you are pregnant, or even single-leg raising unless the muscles are already in very good condition. Nor should you do exercises that entail putting your feet under heavy furniture and then raising the upper body or try any sit-ups without using your hands. Not only can these exercises damage the abdominal muscles, they can also strain the back.

EXPLORING PELVIC MOVEMENT

The bones that form the pelvis are like a cradle for the baby growing inside you, a cradle that can rock in all directions. Feel your pelvic bones with your fingers. Start with your hip bones. Press in over their

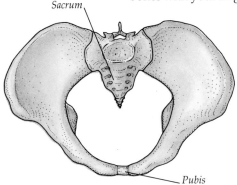

Sacrum

Pubis

upper ridges and then walk your fingers round and down into the small of your back where your hip girdle joins your spine. The point at which it does so is the sacrum, the bone which forms the back of the pelvis and the outlet through which the baby descends. Now walk the fingers around again to the big bones at the side, then down into the groin and around the front till they meet at your pubic bone. This forms the front of the pelvis and the baby dips down under this bridge of bone just before delivery. Notice

Female pelvis
The female pelvis forms a kind of cradle for the developing baby.

that your pubis is much lower than your sacrum. The human pelvis is tilted. Once you have found exactly where these bones are and have a clear picture of them, get your partner to feel them, too. Guide his hands so that he is able to track your pelvis accurately.

PELVIC ROCKING

Lie on any flat surface (it can be a firm bed) with head and shoulders supported by two pillows and your knees bent with the feet flat. Explore the capacity for movement in your pelvis. Experiment with gentle, rhythmic rocking. Then try rolling the cradle around as if you were doing a very slow hula-hoop movement. This is a kind of belly dancing while lying down, in which you tighten your tummy muscles while pressing your buttocks together. As you do so, notice how the different sets of muscles are alternately tightened and released and the way in which tummy and buttock muscles work together in a coordinated fashion.

Now combine this movement with controlled breathing. Each time you pull your tummy muscles *in* and press your buttocks together, give a long breath *out* through your mouth. Then, as you release the muscles and rock your pelvis gently forward (it is a very slight movement), allow your lungs to fill up with air, breathing in through your nose. Do it at your own pace, emphasizing the breath out and letting the breath in take care of itself. This movement done in early pregnancy is a good way of toning abdominal muscles in preparation for the work they must do later.

Now rest your fingers on the big bones at the front of the pelvis on either side. Continue the movement with the breathing and notice the swing up and down of these bones. This is the distance the bony cradle rocks as you walk and move around in pregnancy. The baby is thoroughly accustomed to these movements during its intrauterine existence, and it is therefore not surprising that rocking a newborn baby quiets and soothes it. Research shows that a baby who is being rocked is most likely to be comforted by a swinging movement of three inches to either side of the central position.* This corresponds exactly with the arc of the pelvic rock.

A position with firm support for your spine is best for practicing this pelvic rocking. Other positions may hollow your back, which can be harmful, especially in advanced pregnancy, because it puts stress on the sacroiliac joint situated at the top of your buttocks. Such strain is particularly bad for you when you are pregnant because your ligaments are already softened by hormones released into the blood to make the vagina and cervix more flexible in preparation for the birth. Once these ligaments have softened, any form of pelvic rocking which involves back *hollowing* can cause more backache.

Exercise in pregnancy

Exercises to help you cope with the stresses of pregnancy should be matched by others designed to help your adjustment after childbirth, since this is the time when the speediest and most dramatic physical changes are happening to you. Postnatal exercises are simply a modification of the ones you learn in pregnancy, so there is no need for you to learn completely new ones after the birth. In this book postnatal exercises are described on pages 398–401.

POSTURE AND BALANCE
Good posture maintained every day is more important than pregnancy gymnastics. As the weight load changes during pregnancy you should give conscious thought to balance and body mechanics, something that is usually taken for granted. It is not just a matter of "standing straight, head up" like a Victorian young lady walking with a book on her head, but of understanding how to economize on muscle work and use only those muscles of the body that are needed for any particular task. This results in graceful and comfortable movement without strain and effort.

Standing To achieve good posture, stand with your back to a wall, heels far enough away from it for your seat and shoulders just to touch it. Release your chest, press the small of your back toward the

Aches and pains

In late pregnancy you are carrying more weight which, instead of being evenly distributed, is centered in one area and so affects your balance. This extra weight alone can cause aches and pains by straining muscles and causing you to adopt an unnatural stance, leading to further strain. The way the baby is lying can also cause discomfort and occasionally a sharp shooting pain when the baby is pressing against a nerve. These exercises will help you ease such aches and pains.

Foot exercises

Foot exercises discourage varicose veins in the legs by stimulating the blood flow back to the heart. When you are sitting down or having a rest, practice drawing the alphabet with your feet, one foot at a time, keeping your legs still. You will find that you can easily read or do some work at the same time.

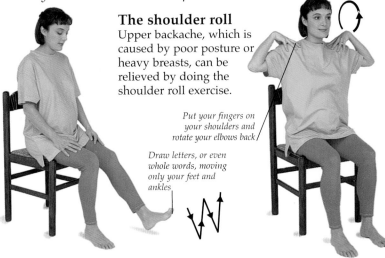

Draw letters, or even whole words, moving only your feet and ankles

The shoulder roll

Upper backache, which is caused by poor posture or heavy breasts, can be relieved by doing the shoulder roll exercise.

Put your fingers on your shoulders and rotate your elbows back

The angry cat

However many exercises you do with your back supported, it feels good to get the weight of the baby off your spine occasionally. You can do this by going onto all fours and rocking your pelvis, an exercise sometimes known as "the angry cat." This is a kind of pelvic rocking reversed.

Spread your shoulders wide

1 *Get onto all fours, keeping the small of your back flat, not hollowed, and your neck aligned with your spine. Your palms should be placed flat on the floor.*

Keep your elbows still

2 *Without moving your elbows or knees, keep breathing as you tighten your tummy muscles and hump up your lower back. Relax back to the flat position after holding for several seconds.*

Incorrect posture

Never, under any circumstances, allow the lower back to cave in while doing this exercise.

Wall stretching

A good way to lift your ribs off your expanding uterus is simply to stretch up your arms. First raise one arm up in the air and then the other, until you are comfortable. A similar result may be achieved if you do the exercise while sitting with your back pressed firmly against a wall to help alignment.

1 *Sit with the base of your spine pressed against a wall and lengthen up as in standing. Keep your shoulders soft and wide as you extend your legs in front of you and breathe easily.*

2 *Keep your seat and legs grounded and your back flat against the wall as you swing your arms out to shoulder height. With your palms pressed against the wall, walk your fingers up it.*

3 *When you have reached as high as you can, turn your palms outward and spread your shoulders wide. With each out-breath let your seat bones drop and your spine lengthen up the surface of the wall.*

The wheelbarrow

Toward the end of pregnancy many women have pain in the groin. This usually occurs as a result of pressure from the baby on the joints of the pelvis. To relieve the discomfort, try this exercise, your partner kneeling very close to you.

1 *Lie on your back with your knees bent. Your partner holds your hips at either side.*

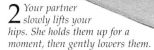

2 *Your partner slowly lifts your hips. She holds them up for a moment, then gently lowers them.*

wall, and feel your seat tucking under and your tummy muscles working to straighten your spine. Make sure not to tighten your shoulders. Keep them dropped. Now imagine that a string is pulling your head up from the center at the top and notice the back of your neck lengthening. Relax your jaw. (Your jaw muscles cannot force your head up!) Walk a few paces away from the wall. You will find that you are now standing in a stiff, exaggerated stance like a soldier on duty. Let the muscles settle into a more comfortable state. The rocking-chair exercise (see page 121) encourages good posture, too, and can be done with the help of your partner.

"I've always been very active physically and was determined I wasn't going to give up because I was pregnant. So I've cycled everywhere and gone on with my yoga and swum every day."

Walking Whenever possible, walk rather than stand. The healthiest, most rhythmic and natural all-around exercise is walking. If you have to stand around, exercise your feet while you do so, even if only by screwing up and extending your toes, going up onto the ball of the foot and down again and shifting weight from one foot to the other. Muscles in the feet and legs pump blood back to the heart, so movement is important to maintain good circulation in the legs.

You can also increase the tone of your buttock muscles and help the circulation in your legs by bridging (see page 122).*

Sitting Sit back on your chair and make sure that your spine is well supported. If necessary, put a small cushion in the small of the back to provide support while you are sitting down. In the last few weeks of your pregnancy you may need more support than this; try sitting well back against a large bean bag or a firm floor cushion. If you have to write or type at a desk or table for any length of time, remember to rest your head down on it occasionally and gently stretch the back of your neck. Use a low footstool (so that your knees are level with or slightly higher than your hips) to rest your back when you have to sit for a long time.

Bending and lifting Use your legs, not your back, when you reach down for anything. This means that, whenever possible, you should bend your knees and get right down in order to grasp the load. Kneel or squat when you are working low down, cleaning the bath or making a low bed, for example. Avoid misusing your spine as if it were a crane. For some household jobs, such as wiping or polishing a floor, it is most comfortable to get onto all fours. This takes the weight of the baby off your spine and is surprisingly comfortable, especially if you do have backache.

Lying down and getting up The front-lateral or "three-quarters-over" position is often the most comfortable when you are lying in bed. It may help to put a pillow under your upper knee. Allow a good amount of space between your legs. Avoid hollowing your back when you are lying down, too. If necessary, put a small pillow under your hips so that your back does not cave in.

Whenever you get up from lying on your back, roll over onto one side first, swinging your shoulders around, and push with your upper arm, drawing up your knees at the same time till you are in a kneeling position; tighten your buttocks and then rise from that position. This movement will avoid unnecessary strain on your abdominal muscles. It may sound complicated but it can come to be a beautifully smooth, coordinated movement, making you feel like Cleopatra rising from her barge.

Aches and pains

Although bad posture is often responsible for aches and pains during pregnancy, you may have other aches and pains that are just the result of being pregnant. If this is the case all you can do to relieve them is concentrate on relaxation and experiment with different positions in which you feel more comfortable.

If you have backache a chiropractor may be able to put it right and show you how to use your muscles more effectively and avoid strain. Chiropractors use a special couch that can easily be adjusted to leave room for your bump, and they can make spinal adjustments right through pregnancy without harming the baby.

Low backache In late pregnancy, if the baby is facing toward your front and engages as a posterior (see page 263) with the back of its head pressing against your sacrum, you may develop backache. Rest in positions in which the weight of the baby is tilted off the spine, and take every opportunity to get onto all fours. Scrubbing a kitchen floor can provide extraordinary relief from backache. The angry cat (see page 128) is an exercise that combines this position with pelvic rocking to relieve your spine of the baby's weight.

Upper backache This occurs when you try to compensate for the weight of your pregnancy dragging you forward by flinging your shoulders back and tightening the muscles in the upper back. To relieve it, roll your shoulders backward whenever you have the opportunity and do the shoulder roll exercise (see page 128).

Pubic pain The cartilage of the joint in the front of the bony pelvic girdle is softened and stretched by hormones in your bloodstream during pregnancy. This makes more room for the baby to come down during birth. Sometimes from around the middle of pregnancy this stretching starts to cause pain. Your pubic symphysis may be tender to touch and you may have low back pain as well as pain along your inside thighs. A pelvic support belt can help, so ask your doctor or midwife about this. A bag of frozen peas or corn wrapped in a cloth placed over the painful area may give some relief when you are resting. When you roll over or get up out of bed be careful to keep your knees together.

Tingling and numbness You may sometimes feel tingling and numbness in your hand. This is known as carpal tunnel syndrome. It results from pressure on the nerves and tendons caused by swelling of the hand and wrist. You will be most aware of it in the morning after your wrists have accumulated fluid during the night. To relieve the discomfort, try the shoulder roll exercise or hold your hand above your head for a few minutes and flex and gradually extend the fingers upward.

Pain under the ribs You may experience pain below the ribs on either side when the top of the uterus (the fundus) is high after 30 weeks of pregnancy (see page 73). This pain normally tends to come on whichever side the baby is lying.

You will discover that you are only comfortable when sitting straight on a rather high chair and will not want to slump down onto your uterus. In spite of folklore about the dangers of an expectant mother lifting her arms above her head, you will find that it helps to stretch upward so that your whole rib cage is lifted off the uterus. You can also do stretching exercises while sitting with your back against a wall for support (see page 129).

Pain in the groin In late pregnancy this is the consequence of the stretching of the round ligaments that go from either side of the uterus into each groin. Avoid rapid movements such as standing up too quickly. Also avoid standing for long periods, and even when sitting change position often. Symptoms can be relieved by doing the wheelbarrow exercise (see page 129). Some women get a stitch in the side of their body because the broad ligament on either side of the uterus is stretched. If you are lying down on your side, you may find it helpful to place a small pillow beneath your uterus to prevent this from happening.

Cramp in the leg Occasionally, pregnant women get recurring cramps because they are trying to go on a salt-free diet. Eating something salty before you go to bed may make the cramp disappear. A magnesium supplement can reduce leg cramps and sometimes calcium tablets are prescribed for cramp on the grounds that your body must be short of calcium. Research shows that this is actually useless as a treatment for cramps.*

"I always wake him up to massage my leg cramps. At least he'll be well prepared for seeing to the baby in the night!"

Avoid curling your toes under while you are sleeping. Use a duvet on your bed or make up the bed loosely so that your toes are not pressed down by the bed linen overnight.

Lifting your feet above the level of your heart will also help circulation and relieve cramps. However, in advanced pregnancy this position may give you indigestion, so you are left with a choice between two discomforts. While you are lying with your feet up, roll them around in circles from the ankles to help stretch the calf muscles, or practice drawing the letters of the alphabet, one foot at a time, keeping your legs still. If you do get a cramp, ask your partner to grip your heel and, using his or her forearm, push your foot up while holding your knee straight with the other hand. It is a useful precaution against getting cramps to do this regularly about ten times before you settle down for the night.

Common problems during pregnancy

Although your baby can grow inside you without your having to think consciously or do anything about it, this growth affects your whole body and every system in it. You may worry about these disconcerting changes taking place if you do not understand what they are and why they have occurred.

VARICOSE VEINS

The valves which help direct the blood through the veins back to the heart may soften in pregnancy and become unable to propel the increased amount of blood through the legs. This causes pooling of blood and swelling of your veins, especially when standing.

Avoid all positions which allow pooling of blood in the legs: prolonged standing, sitting with your legs crossed or with your thighs pressing against the edge of your chair, for example. Foot exercises will help keep the blood moving. If you are advised to wear elastic stockings, choose semi- or full-support styles and put them on *before* you get up in the morning. Bend a knee, put one leg on and wriggle it up; then do the same with the other.

Vaginal varicose veins Sometimes a woman develops varicose veins in her vagina and labia. The discomfort may be eased by wrapping some ice chips in a clean handkerchief, knotting it, and packing it against the sore areas. Obviously you cannot walk around like this, but it is a good excuse to lie down for a while, thus offering a position in which the whole weight of your uterus is not pressing down on the swollen veins. Sometimes vitamin B6 (pyridoxine) can help, and you might take prenatal vitamins which contain B6.

Hemorrhoids (also known as piles) are varicose veins of the rectum and can be caused by constipation. If you have piles avoid any straining on the toilet. This condition should be treated quickly because hemorrhoids can become prolapsed (protrude through the anus), causing extreme pain. Your doctor may give you a prescription for a relieving cream, or a lint pad soaked in witch hazel will help.

CONSTIPATION

You are more likely to be constipated during pregnancy because some of the extra hormones produced while you are pregnant cause the intestine to relax and become less efficient. First of all, ensure that you are eating the right kinds of food (see page 96). Eat plenty of fruit, vegetables, fiber, and whole grains, and drink as much water as you can. When you are on the toilet, allow your pelvic floor to be fully released and bulging down. Take your time over emptying the bowels, and have a brisk walk every day if possible. If you are still constipated, ask your doctor to prescribe a bulking agent.

BLADDER CONTROL AND INFECTIONS

In the first three months or so of your pregnancy the developing baby and enlarging uterus are pressing against your bladder, while the extra progesterone flowing through your bloodstream softens the tissues. So it is quite normal for a pregnant woman to have to urinate very often. This may be even more noticeable at the very end of pregnancy when the baby has gone down into your pelvis.

Cystitis Pressure and engorgement of blood vessels in the pelvic area mean that a pregnant woman is more exposed to the risk of urinary infection. If you notice a stinging, burning feeling when you urinate, this usually indicates that you have developed cystitis. If left untreated, cystitis rapidly becomes very uncomfortable.

If you suspect that you have cystitis, go to your doctor, who will probably prescribe a course of antibiotics. It is sensible to seek help when you first notice the symptoms as delay can allow the infection to take hold more firmly. As a general treatment for cystitis, drink plenty of liquid. Drink a glass of water every time you have used the toilet. Drinking cranberry, orange, lemon or grapefruit juice may help, or an alkaline-based drink such as a mixture of sodium bicarbonate and sodium citrate can be beneficial. One natural remedy that is effective is marshmallow tea.

Wear cotton briefs and avoid any clothing that is tight on the crotch. Wear pantyhose that have a cotton panel or air holes between the legs. Spend time on the toilet to empty your bladder as completely as possible. When the baby is pressing against your bladder in late pregnancy, you will be able to shift position so that the baby moves a little, allowing you to void some more.

Pyelitis If you have a temperature and low back pain, and if it hurts when you apply pressure over your kidneys on one or both sides, you may have pyelitis (a kidney infection). Sometimes the infection also causes nausea and vomiting. Seek treatment immediately, since this is not only painful for you but can affect the functioning of the placenta. Antibiotics are effective, but all the measures suggested for coping with cystitis are also helpful and you will probably appreciate a hot water bottle placed against the painful area. Women with pyelitis are often admitted to the hospital to allow a proper diagnosis of the problem. The right drugs will usually clear it up completely within two weeks.

YEAST GROWTHS

It is normal to have an increased vaginal discharge in pregnancy, but if your vulva becomes itchy and your vagina is red, sore, and burning, you probably have thrush ("candida" or "monilia"). Pessaries of a group of drugs called imidazoles (such as Monistat, Lotrimin, and others available over the counter) are the most effective treatment for thrush. If you get repeated infections, try cutting out sugar and white flour and basing your diet on whole grains, fruit, vegetables, and protein. Painting gentian violet (which you can get from a drug store without a prescription) over the affected area works well but is a messy process; wear a sanitary pad to prevent staining.

BREAST TENDERNESS

The normal breast tenderness of the early weeks of pregnancy can be acutely painful for some women, and they walk about with stiff arms to protect themselves in case anyone brushes against them. A good supporting bra is important even if you do not normally wear one, since if the breasts are increasing in size, as they usually are at this stage, their own weight can be uncomfortable. If your breasts become extra-sensitive like this, you will not enjoy your partner's most gentle touch until about the middle of pregnancy.

INVERTED NIPPLES

Some women have one or both nipples shaped like dimples. These are called "inverted" nipples. If you have a nipple like this but can press it out, or if it projects when you are sexually excited, the baby will be able to get hold of the nipple well and draw it out further. Otherwise you may find it more difficult to fix the baby on to the breast with a good mouthful. However, if you do manage to start the baby off, he or she will soon suck the nipple into a good projecting shape. It is a fallacy to think that you have to have prominent nipples in order to be able to nurse successfully, and there is no point in wearing nipple shells in pregnancy or trying to pull and squeeze your nipples in order to encourage them to project.*

Below
Women with inverted or "dimpled" nipples can still breastfeed.

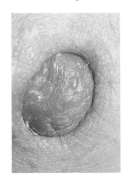

VOMITING

For some women the nausea and vomiting that is very common in the first three months of pregnancy (see page 24) goes on much longer, and this prolonged sickness is known by the medical term of hyperemesis. A woman with hyperemesis is really ill because she cannot take any food by mouth. Surprisingly, the cure may simply be admission to the hospital and often no further treatment is necessary. This is why some psychiatrists and obstetricians have suggested that hyperemesis is a symptom of disturbed relationships and that if the woman has a chance to get away from the relentless day-to-day contact with a partner, mother, mother-in-law, or anyone who is part of the stress to which she is reacting, the vomiting will ease. Part of the cure may simply be that she does not have to do any cooking or smell kitchen odors, however.

If you find that you are vomiting consistently at all hours of the day, cannot be sure of keeping any meal down, and are feeling really wretched, it is worth trying to get right away from your normal daily routine and surroundings, preferably among people you know only slightly or not at all, and who will therefore not fuss over you too much. If this gives you the opportunity to do something that you have never done before (not hang-gliding!) or see something you have never had the chance of seeing before, so much the better. There is a phrase that is sometimes used about a person who is "run down": "she needs to be taken out of herself." A woman who is vomiting almost without interruption may need to be taken "out" of herself and her usual relationships until she can cope emotionally, and then, when her pregnancy has settled down, she can come back "into" herself with new strength.

Nasal congestion

Sinusitis The mucous membrane inside the nostrils and sinuses often swells up during pregnancy because of the action of hormones liberated in the bloodstream which are also, fortunately, softening up your vagina and cervix. Some women seem to have a permanent cold in late pregnancy for this reason. Sinusitis does not interfere with your breathing during labor, so there is no need to worry about this, though you may be more comfortable breathing through your mouth rather than through your nose. This means

"I seem to have had a stopped up nose for months. It'll be good to be able to breathe easily again."

that you will need to take frequent sips of water or have a small spray bottle filled with ice water to spray into your mouth between contractions and lip salve to smooth on your lips to prevent soreness. The symptoms of sinusitis will go away completely after delivery.

Nosebleeds are very common in pregnancy. These, too, are associated with higher hormone levels and congestion. A tiny blob of Vaseline in the nostril will usually stop a nosebleed, and you should avoid blowing your nose hard.

Vaginal bleeding in early pregnancy

Bleeding from the vagina at any stage of pregnancy is always worrying. In early pregnancy it may be that the level of your pregnancy hormones is not sufficiently high to avoid breakthrough spotting. There is no way you can stop this without possibly affecting the developing baby. Cut out unnecessary exertion and, if the bleeding started at a time when your period would have been due, take life gently then and see if you can manage a few days in bed. Practice deep relaxation every day. There is further information about how to deal with a threatened miscarriage on page 372.

VAGINAL BLEEDING IN LATE PREGNANCY

If you notice any bleeding in late pregnancy it may be a sign that labor is about to start. It is usually blood from around the cervix and, except in those cases where there is a polyp in the cervix that has started to bleed, shows that thinning out and some dilation is now taking place. If your baby is due within a month and the bleeding looks like the beginning of a period, a blood-stained mucous discharge (a "show," see page 242), do not worry but accept it as a normal sign that your body is in good working order for labor and that you may start within a week or two.

Bright red bleeding, which flows as if you were at the height of a period, is another matter entirely. It is called antepartum hemorrhage (APH) and, although quite rare, is serious. If you start to hemorrhage, you should call your doctor or go to the hospital immediately. You should actually avoid both vaginal and rectal examination because they can make things worse. Ultrasound is the best way of finding out what is happening.

Placenta previa Sometimes blood flows from the placental site when it is too low-lying and partly in front of the baby's head. Intermittent APH from 27 weeks onward is a typical symptom of this condition, known as placenta previa. Placenta previa occurs in about one in every 200 births and it almost certainly means that the delivery will be by cesarean section. During a vaginal birth, as the lower segment of the uterus thinned out, the placenta would be torn away from its roots, thereby depriving the baby of both nourishment and oxygen. If you start to bleed when you are as much as 37 weeks pregnant, or thereabouts, you will be admitted to the hospital and, if bleeding continues, will be advised to continue to stay there until the baby is mature enough to be born.

In fact, ultrasound at 16 weeks often reveals that the placenta is lying in the lower part of the uterus. Although this tends to be taken by some obstetricians as an indication of the need for cesarean section, it is absolutely normal in early pregnancy and, by the end of pregnancy, when the wall of the uterus has stretched and enlarged, the placenta is usually in the right place in the upper part of the uterus. Only 6 percent of low-lying placentas detected by ultrasound in early pregnancy turn out to be lying over the cervix.*

Abruptio placenta APH can also mean that a part of the placenta, situated in the upper part of the uterus as it should be, has peeled away. This is called accidental hemorrhage (accidental in that the hemorrhage has occurred by chance) or abruptio placenta. Sometimes there is constant pain in the abdomen and the uterus

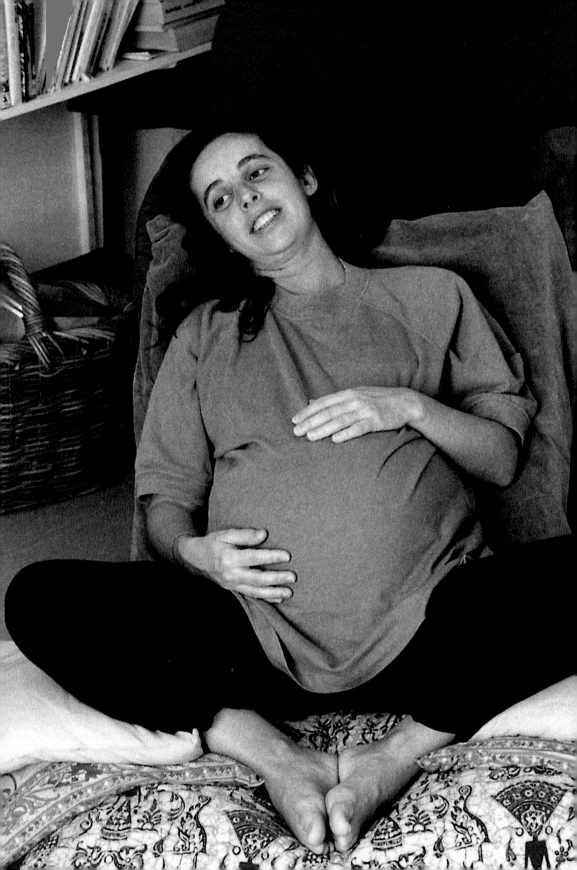

becomes and remains firm. The severity of accidental hemorrhage depends on how large a portion of the placenta has separated from the uterine lining, but it is a potentially serious problem, and the doctor should be informed immediately. You will be advised to go to the hospital for bed rest and, if the bleeding stops and all is well with the baby, will be discharged after four to five days. It is probably wise to avoid intercourse and orgasm until after the baby is born.

HIGH BLOOD PRESSURE

Every time you go for a prenatal visit your blood pressure is checked (see pages 44–45). This is because, although slight fluctuations are normal during pregnancy, any significant rise may be an indication of preeclampsia. If the diastolic figure (the second number) in your blood pressure reading rises by as much as 15, you are considered to have hypertension – high blood pressure.

Low-dose aspirin is sometimes used prophylactically by women who already have high blood pressure at the beginning of pregnancy so that they are less likely to develop preeclampsia. Unfortunately it also increases the risk of abruptio placenta (that is, the placenta starts to separate from the wall of the uterus before the baby is born) and does not reduce risks to the baby.*

Hypertension can be an early signal of preeclampsia. When a woman has preeclampsia the placenta does not continue to work as well as it should. So if you have high blood pressure, bed rest may be prescribed, the idea being that the placenta functions more efficiently if you stay in bed. But hypertension is over-diagnosed. For each woman who has sustained high blood pressure, another is diagnosed as having high blood pressure because it happened to shoot up at a prenatal visit, perhaps because she had to rush to get there, was sitting around for ages worrying about her older child, was made anxious by information she heard in the waiting room, or simply because having her blood pressure checked by a doctor or nurse resulted in "white coat hypertension." If you can, refuse to be hassled and stay as relaxed as possible about your blood pressure. The more checks that are made for hypertension and the presence of protein in the urine in pregnancy, the more often they are found. Frequently they are chance findings.

PREECLAMPSIA

The full name of this condition is *preeclamptic toxemia*, but it is also known as preeclampsia, or *toxemia*. The Australian name for it is *hypertensive disease of pregnancy* or *HDP*, and it is also called pregnancy-induced *hypertension* or *PIH*, and even gestosis. All these names reflect the uncertainty as to its cause. A nineteenth-century doctor called it "the disease of theories" and this remains true today.

Preeclampsia affects between 5 and 10 percent of all pregnant women, but rarely occurs in the early part of pregnancy, unless a woman has been malnourished for years.

Opposite
Take some time to relax each day, breathing deeply and concentrating on the new life within you.

Symptoms Your blood pressure rises, the level of uric acid in your blood goes up, and you retain a lot of fluid. A rise in blood pressure alone does not mean that you have preeclampsia, and neither does an increase in fluid retention. The two symptoms in combination, however, indicate the need for some form of treatment. If mild preeclampsia goes untreated, eventually protein sometimes appears in the urine. Blood tests may show that the liver and kidneys are not functioning normally. Babies of mothers with a high proportion of protein in their urine may be born prematurely; once a woman is excreting a lot of protein, or her blood values are seriously abnormal, pregnancy is unlikely to continue longer than two more weeks.*

The danger of preeclampsia is not so much to you as to the unborn baby. If the condition is allowed to progress, clots and fatty acids build up in the placenta, blocking the arteries and causing the placenta to fail. This means that labor occurs prematurely, before the baby is necessarily mature enough to be able to survive. In its most severe form preeclampsia becomes eclampsia, and it can seriously affect you as well as the baby, causing convulsions and possibly even a state of coma. The following symptoms can all be signs of eclampsia: headache, flashing lights, nausea, vomiting, and pain in the abdomen. Don't make the mistake of thinking that you must have the flu if this happens to you during late pregnancy. Get in touch with your doctor immediately.

Causes No one is certain what causes the disorder, but research at Oxford, England, indicates that it may be because the blood vessels in the placenta are thinner than usual. The problem starts between the 6th and 18th week of pregnancy, when placental cells do not infiltrate arteries in the uterus deeply enough to make the blood vessels expand so that they can nourish the baby (see page 70).

There is another element in preeclampsia, too; it seems to be a process similar to graft rejection. It is as if the baby is a transplant in the mother's body, and her immune system recognizes it and produces cells in order to expel the intruder.

The risk of preeclampsia is highest in the first pregnancy. But it also has something to do with the man; if the woman has a new partner for a subsequent pregnancy, the chances of her developing preeclampsia are about the same as if it were her first baby.

Poor nutrition may play an important part in preeclampsia. You may be able to avoid the disorder by eating well, ensuring you have adequate protein throughout pregnancy (see page 95). If you have had preeclampsia in a previous pregnancy, start out on a program of good nutrition *before* you conceive again. Dietary restriction to try to prevent preeclampsia is definitely harmful.*

You are more likely to get preeclampsia if any of the following apply: you have diabetes or kidney disease; you normally have high blood pressure (140/90 or higher); you are having twins or more; family members have high blood pressure or have had preeclampsia;

you are in your teens or are over 40; you are under 5′ 3″; you have had preeclampsia with a previous pregnancy (in which case there is a one in ten chance of its recurring); you suffer from migraine.

Treatment Many doctors think that staying in bed at the first signs may avoid further developments. Certainly bed rest coupled with relaxation of body and mind will reduce your blood pressure and improve the blood flow to the baby. Don't lie flat on your back in bed, but on your side or well propped up. Left-sided bed rest is most favorable for blood supply to the placenta.

If your blood pressure has risen markedly or you have additional indications of worsening preeclampsia, your doctor will probably admit you to the hospital for bed rest, observation, and medication to lower blood pressure or to prevent convulsions. Once stabilized, you may get to go home on continued bed rest. If the preeclampsia does not improve or if it worsens (eclampsia), early delivery (induction or cesarean section) may be suggested.

Many women feel trapped in the hospital when they have preeclampsia, because they may not feel ill. In these circumstances, knowing what is happening to you and why helps you to care for yourself rather than just put up with having things done to you. Ask questions: find out about your condition and its progress, and understand the reasons for the treatment you are receiving.

DIABETES

For young diabetic women with tightly controlled insulin, childbearing is as safe as for any others. Every diabetic woman of childbearing age should know that it is important to control the condition carefully, particularly before conception and during the very early stages of pregnancy, since otherwise there is an increased risk of fetal abnormalities. The alphafetoprotein test, or the prenatal risk profile, which is the first screening procedure in a series that can reveal the risk of handicap, is more likely to yield an inaccurate result than in non-diabetic women, so this should be anticipated. It does not mean that anything is wrong.

"The diabetes came as a complete surprise, because I'd felt so well right through pregnancy till then."

The accumulation of glucose in a diabetic woman who is pregnant is absorbed by the baby, who then grows very fast. It is now possible for a woman to monitor her blood sugar levels at home using a glucose meter; when linked to a computer at the hospital, the meter provides details of the levels of blood sugar in the average day, so that she can adjust her sugar intake as necessary. A single ultrasound scan is an inaccurate way of trying to find out what the baby's size is likely to be at birth, so the obstetrician may recommend a series of scans during the later months of pregnancy. If it is thought that the baby is growing too big to pass easily through your pelvic outlet, early induction of labor may be recommended. If labor is induced, although the baby may be large, it may not actually be mature, and may need special care after birth (see page 366). Some babies of diabetic mothers are delivered by cesarean section because induction is performed before the mother's cervix is soft and ready to open. There is absolutely no good reason why a diabetic woman should not breastfeed her baby, and many women do so very successfully. In fact, breastfeeding reduces the chances of the child becoming diabetic later on in life.

Gestational diabetes This has been called "a diagnosis looking for a disease." It is much better to consider it more simply as the discovery of sugar in the urine and blood.

SUGAR IN THE URINE

Your urine is tested for sugar whenever you see the doctor or midwife (see pages 44–45). Nearly all women at some time during pregnancy produce sugar in their urine, indicating that they may have raised blood sugar levels, which contribute to a baby's growth. Very occasionally the presence of sugar in the urine can be a sign of diabetes but most of these women are *not diabetics*. It is merely a biochemical variation, not an illness.

When you are pregnant, you have more blood circulating in your system than normally, and there is therefore more blood sugar that must be dealt with by your kidneys. You are more likely to have high blood sugar if you are an older mother, if you are overweight, have had any repeated infections of the urinary tract, or if you smoke.

"I've found that I get sugar in my urine if I eat bananas and sweet things and don't get daily exercise. I also try to eat little and often rather than have a few large meals."

You can reduce the sugar level in your blood by modifying your diet: cutting out sugary foods, bananas, and caffeinated drinks, and by having small, frequent meals instead of a few large ones. If you go for a long time without food, body fat may be burned up and ketones start to appear in your urine. This is definitely not a good idea. It means that you are starving yourself. By all means restrict your weight gain if it makes you feel better, but ensure that you have good nutrition. Sugar levels can also be reduced by making sure that you get some exercise each day.

If sugar is found in your urine your doctor or midwife will probably want to take a blood sample for a *random blood glucose test*. If the glucose content of this blood sample is high you will be asked to take a *glucose tolerance test*. Some obstetricians expect their patients to take the glucose tolerance test as a matter of routine at approximately 28 weeks. It is up to you whether you accept this offer. You are given a sugary beverage to drink (or you may be asked to eat a special prescribed meal with measured amounts of carbohydrates) and then have a blood sample taken one hour later. If the glucose content of this blood sample is high it does not mean that you have "gestational diabetes." If fact, there is an 85 percent chance that you do not but you will be asked to take a longer, more complex, and more sensitive glucose tolerance test. If this indicates "gestational diabetes," you will be asked to monitor your own blood sugar levels and modify your diet. It may also be recommended that you take insulin, on the grounds that this will keep the baby smaller, although there is no evidence that taking insulin reduces the size of the baby in women who are overweight.

Being labelled "gestationally diabetic" and treated as if you were diabetic during pregnancy can be extremely stressful and intrusive: strict dietary advice, frequent blood tests, insulin administration, multiple ultrasound scans, and the likelihood of induction and operative delivery. Most research suggests that this kind of surveillance is unnecessary and even harmful, and it certainly does nothing to help the baby. In the majority of cases a woman's blood sugar level soon falls back to normal once the baby is born.*

ANEMIA
It is normal for your hemoglobin level to fall during pregnancy. Iron used to be prescribed automatically in pregnancy, but now we know that it can be harmful, and that when a woman's hemoglobin level does not fall in pregnancy she is more likely to give birth preterm. Lab tests of hemoglobin concentration and ferritin levels (for which the normal range is 125–150) are not useful.*

If you are genuinely anemic, you can tell because you tend to feel very tired, become exhausted when you do anything vigorous, have dizzy spells, and are frequently short of breath. Women who suffer from anemia in pregnancy are less able to cope with any heavy bleeding at the time of the birth and are more likely to have an infection. Adjust your diet so that you get more iron-rich foods, protein, B vitamins (especially B12), and vitamin C, and take the folic acid supplement which your doctor will prescribe (see page 97). All are necessary to ensure that your blood can carry enough oxygen to all the tissues of your body. Your doctor will also prescribe iron tablets. If they make you constipated, ask for another kind. If you have a very low hemoglobin level (see page 40) after 30 weeks, injections of iron may be prescribed.*

HEADACHE
There is no reason why you should have more headaches when you are pregnant than when you are not pregnant. In fact, some women who usually suffer from migraine find that it disappears throughout pregnancy. You can have tension headaches while you are carrying a baby just as at any other time. If your pregnancy is fraught with anxiety, or you are taking on more than you can handle, you will probably be prone to headaches. Decode the messages from your body, modify your lifestyle, and, if you are worried about labor, find out how you can help yourself (see page 149).

A sharp, blinding headache that affects your eyesight occurring during late pregnancy should always be reported to your doctor as it could possibly be associated with preeclampsia.

DIGESTIVE DISTURBANCES

Indigestion and heartburn are problems of the last three or four months of pregnancy. There seems to be so little room in your abdomen and it feels as if all your organs are being crushed.

It is better to have many small snacks than several larger meals a day, and it is sensible to avoid fried, rich, or spicy foods. Some people find that they cannot digest bread or products containing yeast and that, by cutting out these foods, they can eliminate heartburn. Many women discover they cannot drink during a meal and that meals have to be taken dry. You need to experiment with different combinations of food and liquid to find the kind of diet that suits you personally. There is no perfect diet that is right for everyone.

"When I stopped trying to fight the pregnancy and let myself slow down I began to enjoy it."

Since heartburn results from acid normally present in your stomach flowing back into the esophagus, try to find positions for sitting and sleeping in which the upper part of your uterus is not pressing against your stomach. You will probably prefer upright chairs and at night will feel better if you sleep well propped up with pillows. Make sure jeans, trousers, and skirts are comfortably loose at the waist if you want to avoid indigestion.

SHORTNESS OF BREATH

When the baby is high, after about 34 weeks and before it drops into your pelvis, you will probably find that you are short of breath whenever you exert yourself or even just climb the stairs. Your uterus is putting pressure on your lungs, and your diaphragm may be shifted out of place by as much as one inch. Again, sitting straight and sleeping propped up can help and you will probably discover that you have to take life rather more slowly in order not to become breathless. There is a rhythm to everything in nature, and this is a phase of pregnancy when your body is telling you to slow down.

Daily care and comfort

When you are pregnant you find that you carry around your own efficient central heating system. You do not need to dress as warmly as usual and in hot weather you will probably feel more comfortable in cotton dresses and skirts, and should avoid synthetic materials. Many pregnant women suffer from varicose veins in the legs, rectum, or vagina (see page 133). Boots should not grip so tightly that circulation is impeded. Make sure that jeans or trousers do not interfere with the circulation in the groin.

SHOES

Shoes should allow the feet to keep their normal shape and should not be so high that your weight is thrown forward onto the balls of your feet. In late pregnancy you may find that your feet are wider than usual and so need a wider-fitting shoe or a half-size larger. Although oxfords give good support to the arches, you may not be able to tie them easily in late pregnancy. For the same reason slip-on sandals are better than shoes that have elaborate buckles.

BRAS

Since breast changes and enlargement occur from the first days of pregnancy, you will need to acquire a bra which gives good support and, if you are heavy-breasted, one with straps that are sufficiently wide not to dig into your shoulders.

Heavy breasts, allowed to hang without support, may develop stretch marks (see page 146), which will leave you with silvery streaks after the pregnancy. A woman with large breasts may prefer to wear a lightweight bra at night, too, during pregnancy.

TEETH

Although the baby needs calcium in order to grow strong teeth, your own teeth are no more likely to fall out in pregnancy than at any other time. However, as your gums soften and become spongier along with other tissues in the body as the result of the action of pregnancy hormones in your bloodstream, you may be liable to get a gum infection. Good nutrition (see pages 93–100) is the first line of defense against this. Mouth hygiene is also important, with regular tooth brushing, especially after breakfast and before you go to bed at night. Arrange a dental examination and cleaning but not X-rays when you know you are pregnant. Have another dental check-up when the baby is about 5 months old.

SKIN PIGMENTATION

For many women pregnancy is better than a beauty treatment: skin improves, eyes shine, and hair is in better condition. But some women develop patches of darkened (pigmented) skin on the face, and this can be distressing. The technical term is "chloasma," but it is also called "the mask of pregnancy." It is a result of the high level of hormones and also occurs in some women taking oral contraceptives. It is made worse by exposure to sunlight. The kind of cosmetic cream sold for minimizing birthmarks often disguises it effectively. The mask usually disappears once the baby is born.

You will notice that other parts of the body already pigmented become darker, for example the circles around your nipples and the skin of your labia. You may also develop a dark line down the middle of your tummy from your navel, where the rectus muscle is stretched. It is particularly obvious in dark-haired women. All these colorations should disappear once the baby is born.

STRETCH MARKS

Stretch marks (striae) may appear over your tummy, buttocks, and breasts. They are dark streaks and are a sign that the skin has been stretched from underneath. They never disappear completely but, after the birth, they change from brown or deep violet to a silvery shade, rather like the marks on some fine, gauze-like fabric that has not been properly ironed. Many women use a rich cream or oil to "feed" the skin, and there are some on the market especially for stretch marks. However, these are expensive and any readily absorbed cream, or even vegetable oil, will do. If your skin is very stretched, and especially if you are having twins, it is marked like this because of pressure on the layers underneath which cannot be reached by anything applied from outside. Still, it can be relaxing for you to stroke your tummy; even though you may still have stretch marks, there is nothing to be lost and some pleasure to be gained from gentle massage with a rich, slippery cream.

ITCHING

A pregnant woman may get very itchy and uncomfortable in hot weather. It is important to wear cotton rather than synthetic clothing and underwear that is as loose as possible. Calamine lotion or an equal mixture of a few drops each of camomile, lavender, and bergamot essential oils in some (about 50 mls) witch hazel or rosewater is soothing when stroked into the skin.

If itching is really bothering you, consult your doctor or midwife. Rarely, it is a symptom of liver malfunction – obstetric cholestasis – which puts the baby at risk, and for which the only treatment is the induction of early labor.

SPORTS

Any sport you already do well is probably fine to continue with during your pregnancy: if you are really good at something, you do not waste muscular energy and your movements are smoothly coordinated. As pregnancy advances, you will notice your balance changing as the center of gravity is becoming more concentrated in your tummy. This will almost certainly limit your sporting activities, although I heard of a tightrope walker who practiced daily on the high wire until she went into labor – an exceptional woman! Swimming is splendid exercise during pregnancy, and dancing, too, provided that you are not in a stuffy room. Though strolling through the mall does not provide good exercise, brisk walking in fresh air, wearing comfortable shoes, with arms swinging and breathing deeply, is excellent. Cycling is also beneficial although, if you can avoid heavy traffic and its inevitable fumes, it is kinder to both you and your baby. It is sensible to avoid all competitive sports which might make you overexert yourself.

"I've continued with horseback-riding – it's wonderfully relaxing – but don't do jumps anymore."

TRAVEL

Travel in pregnancy is usually quite safe, but the exhaustion which may easily result from it is not. For this reason it is important to divide up long journeys into short, manageable sections if you can possibly do so; rest in between. Do not sit immobilized in a car, train, or plane for longer than two hours at the most without getting up and walking around for five minutes. Sitting for long periods reduces the circulation of blood in the pelvic area. Also remember to empty your bladder regularly as you are more likely to get a bladder infection during pregnancy (see page 134).

Travel in loose, comfortable clothing and shoes that allow for a little expansion. Soft slipper-socks are usually the most comfortable. Take any opportunity of dropping off to sleep. Pack an eye shade made of soft material to block out light.

Flying On an airplane drink water or fruit juice; avoid alcoholic drinks, as air travel is dehydrating, and alcohol will dehydrate you even further. If you are more than 36 weeks pregnant, some airlines will require a letter from your doctor saying that it is all right for you to travel. Your doctor will probably agree to write such a letter as long as the risk of your going into labor on board a plane is only slight. It would be quite reasonable of your doctor to refuse consent if, for instance, your blood pressure is high, or if you suffered a threatened miscarriage in the early part of the pregnancy. In such cases a change in altitude could bring on premature labor. Similarly, it is unwise to fly in a small unpressurized plane, as the supply of oxygen to the fetus can sometimes be drastically diminished. Some airlines, however, place no special restrictions on travel for pregnant women. You might also bear in mind, if you are thinking of flying a long distance, the strain caused to you by jet lag.

Driving is perfectly safe if you do not find it exhausting and if you are not subject to dizzy spells. It is a good idea to try and avoid the rush hour and breathing in exhaust fumes. If you have a heavy standard shift, the sheer hard work of changing gears can cause discomfort in the later months. Automatic transmission makes lighter work of driving. Make sure your seat belt is strapped under your belly and the shoulder harness is used properly, not so tight as to interfere with breathing or digestion.

REST AND SLEEP

During the first and last three months of pregnancy you will probably feel much more tired than usual, and it is advisable to rest as much as possible, rather than trying to fight off the tiredness. It is much better to rest *before* you become completely exhausted and feel you cannot go on any longer. Toward the end of your pregnancy there may be several reasons why you cannot sleep as much as you would like.

Nearly every pregnant woman goes through a period when she either cannot drop off to sleep or wakes in the night because the baby is kicking her, she needs to empty her bladder, or she has had a violent and disturbing dream and cannot get back to sleep. Sometimes the insomnia occurs because she is lying in bed worrying and in the darkness her fears gain the upper hand.

If you have recently given up work, you may feel that your pregnancy has become a time of passive waiting and is stretching out longer and longer, so that you cannot see an end to it. You probably cannot sleep because you need action, and sometimes vigorous exercise during the day can be a remedy for this problem. You could also try the traditional remedies for sleeplessness, such as hot milk after a luxurious warm bath at bedtime. The problem with this, though, is that you are more likely to have to get up to empty your bladder.

The stillness of the middle of the night provides a marvelous opportunity for practicing your relaxation and breathing techniques and for getting in touch with your baby. Use the time to center down into your body and become more aware of the developing life inside you. Find a comfortable position to relax in, well supported by pillows wherever you need them, and let the pillows take the weight of your body, your limbs, and your head. Concentrate on your breathing and allow it to flow right down through your body to where the baby nestles deep inside you. Cup your hands over the lower curve of your abdomen and breathe deeply so that the wave of the inhaled breath presses your hands up, and as you give a long breath out, your hands sink on the receding wave. Listen to the rhythmic sound of your breathing and think of it as being like waves flowing over shingle.

Relax and enjoy lying there with your baby. Once you have begun to lose yourself in these feelings, you will find that your breathing has relaxed and you are drifting off to sleep. Talk and sing and have private conversations with your baby. In the later months of pregnancy the baby can hear you, and when the baby is jumping around you may find that it soothes you both.

Emotional challenges in pregnancy

Many expectant mothers look and feel radiant. A healthy woman who is looking forward to a much-wanted baby, who has a loving and secure relationship with a considerate partner, and some knowledge about childbirth and what she can do to help herself at that time, often revels in her pregnancy. Many women say "I feel fitter than I ever have felt before" or "I'm really enjoying being pregnant" and are surprised at the vitality and sense of inner fulfilment which they experience.

Yet probably all of us are assailed by darker thoughts at times when we are overtired or under some special stress. Some of the more negative feelings that women experience in early pregnancy have been discussed on pages 24–25. But as your pregnancy advances, more specific anxieties may preoccupy you at times. Anxiety may grip you in the middle of the night when the baby has kicked you awake or when you have had to get up to empty your bladder and cannot get back to sleep again. Every fear is magnified in the darkness as you lie trying to sleep and unable to relax.

WORRIES ABOUT THE BIRTH

Labor can be an intensely pleasurable, all-absorbing, and deeply satisfying activity which it is really possible to enjoy. But just as some people do not like climbing a mountain, even though the view at the summit is magnificent and the climb exciting, and just as some people feel that sex is overrated and not really worth the effort, whereas others think it is one of the best experiences life can offer, different women have very different attitudes towards childbirth. This is not simply a matter of what happens physiologically or how you are treated in the hospital, but also depends on what kind of person you are. Anxiety can cast a shadow over childbirth and produce the speeded-up heart rate, high blood pressure, muscle tension, and other physical results of stress which actually make birth more difficult. It is important to think through it and to understand why you are anxious.

Anxiety about labor is probably best dealt with first of all by finding out more about it – not just its mechanics, but the physical and emotional sensations each phase brings – and learning the relaxation, breathing, and focused concentration which can help you to work with your body instead of against it. The simple process of sharing fears also often results in feeling much more lighthearted, so that women begin to enjoy their pregnancies. A good childbirth education class where discussion is encouraged and you can talk freely about your apprehensions, as well as your hopes, is often

effective in developing self-confidence and helping you to look forward to labor as a peak experience which brings delight and fulfillment, not just an ordeal to be endured.

Pain A woman having her first baby often thinks "I have never had anything really painful. How will I stand up to the pain of labor?" and she has no idea what that pain is like or what contractions feel like, the thought can bring terror. Learning about labor, about how contractions work and how they may feel at different stages of labor, is the most effective way of coming face to face with this anxiety and doing something about it. There is a whole chapter in this book about pain and pain relief (see pages 295–313), but the important thing to understand is that for most women the pain of labor is quite different from the pain of injury. Some women describe it as "positive pain" or "pain with a purpose."

Loss of control For many women anxieties about labor are linked with a dread of losing control. For your whole life you have been taught to control physical processes and your own behavior, and suddenly something is about to happen which clearly cannot be controlled and which will take over your body. You are told that you may cry out or groan, for example, that you may lose inhibitions, be impatient or irritable with your partner or whoever is helping you in labor, and swear and say things you never meant to, and are horrified to hear that during labor you may involuntarily empty your bowels or your bladder.

You also learn that the waters may break suddenly. In any group of women discussing the events of labor, first-time mothers nearly always ask those who have already had babies when their waters broke, whether it was sudden, and if so where it was; they express keen anxiety that they may break in the supermarket or on a bus or in another public place. What these women are saying is that they are fearful of letting their bodies function freely because of the embarrassment and social stigma attached. It is as if degrading physical processes, above all dirty ones which involve getting rid of waste products from the body, are taking place in public.

Think through why you find the thought of your waters breaking in public so upsetting. You are having a baby and it is perfectly obvious that you are going to give birth soon. If your waters do break in public, is it really so very terrible? You will attract interest and sympathy, but not disgust. You may see it as a kind of sexual act in front of other people. You are quite right, and understanding this can help you in labor. Birth, just like lovemaking, is a sexual process. If you can go *with* your labor instead of fighting it the experience can be fulfilling in a strangely pleasurable way. Prepare the way to this through body awareness and relaxation. Touch relaxation (see pages 186–194) is a special kind of release which teaches you to flow toward sensations of pressure and heat. It will help a lot in labor.

Opposite
In a second pregnancy you may worry that you will not have enough love to share between two children. You will.

Loss of dignity and failure An anxiety closely connected with loss of control is the fear of making a fool of yourself. Some women think doctors and nurses will laugh at them if they find themselves making uncontrollable noises, for instance. You may feel that you are on public display in labor and approach it as a test of endurance. You may also be anxious about "letting down" a partner who puts great faith in your ability to cope, or even of "failing" a keen childbirth teacher. Some men who participate in classes and the other preparations for the birth become so enthusiastic and obsessional that they are in effect "trainers," rather like athletic coaches. The woman then feels that she is expected to put on a performance and must excel in it. Childbirth classes which are geared exclusively to techniques used in labor, rather than focusing on wider aspects of the total experience, can reinforce this feeling.

Just as the elaborate techniques performed to "ensure" satisfaction in lovemaking can sometimes disturb the spontaneous rhythm of sex and interfere with the intense feeling and play of emotion between the couple, so breathing exercises and "distraction" techniques can sometimes intrude on the experience of labor. Exercises need to become "second nature" and be made a part of yourself. It is like learning to play the piano: there is a vast difference between laborious scales and playing a sonata. The exercises are important because they prepare you for playing music. But the eventual aim is to let the music flow through you, rather than to superimpose tricks and techniques onto it. Such a physical and emotional surrender is simple in labor because of its intensity. Birth involves mind and body working together in a completely absorbing, exciting, and passionate way. There is no success or failure in labor. You cannot make a fool of yourself, let anyone down, or flunk an examination in birth.

"I was always awkward in my overweight body. But in labor I swam through contractions like a seal or a dolphin. I felt triumphant!"

Fear of managing alone Some women approach labor as a medical incident like having an appendectomy, an unwelcome interruption of normal life rather than an experience which can be satisfying in itself. They feel totally dependent on the technology provided by the hospital and worry about whether they will get there on time, or whether the right people will be present to deliver the baby. Such women's dependence is reinforced by contemporary obstetrics and by every program on television which illustrates the latest marvel of science applied to childbearing. The impression is readily given that women must depend on lifesaving machines, and that without them it is not absolutely safe to have a baby.

The fact is that although these machines can be extremely useful in diagnosing difficulties when a baby is at risk or when special problems are met in pregnancy or labor, the majority of women can give birth perfectly well without them.

It is not advances in medicine but improved conditions, better food, and better general health which have made childbirth much safer for mothers and babies today than it was 100 years ago. The rate of stillbirths and deaths in the first week of life is directly related to a country's gross national product and to the position of the mother in the social class structure.

It is a disturbing thought that it is twice as safe for a professional woman to bear a child than it is for a poor, unsupported mother. The challenge is to find out which mothers and babies are at risk, and to offer them everything which can make birth safer, and to enable all women to give birth naturally if they can.

Loss of autonomy Another frequent anxiety is that of being denied the right to function as an adult and being under the control of doctors, nurses, and even machines. Many pregnant women resent the feeling that they cannot make their own decisions. Increasing numbers feel that they do not want to hand their bodies over to professional caregivers in pregnancy and childbirth, and are seeking maternity care in which they can take an active part, sharing the decision-making with their advisers.

If you are not sure whether your doctor is being quite open with you, or whether the hospital will really let you do the things in labor which you have asked to do, the uncertainty can actually produce a sick fear in the pit of the stomach. Too often pregnant women are treated very much like children or as patients in categories, such as "high risk," "low risk," "primigravida," "multigravida," and so on, who have to be processed through the hospital system, passive receivers of care rather than active birthgivers.

Fear of hospitals For many women hospitals are threatening places. People usually go to a hospital when they are ill. This may be the first time that you have been a patient in a hospital and the sights, sounds, and even smells of hospitals may alarm you. Even more important than the surroundings are the attitudes of members of hospital staff and the ways in which they interact with patients. If you meet cool indifference, rigid authoritarianism, or patronizing behavior you may dread going for your prenatal appointments, and this anxiety may color your whole approach to labor.

There is a certain kind of emotional climate in which anxieties flourish and unfortunately it is one which our society often provides for many pregnant women. If there is no one readily available of whom you can ask questions and be answered in clear terms that you can readily understand, the seeds of anxiety are often sown. Then they are nourished by the insecurity of seeing different members of the prenatal staff at each visit.

Women often feel apologetic about being anxious, about not being "sensible," as if they were revealing some shameful lack of emotional stamina. They are sometimes regarded as having something psychologically wrong with them if they show anxiety. But many of the fears you have during your pregnancy are not the result of inadequacy but a response to stresses caused by an environment which is alien and unfriendly, and by care which is impersonal. In such a situation anxiety is *realistic*.

Although you may not be able to eradicate anxiety about the birth itself, it is sensible to tackle it directly. Take a tour of the maternity ward. You can call the hospital to learn when tours are scheduled. Ask to see around the birth rooms (see page 183), including the machinery which may be used. Though you might prefer childbirth classes that are run independently of the hospital, attend at least some of those at the hospital, too, so that you can get to know some of the staff, and talk with your doctor about the style of childbirth which you would like if possible; ask him or her to note down any particular requests on your chart. Read the section in this book on talking to doctors (pages 47–53) before you go.

Loss of attractiveness Some pregnant women are deeply concerned that their sexual attractiveness may be completely destroyed by childbearing. They are frightened of losing their figures; they may also be anxious that the vagina will be slack and changed in shape, and that as a result they will not be able to make love with their partners in a mutually satisfying way.

The fear of a tear or a cut (see page 320) often discussed in childbirth education classes is not so much about pain resulting from stitches. It is really anxiety about genital mutilation.

Episiotomy In many hospitals episiotomy is routinely used for all women having their first babies and for a large percentage of those having second and subsequent babies. Now this is changing fast. Women are questioning the need for what amounts to surgical intervention in normal birth and the creation of an artificial and painful wound. Obstetricians are asking why this intervention has become so widely used without any proper evaluation. In fact, recent scientific trials have shown that this procedure, except in cases of fetal distress or other rare situations, has no advantage and causes unnecessary damage to the perineum.

Women are often more anxious about episiotomy than any other invasive procedure during childbirth. The thought of being surgically cut, or injured, in such a sensitive place is horrifying, and some women feel as though they are being punished for enjoying sex. Many women worry that childbirth will so damage them that they will never really be the same again.

There are various ways in which you can prepare the tissues of your perineum – the area between your vagina and your anus – to become soft and supple during pregnancy, so that you enter labor fully confident that you can give birth without injury. Pelvic floor movements (see pages 118–119) can contribute to the sensitive awareness, coordination, and control which help you in the second stage of labor, allowing you to open your body for the baby to be born and reducing stress on the pelvic muscles and perineal tissues. Many women find that massaging the tissues with vegetable oil can also help. Certainly getting in touch, literally, with this part of your body and feeling how flexible the tissues are will give you the confidence to know that your vagina and perineum are

"'I can't, I can't' I wailed. 'You can' she said, 'I know you feel you're splitting in two, but trust me, you won't.'"

able to fan out and open wide like a great peony or a rose spreading thick, fleshy petals. Since in late pregnancy it can be quite difficult to reach your own perineum and exert firm pressure, you may want to ask a partner to help you with this gentle massage. It feels especially good if the oil is warmed first and your partner's hands move slowly.

If you are concerned to avoid an episiotomy, discuss the subject with your midwife or doctor in advance. Say that you would like help at the delivery so that you can breathe the baby out rather than push it out, and ask for this to be noted on your chart. It is wrong to think that a woman who is anxious about episiotomy is in any way "neurotic," though doctors sometimes assume this.

It can help you to understand the healing process afterward if you know what has happened, and exactly where. Exploring the vagina with your fingers during pregnancy (see page 116) and after giving birth, and looking at it in a mirror, helps you to feel that it belongs to you; you can gradually rehabilitate the muscles through practicing gentle pelvic floor movements (see pages 118–119).

WORRIES ABOUT THE BABY

Almost every woman wonders at some stage during her pregnancy whether her baby is normal. Fear of producing a handicapped child is often connected with anxiety about not being able to live up to standards set by somebody else, usually either or both of the woman's own parents. It may seem almost impossible that you could produce from the dark interior of your body anything which is completely perfect. This is probably the most persistent, gnawing fear of all, and the only way of coming to terms with it is to develop self-confidence, a process which, not surprisingly, takes time. This is where regular attendance at childbirth education classes, which encourage you to have trust in your body and in your ability to give birth, rather than depending on others to get the baby born for you, can help enormously.

One woman who had disappointed her parents academically became pregnant outside marriage, in a desperate effort to show them that at least there was *something* she could do. She then lay awake wondering if her baby was deformed. Talking about this fear in a childbirth discussion group led her to reveal that she was having awful dreams. It then emerged that five out of the twelve women in the group were having very vivid dreams, and that even some of those who had not admitted to any worry about whether the baby would be "all right" were having dreams in which the baby was disposed of because it was not "good enough," or was taken away and looked after by other people because they, the mothers, were not themselves good enough. She felt relieved and reassured that she was not alone. Dreams can often reveal emotional tangles which cause distress in pregnancy until they are brought out into the open.

Most women who fear bearing an abnormal baby have little reason to expect that the baby will not be perfect. The minority of women who are aware of the possibility of inherited diseases or handicaps in their or their partners' families, or who are pregnant after the age of 40, will realize that they can seek genetic counseling and can have alphafetoprotein (AFP) or prenatal risk screening (see pages 220–226) and, if necessary, amniocentesis (see pages 227–228).

WORRIES ABOUT THE FUTURE

Loneliness Some women having their first babies move during pregnancy, to a larger apartment or house, and they find themselves in an area where they know nobody at all. Your doctor or midwife may be able to tell you about other pregnant women or mothers with new babies who live near you. It is worth investigating the possibilities while you are still pregnant. When you are busy with a baby it may be difficult to make new friends, especially during the winter months, so take the opportunity of making them now.

Change When a woman expresses anxiety about "things never being the same again," it helps to think through what exactly this means for her. One couple who had a deeply satisfying relationship saw the pregnancy and the birth as an "interruption": "We don't want to change our lives for a child," the woman said, "to be swamped by it. How long will it take before we get back to normal again? Sometimes I'm frightened we'll *never* get back to normal."

"We were happy and didn't want things to change. But now we're falling in love with the idea of each other as a mother and father. We're falling in love again."

When I asked what she found frightening, after some thought she said she did not want to become the same kind of woman as her mother. Most of all she was afraid her partner would not love her anymore and that she would be desexed by maternity.

Social expectations Another woman said that her pregnancy made her feel that at last she was fulfilling a socially acceptable role and that her own mother was proud of her for the first time in her life. In a way, she resented this. Other women acted as if they knew how she felt and what she thought and wanted. The doctors at the hospital expected her to be a "good patient" and be processed through the busy prenatal clinic like all the others with their swelling bumps. She suddenly felt miles away from her former colleagues and the others with whom she had worked, separated from them by the inescapable fact of her pregnancy. But by the end she felt guilty that she had resented the baby at the beginning of her pregnancy. At night as it moved inside her she lay wondering whether she would ever be a good mother. She said, "I sometimes feel so sorry for the little thing in there that I end up crying."

In a prenatal discussion group both women had the chance to talk about their feelings. It emerged that several of the others were also lying awake at night worrying. What had seemed personal handicaps proved to be an experience shared by a number of women.

If you realize that you are not alone with your fears, and are not being "odd" or neurotic, the anxieties usually become much less disturbing. Thinking about inevitable change may worry you in different ways: you may be afraid that the relationship with your partner will deteriorate; that you have no maternal instincts; that the loss of a job and the money and sense of freedom associated with getting out of the house and earning your own living may bring a real deprivation. You may wonder if you may be able to tolerate being at home all day with a "screaming brat," and whether you will miss all the interesting people at work.

Although such anxiety is realistic in the sense that these changes are dramatic and demanding for many women, most expectant mothers worry more about labor and the baby than about how they will cope after the birth. Many take the unknown "afterward" more or less for granted. It is as if they can see only as far as the birth, which dominates the horizon. The postpartum experience may then come as a shock. So some anxiety about life after the baby arrives is a healthy sign, and indicates that the emotional work is taking place which prepares a couple not only for birth but for parenthood.

Many anxieties during pregnancy, for both the woman and the man, offer clues to the challenges confronting the couple. It is a waste of emotional energy to try to "forget" them or put them to the back of your mind. They are there to be worked with. It is often the man and woman who are determined to take it all in their stride and carry on as usual, and who do not acknowledge feelings of apprehension on the threshold of the unknown, who face the most shattering crises when they have a baby in the house.

The discomfort produced by anxiety can force you to think through the meaning for you and your partner of the coming of a child into your lives. Without stress and challenge of this kind, emotional preparation for birth and parenthood may be overlooked. Fears and anxieties are an important element in the emotional changes necessary if you are to face up to the reality of birth and then to the astonishing reality of the new baby.

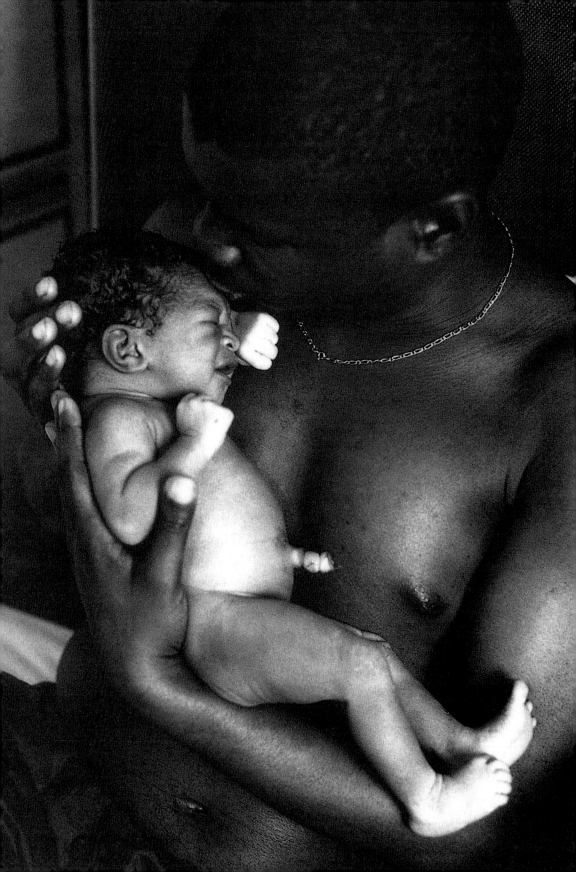

Becoming a father

Becoming a father is a major step in a man's life. It can also be a daunting one. Yet it is an experience usually treated as insignificant in comparison with that of becoming a mother. As a result the emotional upheavals and stresses of the future father are little understood and men are not prepared for the impact of pregnancy. If people do notice that a man is finding the going difficult they tend to laugh rather than sympathize. In fact the nervousness and anxiety of the father-to-be are favorite subjects of jokes and anecdotes, ranging from the picture-postcard variety – showing a man wide-eyed and desperate in the hospital corridor as his wife produces triplets – to those amused tales about male ignorance and incompetence shared between women over coffee.

In childbirth classes and hospital lectures for parents-to-be a man is often discussed only in terms of how he can help his partner, and his own emotional needs are neglected. One result of this is to make him feel isolated and resentful, finding it difficult to reach out and give his partner the support she needs. She is the princess going to the ball and he feels a bit like the back legs of a pantomime horse.

An expectant father may feel jealous of all the attention given to the future mother, absurdly envious of her reproductive powers and sometimes even jealous of the coming baby. Then he feels guilty about succumbing to these emotions and decides to concentrate on his work – because that at least is one thing he can do properly. And the more he immerses himself in his own preoccupations, the more isolated and left out of the pregnancy he feels.

Some men become depressed during pregnancy or experience violent mood swings similar to those that a pregnant woman may go through. A few even walk out of the relationship because the stress is too great for them to handle. So it is important to remember that usually there are *two* people having a baby and that the man also goes through a transitional period of stress when deep emotions may be stirred and his behavior may be difficult to understand.

REACTING TO FATHERHOOD

The sheer responsibility of having a baby can be frightening. The woman may be planning to give up work for a time, or even for good, and the man is expected to support the family. The financial burden may be too great for some men to shoulder without anxiety. For many men money problems constitute a rationalization, a socially acceptable explanation for anxiety, without getting to the root of what they really find disturbing. In fact, some men find that the prospect of becoming a father brings with it a crisis of identity. Although it is a common occurrence and one which in due course brings about creative change, it is nevertheless still a crisis.

Opposite
A father discovers new depths of compassion and love, and life becomes more precious.

159

The changing relationship One element in this crisis involves grieving over a relationship that is bound to change. The easy ways, the lack of routine, the spontaneity of the early stage of the relationship, all have to give way to an existence centered around a baby. Some men see their partners as their mothers. When the woman becomes pregnant it is as if the man is losing a mother and is being replaced in her affections by a new baby. As his partner becomes more involved in the pregnancy and the baby to whom she is giving birth, he feels increasingly rejected and finds this inevitable shift of focus very threatening.

The changing woman Some men acquire a woman as a kind of showpiece, proof of their success in hunting down and possessing a desirable sexual object, or evidence of their social success, a demonstration and the symbol of a lifestyle which embodies achievement. Delighted as such a man may be to be fathering a child, he may find it quite difficult to cope with his partner's new concentration on the pregnancy rather than on him. He feels that the physical changes in his partner's body are upsetting as conventional attractiveness is replaced by a very different body – no longer the outline of a neat figure but a melon-shaped abdomen and heavy, swelling breasts covered with a network of tiny blue veins. A man who has valued a woman as a status or sex symbol may feel that he is being cheated.

The developing baby It is sometimes difficult for a man, who does not have the baby growing inside his body, to acknowledge its reality. He often begins to become more aware of the child at about the time he feels it bump and kick at night. Some men find this sensation not only astonishing and exciting but rather eerie, and they take a while to adjust to the idea of another being living and growing inside the body of the woman they know so well.

The future grandparents When a couple have a first baby they may have to work through a painful transitional period in which they must forge a new adult relationship with their own parents, which allows for the responsibility and commitment they have to the child they are bearing. This may produce stresses with the future grandparents, and a man may get caught up in a difficult relationship with his own mother just as a woman may with hers. When a man's mother is fearful that she is losing her son she becomes demanding. He may feel the pull of her possessive love drawing attention away from the needs of his wife and baby. Sometimes a woman sees this, whereas the man is completely unaware of it. It is important to understand that the older women, the ex-mothers, are being replaced, and they may feel hurt and unwanted. If there is a problem of this kind, the couple should talk about it together and be honest about their feelings.

THE FATHER'S NEW ROLE

Having a baby used to be solely the concern of the woman, with her mother standing in the background giving advice. Nowadays it is much more something for a woman and a man to share.

There are still some men who say they do not want to get involved in "women's things" and who feel that their manliness is being threatened. They have the uneasy suspicion that learning about childbirth means that they will no longer be potent, virile males. Some imagine that it is expected that they will be able to hand the woman over to the experts and retire from the scene. They believe that the professional must know so much more than they do, that they are bound to be in the way during the birth and have no function in the delivery room.

Thirty years ago some midwives and obstetricians looked askance at men who became involved in the process of childbirth, as if they were slightly odd. Go back fifty years or so and men kept well away from anything to do with birth; pregnancy was a "certain condition" which a man pretended he knew nothing about.

My mother told me that my father felt embarrassed to go out with her in advanced pregnancy, so that walks they took had to be after dark, with her enveloped in a wraparound coat. And as for a father wheeling a stroller, or changing a diaper – it was unheard of; even a man who might have liked to try his hand at such things rarely got the chance. This was partly because in those days there used to be what one perceptive psychoanalyst called a male "taboo on tenderness." Men were frightened that to be seen to be involved with women's activities would humiliate them in the eyes of other men. And childbirth was the epitome of all feminine mysteries. Both women and men were prevented by these rules from discovering their full potential.

"He often begins to become more aware of the child at about the time he feels it bump and kick at night. Men find this sensation astonishing and exciting."

Many modern men are determined to share as much as they possibly can in pregnancy and birth. They enjoy the woman's changing shape and the reality of the baby's kicking against their hand. But a man often still feels he will be a novice at fatherhood. He wonders just how much he can do, since the baby is growing in his partner's body, not his. In a way, the partnership between the mother and her unborn child is already complete. And pregnancy often seems to be so carefully managed by the obstetric team that a man can sometimes feel like an intruder.

But a woman depends on her partner's support and needs the special relationship with him, which is quite different from any others that she has. She may not realize just how much he is sharing in the pregnancy emotionally and the heights and depths of his own feelings about it. There is no longer any need for a man to square his shoulders and pretend he is not stirred by what is happening. Take the opportunity to talk together about your feelings.

Feelings about being present at the birth

Most expectant fathers today approach childbirth with curiosity and interest and in a very different spirit from that thought suitable by their fathers and grandfathers. Though they may wonder whether they are going to make fools of themselves while playing an unfamiliar part, and may be nervous about unpleasant procedures involved in labor, they want to understand what is going on and to help and support their partners. They realize that hospital staff are usually extremely busy and working with more than one patient at a time. It is therefore impossible for other people to give the constant companionship and loving care which a woman craves as she is swept through the intensely powerful physical and emotional experiences of labor, and the very unfamiliarity of the surroundings can make the most courageous woman apprehensive.

"I wouldn't have missed it for the world. I wasn't sure that I wanted to be there, but it turned out to be an incredible experience."

She needs her partner or someone else who loves her. She needs someone who is there not simply as an onlooker but as a companion, who understands what happens in childbirth, who knows what the prenatal preparation has been like, and who is able to help her in labor. (For more about the father's role at the birth, see page 277.)

The man who fully involves himself in the birth shares in an experience which is exciting, challenging, intensely moving, and deeply satisfying. It is a question not only of helping his partner have their baby but of an often surprising encounter with his own emotions and the discovery of a peak experience which is bigger than anything he anticipated. There may be an astonishing, an incredible joy and wonder at being so close to the beating center of life. In a very direct way, love is made flesh.

Being supportive about prenatal care

Pregnancy can be a time of great emotional upheaval as a woman adapts to the extraordinary things happening inside her body. She has to go through all sorts of physical examinations that are not always conducted in a warm, sympathetic way. It is clear that many women are made anxious by the kind of prenatal care they receive.

The doctor's office

Some men find a woman's anxiety difficult to understand. They say that they find the sophisticated technology which is used today reassuring and fascinating. But if the man imagines something happening inside his own testicles or penis, he may find it easier to comprehend. How would he feel if his testicles started to swell up and change shape dramatically, forcing him to visit a doctor regularly and be prodded, poked, and examined by strangers who seemed concerned only with the lower end of his body? He might find it impossible to get information about what was happening to him, knowing only that he faced an ordeal at the end of nine months when whatever was occurring must be terminated and the thing inside him somehow got out. How would he like lying flat on a high table, sometimes with his legs up high and wide apart in metal stirrups, while various women in white coats peered at him with little lights and probed his body with special machines? Out of the corner of his eye he could see them writing up case notes full of technical terms and abbreviations apparently suggesting a disease.

A man has to go to the doctor's office only once to discover how intimidating it can be. In the atmosphere of a busy doctor's office women often feel that they have become part of a factory process. Questions about treatment or requests for advice go out of their heads, or else seem to interrupt the smooth running of the office and mean that other women waiting their turn have still longer to wait. Often a woman returns from the doctor depressed and anxious. If her partner can attend occasionally and meet the doctor, he can give her moral support and build the foundation for a good working relationship with those who will be present during labor.

Even if this is not possible, he can still help his partner by providing comfort and security if this is what she needs, and by talking to her about the things that ought to be discussed with the doctor. It is helpful to write questions down and keep a notebook for this purpose, together with information that you want to consider.

CHILDBIRTH EDUCATION CLASSES
By attending classes in preparation for the birth with his partner, a man can learn a good deal about the physiological processes and emotional changes of labor, can understand his own part in it, and often has the chance to see films of birth where men are giving support to their partners using skills learned in class.

EVERYDAY HELP
In the last three months a man can help by seeing that his partner takes more rest and lies down every afternoon or evening. Extra labor-saving equipment or additional help in the house can ensure that she does not get worn out. She should not be doing heavy shopping, so he may take over supermarket duty, or go with her to load the bags of groceries into the car. If there are jobs in the house like moving furniture, these are his now. And if she cannot get down to bathe the toddler or strip the bed, the man can make these his responsibility now while she does some of the easier tasks. On the other hand the woman does not need to be treated like an invalid, and the couple can enjoy going out together, especially at the end of pregnancy when time may seem to pass very slowly and she feels she has been pregnant forever. A man can also protect his partner from all the well-meaning and often confusing advice that comes from other people both before and after the birth. He can support her in doing things the way they have both decided.

Your changing relationship

Pregnant women are not only obstetrical patients or even just future mothers. They are also usually in a loving relationship with a man. Pregnancy can be a time of great opportunity for both partners in the relationship to discover things about themselves and each other. However two people feel about each other, the emotional changes of pregnancy are bound to affect them. If they do not communicate easily it can be a time when small irritants turn into major crises.

THE COUPLE UNDER STRESS

There are some couples who find the transition period of pregnancy an especially difficult time. It can put stress on the couple who have an informal, even casual, relationship and who have not attached particular importance to getting married, but who perhaps marry when a baby is on the way. It can put equal stress on a couple who both enjoy their careers and have never seen themselves as parents, but who nonetheless decide to continue with the pregnancy when the woman conceives by mistake. It can bristle with challenges, too, when a woman has been on the pill, stops taking it because the couple think it might be a good idea to have a baby, and then immediately becomes pregnant before she has had time to switch her mind to the actual possibility of motherhood. In these situations rapid adjustment is necessary, and either or both parents may feel trapped at the same time as they are feeling delighted.

As soon as they tell other people about the pregnancy they may feel that a social machine has swung into action. Some couples say that they felt strong disapproval from relatives, especially their parents, when they put off having a baby because they were both busy with their careers. Then when the woman eventually did become pregnant they were overwhelmed by the relief and pleasure these people expressed, as if at last they were doing the socially acceptable thing. Even positive reactions may feel like a public intrusion on their intimate and personal relationship with each other.

SHARING THE PROBLEMS

When a pregnancy starts, a man and a woman often begin inhabiting different worlds. He may think that she has become psychologically unpredictable and vulnerable. She may see him as unsympathetic, unloving, and crude. He may feel he can no longer talk to her about "rational" matters, and that she has lost interest in everything except the baby. He may even feel pushed out into the cold, as if he were living with a different woman. Because they are often isolated from other couples facing similar difficulties, they may be under the impression that such problems are unique to them. Talking to others expecting babies can help them to detect the social pressures on prospective parents and the cultural style of childbirth in modern Western societies, which often creates emotional stress. Attending classes together can provide a bridge between the different socially assigned gender roles of man and woman, and can help draw them closer.

TALKING IN A GROUP

At one prenatal group couples discussed together the effect of pregnancy on their relationship. One woman, who was feeling that she had lost her individuality in the universal category of expectant motherhood, remarked that she was frightened of what this was doing to her relationship with her husband. Would they, she worried, become just "Mom and Dad" and cease being lovers? Her concern about this was even making her resent the baby at times.

In discussion the members of the group found that other couples, too, were experiencing these pressures and the same kinds of anxiety. Some of them felt strongly that they wanted to be different kinds of parents from their own parents and to have a happier marriage than their parents had. It was agreed that it was important for a couple to share these thoughts with each other and to discuss not just the practical arrangements for the baby, but their ideas about the kind of parents they hoped to be, and what they thought about their partners as prospective parents as well. Becoming a mother involves emotional "growing pains" which can be as disturbing as those of adolescence. A similar psychological process often occurs in a man, too, but he usually feels he has even less justification to talk about it because *he* is not physically pregnant. Yet to be able to nurture their young, both the man and the woman have to change and become different kinds of people.

Another couple who had been through this process with an earlier pregnancy said that talking about it had helped them to understand each other better and that they came to like their changed roles. At first they were merely playacting the parts of "Mommy" and "Daddy," but then they found they were good at them. As they grew to become confident parents they became aware of qualities they had never imagined the other possessed.

DEVELOPING CONFIDENCE

Many couples have a funny name for the unborn child, and talk about it as if it were a friend whom they know well by reputation but have never met. When doctors prod and poke and the hospital takes the woman over at the prenatal clinic or when she goes into labor, the couple can sometimes feel as if a very personal and intimate relationship between the three of them has been invaded. "Our" baby has become "the" baby, or even "the hospital's" baby. A woman needs to feel that the baby belongs to her. Other couples have problems in family relationships (especially with their in-laws), which they imagine to be peculiarly their own and which they do not realize are shared by many others. Each partner may be resenting the other for his or her insensitivity and ineptitude at handling these situations, or for being overdependent on their parents. A childbirth education class may well offer an opportunity to talk through these problems with others and to discuss the future grandparents' feelings and any other situations which might be causing stress. The very fact of finding that they are not alone with these kinds of difficulties may help a couple to overcome them.

GROWING THROUGH THE EXPERIENCE

Many couples have their babies before they are really emotionally ready for them. As a result, some babies come into the world in spite of, rather than because of, what their parents feel about each other. When a woman decides to continue with an unplanned pregnancy, she needs special emotional support. If a man has nothing else to offer he can at least give her this.

It is bound to be painful for them both if they decide to part with the baby, but the experience can be important for both of them and can help them to grow in understanding. When a couple is unhappy together, there is an even more compelling reason to use the months of pregnancy for joint preparation for the birth of their child, if only because the task can in itself bring with it a new perceptiveness and sensitivity to the other's needs. So, in all circumstances, preparation for birth is not merely the acquisition by the woman of a set of instructions and exercises, but a process in which two people start out together on a shared enterprise. It provides opportunities for increased understanding of each other's needs and enrichment of their whole relationship. For both parents pregnancy can be a rewarding time of growing up. If a man and woman can fully understand what the pregnancy means to the other partner they are well on the way to growing up together.

The emotional changes of pregnancy occur for all couples who are expecting a baby, and it helps to realize that others share these experiences and find them challenging. Sharing brings relief from anxiety and a new understanding of the emotions involved.

Sex in pregnancy

It is important for your sense of wellbeing that you are physically loved in pregnancy, whether or not this involves sexual intercourse. Stroking, massage, loving touch, and sexual pleasuring are all part of this physical expression of the relationship.

ATTITUDES TOWARD SEX

Many couples make love right through pregnancy. At the beginning nausea and vomiting can mean that the last thing you want to do is to make love, but usually by the middle months lovemaking is enjoyable and satisfying, sometimes for the first time. Pregnancy is a good time for you to learn more about how your body works. A woman who begins to learn about her uterus, vagina, and pelvic floor muscles may become sensitively responsive to this part of her body as she was not before. Many do not realize the function of the pelvic floor muscles in lovemaking and some have never explored the way in which the vagina, labia, and clitoris are constructed. Some women have their first orgasm during pregnancy.

But this is not just a matter of intellectual information and diagrams of the female genitals. Some women dislike and have a profound distrust of their bodies. For the first time in pregnancy they can come to know and be comfortable with themselves. If you have never before allowed feelings to sweep through you, you may find that preparation for the intensely emotional experience of labor, with its storms and currents, and the extraordinarily powerful drama of delivery, unlock a capacity for "letting go" which can apply to lovemaking also. But some couples (especially in the later months) feel that they do not have the doctor's approval for lovemaking. You may have guilty feelings and be anxious that you are somehow harming your unborn baby. This is one of the subjects that expectant parents often want to talk about in childbirth education classes. Many couples say that they often find sex a very difficult subject to discuss with their doctor.

POSITIONS FOR LOVEMAKING
The conventional "missionary" position (with the man lying on top of the woman) is rarely comfortable, unless the man gets on all fours and puts no weight on the woman. It is worth experimenting with some other positions in which the woman is uppermost or in which entry is from the side or from behind (see pages 168–169). You can be sure that no harm will come to the baby: the bag of waters cushions it and a seal is provided by the mucous plug, which is like a stopper in a bottle. Even when your abdomen is bumped hard in lovemaking, the baby bobs like a cork in a glass of water.

CAN ORGASM START LABOR?
Although the female orgasm involves contractions of the uterus, it will not trigger labor unless everything is ready to start anyway. But it is quite natural after intercourse to feel contractions, which usually die down after a few minutes. The uterus is an active organ and contracts from the time of a girl's first period right through to menopause. It is especially active in pregnancy and the contractions (Braxton Hicks contractions) which you feel in the last months are rehearsals for the labor. If you have had a premature labor before, if you notice spotting of blood, or if the mucous plug has already gone, it is wise not to have intercourse. Once the cervical mucus has been disturbed by contractions (and this *can* happen in the last four to five weeks), ascending infection is a possibility.

USING SEX TO INDUCE LABOR

If you are "due," especially if induction of labor has been suggested by your doctor, lovemaking is one of the ways in which you might be able to start things off naturally. Some women are thought to be especially sensitive to prostaglandins in semen. (Prostaglandins cause the uterus to contract, and semen has a higher proportion of them than any other body substance.) It is best to choose a position in which the woman lies on her back with her legs raised on the man's hips. But since such a position may be very uncomfortable at this late stage of pregnancy, it should be done gently.

Breast stimulation in late pregnancy also sometimes produces a strongly contracting uterus. This worries some people, but unless you have reason to think that the baby may come too early it is

Lovemaking in pregnancy

Some women find that pregnancy makes lovemaking more exciting. Others want nothing to do with sex. Both reactions are normal. Sex in pregnancy should always be gentle and tender. For many couples it presents an opportunity to find new ways of making love.

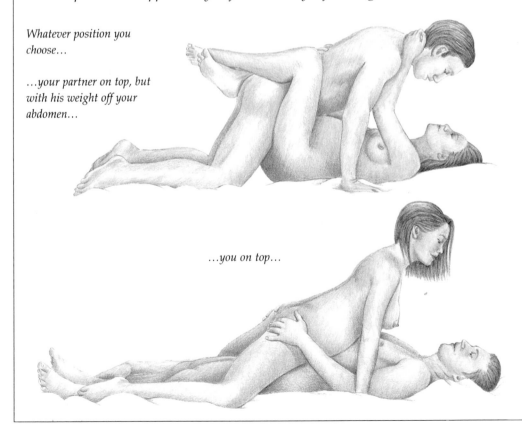

Whatever position you choose...

...your partner on top, but with his weight off your abdomen...

...you on top...

harmless, and may be a good thing, because the contractions which result help to prepare the way for labor, softening and drawing up the cervix and dilating it a little even before labor begins.

NIPPLE STIMULATION DURING LABOR

Stimulation of the nipples can restart a labor that has come to a halt. Some doctors have tried it in place of the oxytocin drip. But it does not always work. It may depend on how the stimulation is provided: perhaps someone you love may be more effective than a breast pump. The midwife or doctor may agree to go out and leave you. It makes sense to try the natural way of stimulating the uterus first. The emotions you have as lovers are not in conflict with the feelings of compassion and tenderness you have about a baby.

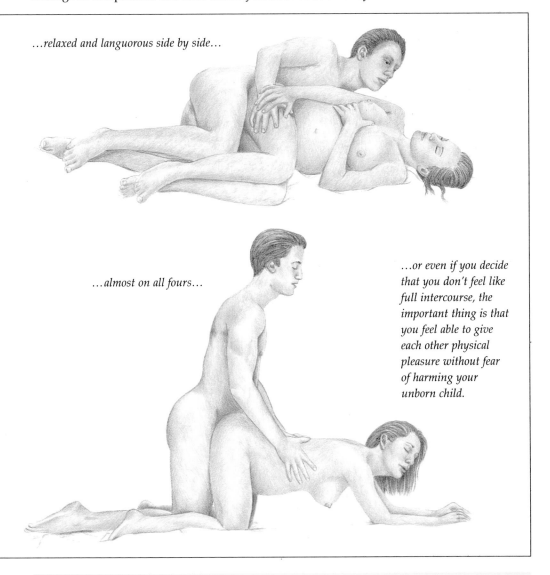

...relaxed and languorous side by side...

...almost on all fours...

...or even if you decide that you don't feel like full intercourse, the important thing is that you feel able to give each other physical pleasure without fear of harming your unborn child.

Pregnant again

Pregnancy the second or third time around is a new experience. It will not be exactly like the first time. It holds different challenges. Coping with them involves flexibility and resourcefulness on the part of both parents. In some ways things are much easier: you know what to expect and have probably developed self-confidence in your role as a childbearer. You may sail through the pregnancy with style. But there may be difficulties which come as a surprise because you thought it would be simple this time.

REACTIONS TO ANOTHER PREGNANCY

Other people's reactions The first problem you may encounter is the reaction of other people to a new pregnancy. Whereas your first was greeted with delight, friends and relatives are usually far less interested in the next pregnancy and may even raise their eyebrows and criticize you if you already have three children or if you are pregnant again after a very short interval. They can make you feel that what you are doing is not very public-spirited and even socially harmful. Some women say they were asked "Do you want it?" or "Don't you think you've had enough?"; others cite sympathy offered by well-meaning friends: "How ever will you manage?"

Your partner's reaction You may find that your partner is not so excited about the next pregnancy. He may be busy and preoccupied and even seem totally uninvolved. Many men feel an extra burden of responsibility and financial anxiety when a second or subsequent baby is on the way. One baby was fun but now he feels "trapped" into having to provide for a growing family for years to come. Some women are desperately disappointed at their partners' reactions to later pregnancies and feel that they are missing out on all the joy of the first baby and the companionship that drew them close together the first time around. Talk about your feelings together so that you can come to appreciate what the experience means to each of you.

FINDING TIME TO RELAX

When you already have a lively two- or three-year-old or a group of energetic youngsters to look after, pregnancy can be very tiring. The first time around you were able to look after yourself and even occasionally luxuriate in afternoon rests, with time for thinking, planning, and dreaming. Caught up in the hustle and bustle of family life, ferrying children to and from school, coping with the enormous meals they can consume and facing the everyday battle with tricycles in the hall and crumbs on the carpet, you may have to relegate pregnancy to the back of your mind. You simply do not have time to think about it. This may result in your neglecting yourself, your nutrition, and your relaxation, and also missing out on times when you can just focus your thoughts on the baby and yourself. When you realize this, in the short and infrequent intervals between your commitments as wife, mother, nurse, psychotherapist, teacher, hostess, chauffeur, house cleaner, chief cook, and bottle washer, the chances are that you will feel guilty. You begin to feel apologetic to the little baby who is growing inside you, and perhaps also fearful that you cannot give him or her the time or even the love that you have devoted to the others.

This feeling may be intensified after the birth, when to some extent the new baby has to be fitted into family life rather than your own activities being modified to the baby's needs. If you are sitting a two-year-old on the potty, or calming down three children in the bath having a very splashy game which threatens to submerge the toddler, it is difficult at the same moment to fix the new baby comfortably on the breast and to enjoy the release of milk.

Talk about these feelings of inadequacy with other women who are facing the same problems. If you do feel guilty, the only solution is to try to organize your life so that every day you have at least some time to think about and plan for the coming baby, or, once the new baby has been born, to give him or her your whole concentration. It is certainly difficult to find even a short space of time for such attention; but you may be able to enlist someone who is willing to take your other children for a walk some afternoons, or your partner might bathe them and put them to bed every evening, giving you time to concentrate on yourself and your new baby.

TAKING CARE OF YOURSELF

A new pregnancy may produce aches and discomforts which you have not experienced before. Lifting bigger children and the inevitable clearing and cleaning may contribute to backache associated with bad posture. This is accentuated by fatigue and doing things in a rush. If your child still wakes in the night, doesn't *ever* like the idea of an afternoon nap, or wakes very early in the morning and comes jumping into your bed during the hours after dawn, a restless bundle, you may be running short of sleep and long for a solid uninterrupted 10 or 12 hours. Perhaps it is possible to arrange this when your partner is at home on the weekend.

The chances are that you look and feel more pregnant with this baby, too, partly as a result of poor posture and tiredness, but also because of the stretching your uterus has already withstood during the previous pregnancy or pregnancies. This may mean that you don't feel at all happy about your body; such a lack of pleasure in yourself is then expressed automatically in the way you stand, walk, and sit. It is a vicious circle only too easy to get into.

Ask your childbirth educator to help you firm up your abdominal muscles. Use your buttock and leg muscles in order to help support your spine and tummy and do a few rhythmic exercises each day

Above
Birth provides an opportunity for a child to learn about and share in a major life transition, and to develop new social skills and awareness.

(see pages 124–125). Your older child may enjoy doing them with you. Then make an opportunity to cherish yourself a bit. Ask your partner for a massage. Think about what would cheer you up.

Preparing the older child

Some parents worry a great deal about how to prepare an older child for the new baby. This problem can seem almost insurmountable if the older one is clinging and very dependent. Childbirth educators* have come up with the idea of making a book for such a child, with photographs of himself and starting with a simple description of how a baby grows inside its mother, complete with line drawings and a photograph of the mother when she was pregnant. You could show preparations for the birth, and then your child as a newborn baby, being suckled or bathed. These pictures could be followed by a series of photographs of the older child eating, drinking, playing, helping in the house and yard. Perhaps the last page could be left blank for a photograph of the new baby. All this helps the older child to prepare for the new baby and to realize that he was once just as small and incapable as it will be. If possible borrow a baby for a few hours or have a mother and her small baby in the house for half a day or so. This will help your child to confront the reality of a baby and also observe how a mother cares for it. Many older children expect a new baby to be either a passive bundle that can be handled like a doll or a playmate who can join in their games immediately.

If you are moving the older child from a crib to a bed, do so several months before the birth, so that it does not seem a consequence of the baby's arrival. And if you are going to have extra help after the birth, encourage the helper to become friends with the older child well before the advent of the new baby.

When another baby is on the way, the relationship between the father and the older child is of great importance. It is a time when the two can draw closer together and enjoy each other's company for longer periods, something that will help you a great deal after the birth when you are busy with the new baby.

SIBLINGS AT THE BIRTH

If you are thinking about having your older child or children present at the birth of this baby you will need to involve the child in your prenatal care and prepare him or her for the experience of birth by giving simple but vivid descriptions of how the baby is born, what happens in labor, and how you may behave. Children are fascinated by how the baby grows in the uterus, and there is a book of mine which may help with this. It tells the story of how the baby grows inside the mother through photographs and text describing what the baby can do at each stage of pregnancy.* But remember that children need not only see pictures of giving birth but can get familiar with the breathing and other sounds you may make. Only you can know if this experience will be right for a child. It can be a great education.

Each child should have an adult companion whom they like who is responsible solely for that child. Labor is often long and children get bored. They want to play, to run around outside, to eat, drink, and sleep. They also need explanations of what they see and hear at the time: "She is grunting because she wants to push"; "That creamy white stuff kept the baby's skin soft, smooth, and watertight so it did not get all wrinkly inside." The child's companion should be well informed as well as comfortable with being at the birth. An anxious adult conveys this to a child. Whenever a child expresses the wish to leave the room or do something else the companion should respond instantly. Your midwife or doctor should be involved in planning ahead for a child's presence at birth, and have a chance to get to know the child and build a friendly relationship. By the time a child is around four years old you can help him or her to construct and write a birth plan: "I would like to cut the cord . . . hold the baby after mommy has cuddled it . . . cut the cake at the birthday party after the baby has come out." It is best to arrange for other children to be present if you are having a home birth, and for some women this is a reason for choosing not to have a hospital birth.

Anticipating the birth

In tune with your body for labor

Part of preparation for birth consists of exercises, but it is even more important to *think* about labor in a constructive way. Give yourself time to imagine what is going to happen in your body and what you may feel, and so build up a picture that has meaning for you. This picture will be quite different from illustrations in obstetric textbooks: it is vital that it relates to *feelings* and is not just composed of intellectual information. Only then can the subjective sensations you experience in labor fit into a pattern that makes sense to you and that can help you adjust to each challenge as it comes.

So during pregnancy take time to imagine the birth of your baby. Think of different kinds of birth (see pages 262–276) and how to cope with them. Avoid restricting your fantasies to only one kind of labor when it may turn out that the labor you have is very different.

CHILDBIRTH EDUCATION

If you are having a baby without having been to childbirth education classes, your body will probably respond naturally to the situation. However, education for birth helps you to know more about your body and so feel happy with it during pregnancy. You learn how to prepare yourself so that when you are in labor you can work *with* your body instead of fighting it, so that you understand the activity of the uterus, and so that, through relaxation, breathing, and focused concentration, you can gradually come to achieve harmony with the birth process. This is important not only for the hours that you are actually in labor, but also for how you feel about the whole experience, yourself, and the baby afterwards. Birth is not "just another day in a woman's life." Women remember their births and the intense emotions that were stimulated with extraordinary clarity years later, often into old age. They remember vividly how they felt when labor started, when the bag of waters popped, how it was when they got to the hospital, what doctors, nurses, midwives, and their partners did, interventions that occurred in the birth, and, of course, their first meeting with the baby. Positive experiences remain as good memories. Negative experiences, far from being forgotten, intensify over time.*

Choosing a prenatal class

Once you have begun your prenatal care, it is time to think about arranging childbirth classes, so that you and your partner can learn about the physiological changes of pregnancy and labor and the possible emotional impact of the stresses likely to be involved.

It pays to shop around for classes and discover different ones available in your area. You would not dream of walking into any hairdresser's and asking them to cut and style your hair without finding out what sort of work they did. Learning about childbirth is even more important, and so you should approach childbirth education classes with the same discrimination. For the quality of teaching to improve, more critical, informed consumers are needed. Any prenatal teacher worth her salt learns from her students, and continues to modify her teaching on the basis of the feedback she receives from them and the ideas they share with her.

FINDING OUT ABOUT CLASSES

When you inquire about classes, do not assume that they are successful only if those who have attended them have had easy labors and births. If you have to have a forceps delivery or a cesarean section it does not mean that you have "failed" in applying what you have learned. Having a baby is not like passing an exam or winning a race. You are not expected to come out "on top" with a two-hour labor, or no pain-relieving drugs or whatever. It is

"I was working hard in the office through most of my pregnancy and the classes gave me special time that was just for myself."

much more a question of learning how to adapt your responses – mainly those of breathing and relaxation – to the particular challenges of your own labor. So it can be useful to talk also to women who have had labors that were not straightforward, and to find out from them if attending classes helped them at all.

Even though women all the world over have babies in much the same way, birth can be a vastly different experience for different women; just as sexual intercourse involves certain mechanical and physiological processes which are the same everywhere, what people feel about it, exactly what they do, and the meaning the total experience has for them varies with the individual and the occasion. Childbirth is not primarily a medical process, but a psychosexual experience. It is not surprising that adapting your responses to the stimuli it presents should involve a subtle and delicate working together of mind and body.

When looking into classes, ask a woman whether she found the skills that she learned in class helpful when she was actually in labor, and whether she felt confident and understood exactly what was going on. If she says "Nothing helped," it implies that the classes did not relate in any way to the reality of labor; if she says that she was absolutely terrified from beginning to end, it sounds as if the classes did not help her either, though she may have enjoyed getting to know the other expectant mothers.

Your local hospital may offer prenatal classes, although frequently they focus on the routines and procedures you may expect to have done in that hospital, rather than on the choices. Your doctor or midwife may know of other prenatal classes. Alternatively, write to the International Childbirth Education Association (ICEA), the American Society for Psychoprophylaxis in Obstetrics (ASPO), or the American Academy of Husband-Coached Childbirth (AAHCC). Addresses for all of these are given on page 413. They will let you know where classes are held by their teachers, or put you in contact with the organizer of a childbirth group in your area.

WHAT MAKES A GOOD PRENATAL CLASS?

Good classes are progressive in the sense that you learn a little more each time; you should not feel at the third or fourth lesson that you have sat through it all before. There should be opportunities for you to ask questions, discuss freely, and practice the exercises rather than simply listen to a formal lecture. Breathing and relaxation exercises which can be of practical use in labor should be included. Their relevance to labor should be specifically described, and why and how they are used. Relaxation is not as simple as it might sound. It is not just a question of flopping in front of the TV screen or of lying down with a bar of chocolate and a good book, but of learning complete awareness and control of muscle groups all over the body so that they can be contracted or relaxed at will, including muscles you may not even know you possess. Relaxation also means learning how to relax *under stress*, not just lying in a deck chair on a sunny day or in a classroom while a cool voice tells you that a contraction is beginning, continuing, and then fading away.

It helps to learn different patterns and rhythms of breathing for the different phases of labor (see pages 201–208). So when you are asking about classes, try and find out from any woman who has been to them whether she learned breathing in detail.

An effective teacher helps her students realize something of what labor feels like, and the reality and power of its challenge. She also explains things fully, without fear that she is burdening her students' minds, and does so honestly and clearly. Unfortunately, in some classes there is far too much talking down to pregnant women. You have a right to understand what is happening to your own body and what people are proposing to do to you. A good teacher does not answer a query with "Oh, you don't have to bother about that," or imply that everyone will do what is best for you and your baby, and that all you need to do is have trust in your birth attendants. Discussion should always be a real exchange of ideas, not simply a few questions to which answers are fired back without recognition of the apprehension and the sometimes nightmarish fears that can lie behind them.

"I didn't want reassurance and talk about 'discomfort.' I wanted complete honesty so that I could make rational choices for myself."

You can see from this that a good deal depends on the personality of the teacher. It is not so much "the method" that is good or inadequate as the quality of the teaching itself, and perhaps most of all the relationship that the teacher has with her students. I have seen teaching which seemed woefully inadequate or mechanized, or which involved learning a number of rather irrelevant physical exercises, and yet, because of the personality and attitude of the teacher, the women participated joyfully in their labors.

The Read method

There are different approaches to childbirth education and the names associated with them can be confusing for expectant mothers. The Read method is named after Dr. Grantly Dick-Read;* it is the oldest method and is usually associated with "relaxation classes." The philosophy behind this approach is that ignorance produces fear, which leads to tension, which in turn quickly produces pain. So teachers concentrate on overcoming fear by teaching deep relaxation and the breathing that accompanies it, along with providing full and accurate information about the childbearing process, exercises to keep you supple and poised, and discussion of breastfeeding. Today, there are few Read method teachers, but most childbirth educators incorporate his concepts into their classes.

Psychoprophylaxis

Psychoprophylaxis is a highly systematized training centered on techniques of breathing rather than relaxation. This method originated in the USSR, was developed in Paris, and was then adapted in the United States by Elisabeth Bing.* Psychoprophylaxis classes start by deconditioning the women from their fear and doubts about childbirth, and then proceed to recondition them to respond to labor contractions as helpful stimuli and not as pains. Exercises are taught both for limbering up and for using in labor. Full information is given about the anatomy and physiology of pregnancy and labor. This system is taught by American Society for Psychoprophylaxis in Obstetrics teachers and is one of a range of approaches taught by International Childbirth Education Association teachers. Those organizations can refer you to childbirth educators in your area (see page 413).

In the US, women know psychoprophylaxis by the name of its French originator, Lamaze, whereas in France itself it is often called *accouchement sans douleur* (birth without pain), or *asd*. This name is thoroughly misleading and might make any woman having pain in labor feel that something is going wrong. For most women who have been to prenatal classes the pain of labor is not the most salient thing about the experience but is a side effect with which many of them, helped by techniques of adjustment and by emotional support and guidance at the time, can cope very well without any pharmacological aids. Other women may want some additional pain relief in labor, and should certainly have it.

In North America and Britain, psychoprophylaxis methods have changed radically since they were first introduced. Dogma has disappeared, breathing is no longer regimented, and the whole approach has become more relaxed. Many teachers have learned to be skilled in group dynamics and psychological counseling, and different educators have evolved their own approaches to childbirth.

THE BRADLEY METHOD

An American obstetrician, Robert Bradley, has created "husband-coached" childbirth, in which the man acts as the woman's teacher and supporter in pregnancy and labor, breathing is slow and full, obstetric intervention is kept to the minimum, and pain-relieving drugs are not used. Many Bradley enthusiasts opt for home birth. The American Academy of Husband-Coached Childbirth can refer you to a Bradley instructor nearby (see page 413).

THE AUTOGENIC METHOD

On the European continent, a system of training for labor based on the Schulz methods of relaxation and breathing is taught in many prenatal hospital classes. A woman is taught to relax by conceptualizing warmth and weight in different parts of the body; her breathing should be slow and relaxed.

ACTIVE BIRTH

Janet Balaskas has developed an active method of preparing for birth based on hatha yoga, with the focus on moving around and changing position throughout labor, and giving birth squatting, kneeling, or on all fours. To be able to do this freely and with comfort, it is very important to practice "stretching" exercises beforehand, and a woman learns how to adopt "open" positions with help from her partner.* Some methods of preparation for active birth are now often incorporated into other classes, and Janet Balaskas's great achievement is that in many hospitals all over the world she has succeeded in getting women off the labor bed and the delivery table and onto the floor.

THE ODENT APPROACH

Although a surgeon, Dr. Michel Odent perceives that childbirth is different from surgery. For him, it is important to provide an environment that facilitates a spontaneous psychophysiological process in which the woman who is left undisturbed will feel as if she is "on another planet."

Instead of holding childbirth classes, Odent organized singing get-togethers in which new parents, pregnant women, and their partners, midwives, doctors, and little children all joined. He has rediscovered the use of water in birth, offering the woman a deep bath of warm water in which she can float in a peaceful, darkened room. For delivery, he favors the standing squat, with the woman supported from behind by her partner or another helper. Michel Odent's ideas have been incorporated into many classes run by birth centers, by midwives, and by other childbirth educators.

THE KITZINGER PSYCHOSEXUAL APPROACH

My own "psychosexual approach" originally grew out of both the Read and psychoprophylaxis systems and now incorporates many active birth positions and movements. The approach is based on the idea that the woman is an active birthgiver rather than a passive patient. It focuses on birth as an experience rather than as a series of exercises in breathing and relaxation.

Psychology and social anthropology have contributed much to my own approach, and especially my observations of how women behave in and feel about labor in many different cultures. I have learned most from women themselves. Labor often involves barely glimpsed feelings about ourselves which have developed through the formative years of childhood: attitudes to and fantasies about our bodies, feelings about the relative size and positions of organs and orifices, and concepts of cleanliness and pollution, beauty and ugliness. All of these are partly social in origin, products of our upbringing and family relationships.

Being in labor is a social situation, not just a physiological or even a private emotional experience. Because it involves human relationships at a sometimes tense and demanding time, it helps to know how to talk with the different people assisting at the birth and how to understand what may be in the doctors' and midwives' minds. All prenatal teachers agree that students need plenty of information about *"The role play helped a lot, exploring ways of engaging with doctors and nurses, and how to handle resistance."* how their bodies work and what goes on in hospitals. Most classes make a visit to the hospital and a tour of the delivery room. Yet it is not just a matter of knowing what will happen to you, but of learning how to negotiate to have the kind of birth you want.

THE AIMS OF CHILDBIRTH EDUCATION CLASSES

So you will see that there is wide variation in exactly what is taught and how, although there is general agreement that six sessions of one and a half or two hours each are the minimum required. The aim is not to retreat from contractions but to adjust to them and respond actively. There is more and more emphasis on a woman's being in the kind of setting and having the loving emotional support which enables her to be confident in her own powers and to behave spontaneously, without having to do "exercises" or wondering whether her performance is good enough. In the classes partners can learn how to help in pregnancy and labor and understand something about the feelings involved in becoming a parent. It is important that a woman be allowed to bring a woman partner if she wishes, and classes should not be restricted to heterosexual couples.

Your partner in childbirth classes may be male or female, a lover, husband, friend, or relative. If you are offered less than this in the classes you attend, you will probably feel the need to supplement them with other classes, reading, or extra private tuition.

WHEN TO START CLASSES

Whatever method you finally opt for, do not leave registration for classes or your reading till the last moment. Start finding out what is available and begin your course of reading four or five months before the baby is due, even though classes may not be offered till the last nine weeks or so. Where teachers run classes only for those in the last two or three months of pregnancy there is often an opportunity to meet the teacher earlier. This is an excellent idea, although some teachers of Lamaze believe that students get bored if they start too soon. Even if you do not start to practice any breathing techniques till the last weeks, it can only be beneficial to learn good posture in early pregnancy, and something about how the baby develops inside you and how to cope with any minor discomforts of pregnancy. It is also an advantage at any time, whether or not you are pregnant (and for men as well as women), to know how deep relaxation can help you get to sleep.

Whatever approach you select, provided you are happy with your teacher and develop confidence in yourself through the instruction, the teaching will be right for you, and you will find that you have a variety of suitable tools with which to adapt to contractions in labor. Labor need not be a fearful ordeal, but should be a positive, rewarding experience, and a really happy birthday.

MAKING YOUR OWN SPACE

Some women want to be absolutely alone during labor. Most women, however, welcome understanding support from someone else in whom they have confidence and with whom they can "be themselves" and do what comes spontaneously.

Labor should not have to be a public performance. Unless there are especially urgent and demanding reasons why total strangers – nurses, doctors, students, medical auxiliaries, hospital porters, and cleaners – should be there you have the right to ask for privacy and have only those people with you whom *you* have chosen. You could make this absolutely clear in the birth plan which you hand over to be inserted in your chart (see page 50).

When women talk about their birth experiences in hospitals, especially large ones, they often talk about all the people who wandered in and out, anonymous faces looking through the porthole window in the door, and conversations about them, not *with* them, conducted over their supine bodies. Can you imagine the effect of having strangers and other observers around you when you took a bath, sat on the toilet, tried to sleep, or were making love? Birth is a psychosexual activity that involves revealing that which is usually physically and emotionally private. It is patterned by rhythms similar to those in other physiological functions that entail letting your body open up. It involves strong emotions like those of intense sexual arousal. The tides and waves of labor culminate in the birth passion. To be watched by someone with whom you have no

A typical birth room

If you plan to have your baby in a hospital it is a good idea to look at a birth room. Some equipment seems daunting until it is explained to you. Many hospitals arrange tours of their maternity departments so that expectant mothers can see them in advance of labor.

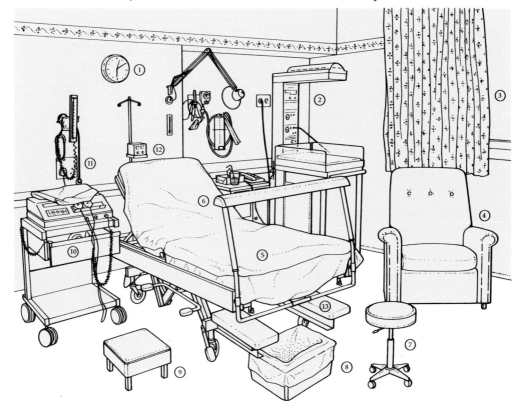

1 The clock is used to record the length of each stage of labor and for noting the time of the baby's birth.

2 The resuscitation cart for the baby is equipped with oxygen and suction apparatus to extract any mucus from the baby's lungs.

3 Curtains screen harsh daylight so that it does not disturb the mother. They are intended to provide a homey and reassuring element in the birth room and enable you to darken the room for your first meeting with the baby.

4 Some hospitals have a chair bed, a comfortable seat for the birth partner which can be folded out for an overnight stay.

5 The birth bed has three sections: head, middle, and foot, which are adjustable. The head can be raised or lowered. The entire bed can be raised or lowered. The foot can be lowered or removed as shown here.

6 The squatting bar gives a firm support to hold on to if you want to adopt a squatting position.

7 The adjustable stool is for the doctor or midwife.

8 A plastic container catches fluids and waste products during the birth.

9 A low footstool is usually provided and is useful for helping you get into bed.

10 An electronic fetal monitor with sensing devices that are attached to your abdomen. It can be used intermittently or continuously during labor, or not at all. It detects and records the fetal heart rate and your uterine contractions.

11 Behind the bed is the apparatus for measuring blood pressure. There is also a supply of oxygen available should the mother need it and spare electric sockets for other purposes.

12 The IV pole will hold the fluid if a doctor decides to set up an intravenous drip for the mother.

13 Adjustable foot rests are on either side of the bed. When the mattress at the foot of the bed is removed, the mother may place her feet here.

intimate and trusting closeness, to be inspected, criticized, applauded, and urged to do better, can interrupt and prove an obstacle to psychophysical coordination. This is why it is important to create your own space for birth, and to arrange to have one or more companions with you with whom you feel not just comfortable, but completely at ease. If you are giving birth in a large hospital with people whom you have never met before it is all the more vital to choose a birth companion who can be like an anchor in a stormy sea.

CHOOSING A WOMAN BIRTH COMPANION

Research in various countries shows that if a woman has another woman with her during labor and birth she has less need for pain-relieving drugs and her labor is shorter. There are fewer operative deliveries (forceps, vacuum extractor, and cesarean sections), and fewer episiotomies; babies are in better condition at birth, and mothers are much more likely to look back on the birth as a positive experience. Some studies also reveal that such women have fewer perineal lacerations, are more likely to be breastfeeding at six weeks, and are less likely to be depressed.* Ten randomized controlled trials involving 3,000 women in childbirth who did not even know their companions before they went into labor have confirmed the benefits of having a support person through labor and birth.*

"My sister was marvelous during my labor – really supportive – and it was lovely having her there and sharing the miracle of the birth with her."

The evidence is that the constant presence of a birth companion who is focused on your needs is one of the most effective forms of childbirth care introduced in the last 25 years. It is the rediscovery of a practice that was elemental to birth in many different cultures all over the world, including Europe and North America, until professionals took over. Women have always had other women with them. In medieval Europe women birth companions were known as "God sibs" – literally, "sisters in God."

In the United States today the term "doula," which is a Greek word meaning "a female birth companion," is often used. A doula can be present at the birth either instead of the baby's father or to support the couple who want to be together.

Doulas are women who are especially interested in birth and in helping women through birth. They have had training and experience in providing emotional, physical, and informational support. It is now possible to meet and select your doula. For referrals, contact Doulas of North America (see page 413), or if you prefer, consider your childbirth teacher, a student teacher, a close friend, or anyone in your family whom you feel has the right personality and who will give you loving emotional support. A "doula" is often described as someone who will "mother the mother." In fact, this may not be exactly what you want. Many women do not look for mothering, but welcome woman-to-woman understanding and practical help from someone more like a sister.

Hospitals used to lay down strict rules stating that only one other person could be with a woman in childbirth. This has now changed. More and more hospitals recognize that having not only your partner but a friend or family member whom you know and trust, and whom you have yourself selected, helps you relax and increases self-confidence, with the result that labor is more likely to go well.

Relaxation and massage

Relaxation is the art of letting go and allowing peace to flow through you. The skill is in being able to release your muscles at will and not only when you are in a special mood to relax. It is not just an exercise, but as necessary a partner to – and interlude in – strenuous activity as is the breath out to the breath in.

THE IMPORTANCE OF RELAXATION

Relaxation is vital for labor. If you cannot relax you are likely to become exhausted as a result of muscles tightening up all over your body in reaction to the challenging stress of contractions. By tensing muscles unnecessarily you are wasting energy, and if you are exhausted any pain will be felt more keenly and your ability to control it is bound to be diminished.

Generalized tension and anxiety can sometimes affect the way the uterus contracts, producing incoordinate uterine action, which causes painful contractions that are not very effective in pulling open the cervix. Because it alters your whole body chemistry, marked tension lasting a long time can also reduce the oxygen supply to the baby. Just as the smooth coordination of your digestive system, the beating of your heart, and your breathing are all affected by acute tension, so stress and anxiety can slow down the unfolding process of childbirth and make it more difficult.

When you know how to relax you can adjust to your labor with special breathing, positions, and other techniques. Relaxation helps keep your mind clear so that you are able to understand what is happening and can respond to it purposefully and creatively.

CENTERING DOWN

To explore and enjoy the skills of relaxation, you need to be able to "center down," to use an old Quaker term, and be still, and enjoy peace of body and mind. Lie down on your side, well supported with plenty of pillows, back rounded, head and shoulders forward, legs and arms bent. Or sit in a comfortable chair with cushions supporting all of your back, including the back of your neck. You may also like a cushion under each arm or underneath your thighs. Before starting any exercises spend time thinking of the journey the baby makes to be born. Read pages 252–253 and then focus your thoughts on that part of your body. Concentrate on feeling your muscles and flesh heavy, all tension released.

Touch relaxation

Tension makes childbirth unnecessarily painful. Learn how to relax to your partner's touch so that this is a spontaneous reaction in labor. To practice touch relaxation, first sit on the floor, well propped with cushions and with legs and arms bent and spread a little. Give a long breath out through a relaxed mouth. Now you are going to contract different sets of muscles – especially those you tend to tighten under stress – noticing how you feel when they are tight. Your partner rests one or both hands over the area you have tightened. As you feel the touch, relax as if you were flowing out toward the touch.

Relaxing your abdomen

Under stress the abdominal muscles tense up and this can lead to a more painful labor than need be the case. Tense abdominal muscles also cause shallow breathing. Massaging your lower tummy can relieve your tension and contribute to an easier labor. During labor the pull of the dilating cervix often feels painful and then light massage over the area just above your pubic bone can also be helpful in easing pain and tension. Practicing how to relax abdominal muscles allows you to learn how to respond to your partner's touch in advance of labor.

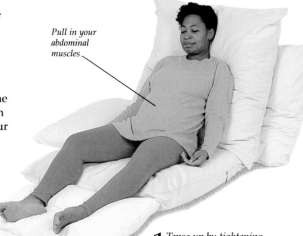

Pull in your abdominal muscles

1 *Tense up by tightening your abdominal muscles and pulling them in toward your spine. As you do this, notice how the tension feels. You will find you have also tightened the muscles at the bottom of your back and that your breathing is affected too.*

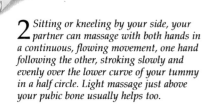

2 *Sitting or kneeling by your side, your partner can massage with both hands in a continuous, flowing movement, one hand following the other, stroking slowly and evenly over the lower curve of your tummy in a half circle. Light massage just above your pubic bone usually helps too.*

Relaxing your shoulders

Most people tighten their shoulders when under stress. Tight shoulders result in strained breathing and, because the tension is in the back of the neck too, can cause a headache. In labor, tension in the shoulders very soon results in heavy, panicky breathing, which in turn leads you to hyperventilate. A side effect of this is a reduction in the amount of oxygen reaching the baby. If you know how to release your shoulders, you will not hyperventilate. A woman may tense her shoulders when she is finding it difficult to cope with strong contractions in the first stage of labor. She presses her shoulders and her head back into the pillows. Try doing this while lying down and notice how you feel. Is it affecting your breathing?

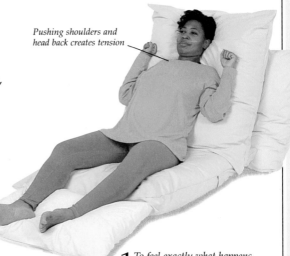

Pushing shoulders and head back creates tension

1 *To feel exactly what happens when your shoulder muscles become very tense, concentrate on pressing your shoulder blades back toward each other as if they were angel's wings and you could make them meet at the back.*

2 *Now your partner rests one hand firmly over each shoulder, applying pressure with the heels of the palms at the front of your shoulders. You release immediately, flowing out to the touch. Then the hands are slowly removed.*

3 *When tension is building up in labor, firm pressure on your shoulders, or the shoulder on the side nearest your partner, enables you to release this tension.*

187

Relaxing your head

This exercise helps to release tension in the muscles of the scalp. We often forget about the scalp muscles because they are under our hair, but tension here can lead to a frozen, strained facial expression, as well as giving you both head- and neckache.

Release tension in response to pressure on temples

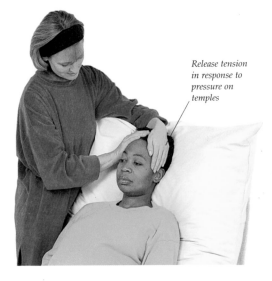

1 *Push your eyebrows up toward the top of your head. Notice how you feel when you do this. The scalp muscles can become this tense during labor.*

2 *Your partner forms his or her hands into a cap, which is rested against the top of your head. As you feel the pressure, release. Let your eyes close slowly. As your partner becomes aware of your tension easing, he or she reduces the pressure slowly. As this happens you visualize any residual tension flowing out of your head.*

Relaxing the face

If a woman in labor is concentrating hard, or feels anxious about what her body is doing, the muscles around her eyes become tense and her brow furrows. Her jaw stiffens, her mouth gets tight, and it becomes difficult to release the vagina and perineum too.

1 *Frown as if you had a headache and were in a very bright light. Notice how you feel when you screw up your eyes and forehead. This is how you may feel while concentrating hard in labor.*

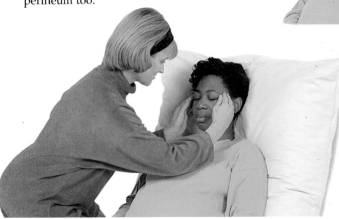

2 *Using two fingers placed on each side of your head, your partner presses gently on the bone of the temples. Release muscular tension as soon as you feel this touch. Then very gradually your partner reduces the pressure, as you visualize any residual tension flowing out and away.*

Relaxing your arms

When you are experiencing a very strong contraction, it is tempting to grip someone or something with your hand and to contract muscles in your arms. This makes pain worse and, along with tension in the shoulders, interferes with breathing, so that you start to gasp.

Hold tension in arm

1 *Tighten the muscles in the arm that is nearest your partner. Notice how your arm feels. Your partner watches to judge when the muscles look tight and then applies gentle pressure on the arm.*

2 *Your partner places one hand firmly on the front of your shoulder, with the other hand over the inside of your upper arm, cradled around the big muscle there, the biceps. The hands are held as if they are molded to your body. As soon as you feel the warmth and pressure of the touch, release your arm muscles completely.*

3 *Then the hand on the inside arm moves slowly and firmly, stroking right down to your wrist. The other hand stays firm on your shoulder. As the hand moves, focus on the feeling of any residual tension flowing down your arm, out and away. Movements like this, from the center of the body toward the periphery, are helpful because tension always flows from the center, out and away. This slow, firm stroking down the inside arm can feel very good in labor. Try it at the start of each contraction.*

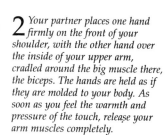

Relaxing your legs

When a woman feels her baby pressing down to be born she often tightens the muscles of her inner thighs in direct response to the pressing sensation. A vital part of opening up in order to allow the baby to be born is the complete release of any tension in your thighs.

1 *Press your knees very firmly together. As you do so, notice how tense the muscles of your inner thighs feel.*

2 *Your partner rests one hand on the outside of each leg and you relax toward the touch, letting your knees roll outward naturally.*

Easing cramps

Sometimes in labor the inner thigh muscles get so tight that the woman's leg becomes stiff and her foot drawn up so that she gets a painful cramp. This can be released with massage.

1 *Stretch one leg out straight, so it feels stiff and taut, then flex your foot. Concentrate on feeling the muscular tension that results.*

2 *To help release the tension in the muscles, your partner places one hand on the inside of your thigh, molding the hand to the leg, then strokes slowly and firmly down to your ankle. You release to the warmth of the touch.*

Releasing tension

This massage is particularly useful as you reach the end of the first stage of labor, when contractions are coming about two minutes apart, and last a minute or more. At this time a woman often feels that her legs are cold and tense. She may begin to shiver and shake, until her whole body is trembling. If this is your experience, you will find that massage of the inner thigh muscles warms your legs so that you feel they belong to you again and you can consciously release tension in them.

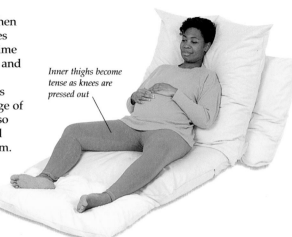

Inner thighs become tense as knees are pressed out

1 *See what happens when you press both your knees outward so that your inner legs are uppermost. Concentrate on feeling the tension in your inner thighs as you do so.*

2 *Your partner now rests both hands on the inside of your upper thighs, and you then relax to the touch. With hands shaped around your inner thighs, your partner strokes slowly from the top of your legs down to your knees. She should use a very firm stroke as the hands slide down the inside of your thighs, and a gentle stroke coming up over the outside of the legs in a continuous flowing movement, helping tension flow out from the center of the body, down, and away. It is as if the hands are giving the message "Open up, open up, the baby's coming out."*

Releasing your pelvic floor muscles

This type of massage reminds you to release your pelvic floor muscles so that you can help the baby's head bulge forward in your vagina. Each downward movement of the hands has the effect of releasing the muscles through which the baby is coming to birth.

To focus on this feeling, first contract your pelvic floor muscles as if they were an elevator going up to the second, third, and then fourth floor of a building. Pull them up and hold them. Then your partner rests both hands on your inside thighs, and you release the pelvic floor muscles down to them, as if the elevator were going down to the basement. As your partner slides her hands toward your knees, release still more, bulging your perineum forward.

Relaxing your back and shoulders

For the next set of exercises, lie on your side, making yourself comfortable with pillows. Your back should be rounded, your head and shoulders well forward, and your underneath arm behind your back. If a woman is lying on her side during childbirth and she becomes tense, she often adopts a fetal position. Having someone hold your shoulders in this position is helpful if you tend to overbreathe during contractions. A thumb massage over your upper back and shoulders or each side of the spine may help too.

1 *Curl up into a fetal position and hunch your shoulders. Notice how you feel when you do this. Your shoulders will have tightened up so that they are now near to the level of your ears. Your breathing will probably be affected too.*

2 *Now your partner rests his or her fingers on your shoulders and applies firm pressure with the palms. You release, flowing out toward the touch.*

Cushion gives extra support

Locating tension in the small of your back

Many women experience backache in labor, usually around the sacrum – the bone in the small of the back where the pelvis joins the spine. The tension that results from such backache means that you suffer more pain from your own stiff muscles.

1 *To find out exactly where the sacrum is, ask your partner to place his or her fingers over the large bones at the side of the pelvic cradle and then trace the shape of the pelvis around to where it dips downward at the back to meet your spine.*

2 *Still lying on your side, imagine that you have a bad pain around your sacrum. Pull in the small of your back to tense up muscles all down your back. You will find you are sticking your bottom out and throwing your shoulders back. This is what happens when a woman has back pain in labor.*

Tension is created when the small of the back is pulled in

Relieving backache

The tension that results from backache can be greatly relieved if your partner applies firm pressure over this area. Relax your muscles and let go of tension while your partner presses along each part of your lower back.

To help you release, your partner now presses firmly and steadily over the sacrum, using the heel of the palm (not the fingers). As soon as you feel the warmth and pressure, you relax, letting go and flowing out toward the hands. Muscles right down your back soften and loosen immediately.

Relaxing your back with massage

In childbirth, firm counterpressure, as above, may feel good, or you may prefer to be massaged. Massage is usually best done by moving the flesh – both skin and muscle – on the bone, rather than by merely creating friction.

Your partner can use either a firm, circular motion with hands more or less stationary, or slide the hands across the top of one buttock to the top of the other and back again.

Relaxing your partner's back

Partners using counterpressure or doing back massage often develop backache too, because they are relying on muscle strength in the arms rather than allowing their own body weight to flow down *through* their arms. Your partner may want to rest one hand on your hip, but should be careful not to exert pressure there or lean on you, since that will cause you discomfort.

The exertion of giving a massage can give your partner backache too. She may want to relax by resting one hand on your hip.

Relaxing your buttocks

A woman in labor may tense her buttocks because the baby is pressing against her rectum and anus as it comes around the curve of the birth canal, and she feels as if it is coming out of the wrong hole. She is often convinced that she wants to go to the toilet. She resists the sensation by tightening up her muscles. When she tightens her buttocks she also tightens her pelvic floor muscles against the baby's head, as if shutting the door on it. Contracting these muscles can hold up the descent of the baby's head and cause unnecessary pain.

1 *To tense up the muscles, press your buttocks tightly together as if you have a piece of paper between them and somebody is trying to take it away from you. As you hold on to it, notice exactly how you feel. This is how tense you may become during labor. Your partner watches for the tension, then rests one hand on each buttock, on the lower inside curve, and as you feel the warmth and pressure you release. Your partner will feel the tension slide away.*

2 *Your partner can help you relax by firmly massaging your buttocks as if kneading bread dough. It is important for her to get down into the fat and muscle, very slowly kneading both buttocks at once. As soon as you feel the firm, reassuring touch, you will relax.*

Relaxing your "tail" muscles

Firm pressure, or rhythmic "rocking" massage, at the very base of the spine relaxes the "tail" muscles. These muscles form part of the pelvic floor.

Imagine that you have a tail like a kangaroo. You can lift it off the ground and then drop it down again. Now kneel in front of a chair with your forearms on the seat, and lift your "kangaroo muscle" up. Your partner firmly rests a curved hand at the very bottom of your spine, just around the curve where your anus is. You release toward the touch.

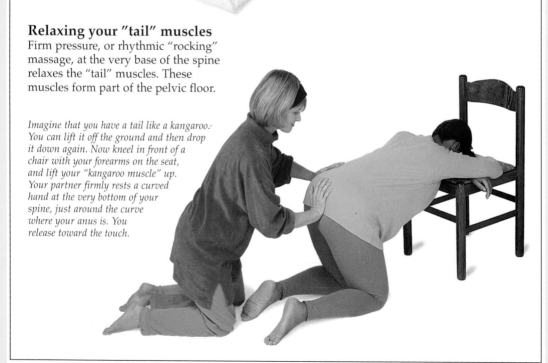

TOUCH RELAXATION

With touch relaxation, a partner gives you a message of touch to say, in effect, "release here." You respond to the pressure and warmth of the hands with immediate relaxation. If you learn to respond to your partner's touch in this way during pregnancy, it will be a spontaneous reaction when you are in labor. In effect, it will amount to your partner's being able to draw the tension out of you.

To practice the technique, you contract different sets of muscles one set at a time. Your partner then rests his or her hands over the area that feels tight, and as soon as you feel the touch, you release, as if you are flowing toward it. Sometimes it helps if the touch develops into a gentle massage over the part of the body that is tense. This massage should be very slow; a partner who is worried or excited may massage in fast, jerky movements and this has the effect of communicating tension rather than relieving it. Whenever massage is performed on bare skin, it is a good idea to use a little powder or warm oil, so that the hands glide smoothly and you do not feel itchy.

Between each exercise it is important to discuss whether it feels right for you – whether you want the touch firmer, lighter, or in a slightly different place. During labor, too, you can talk together between contractions so that your helper understands exactly what you want. Some examples of touch relaxation for different parts of the body are given on pages 186–194. In childbirth, touch can be enormously comforting. It helps you release all the muscles you do not need to use in order to have the baby. It relieves psychological stress, too, because you are able to feel secure and nurtured.

On the other hand, some women find that the experience of giving birth is so total, so overwhelming, that touch would be superfluous. While touch relaxation can be an important part of preparing for the birth, when you are in actual labor you may come to a phase when you do not want to be touched at all. If so, simply tell your partner this. It is vital that you have the kind of support *you* want and that your partner be willing to stand back and let you do things your way.

Release of tension By practicing relaxation techniques with you like this, your partner becomes aware of any tensions you are feeling and, when you are in labor, will be able to notice if there is a build-up of tension in your body long before anyone who does not know you well realizes what is happening. Then, all that is needed is to reach out a hand with the message: relax! If your shoulders are getting tense, for example, a firm hand rests on your shoulder. If your legs are knotting up, loving hands stroke your legs firmly.

One great advantage of this is that it does not involve giving directions and "coaching" in labor. There may be times – especially at the very end of the first stage – when positive guidance is invaluable, but there is no place at all for bullying a woman in childbirth. Through learning touch relaxation, your partner will have the self-assurance to give you just the kind of help you need.

Responding to the doctor or midwife Experiencing touch relaxation together also prepares you to respond to the touch you receive when the doctor or midwife examines you. Instead of feeling threatened, tensing up, and pulling away like a snail drawing in its horns, you will be able to relax. This makes having your tummy palpated and pelvic examination much easier and more comfortable.

Pressure from the uterus During childbirth the stimulus coming from the uterus feels remarkably like a strong, intense kind of touch radiating from inside. As the uterus contracts it squeezes tightly. A powerful pressure builds up and there is a sensation of heat. When the cervix is being opened and pulled wider, still more pressure is exerted. Then, as the baby moves down through the cervix, pressure is produced by the ball of its head. It feels as if a grapefruit were being pressed down first against the anus and then through the vagina. To all these stimuli a woman may respond either by tightening up or by releasing her muscles.

"I hadn't realized that I clenched my jaw when I tensed up around my eyes or how often I curled my toes when I concentrated."

Learning to flow with a contraction Now imagine that you are in labor and that the pressure of the uterus is increasing with each contraction. Visualize the pressure of the baby's head, too, then release and flow toward these sensations. Some women experience each contraction as warmth building up to heat and then dying down again. One woman told me that every contraction was like an oven door swinging wide open; at its peak she received the full blast of the heat and then the oven door closed again.

When the baby's head is on your perineum and coming through the vagina, all the tissues fan out like the petals of a flower. As they open you may feel a warm, tingling sensation, as if the whole area is being flooded with heat. In addition, if you have learned always to relax in response to the pressure and warmth from your partner's hands, you will be able to respond to these physical messages from *inside* your body too, not by pulling back, but by releasing and *flowing toward* them. In this way the sensations you get from within your body can serve to guide you in labor.

PUPPET-STRINGS RELAXATION

Of course you do not always have someone to help you with relaxation. You can practice relaxation by yourself, using a method that I call the puppet-strings method.

Lie in whatever position you usually sleep. Make yourself really comfortable, well supported by pillows, and give a long, sighing breath out and relax. Imagine that strings are attached to all your joints. Think of one fixed to your elbow, being tightened gradually so that your elbow is pulled up with the string. Depending on the position in which you are lying, your elbow may be moved a lot or a little. Then let it go. Notice the different feelings. Now the angle of the string is different, so feel the pull in a different direction. It lifts your elbow higher and higher. Now the string is released. It may take a little practice, but try not to allow any parts other than those operated by the string to move. The hand hangs limp at the wrist. The shoulder is not lifted. Only the elbow is activated.

Now do the same thing with an imaginary string attached to the other elbow. Let it be pulled in various directions. Continue as if a string were fixed to one big toe, then the other one, the back of one ankle, then the other, the left knee, the right knee, the left wrist, the right wrist, the index finger, the middle joint of a finger, one shoulder, the other shoulder, your left hip, your right hip.

Then imagine two strings, attached to your right elbow and right wrist, for example, tightening one after the other till both are drawn taut; first the wrist string is released, then the elbow string. Experiment with the strings working in a different order. Keep your mind focused on the tightening string rather than on the muscle you are contracting. Only when the invisible string is taut should you turn your mind to analyzing which muscles are tightened.

Imagine one string fixed to the top of your head, another to the base of your skull. First one is pulled, then the other. One goes slack, then the other. You will find that you can make the strings pull in different directions and at varying angles. This saves it from being a repetitive exercise that you do from habit, not focusing on what your body is doing. It is important that any body movements you do bring awareness, an increased sense of working *with* your body. Mechanical exercises have no place in learning to relax.

STANISLAVSKY RELAXATION
There are acting techniques for increasing body awareness and learning which muscles contract and work together. The precise combination of muscles working together varies with each individual and the nature of the task, the angle at which you tackle it, the weight, dimensions, and even the texture of the tools used. You will find that tasks you perform, even ordinary, everyday tasks, often cause you to change your breathing, and sometimes you hold your breath altogether. You may also discover that you tense up muscles that you do not need to use because you tackle a job in the wrong way or overwork at it, or because you are emotionally keyed up about what you are doing. All this is a valuable process of self-discovery as you can gradually learn more and more about yourself.

The method of relaxation that is based on Stanislavsky's acting techniques explores different sets of muscles in the body that naturally function together and the ways they work in response to different imagined activities and tasks and even thoughts and feelings. You think of certain situations – things you might be doing with your body – and mentally involve yourself in these situations as if you were actually performing them. Notice which muscles have become tense. Once the observation is made, switch off the picture in your mind and deliberately release those muscles. Start by sitting or lying against a firm support and let the pillows take the whole weight of your body. Listen to the sound of your own breathing. Breathe so that you can just hear yourself – in through your nose, and then out through your mouth. Allow the breathing to flow through your mouth, letting the breath out be long and slow. The sound is like a little sigh as you breathe out. You may notice that there is a slight pause after you breathe in as if you have reached the crest of a wave. Enjoy that slight pause. Then give a long breath out. And with each breath out, relax a little more.

SUGGESTED EXERCISES FOR STANISLAVSKY RELAXATION

The jaw Imagine that you have some very sticky taffy in your mouth, and chew it well. It is sticking to your teeth. Work this great hunk of taffy out of your teeth. Notice what is happening. Then rest and drop your jaw. Let it relax, quite soft and loose. Notice the different feeling of complete release of the jaw muscles.

The eyes We do not usually notice when our eye muscles become tense. Imagine that there is a fireman climbing a ladder to rescue a little dog stranded at the top of a house. Focus on the firefighter as he climbs all the way up. Observe the feeling in the muscles behind and around your eyes. Follow him with your eyes – up and up – until he is at the top. He has the little dog under his arm and is bringing it down and down. Now he is at the bottom. Relax your eyes, and if you want to, let them close. Notice how different they feel.

The feet Imagine that you are at the seashore standing on a very pebbly beach with no shoes on. Making very slight movements, imagine that you are walking on the beach with the sharp pebbles underfoot, and really feel them under your bare feet. Pick your way carefully over them. Oh! That was a sharp one! Observe the tension in your feet. Now go on to the soft sand. Really feel the difference. Then imagine lying down and letting your feet relax completely.

The hands Can you recollect the feeling of making a snowball? Imagine that you are picking up snow and are patting the hard cold mass into a firm snowball. You are hurrying so that you can throw it at someone. As you quickly make your snowball, notice the tension in your hands. Then drop them and let them relax beside your body on the bed or floor again and notice how warm, soft, and loose they feel.

Taste Imagine that you are sipping some water. Place the glass to your lips. It is sharp, neat lemon juice! Really taste it. Notice what is happening in your mouth and the tension that is spontaneously produced. Now it is gone. Let the muscles of the mouth soften. Now you have a large, ripe peach. Take a good bite of it. It is very juicy and the juice is dribbling down. You need to suck it and draw in the juice. Smell it, too. Chew it, swallow it. Now it has gone. Notice the very different feeling in your mouth. Relax completely and think through what happened to the muscles inside your mouth and nose and to the other facial muscles as you imagined eating the peach.

Smell Muscles around the nostrils and in the cheeks and the mouth work together as we smell and taste things. Imagine that you have in your hand a bottle of liquid. Take out the stopper and take a good sniff – it is ammonia! Notice how you have become stiff down the back of your neck. Then deliberately relax. Breathe in fresh, pure, clean air. Let yourself breathe easily.

Here is another bottle. Do the same with this one. It is perfume this time: lily of the valley. You will find yourself drawing in the scent of lily of the valley in long, slow breaths, holding the fragrance as if it were suffused behind the surface of your face. Now the fragrance has gone and you are just breathing air. Relax.

Go on from this to recreate in your imagination actions that you usually perform without thinking, simple things like writing a shopping list, tying shoe laces, or unlocking a door, and discover exactly how you use your body.

Visual imagery in childbirth

Preparation for birth is not merely learning techniques for "coping" with pain. It is much more positive than that, and at best enables a woman to draw on her own inner power. Ninety percent of birth, like 90 percent of sex, has to do with what is going on in her head. One woman experiences a long or physically difficult birth with elation. Another finds a straightforward birth distressing. It is in large part a result of the particular quality of the relationship between her and her caregivers. It is quite difficult to have a positive experience in an unsympathetic or hostile environment. The mental images a woman has of labor and birth are vitally important, too: how she imagines all the intense physical sensations as they well up in her, and the meaning that these have as contractions sweep through her body and the

"I enjoy windsurfing, so that's how I pictured myself while I was giving birth – an active image that fitted my strong, rapid labor exactly."

baby's head descends. Pain may be seen as destructive and produce pictures of internal organs tearing and the baby being damaged. Or it may be seen as pain with a purpose, as the pain of strong muscles working and the body opening. It helps to focus on creative images, and to rehearse them ahead of time. It is good preparation to imagine being in labor, welcoming each contraction with relaxation, rhythmic breathing, and a vivid mental picture which enables you to go *with* the work of your birthing body, instead of resisting it. It may be that these pictures inside your head are enough by themselves for you to get in tune with your labor. You may want an entirely internal focus and anything else may be distracting. But it often helps to have something which you can see and on which you can concentrate during contractions: a photograph, painting, pattern on your partner's T-shirt, or an object such as a beautiful piece of pottery, small sculpture, or some intricate tiles – something which represents for you the energy and flow of birth. Sky and seascapes, a range of mountains capped with snow, a path through the forest, great trees with their branches spread wide, a waterfall cascading into a lake, a field of ripe wheat with the wind sweeping across it, a flower opening from bud to full bloom – perhaps a waterlily, rose, or peony – are images which may be right for you. In some Mediterranean peasant cultures women have a flower beside them when they are in labor. It is the rose of Jericho, which looks dried up and lifeless but in the heat of the birth room it opens up and spreads its petals wide. In southern Italy they call it "the hand of the Mother of God." It is both a symbol of the help that Mary gives them in childbirth and of the cervix that is opening wider and wider so that the baby can be born.

> *"A painting of Mary giving birth to her baby, his head crowning in a halo of light, was my visual focus."*

In Mediterranean cultures, too, there is a tradition of ritual actions that provide a powerful sense for the woman in labor of everything being opened and released, so that she can feel her body opening in a similar way. In Greece grain or water may be poured, windows and doors flung wide, and clothing unbuttoned. As labor progresses and contractions get stronger and longer, you may want very active images that express the extraordinary power that you feel unleashed in your body. It often helps to focus on imagined actions, and to feel that you are swimming over waves, windsurfing, climbing a hill and then skiing down a slope, swinging, and flying or roller-coasting over contractions. You can use music in a similar way, selecting tapes that echo your images of birth and represent for you the elemental forces of earth, air, fire, and water.

In many different cultures women are drawn to images of water. Contractions are like great waves bringing the baby to birth as if on the swell of the incoming tide. Women poets writing about birth use water imagery, too. For Kathleen Raine contractions are "waves that break on the shore of the world" and she calls to her baby, "Child in the little boat, come to the land." An ancient Armenian poem expresses the overwhelming feelings of birth: "The skies were in labor and the muscles of the earth and the ripe red seas were in labor."* For some women a poem, a chant, a prayer, or a song can have special significance and help them keep on top of contractions.

If when you are in labor an image turns out to be unsuitable or irritating, simply discard it and choose others, or focus on your uterus squeezing in and hugging the baby, your cervix opening in increasingly wider circles, the tissues of your vagina fanning out, your baby pressing deeper and deeper to be born, and reaching down to lift your baby into your arms. The essential element in the use of images like these is to achieve focused concentration, rather than letting your thoughts be dispersed by pain, and interpreting physical sensations in a positive, creative way, instead of feeling under attack. A woman uses the power of her mind, in harmony with the power released by her uterus, to help her body work freely.

Breathing for labor

Relaxation and breathing are so closely associated that it is important to explore them as parts of a unity. You cannot breathe correctly for labor unless you are relaxed. As labor progresses you may spontaneously breathe more rapidly. If you breathe more

Below

Having someone you love with you makes for the best atmosphere in which to relax.

quickly and at the same time heavily, you will hyperventilate and flush carbon dioxide out of your bloodstream. This can make you feel uncomfortable and, if severe enough, you may even pass out. Ironically, when you hyperventilate, you feel you cannot get enough air in, and you tend to gulp air which makes the hyperventilation worse. In fact, it is possible to correct the effects of hyperventilation by holding your breath for short periods, or by rebreathing carbon dioxide (by breathing in and out of a paper bag). This restores carbon dioxide levels and the symptoms disappear. The opposite – underbreathing or even not breathing at all – results in lack of oxygen and is more likely to happen if you have Demerol to relieve pain. Though you can cope with this, your baby needs you to go on breathing. Overbreathing, "forgetting" to breathe, and holding your breath are all harmful to the baby during childbirth.

"As massive contractions swept over me I couldn't help holding my breath. My midwife said, 'shout, moan, sing! That'll help!' "

In many cultures breathing in labor is deliberately regulated to help a woman work with the forces bringing her baby to birth. Among the Zulu, for example, breathing exercises are taught in pregnancy. A woman goes to the door of her hut each morning as the sun rises and takes careful, controlled, full breaths through each nostril alternately.* She uses the same breathing in labor. In other cultures breathing is regulated by background sounds, including prayers, music, the beating of hands, repeated phrases of encouragement, or the swaying of attendants holding the mother.

Breathing for relaxation

Smooth, easy breathing rhythms can also help release tension and create a state of pleasurable relaxation. In labor this is particularly important because, since contractions come like the waves of the sea, there is a strong natural rhythm built in to the physiological activity. A woman can either resist this, trying to "switch off," escape from, or dominate it, or she can go with it and adjust her breathing to the compelling sweep of uterine power. She can only go with the rhythm if she can accept what is happening in her body and assent to it.

So the breathing taught for labor is not to do with "distraction techniques" and is no magic method of eradicating sensation or guaranteeing that you do not feel pain. It is simply another way of getting in tune with your body and especially with your uterus.

Rest your hands over the lower curve of your abdomen. In late pregnancy you have a lovely melon shape there. Breathe as slowly as you comfortably can. As the breath enters your nostrils, allow them to dilate, notice the slight pause between the breath in and the breath out, and then breathe out through a soft, relaxed mouth as if you had on a new, glossy, and rather expensive lipstick. Enjoy that breath out. Notice what is happening to your abdomen. Feel it rising under your hands as you breathe in – a gentle swelling, like a wave building up. Then as you breathe out, the abdomen sinks back again and the wave recedes. Be aware of the slight pressure under your hands as you breathe in, and feel the pressure withdrawing as you breathe out and the abdomen goes back to its former position.

BREATHING DOWN YOUR BACK

You need someone to help you rehearse this. Try kneeling in front of a chair with your forearms and head resting on the seat and your knees well apart. Ask your helper to rest one hand firmly on each side of the base of your spine. Then breathe slowly right down your back, noticing the pressure against the hands as you inhale and how it gradually falls away as you exhale.

THE GREETING BREATH

When you are in labor, meet each contraction with your breathing, giving first of all a complete greeting breath. This is a deliberate, slow breath *out*. Imagine an early first-stage contraction lasting 45 to 60 seconds. Breathe slowly through the contraction, with the lower back spreading out and pressing slightly against the bed or floor as you breathe in, and the pressure being lifted as you breathe out.

THE RESTING BREATH

As a contraction fades away, you give a long, slow, complete breath out through your mouth – a resting breath. This is important partly because it offers you complete relaxation at the end of a contraction so that you can rest and get refreshed before the next one, and partly because it signals to everyone in the room that a contraction is over. If the midwife or obstetrician wants to talk to you, or ask you to turn over, now is the time, between contractions – never during them.

In strong labor you may want to give several of these complete resting breaths once a contraction finishes. Do whatever feels good. If you always respond to the end of a powerful contraction by one or more resting breaths you can be sure that, however difficult contractions are, you are giving your baby oxygen by breathing fully.

FULL CHEST BREATHING

You need a partner to help you practice this. Lie on your side with your back rounded, head and shoulders curved forward, legs well apart, and the upper leg drawn up and bent at the knee. Now lift your head as if stretching your spine all the way up the back so that you feel taller. Stretch your neck at the back, stretch all the way up your spine, and then simply let it drop back into place; let your head settle comfortably on your shoulders. See that there is a good space between your legs. Then give a long breath out and relax completely. Allow your eyes to close if they feel heavy.

Think of your back. Your spine is not stiff like a lamppost. It is constructed of small vertebrae in a curving shape like a string of sausages. We often act as if our spinal columns were very stiff.

Yet think of the way a cat moves and how the movement ripples up and down the back. Now your partner rests one hand on each of your shoulders and massages with the flat of both hands from the top of your back right down to the bottom. The hands should be relaxed. Say if you would like the massage to be heavier or lighter, slower or quicker. Is it in the right place? It should feel good. Concentrate on relaxing toward the hands.

Then your partner rests the palms of both hands firmly above your waist on either side of the spine over the ribcage. They should be in a position that is comfortable for you and should not be pressing in on your waist (or where it once was!). Notice their warmth and strength. Breathe in through the nose and out through the mouth again so that the main level of breathing awareness is just where you feel the pressure and warmth of the hands, and listen to your breathing. Breathe right down to where you feel the hands, expanding your ribcage, so that it is swelling out under the hands as you breathe in, and then it falls away from the pressure of the hands as you breathe out. Listen to it for a moment. Can your partner feel the pressure, building up as you breathe in and falling away as you breathe out? This is full chest breathing. This kind of breathing can be very useful, once labor starts, to help you to meet the earliest contractions of the first stage of labor. You may be able to breathe like this all the way until you are about 5 cm dilated, concentrating on breathing into the area against which your partner is pressing the hands. When you are actually in labor you will not need the hands there because you will do it automatically and the contracting uterus itself will provide sufficient stimulus.

UPPER CHEST BREATHING

As contractions strengthen, you may want to lift your breathing above them, as if over the crest of a wave. Contractions come like waves and you may find that you can cope with them more easily if you breathe more lightly and more quickly. At this phase they may be coming every four or five minutes and lasting about a minute.

To practice breathing with these contractions, your partner should rest the palms of both hands on your upper back just below your shoulder blades. You breathe so that your main level of breathing activity and awareness is where you feel the pressure of the hands. You may find that you want to breathe more rapidly, perhaps through parted lips. You should be able to hear a crisp little sigh or "huff" with each breath out. Now if you rest your hand over your upper chest you will feel it rising and falling at the same time, rather like a seagull floating on a wave. In labor the wave of a contraction will be underneath and you will be breathing over the top of it. Relax your shoulders; they are not doing any of the work. If you find that you can still breathe with your full chest, do so. Only "lift" your breathing if you really need to.

Practicing for breathing

Prepare yourself to ride the waves of contractions during labor with the type of breathing that feels right for you. Breathe easily and without strain as contractions sweep through you. There are no rules about how you ought to breathe. When you are in labor your body will tell you what to do.

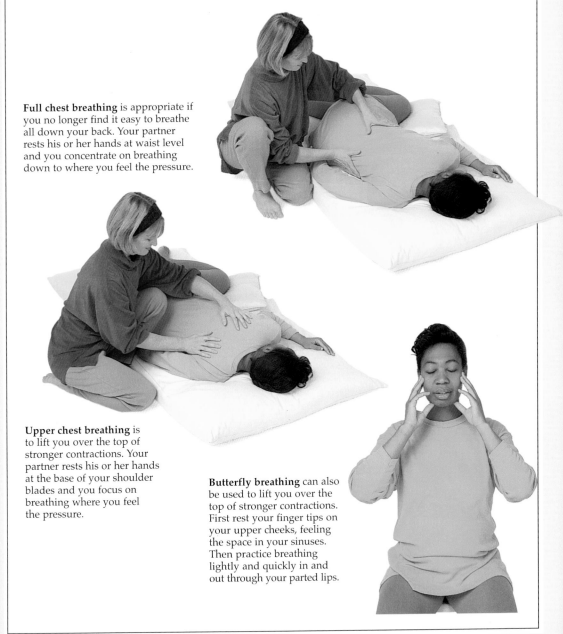

Full chest breathing is appropriate if you no longer find it easy to breathe all down your back. Your partner rests his or her hands at waist level and you concentrate on breathing down to where you feel the pressure.

Upper chest breathing is to lift you over the top of stronger contractions. Your partner rests his or her hands at the base of your shoulder blades and you focus on breathing where you feel the pressure.

Butterfly breathing can also be used to lift you over the top of stronger contractions. First rest your finger tips on your upper cheeks, feeling the space in your sinuses. Then practice breathing lightly and quickly in and out through your parted lips.

Practicing for contractions

By simulating contractions you learn to respond to painful stimuli with the use of appropriate breathing techniques, so that you become able to work with your body in a positive way instead of fighting pain, which only increases tension and makes labor more difficult.

Simulating the action of the uterus

It is best to practice this technique with your partner, who acts as your "uterus" by pinching a little flesh on your inside thigh between his or her fingers. Be careful that this pinching is not over a varicose vein or so strong that it leaves you with a bruise. There is no need to press down on blood vessels. Simply lift a fingerful of flesh off the leg, gradually increase the pressure for 30 seconds or so, and then reduce it.

1 *If you need to, allow your breathing rhythm to get lighter and quicker as the pressure builds to the maximum. Then breathe slowly and fully as the contraction fades.*

2 *After a while it may be a good idea to change places with your partner. "Contractions" – like the real ones – can vary: some short, some long, some easy, some harder; some may even have double peaks. For your partner it may be the first real inkling of what labor can be like.*

BUTTERFLY BREATHING

This is a kind of breathing that you may never need to use, but which feels lifesaving in a speedy labor when contractions seem to hit you like huge waves in rapid succession.

When the going is hard, women tend to raise their chins in the air, tense the muscles of the neck and jaw, and start to gasp and overbreathe. Instead, let your head drop forward onto your chest like a heavy flower on its stalk. Remembering to keep your shoulders loose, the back of your neck long, and your jaw released will help you to keep a steady rhythm and let your breathing "dance."

Butterfly breathing is the lightest, most rapid breathing you may want in labor. With most breathing techniques you are consciously using your diaphragm and lungs, but butterfly breathing is easier if you think of it as being centered in your mouth and behind your cheeks and not in the throat. If you center your breathing in the throat, you will probably tense up your neck. Think of the space in your mouth, the space behind your warm, plumped-up cheeks. Either sit up in a chair or lie well propped up on the bed for this exercise. If you are lying flat, you can find yourself gasping and panting heavily when you are doing this breathing. So pile three or four pillows behind you, or try a squatting, kneeling, all-fours, or standing position.

Resting the plump pads of the tips of your fingers against your cheeks will help you to concentrate on this area. Part your lips in a slight smile like the Mona Lisa. Relax your mouth and you will probably find that you are salivating a little. Breathe lightly in and out through your parted lips. Start gently, then allow your breathing to speed up till it is like little dancing waves.

Butterfly breathing may be quite difficult at first. You may feel that you are taking in or letting out too much air. Most people do to begin with, and find this the most contrived kind of breathing to learn. They think that they will never be able to manage it in labor, but then it comes quite naturally and they do not know how they could have coped without it. You may find that it helps to think in terms of a definite rhythm in which one beat is slightly accentuated: *one,* two, three, four; *one,* two, three, four; or *one,* two, three, four, five, six. If you do this, be careful not to expel a great deal of air on the accentuated breath or you will gasp in the following breath and start to hyperventilate. If you find it difficult to keep the rhythm, or find your throat getting tight, give a quick blow out through pursed lips and carry on with the light breathing immediately after.

After you have experimented with this breathing, try it once again, and this time notice especially if your shoulders or the back of your neck becomes tense. Drop your shoulders and relax. Under stress, it is tempting to breathe too heavily and sound as if you are a chugging piece of machinery. Try to keep your breathing as light as a whisper. When you rehearse, think of the sound of leaves in the forest floating to the ground, but bear in mind that in actual childbirth you will naturally make more noise than that. You will want to use this sort of breathing only when you are coping with the strongest contractions, at the end of the first stage. You may discover that full chest, upper chest, or even breathing all down your back works well for you at this time. Do whatever feels right for you. When you reach this point, you may feel like a little ship in a storm at sea in the midst of huge waves and confusing cross currents. For most women this is the most difficult time of labor. Grantly Dick-Read used to call it "the pain period of labor." This does not mean that you may not feel pain at other times, but it is the time when you will need all your concentration and control.

SHEEP'S BREATHING

If we watch any mammal giving birth, a cat, for example, or a sheep, we notice that she does not take great breaths in and then "block" the birth canal by holding her breath. A sheep gives birth with rather light, quick breathing. Her breath is involuntarily held as she bears down and then she continues the light, accelerated breathing again.

During the second stage of labor, when the baby is traveling down the vagina or birth canal (see pages 252–253), most women feel the urge to push during contractions. As a contraction builds you move from full to lighter, quicker breathing, your cheeks plumped up. Then the surge of desire to bear down comes and you hold your breath. As soon as you can breathe again you do so, then feel you have to bear down again – and so on until the desire fades, your breathing slows down, and then the contraction ends. Practice this with only a very slight push, with a hand resting over your perineum so that you can feel its gentle bulge forwards.

Different movements for labor

Once you are fairly confident about your ability to relax and breathe rhythmically, explore some different positions which you may want to use in labor. There is no reason why you should have to be tucked up in bed all the time. There are definite disadvantages to the supine position (lying flat on your back) for your baby, since the blood flow in the large veins in the lower part of your body may be obstructed by the heavy weight of your uterus and this can reduce the blood flow through the placenta to and from the baby.

Through the first stage of labor you will almost certainly feel happiest walking about or standing up. During contractions you will probably want to lean against a wall or your partner. If you have low backache, you can lean forward onto a heavy piece of furniture. Once labor is advanced, it will be easier if you already know the positions in which you are likely to feel most comfortable. Avoid getting stuck in one position; the essence of labor is movement. Explore ways in which you can rock, circle, and tilt your pelvis. You can try kneeling, leaning back over your heels or forward onto a pillow placed on a chair or bed or over the top of the headboard; a knee-chest position with your knees placed either side of your body, rather like a frog; on all fours or squatting, with your back firmly supported. Some of these positions are illustrated on pages 210-215.

Your aim is to give the baby as much room as possible in your pelvis by keeping your knees well apart and allowing the uterus to tilt forward onto your abdominal wall and away from your spine. In this position the uterus assumes an egg shape, whereas when you are lying flat on your back it tends to be distorted from this natural shape. When you are upright you are also allowing gravity to help the baby down. In all these positions contract only those muscles you need to use to support yourself, and whenever possible use pillows, furniture, or another person to help you.

You can relieve low backache in labor, especially common when the baby is in an occipito-posterior position (see page 263), by assuming a posture in which your abdomen can hang forward, tilting the baby away from your sacrum, and by gently humping your lower back up and letting it drop down, or circling your pelvis – whichever feels right for you at the time. This position is also convenient for back massage and counterpressure, and because the longitudinal axis of the uterus is then in line with the birth canal it may help the baby

"It was agony to lie on my back during my labor, so though the nurse said it might interfere with the printout from the monitor, I knelt and held on to the bed. That way, I could cope much better."

to rotate into the correct anterior position. If the baby is lying in a posterior position, you will probably have bearing down sensations before you are fully dilated, and are more likely to be able to control the urge if you take some of the pressure off your rectum.

Pressure on the umbilical cord interrupts the baby's blood flow through it. Resulting decelerations of the fetal heart which last after the end of the contractions may be noted if you are having continuous electronic monitoring (see pages 333–334). Decelerations of the fetal heart will lead your doctor to consider undertaking a forceps delivery or cesarean section for fetal distress. If you adopt a position in which your tummy is hanging forward, however, such as on all fours, both the baby and its cord will be tipped away from your spine and the pressure on the cord may be relieved.

Incidentally, it is a good idea to adopt an all-fours position for delivery if the baby has large shoulders that might get stuck (shoulder dystocia). It gives the assistant more room to maneuver, as the baby's head can be extended and drawn out and up toward your anus. Thus the baby's shoulders are delivered nearer your front, and the rest will then follow easily.

Sometimes contractions are inefficient from the very start of labor and do not seem to pick up or, having been effective at first, become weak. In either of these cases it is worth trying a position in which the uterus can most easily form a sphere. It may help to stand facing a wall, with your legs well apart, and leaning forward with your hands resting against the wall.

Practicing movements for labor

There is no reason to spend labor in bed. In fact, lying flat on your back diminishes the oxygen supply to your baby and prevents the uterus from contracting efficiently. While you are pregnant, try out different positions to find those which are most comfortable for you. Always keep your neck free and breathe with the movement, letting go of any tension.

Keep back flat

On all fours

To relieve low backache in labor, get down on all fours and place your hands flat on the floor, as wide apart as your shoulders. Remember not to arch your back.

Keep hands wide apart

Standing lunge

1 *Stand with your feet well grounded and wide apart. Place the flat of your hands against a solid surface, such as a wall. Try rocking and rolling your hips in this position.*

2 *You can step nearer the wall and lean your forearms against it. Rest your head on your forearms. Remember always to keep your shoulders and neck relaxed.*

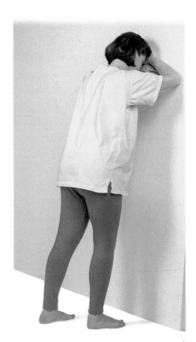

Kneeling up

Kneel on the floor with your back straight, legs apart, ankles turned out, and toes turned in toward each other. This position opens the pelvis and releases any tension in the back.

Kneeling forward

In the same position as before, lean forward with your forearms flat on the floor. This is a good position for opening the pelvis, too, taking the baby's weight off your back and relieving backache.

Hanging abdomen

Try kneeling on all fours, with your forearms on the floor, your knees spread wide, and your abdomen hanging between them. In this position you may like to rock backward and forward. Keep your lower back flat.

Ankles turned out
and toes turned in

Keep knees apart

Lying down

You can relax almost on all fours, but flopped forward onto several pillows, a big floor cushion, or bean bag to support the weight of your uterus.

211

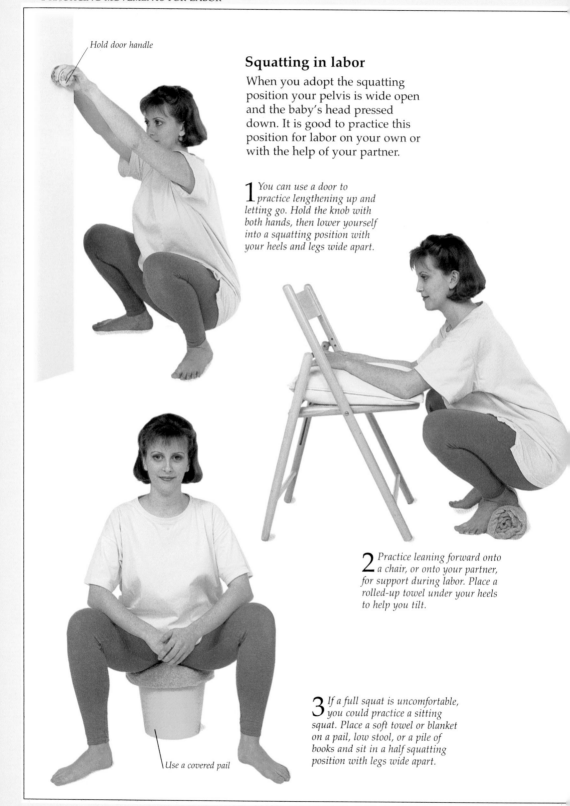

Hold door handle

Squatting in labor

When you adopt the squatting position your pelvis is wide open and the baby's head pressed down. It is good to practice this position for labor on your own or with the help of your partner.

1 *You can use a door to practice lengthening up and letting go. Hold the knob with both hands, then lower yourself into a squatting position with your heels and legs wide apart.*

2 *Practice leaning forward onto a chair, or onto your partner, for support during labor. Place a rolled-up towel under your heels to help you tilt.*

3 *If a full squat is uncomfortable, you could practice a sitting squat. Place a soft towel or blanket on a pail, low stool, or a pile of books and sit in a half squatting position with legs wide apart.*

Use a covered pail

Supported squat

This type of squatting can be practiced with your partner, who supports you as you adopt the squatting position.

1 *Stand facing your partner. Grasp each other's forearms. Your partner bends her knees and leans slightly backward, one foot in front of the other.*

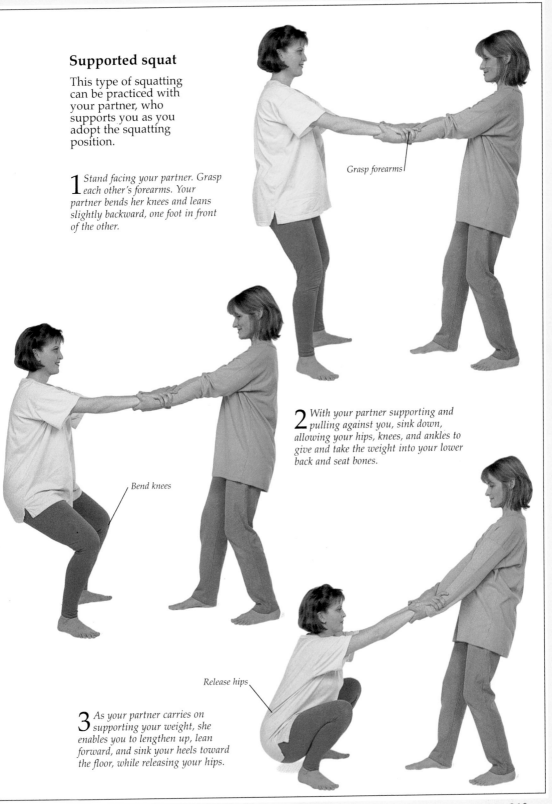

Grasp forearms

Bend knees

2 *With your partner supporting and pulling against you, sink down, allowing your hips, knees, and ankles to give and take the weight into your lower back and seat bones.*

Release hips

3 *As your partner carries on supporting your weight, she enables you to lengthen up, lean forward, and sink your heels toward the floor, while releasing your hips.*

Practicing movements for delivery

Try to explore different positions for delivery with your partner or the people who will be helping you at the birth, so that everyone has some idea of what to expect. Use a doll, a ball, even a grapefruit, as a substitute for the baby.

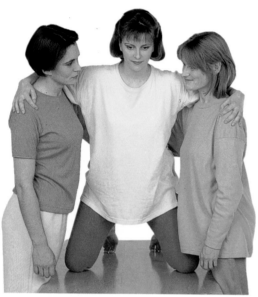

Supported kneeling

Kneeling opens up the pelvis fully and aids the baby's descent. You will feel most secure if you have the support of two helpers, one on each side of you. Practice on a flat surface as a substitute for the bed or delivery table.

Supported squatting

You may find it more comfortable to squat. Again, you will need two helpers, who can support your knees when you are bearing down.

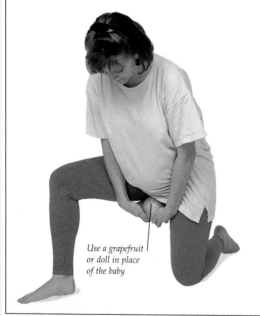

Use a grapefruit or doll in place of the baby

Half kneeling, half squatting

Kneel on one knee with the other leg bent, foot flat on the floor. This half kneeling, half squatting position is the easiest if you are lifting out your baby yourself. It should give you greater stability than kneeling or squatting and allows you to guide the baby out.

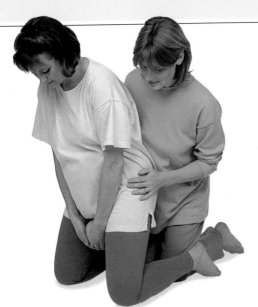

Kneeling upright

Kneeling with your body upright speeds up a very slow second stage. The midwife can deliver your baby from behind and pass her through your legs, or you may be able to lift her out yourself.

Knee-chest position

Kneeling on all fours, with your head down and bottom up, will slow down a second stage that is happening very fast. This position will help you to feel more in control, as well as allowing your vaginal tissues time to soften and stretch so that they are less likely to tear as the baby is born. This can also be useful during the first stage to help turn a posterior baby, and during the transition stage to encourage dilation of an anterior lip (by slowing down the urge to push).

Leaning forward

This is especially good if the second stage of labor is fast, since it will slow you down a little. The midwife will guide your baby out, and then you can turn around and take the baby into your arms.

Practicing for contractions and pushing

The experience of labor is difficult to imagine before you have had a baby. Will contractions be unbearably painful or hardly noticeable? Some women think of the contractions as bigger and bigger hills they have to climb, each hill having its own peak, until they reach the mountain range at the end of the first stage.

THE ACTION OF THE UTERUS

When the uterus contracts it is tightening up, just like any working muscle in the body. Make a very tight fist with one hand and raise your arm so that the big muscle on the inside of your upper arm, the biceps, tightens; then feel it with your other hand. You will notice that the biceps has become hard and is sticking out. If a man does the same thing, his biceps may stick out a good deal more than yours does, because his is probably a bigger muscle. The biceps gets hard as it contracts and it also protrudes. This is because the muscle fibers are shortened and thickened. The same thing happens, on a much larger scale, when the uterus contracts. Like your bulging biceps, the uterus bulges forward in your abdomen when you have a really strong and effective contraction. The strong contractions are the best of all for helping the baby to be born.

Place your hand just above your pubic-hair line at the very bottom of the abdomen. The cervix lies under this area and it is here that you are likely to feel the strong, rhythmic pull as it opens, a pull that will feel tightest at the height of each contraction (see page 246).

You cannot do anything actively to help the baby down the birth canal until the cervix is wide open. A relaxed body and a mind at peace are the most important contributions you can make to the birth process at this stage. It is possible to train yourself to respond with neuromuscular release whenever you want to. Your breathing techniques can help your relaxation and your relaxation can help keep your breathing smooth and rhythmic.

SIMULATING CONTRACTIONS

Contractions are felt mainly as powerful pressure which comes whether or not you want it to, so when you are practicing for them work with a partner and allow him or her to simulate the contractions, deciding when they start, how strong they become, and how long they last. Meet each contraction with a welcoming breath out and use the rhythmic breathing you have learned right through each one, with a long resting breath out at the end. Your partner sits beside you so that you have eye contact with each other. He or she pretends to be your uterus by taking hold of a piece of your flesh, the inner thigh, say, and squeezing it. He will find that grasping a small piece of flesh rather than a big area is more effective. He should be particularly careful if you have a varicose vein, lifting the flesh up off the leg instead of pressing down into the leg, and avoiding the area around the varicose vein. First he squeezes gently, and then tightens his grip to a strong pinch that lasts for about 15 seconds, after which he gradually releases his hold. The contraction should last about 45 seconds in all. This exercise will help him to be aware of what you are feeling and how you react to stress of this kind, so that he can give you emotional support and encouragement. If you do not want him to do this, because you cannot rely on him to be perceptive and sensitive, omit this method.

In between these mock contractions, you can discuss with him how each one felt, and perhaps how he can improve his performance and you can improve yours. In labor this rest space between contractions should be used to prepare you for the next one: do not waste time discussing the contraction that has just ended. It is a good idea to change places so that you become your partner's "uterus" and he can experience this firm gripping sensation and learn how to respond to it. This is important if he is going to be with you during labor and wants to be able to help you by breathing with you when and if contractions become difficult.

PRACTICING FOR STRONGER CONTRACTIONS

Switch roles again and imagine that labor is progressing, with longer and stronger contractions, each reaching its peak about halfway through. Always remember, however, that contractions vary and that it is no good wishing for a "textbook labor" if your own labor proves to be quite different. Some contractions have their peaks about a third of the way through; some may even have two peaks. The important thing is that if you go with your uterus, you tune in with it rather like an orchestra responding to a conductor. The conductor in this case is the uterus. You have to be able, as it were, to "listen" to your uterus to react appropriately to it and be in complete harmony with it. For these stronger contractions your partner grips the flesh of your thigh for a minute or a little longer.

"My partner was very responsive. I never felt he was too tough on me. But it helped me prepare for strong contractions."

When necessary during these longer contractions respond by lifting your breathing above the contraction – breathing more shallowly and more quickly (see page 204). Relax your shoulders and toes; then, as the contraction becomes slightly less intense, allow your breathing to become slower and fuller.

PUSHING

Pushing or bearing down is often described as an extraordinarily athletic activity, as if you could learn to do it the way you learn to do an aerobic exercise. It should not be like this. It is, rather, a spontaneous welling up of energy which culminates in a triumphant push and an opening of the vagina. A woman in the second stage experiences mounting excitement. She feels that she stands on the edge of a chasm with life at its most elemental surging up from the depths, until every nerve and every pore of her body tingles with an urgent desire. She does not have to ask for any instructions. She does not have to ask doctors and midwives if she can "push now." The creative power in her body is intense and overwhelming.

However you are sitting now, rest your hands beneath the lower curve of your abdomen. Take a breath and hold it. Drop your chin forward on your chest and at the same time allow the bulge underneath your hands to press downward and forward, so that from inside your abdomen you are pressing your hands out and moving them forward. You probably feel your perineum moving forward, too. Allow the movement to carry right down through you until you feel the tissues of the vagina spreading out, and then rest. Did you get that feeling of something moving forward? When the baby is ready to be born, this movement helps its head to bulge farther down the birth canal. Though it is useful to learn how to do this beforehand, especially if you practice it without straining and useless effort, most women who are free to do whatever they feel like doing have a spontaneous physical and emotional urge to do it anyway during the second stage of labor (see page 251).

"It felt wonderful to swing into second-stage pushing. I know now what you mean by 'the birth passion.'"

Before going on to practice this pushing movement, make sure that your bladder is completely empty. You can adopt any of the positions suggested on pages 210–213.

One of the best ways of rehearsing pushing is on the toilet since we also release pelvic floor muscles for defecation, so they are not put under unusual strain. If you happen to be constipated, as many women are in late pregnancy (see page 134), this movement will help relieve the constipation and is an excellent way to encourage spontaneous, easy bowel movements.

Each time you practice you will feel more comfortable in an upright position. This will be an advantage during labor, too, as you are more in control of what is happening, can open up more easily for the baby to be born, and can see over the bulge to watch the birth if you want to. Gravity can help you. If you are lying flat, or almost flat, you are pushing the baby uphill, because the uterus is almost at right angles to the vagina (see pages 244–245 and 252–253). In an almost upright position you can lean on your uterus and press the baby down.

After you have done this gentle pushing a few times, begin to work with your partner. To start, you might like to try sitting. Your partner sits near your head with a pillow over the forearm and supports your head and shoulders with it. This gives you a very wide base of support. With your helper's hands over your lower abdomen, you can both feel what is happening inside. Drop your head forward onto your chest, so that you do not strain with your throat muscles and produce a grunting sound. Take a breath. Lean forward and press from inside steadily out, slowly, gently; a little bit more; let it go; let the breath out and rest. While you are practicing, your partner's hand pressed firmly against your lower abdomen gives you something to press against and guide you. It is easier to bear down when your baby is actually in the birth canal waiting to be born because you have something to press against. Allow your pelvic floor muscles to bulge forward like a heavy sack of apples. When you have felt and noted the sensation this produces, lift your pelvic floor up again so that it is well toned and not sagging (see page 118). Think of it as smiling.

TRYING OTHER POSITIONS

When you are confident that you have the feeling of pushing with complete release of your pelvic floor muscles in this position, go on to explore other positions which may feel right when you are in labor. Experiment with every open position – on a mattress on the floor, on the bed, leaning over or against furniture, using cushions and other kinds of support, cradled by another human body – in which you can feel in touch with what is happening and free to let the energy of the uterus sweep through you to birth. An almost impossible posture in which to do this is, as you can imagine, lying flat on your back with your legs in the air in the standard lithotomy position, or with your knees scrunched up to your chest while you try to roll yourself into a ball – both of which used to be standard positions for the second stage of labor and delivery in contemporary hospitals.

Since the eighties, however, there have been widespread changes in practice. Now in many hospitals in the United States, women are encouraged to find any position, and make any movement, that is going to be comfortable for them, and to give birth kneeling, sitting, squatting, or on all fours, if they wish.

Windows into the uterus

Apart from the routine urine and blood pressure tests you have every time you go to the doctor or midwife (see pages 44–45), other investigations may be done during pregnancy. Whether they are done at all, or how often they are done, will depend not only on there being some specific reason for them, but on the part of the country you are in and therefore on the sort of hospital or clinic you attend. Teaching hospitals have far more sophisticated equipment and are also engaged in research, so, for example, if you are in a large city you may have ultrasound two or three times during your pregnancy (see page 223). It is up to you whether or not you accept it. Some physicians have an ultrasound machine in their offices, and tend to use it frequently during pregnancy.

Screening for genetic disabilities

Screening aims to identify pregnancies in which the risk of abnormality is higher than usual. *Most women whose screening tests reveal possible abnormalities have normal babies.* Screening may be followed by diagnostic tests. These are much more precise.

You have the right to say no to any tests. You may have ethical or religious reasons for refusing them or simply not feel happy about having them. You do not have to give a reason. All invasive diagnostic tests which entail entering the uterus bring some risk for the baby. Your doctor should tell you what this risk is.*

But every screening and every diagnostic test, even a simple blood test for sugar in the urine, and measurements of blood pressure and weight gain, can be emotionally invasive. If a test raises the question of possible termination of a pregnancy it is bound to cause anxiety, and even after this anxiety is relieved theoretically by a negative test result, a woman is often left feeling anxious, and sometimes can be convinced that there must be something wrong with her baby. She may feel that a screening test that has produced a positive result must mean something bad has happened. She may feel that she has not been told the whole truth. So all screening and diagnostic tests have side effects, although it is difficult to measure these because they are emotional, rather than physical.

AFP screening

Alphafetoprotein (AFP) is a substance produced in the early phases of pregnancy by the embryo's yolk sac and later on by the fetal liver. It is known that when the levels of AFP are abnormally high a large proportion of babies are found to be suffering from neural tube defects such as spina bifida (when part of the spinal cord is outside the baby's body) and anencephaly (the absence of a brain). The baby without a brain cannot live, but babies with spina bifida do sometimes live, although they are usually paralyzed below the waist and will often develop hydrocephalus (water on the brain) as well. If the AFP level is unusually low, one possible cause is that the baby has Down's syndrome.

Levels of AFP in a pregnant woman's blood double about every five weeks in the fourth, fifth, and sixth months of pregnancy, but earlier than this they are usually low. The best time to screen your blood for AFP is therefore in early pregnancy, before the 18th week. Results come through in two to three days.

If your dates are wrong and pregnancy is more advanced than you think, you may find that the AFP level is suspiciously high. The proportion will also be high if you are expecting twins. It may be low if your pregnancy is less advanced than you think. In both these cases ultrasound will be used to help figure out the real age of the baby and whether you are expecting more than one.

If the rate appears to be high or low for no obvious reason, another blood test may be done to double-check; if the level of AFP is then found to be two or three times higher or lower than the median level of a sample group, you will be offered an ultrasound and/or amniocentesis. This means that two or three out of every hundred women will agree to amniocentesis, and suffer the risk attached to it (one or two babies out of every hundred are miscarried as a result of amniocentesis). If your AFP level is high the risk of having amniocentesis can be greater than the risk of bearing an affected baby. Although there are differences of opinion within the medical profession, AFP screening is now done routinely in the United States; the point at which you are offered amniocentesis will vary depending on the center where your blood is tested.

"I was terribly worried when I had the news that my AFP level was abnormally low, but it turned out that my dates were wrong."

As with all medical intervention, solving the problem is a matter of a delicate balance between risks and there is no easy answer. If AFP testing shows that your level is high or low, discuss the matter with your doctor, taking your partner or a family member with you so that you can talk it over together afterward and make a shared decision about whether or not to have amniocentesis.

The triple screen, or Prenatal Risk Profile, is a mix of AFP and other blood tests and is done at 16 weeks. With this test AFP and the pregnancy hormones human chorionic gonadotrophin (HCG) and estriol are measured. It is fast replacing the AFP screening test because of its added accuracy. Still, however, it cannot pinpoint whether the baby has chromosomal abnormalities such as Down's or Turner's syndrome, or abnormalities of the central nervous system, but it can show whether the risk is higher or lower than

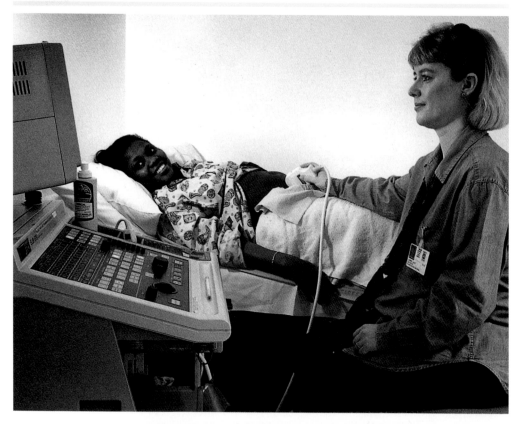

Above

Ultrasound scan in
progress. You may
be given more than
one, or even a series
of scans, every few
weeks during
pregnancy. Or, in
smaller hospitals,
you may not be
given a scan at all.

Right

This image shows the
baby's shape clearly,
but it is often more
difficult to identify the
different parts, some of
which may be hidden
behind other of the
baby's organs.

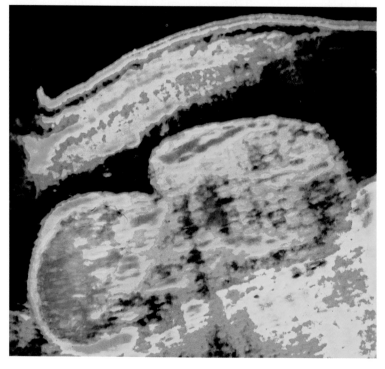

usual. One in 30 women has a high AFP result. Most positive results are followed by the birth of a normal baby. A baby who has Down's syndrome tends to be small and produces less AFP than usual. If there is also a combination of a high level of HCG and a low level of estriol there is more chance of having a Down's syndrome baby.

Ultrasound

Ultrasound (also referred to as a scan, an ultrasound scan, or a sonogram) works on the principle of bouncing very high frequency sound waves (far higher than the human ear can detect) off solid objects. It is a method which has been used for many years by navies to locate submarines in wartime, and by fishermen to locate schools of deep sea fish. Echo sounders in yachts work in a similar way.

USES OF ULTRASOUND
In pregnancy ultrasound is used to obtain a picture of the baby in the uterus. It is possible to see the tiny fetus kicking from the end of the second month, and after 28 weeks breathing movements can be observed. There are a number of reasons why scans are done:

To confirm pregnancy A scan can be used to confirm pregnancy very early on, before clinical tests are effective: it is capable of detecting changes in the uterus that cannot yet be revealed by physical examination. From eight weeks it can show the embryo with its heart pulsing. You can find out if you are having twins, for instance, when you are only eight weeks pregnant, although this is unnecessary, does not make birth any safer for them, and is more likely to result in the pregnancy and birth being medicalized.

To establish the estimated date of delivery Scans are frequently used routinely in large hospitals, where you may expect to have them done at least two or three times during pregnancy. A scan will probably be offered at about 16 weeks in order to establish the estimated delivery date. At this stage the age of the baby can be established to within 10 days (later in pregnancy it is more difficult to be precise because babies of the same age may grow at very different rates). It may be suggested that you be scanned again in the middle and at the end of pregnancy, or even more frequently, at intervals of a few weeks. This is called serial assessment and does not mean that anything is wrong. Only when the scan is used in this way can the clues that it gives about the rate of fetal growth be taken seriously. In smaller hospitals you may never have a scan at all, unless there is a specific reason for it.

To detect certain handicaps At 20 weeks, ultrasound can be used to detect certain abnormalities in the fetus, including congenital heart defects, gastrointestinal and kidney malformations, and spina bifida. This is called an *anomaly scan*. These physical defects can be detected earlier in the pregnancy if the ultrasound probe is inserted into your vagina instead of being placed on top of your abdomen. Most babies with severe chromosome abnormalities have extra fluid behind the neck, and this can be detected by a scan with an experienced radiologist at 12 weeks.

To assess maturity in late pregnancy Late in pregnancy a scan is sometimes used to indicate whether or not a baby is ready to be born. The scan cannot show whether the baby's lungs are mature enough for breathing, but by accurately measuring the size of the baby's head it can establish the approximate age of the baby as well as its current stage of development.

To detect how the baby is lying It may be important to find out how your baby is lying in the uterus (for example, whether the baby is lying head down or is in the breech position), but the doctor cannot know this information for certain from carrying out a standard manual examination. Ultrasound can, however, tell with accuracy. This knowledge may actually make all the difference to you and have an effect on your decisions about the birth, particularly, for instance, if you want to have your baby at home.

If the baby is shown to be lying in a good position, you can proceed with confidence in your plans for a home birth. However, if the baby is seen to be lying awkwardly, you will accept that it might be more sensible to go to the hospital for the birth. Either way, you and your doctor can be guided by the information provided by the scan. But this scan should not be a condition for you having a home birth. You are free to decline to have it.

To assess the condition and position of the placenta When there is bleeding in late pregnancy ultrasound can be used to locate the accurate position of the placenta. The potential danger is that the placenta might be blocking the baby's way out of the uterus (this is a condition known as placenta previa and it is described further on page 137). In fact, a scan done in the first few months of pregnancy often gives the impression that the placenta is lying low on the wall of the uterus, but as the pregnancy progresses and the uterus enlarges the placenta usually proves to be in the right place after all. Occasionally bleeding in late pregnancy means that the roots of the placenta are becoming dislodged with prelabor contractions, indicating that the baby's oxygen supply would be cut if labor were allowed to proceed. A scan can show this clearly, and a cesarean section can be performed to save the baby. Used in this way, or as a preliminary to amniocentesis (see page 227), ultrasound has undoubted advantages.

"I found the scans at sixteen weeks and thirty weeks exciting because the images on the screen were explained to me so that I could understand them."

How ultrasound works

You undress, put on a hospital gown, and lie on your back beside the scanner. Your abdomen is oiled and then a transducer is slowly passed over it in different directions. The transducer is a machine which picks up echoes from the different planes of your own organs and also the developing baby's tissues, and which then translates the information it has picked up into the form of a map on a screen that looks like a television screen.

A scan done in the first few months of pregnancy gains in clarity if your bladder is full and therefore clearly visible, so you will probably be asked to drink a lot of water first and not urinate for an hour or so before the scan. Do not expect to see an immediately recognizable picture of your baby, even in late pregnancy; if a doctor is present, ask to have the picture interpreted, because it may look more like a map of the moon than a baby, and you may find it difficult to make out the different parts of the baby.

Another technique involves the use of a specially designed intravaginal transducer which is sometimes used in very early pregnancy and also for other specific purposes.

Is ultrasound safe?

As far as we know, ultrasound is safe, and is certainly much safer than X-rays (see page 110), which provided the only method of gaining information about the baby in the uterus before the scan was developed. On the other hand, it is known that high frequency sound waves continued for a long time can cause damage to hearing in an adult. Questions have therefore been raised about the possible effects on the baby's hearing since, although the sound waves are bounced off the baby for only a short time, the baby may be vulnerable at certain stages of its development. Babies are not born deaf after having ultrasound, but no one yet knows if any of them will suffer delayed effects in later life.

Ultrasound does have other effects on the body that are not yet fully understood. It causes heat to be generated in body tissues, and tiny bubbles inside tissue may dance in reaction to the sound waves. This does not necessarily mean that diagnostic ultrasound at the level at which it is normally used in pregnancy is dangerous. But it does imply that we should be asking searching questions about possible long-term effects. It could be that ultrasound has some subtle deleterious effects on especially vulnerable babies in the first 12 weeks of pregnancy, during the time that the major organs of the body are in the process of being formed.

Research carried out to date suggests that, in the words of the British Chief Medical Officer of Health, "All ultrasound exposure should be justified and limited to the minimum necessary for the diagnostic purpose. The greatest risk with ultrasound is from inaccurate interpretation of the image, rather than from any physical hazard of the ultrasonic field."*

SOME SAFETY MEASURES

It makes sense to expose pregnant women and the babies inside them to ultrasound only when a diagnosis is needed which cannot be made without ultrasound, and when that diagnosis would result in some change in the kind of care that is given. This rules out routine scanning at 16 weeks – now the accepted practice in many countries. It also rules out using ultrasound simply because parents would like to see a picture of the baby or to enable a woman or her partner to "bond" with the fetus. Many obstetricians are rather keen on this and believe that they can make a contribution toward ensuring that babies are well mothered by doing routine ultrasound scans. They do not realize that there are other – better and more intimate – ways of becoming aware of the baby (see page 237).

When ultrasound is used, the length of time you are exposed to it should be limited, and when you are discussing what you can see on the screen, ask for the image to be frozen. Understandably, a woman is fascinated by seeing her baby's movements on the screen; in Denmark the scanner is linked to a video camera so that the examination can be replayed later, the woman can see her baby moving, and there can be full discussion about it without exposing the baby unnecessarily to ultrasound.

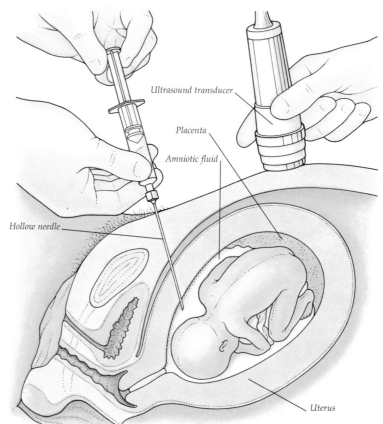

Ultrasound transducer

Placenta

Amniotic fluid

Hollow needle

Uterus

Amniocentesis
This can be performed under ultrasound. When amniocentesis is done under guided ultrasound there is a much reduced chance of the needle touching or in any way harming the baby.

Amniocentesis

Amniocentesis is a procedure which has been developed in order to detect any abnormalities of the baby's central nervous system (spina bifida and anencephaly) and some other genetic abnormalities such as Down's syndrome (mongolism). The sex of the baby can also be determined by this procedure, so you can discover if any sex-linked disorders might have been inherited.

HOW AMNIOCENTESIS WORKS

Under a local anesthetic a hollow needle is inserted through your abdominal wall into the uterus, where about half an ounce (14 g) of the water in which the fetus is lying is sucked out. This fluid has been swallowed by the fetus and passed out of its body again either through its mouth or bladder; it is full of cells from the skin and other organs which, when analyzed, can provide valuable clues to the baby's genetic makeup. The fluid is then spun in a centrifuge to separate the cells from the liquid. The cells are left to multiply and are then analyzed. Results are available in two to four weeks.

In the 1950s, when amniocentesis was first invented, mistakes were sometimes made and the needle penetrated placental tissues, causing occasional miscarriage. But now ultrasound techniques are used to locate the placenta and the risks of damage to the placenta have been very much reduced. There still remains a 1 or 2 percent chance, however, that amniocentesis may cause miscarriage.

Because of this small but definite risk, there is no point in having amniocentesis unless there is a well-above-average chance of your baby being born abnormal. You will have thought carefully about the implications of discovering that something is wrong with your baby and have decided that you would opt for termination. In some parts of the country, amniocentesis is offered to all women over 35, since the incidence of some disorders it is designed to detect rises sharply with age. You should be able to talk to a counselor *before* an invasive diagnostic test. If an abnormality is revealed by the test, counseling should be immediately available to both parents.

There is a 1 to 2 percent risk of miscarriage when amniocentesis is performed after 16 weeks. Experiments have been done with amniocentesis as early as nine weeks, but the miscarriage rate then is between 3 percent and 7 percent, depending on the skill of the operator. Since less fluid is available at that stage of pregnancy, the lab is unable to grow a cell culture in up to 21 percent of cases, so the amniocentesis has to be done again.*

When amniocentesis is done between the 14th and 16th weeks of pregnancy, when many women have felt the first fetal movement, the decision to terminate a pregnancy is a distressing one to make and the termination is riskier than one that is performed earlier in pregnancy. The woman who is going through this experience needs generous emotional support from her partner and family.

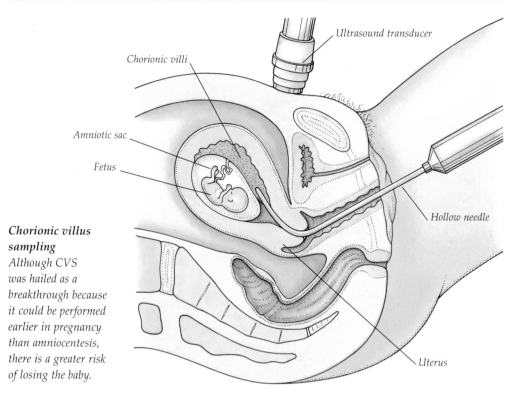

Chorionic villi

Ultrasound transducer

Amniotic sac

Fetus

Hollow needle

Uterus

**Chorionic villus
sampling**
*Although CVS
was hailed as a
breakthrough because
it could be performed
earlier in pregnancy
than amniocentesis,
there is a greater risk
of losing the baby.*

Amniocentesis is sometimes performed late in pregnancy if it looks as if the baby may possibly be born preterm or if there is a complication such as placenta previa (see page 137), in which case the risks of continuing the pregnancy must be weighed carefully against the risks of delivering a child with immature lungs. The amniotic fluid can reveal vital information as to whether the fetal lungs are mature, that is, whether they are now strong enough to allow the baby to breathe normally after birth. If the lungs are discovered to be still immature, then labor will not be induced, nor will the pregnancy be terminated via cesarean. Instead, appropriate drugs (corticosteriods) and some more time will be allowed. Results of amniocentesis for lung maturity are available immediately.

Chorionic villus sampling

Chorionic villus sampling – CVS for short – entails taking a sample of tissue from the part of the outer membrane around the embryo that will later become the placenta, in order to diagnose whether or not a fetus will have a genetic handicap. One of the handicaps this process of testing cannot detect, however, is spina bifida. CVS can be carried out before the pregnancy runs to 12 weeks – even as early as 10 weeks after conception – so that an abnormal fetus can be terminated much earlier in the pregnancy.

The risks of CVS, however, outweigh any of the benefits. There is a high incidence of infection, bleeding, and miscarriage following CVS. It has also been linked to limb defects. This was not discovered by a medical researcher, but by a woman who had CVS and gave birth to a child with deformed limbs. After meeting another woman whose baby had been diagnosed with similar abnormalities after she had CVS at the same hospital, she reported it to a genetic counselor. She was told by doctors that there was no connection. But she continued to ask questions. A study was then conducted that suggested that there was an association. The earlier the CVS the more likely a limb deformity will occur, probably as a result of interfering with the blood supply to the limb.* Amniocentesis in the second trimester of pregnancy is safer than CVS.

Umbilical vein sampling

At the end of the seventies, fetoscopy – photographing the baby with a telescope introduced into the uterus – was the latest technique for finding out exactly what was happening to babies known to be at risk. Unfortunately, the risk of miscarriage after the procedure proved to be as high as 5 to 10 percent. Fetoscopy has now been superseded by umbilical vein sampling (cordocentesis), hailed by Dr. Stuart Weiner of the University of Pennsylvania as opening up "a whole new area of fetal medicine."*

In umbilical vein sampling, a very fine needle is passed through the mother's abdomen and uterus into the fetal vein in the umbilical cord and blood is withdrawn so that it can be tested. Intrauterine blood transfusions can also be given in this way, and drugs can be injected directly into the baby. Because the fetal vein is frail in early pregnancy, the technique cannot be performed until after 18 weeks.

Umbilical vein sampling is now being used in addition to amniocentesis and ultrasound; it is also used when there is Rhesus disease (see page 113), in order to diagnose hemophilia in a baby, and to check for any metabolic disorders as well as any infections such as toxoplasmosis and rubella.

Dr. Kypros Nicolaides, of King's College Hospital, London, estimates that when the method is used by experienced doctors, the risk of losing a baby is only 1 to 2 percent – the same as that for amniocentesis and chorionic villus sampling in that hospital. He emphasized to me that "the greatest risk of any operative technique in pregnancy is always the skill and experience of the operator."

ETHICAL DILEMMAS

The developing science of prenatal diagnosis presents ethical dilemmas. In many countries it is unregulated. In some countries no counseling is offered. In others, telephone counseling is available. Some firms offer do-it-yourself tests for conditions such as cystic fibrosis – a disorder of the lungs and digestive system.

Making decisions about whether or not to have screening, and if so, exactly what to screen for, is becoming increasingly complex. Would you want to know if a child you were bearing, or yourself, or other members of your family, run an increased risk of having heart trouble in middle age, developing breast cancer at some stage, or Alzheimer's in old age? If you did, how great would the risk have to be for you to go through genetic tests? And how great the risk for you to decide on termination of a pregnancy? How accurate would tests have to be? Suppose there was nothing you could do to prevent an illness from developing or to treat it effectively if you or your child did get it; would you still want to know? Would you want to have this knowledge if future employment prospects and insurance depended on test results indicating that there was no additional risk?

"I didn't want these tests, but I knew that everyone would blame me if I had an imperfect baby that I could have aborted."

The decision to terminate pregnancy is implicit in screening procedures that are now readily available, such as those for Down's syndrome and neural tube defects. You may feel absolutely sure about what you would want if it turned out that there was a high probability of the baby's being handicapped. But now screening is becoming available for conditions which do not produce serious handicap, which are not life-threatening, and which may develop only in adolescence or later. How can you weigh up the pros and cons of such tests? You may want to discuss these issues with your partner, a close friend, or your doctor or midwife, who can put you in touch with a genetic counselor.

The genetic counselor may be of real assistance in helping you establish your priorities. She will give you the facts that are known and discuss your options. She will not advocate termination, though she will support you if that is what you want. She will not persuade you to go on with a pregnancy, but will support you if that is your choice. It is up to you. You cannot predict how you would react to a positive test result. Even if you are certain that you would not terminate a pregnancy, you may wish to know ahead of time that a baby is not going to be perfect, so that you can plan ahead, or you may prefer not to have screening, and to wait and see.

The last few weeks

Your baby is almost ready to be born. The firm body is nestled in the cup of your pelvis, and the little arms and legs are plumper as the last layers of fat form to help the baby's temperature control system function efficiently after birth. Sometimes the baby gains as much as 8 oz (226 g) in a week at this stage of pregnancy.

PHYSICAL SENSATIONS

You may feel fewer big body movements but an insistent kicking underneath your ribs on one side or the other. If your abdominal wall is thin you may even be able to hold your baby's foot. There may be other strange movements, perhaps a sudden urgent knocking which continues intermittently for half an hour or more. This can be so pronounced that you may worry in case your baby is having something like an epileptic seizure. But it is definitely not that. The baby may have hiccups, perhaps because he was gulping amniotic fluid; or he may have lost his thumb which he was contentedly sucking, and is "rooting" to find it again, with quick, darting movements of the head from side to side, just as after birth he will search for the nipple. The baby's head feels like a melon or coconut pressing through your bulging perineal tissues.

There may also be odd sensations in your vagina. Sometimes there is a sharp buzz like a mild electric shock or a tickle. The baby may be lifting and lowering her head against your pelvic floor muscles in another movement which she will do naturally after birth too, when put down on her front in an alert state. There are times when your baby is sleeping or drowsy, and other times active – often in the evenings.

MIXED EMOTIONS

Conflicting emotions are characteristic of these last weeks. You may be tired of being pregnant, but on the other hand the state you are in now is a condition you know and understand, whereas in front of you there is an unknown challenge. So sometimes you want the baby out and long to get on with the labor. But at other times you feel safer as you are, and anxious about the future. Some women say that as the birthday draws nearer they feel irritated with the pregnancy. This produces an emotional state which makes them welcome the start of labor. Other women relish these last weeks.

PRENATAL DEPRESSION

It is common to feel low some time in the last six weeks of pregnancy. If you have been practicing and preparing for a natural birth you may experience a kind of stage fright and be convinced that you are going to forget everything when you are actually in labor. You may also be feeling physically tired and heavy with the weight of your burden.

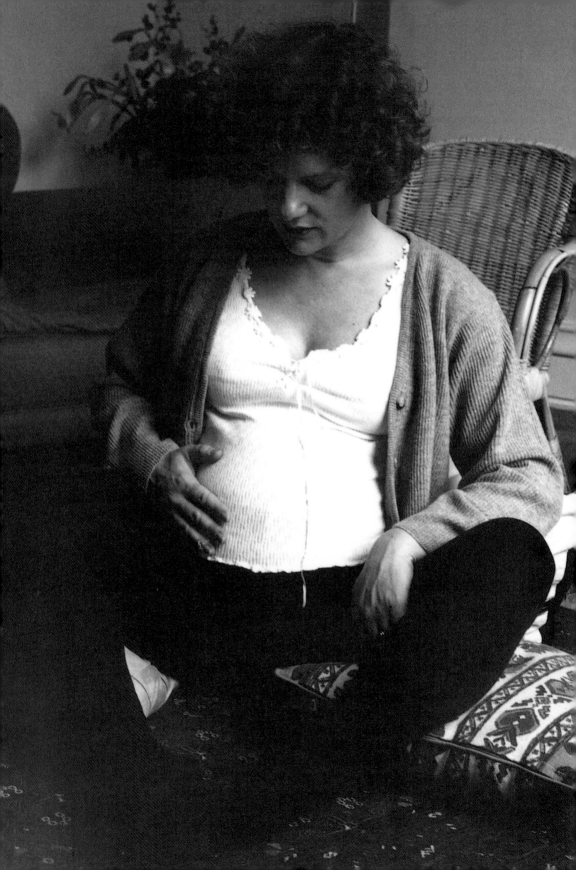

Prenatal depression, though usually shortlived and spasmodic, is a fact of life for some women. It may suggest a need for more rest. You may feel very different if you lie down to rest in a darkened room in the middle of the day, have some early nights, and adjust your activity to slower, gentler rhythms if possible.

If you find yourself becoming depressed at this stage of pregnancy, have a talk with your childbirth educator who, probably a mother herself, will understand what you are feeling.

Thinking ahead to labor

You will probably be thinking a great deal about labor in the last few weeks, wondering what it will be like. One of the things you can find out is the position your baby is in; remember to ask when you are being examined by the doctor or midwife. The ideal position for a straightforward labor (and by far the most common) is head down and anterior. Some babies present in different positions, as posterior or breech, for example. Delivery may be less straightforward with the baby in these positions (see pages 262–276).

THE BABY WHO IS PRESENTING AS A POSTERIOR

If your baby is lying head down with its back against your spine, limbs toward your front, it may be because it is still rather small or you have a roomy pelvis so that it can still move freely. Women who think they are due but who really have another two weeks or so to go before delivery can have a baby who is still moving like this – sometimes posterior, sometimes anterior. Pre-labor and early-labor contractions usually work to turn the baby into an anterior position in a matter of hours.

If your baby seems to have settled in a posterior position, you may find that you can coax it to change during one of its waking periods by very firm hand pressure. The posterior baby is usually lying with the ball of the head on your right side. You want to shift the baby's body round and over toward the left. Treat the baby as if it were a sleeping kitten which you were trying to scoop off the middle of a sofa and move over to the left side. Curve the side of your hand around the most solid section of its bulk and firmly, little by little, edge it over. Keep the fingers of your other hand over your navel. If you are successful the saucer-shaped dip there (the space between the arms and legs of a posterior baby) will become – at least temporarily – a hard convex curve (the back of a baby in an anterior position). You will be able to detect the change as your navel will probably stick out. Talk to your baby as you move it. This is not simply a clinical exercise, but a bit of maternal persuasion.

Once the baby is stretching the uterus to its utmost it is a tight fit and you will probably not be able to move it. Wait and see whether the first-stage contractions will do it for you, and explore the positions and movements which aid rotation while you are in labor.

Opposite
Toward the end of pregnancy, especially with the first baby, it is natural to feel a kind of stage fright as the great day approaches.

Helping a breech to turn You can try to tip the baby up out of your pelvis yourself by adopting a position with head down and bottom in the air for 15 minutes three times a day (before meals). Some babies turn a somersault once clear of the pelvis – even after 37 weeks.* A knee-chest position, leaning over a firm bean bag on your front with your head on the floor and your hips as high as possible, or lying in this position on a steeply sloping, cushion-padded ironing board propped between the bed and the wall or a solid piece of furniture, offers a range of options – none of them, it must be admitted, very comfortable in late pregnancy! But if you are able to turn the baby, it may make the difference between a vaginal and a cesarean birth.

THE BABY WHO IS PRESENTING AS A BREECH
Most babies tip head down – in the vertex or cephalic position – between the seventh and the eighth month. If your baby is still presenting buttocks first (breech) after 36 weeks, the doctor may try to turn the baby – a procedure known as external version. There is little point in doing it earlier, as the baby often turns back again.*

How external version is done You empty your bladder and then lie down on your back with your knees drawn up. The doctor will probably do an ultrasound scan to find out exactly how the baby is lying and will listen to the baby's heartbeats before and after turning the baby. You may be asked to lie on a sloping examining table with your legs up and head down for about a quarter of an hour before the maneuver, so that the baby is encouraged to move clear of the pelvis. Spend this time relaxing as deeply as you can; use abdominal massage to help you release your tummy muscles and use your breathing to help you as well. The uterus often contracts when the doctor's hands are pressing on it, and this makes it more difficult to turn the baby.

When you feel the doctor's hands on your tummy, release and flow toward the touch. Give a long, slow breath out and let your lower tummy bulge out in a great wave as you do so. If the version is successful and the baby turns, walk around for an hour or two so that there is the best chance of fixing the baby head down. Some babies turn back into the breech position. Seven times out of ten, however, external version at 37 to 39 weeks is successful.* But if the baby tips back again you will have to accept that she prefers it; discuss with your doctor the sort of delivery you will have (see page 267).

Being "overdue"

Concern about the best things to eat, the position of the baby, and whether labor will be straightforward can be preoccupying in the last few weeks. If you actually go *past* the estimated date of delivery you may really begin to worry; you are now consigned to the category of the woman who is "overdue."

THE ESTIMATED DELIVERY DATE

The date that you are given at the beginning of pregnancy for your baby's birth (EDD or EDC) is only a statistical mean. Studies show that only 5 percent of babies arrive on that day. If you look at the 95 babies out of 100 who do not put in an appearance on the "correct" date you find that three out of ten babies come before the EDD and seven out of ten come *after* it. This is partly because women's menstrual cycles are of different lengths, and ovulation – and hence conception – may occur at different times within it. But by the time you reach the end of your pregnancy you may not be able to prevent yourself from fixing on the expected delivery date as your goal. If it comes and goes and nothing happens, you may become very depressed. Each day that passes seems like a week, and each week

---

CHOOSING WHAT TO PACK

Now is the time to think about the comfort things you want available during and after birth. Select a small number of items that you think will be most useful, and gather them together in a lightweight, easily carried duffel or suitcase. Choose from the following:

Comfort aids for birth

- Cotton pyjama top, short nightdress, or baggy T-shirt.
- Face cloth.
- Two small sponges to be dipped in ice water and used for sponging your face, wetting your lips, and sucking between contractions.
- Lip salve or vaseline for dry lips.
- Lavender and other essential oils.
- Talc, cornstarch, or massage oil to avoid skin friction when massaged.
- Cassettes and cassette player.
- Candles, matches.
- Swimwear so that your birth partner can go with you under the shower if you wish.
- Camera and plenty of film, including fast film for night-time if you do not want to use a flash/video camera.
- Small spray bottle for moistening the face with cold water.
- Baby's hot water bottle or a picnic thermal pack to be heated up in water for use as a hot compress in the small of your back, between your legs, etc.
- Rolling pin with cloth tied over it to iron away backache.
- Honey to keep your strength up in early labor.
- Paper bag to breathe into in case you hyperventilate.
- Beautiful object to use as a visual focus if you wish, e.g., painting, photographs, or sculpture.
- Nourishing snacks for your birth partner.
- Notebook to serve as logbook.
- Hairbrush and ribbons or bands if your hair is long; comb.
- Books, magazines, playing cards, chess, scrabble, crosswords, etc.
- Herb teas or glucose drinks.
- Bendy straws.

Comfort aids for after the birth

- Calendula and hypericum cream from a homeopathic pharmacy, for a sore perineum.
- Bottle of witch hazel lotion with which you can soak the sanitary pad next to the stitches.
- Sanitary pads, largest size.
- Soft toilet paper.
- Cotton nightgowns and robe.
- Nursing bras.
- Toiletry bag, and makeup if you wish.
- Earplugs.
- Writing paper and envelopes.
- List of telephone numbers.
- Coins for the phone/cellular phone.
- Deodorant (you will perspire heavily in the few days after birth).
- Baby clothes.
- Clothes to wear going home.
- Baby seat for car.

more like a month. Unless you plan for activity and recreation during this time your morale will drop to rock bottom. If you find that you are getting despondent, remind yourself that, though very few babies are born on the day predicted for their birth, nine out of ten do put in an appearance within ten days of the expected date. There is nothing abnormal about a baby who is nine days "late." Many women, however, are made to feel "under sentence of induction" if they go as little as a week past their expected date. Some obstetricians induce labor when the woman goes even a few days beyond the estimated date, and this is done without further investigation. If your pregnancy is normal and you are in good health, being ten days "late" is a very poor reason for induction.

Whether induction (see pages 324–328) is really necessary or not depends entirely on the baby's wellbeing toward the end of your pregnancy. The baby's wellbeing, in turn, actually depends on the condition of the placenta.

The aging placenta

At the end of pregnancy the placenta looks like a piece of raw liver about the size of a dinner plate and the thickness of your little finger. Like every other human organ, it has a youth and an old age. An elderly placenta works less well. If labor does not start at the right time (which may be anywhere between two weeks before and two weeks after the estimated date of delivery – and very occasionally later still) the placenta may fail to support the baby in the uterus. The baby is then deprived of nourishment.

This is why obstetricians become concerned if a pregnancy is prolonged much past the date worked out for the birth. Even so, a baby who is thought to be overdue may prove at birth not to be postmature at all. There are various ways in which the baby's condition can be assessed. Some are tests which doctors do to you; probably the most reliable method is one which you can do for yourself (see page 237).

Urinary estriol tests

Some doctors still try to test whether the placenta is functioning well enough by measuring the output of estriol in your urine or blood. (Estriol is a form of the hormone estrogen which is very important for the baby's growth.) The level of estriol produced by the placenta rises during the course of your pregnancy. But just before labor starts, the level of estriol drops.

The proportion of estriol in your urine varies by as much as 30 percent with different readings, however, and there are day-to-day variations even when everything is normal. When levels of estriol output are compared with the information provided by an ultrasound scan to assess the baby's growth, there is often a discrepancy. Recent research has shown that the measurement of placental proteins and hormones is unlikely to be beneficial.*

ELECTRONIC FETAL MONITORING AND ULTRASOUND

Ultrasound may be used to check both the flow of blood through the umbilical blood vessels (Doppler flow studies) and the volume of amniotic fluid. Electronic fetal monitoring (called a non-stress test) can reveal whether the baby's heartbeat shows the usual variations when the baby is active and at rest. If the baby's heartbeat is normal, induction of labor has no advantage, and may be harmful.

FETAL MOVEMENT RECORDING

One of the most accurate ways of knowing if a baby is doing well while still inside the uterus in late pregnancy is something you can do for yourself. This is to note the baby's movements. In the last weeks of pregnancy, until it engages, the baby usually wriggles, dips and turns, bangs and kicks, and moves like a porpoise from side to side in great sweeps of activity which you can actually see through your clothing. Once it has engaged it often moves less because it is a rather tight fit. Even so, a vigorous baby moves even after it has gone down into the pelvis, though the movements then tend to be just the knocks from knees and feet. You feel as if you have a rolling coconut in your groin or just behind your pubis (the head turning), and later the strange buzzing sensation of the engaged head bouncing against the pelvic floor muscles (see page 231).

You may not normally be aware of most of these movements while you are busy but as soon as you sit down to rest, or lie down hoping to sleep, you cannot help noticing them. They are a good sign that your baby is healthy. Studies of fetal activity show that every baby has its own individual pattern of waking and sleeping inside the uterus, and by late pregnancy you will have probably noticed what your baby's pattern is. But sometimes you may be awake and expect a kick; if nothing happens it can be disconcerting. In fact, the baby is probably fast asleep; if you have had an alcoholic drink or taken sleeping pills, your baby will probably be affected by them too.

Mothers do vary in the extent that they observe fetal movements. Sometimes this awareness is related to the amount of amniotic fluid, since the fluid cushions movements. If you are preoccupied and concentrating hard on something you may also be less aware of fetal activity. If you are still working outside the home, or busy inside it, there may be too much going on for you to notice any fetal movements. Each woman's experience of the movements is fairly consistent if her baby is thriving in the uterus, bearing in mind that the nature of movements changes after the baby has engaged, as described above. If for any reason it is thought by your doctor or midwife that your baby may be "at risk" (usually because you have not put on weight for two or more weeks, your tummy has not got bigger during this time, or because you are "overdue"), you can use your own sensitive awareness about your baby's movements to keep a check on its wellbeing inside you.

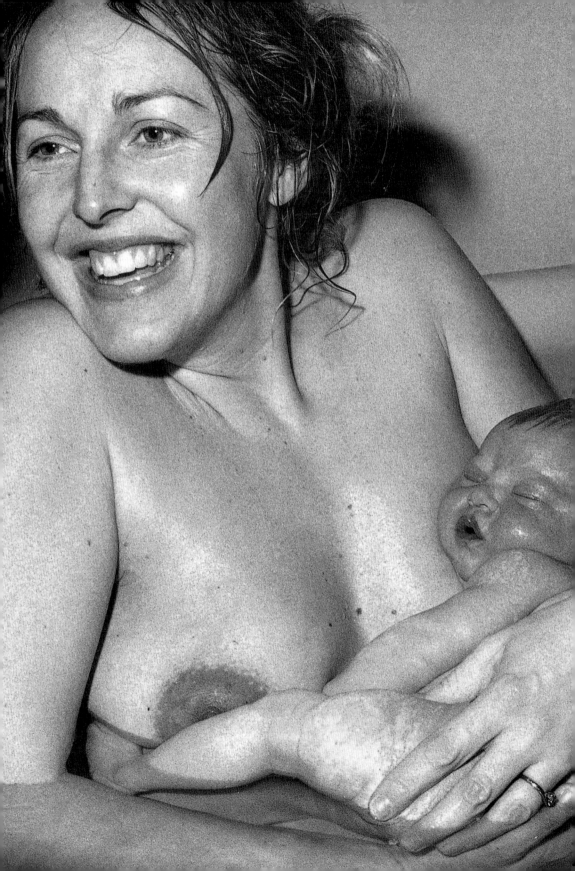

The experience
of birth

What happens in labor

Language shapes the way we think. It is never neutral. The language used by men about women's bodies – especially their genitals – is often degrading. In some languages the only words available for parts of women's bodies express disgust. In Swedish, German, and Dutch, for example, a nipple is a "breast wart." In Polish and Swedish the vaginal labia are called the "shame lips" and the pubic symphysis is the "shame bone." In Japanese pubic hair is the "shame hair." Terminology like this must make it difficult for women to feel positive about their bodies, in particular the organs involved in childbirth, which are associated with a sense of shame and pollution.

Today the language that is used about childbirth is medicalized and imposes a medical view of birth. This does not mean that you should not understand medical terminology about your body and the process of labor. But it does mean that it is important to find words for your own personal experience of pregnancy and birth too, both negative and positive aspects of it.

Women in the childbirth movement have been working to create a language of birth that is not medically dominated. They have invented or adapted words like "rushes" for uterine contractions and "visualization" for the mental pictures which help a woman adjust to the different sensations of birth. Some have analyzed the inappropriate and often sterile or destructive language that is employed by obstetricians, and sometimes nurses and midwives, too, to describe the stages of the birth process.

The medical model for childbirth incorporates an image of the pregnant woman as an ambulant pelvis, and for a woman having her first baby this pelvis is "untried." During labor she becomes a contracting uterus, and the birth process is an equation between the "powers," the "pelvis," and the "passenger," for the baby is seen as an inert passenger through the skeletal structure. Metaphors of war and conflict are often employed: obstetricians talk about "the aggressive management of ruptured membranes," "the oxytocin challenge test," "a trial of labor," and "the trigger factor for labor," and as the baby is about to be born its head "hits the pelvic floor." Midwives and nurses sometimes urge a woman to push in the second stage by telling her to "get angry with her body" or even to be "angry with the baby." A woman may be made to feel that she is being blamed for failing to function effectively: she is in "false labor." Her cervix is "incompetent," "sloppy," or "rigid." There is "failure to progress" because her uterus is "lazy" or the fundus is "boggy." Some terms, such as "elderly primigravada" and the term "abortion" when it is used to mean miscarriage, have all but disappeared from medical vocabulary because they were so obviously offensive. But there are plenty that are still around.

In this chapter, as we explore the feelings of birth and ways in which you can adapt to your physical sensations, I shall try to use not only medical words but also those which convey sensory meaning and which express the personal experience of birth.

The stages of labor

There are three stages of labor. During the first the cervix is being drawn up into the main body of the uterus and dilating (opening); in the second the baby is pressed down through the birth canal, and this stage culminates in the birth; during the third the placenta and membranes are sloughed off the lining of the uterus and expelled.

Having said this, it is important to add that for many women labor is an overwhelming and dramatic experience, and you are certainly not sitting around thinking in terms of neat stages. There is no fanfare of trumpets to tell you when the first stage is really under way or when the second stage has started. Some women have a clear physiological message, such as the breaking of the waters and sudden strong, regular contractions, leaving them in no doubt that labor has begun and that this is unmistakably it, and when they reach the end of the first stage they know with equal certainty that they are now in the second stage and have to push. For a great many women, however, the different stages of labor shade over into each other. The experience is rarely as tidy and compartmentalized as birth books seem to suggest, and the third stage may even pass completely unnoticed as you hold your newborn baby in your arms and marvel at him or her.

THE BABY SIGNALS THAT IT IS READY TO BE BORN

The *baby* initiates labor by sending endocrine signals to the placenta to produce enzymes that stimulate production of estrogen. These signals consist of catecholamines. Simultaneously, the same hormonal signals help the baby's vital organs to mature. If labor is induced artificially, the timing may not be right either for the uterus to work most effectively or for the baby to be ready for life.

BUILD-UP TO LABOR

Labor starts with the gradual softening and ripening of the cervix at the base of the uterus. This can take days and days or can happen overnight, especially if you have had a baby before. Once the cervix is soft and stretchy the uterine contractions – which are occurring anyway in late pregnancy – tend to draw it up bit by bit, so that it gradually changes from being a long canal hanging down in your vagina to being a dip in the bottom of the uterus, the tissues having been pulled up into the lower segment of the uterus.

You are not considered to be in labor when all this is happening. Your labor has not started in medical terms until you are having regular contractions which are effectively dilating the cervix; it is

Muscle bundles
The uterus is composed of spiral muscle bundles which in early pregnancy start to unfold into an open-latticework formation at the top of the uterus. If you think of the uterus as a clock, the muscle bundles are spaced out most between 9 and 3 – that is, over the fundus of the uterus. By the end of the pregnancy these bundles of muscle have unfolded much more and are stretched lengthways.

 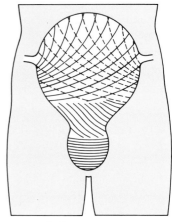

Early pregnancy   *Late pregnancy*

work that has to be done before it is possible for the cervix to open wide. Usually this means you are at least 3 cm dilated (see page 251) before you are considered to be in labor. In fact many women already have a partially dilated cervix by the time they begin to realize that they are having contractions.

It is obviously more pleasant for you if your body is working for you while you are carrying on with your work, shopping, eating and sleeping, and seeing your friends. You cannot possibly be tensing up and fighting your body when you are busy doing all these things and leaving your uterus to work undisturbed and unremarked on. So carry on normal living for as long as is comfortable.

FIRST SIGNS OF LABOR
Three things can indicate that labor has started or is about to start: you see a show, the waters break, or contractions begin.

A show This is the bloodstained mucous discharge that you have when the cervix is beginning to stretch. Until the start of labor this mucus has acted as a gelatinous plug in the cervix, sealing off the uterus. Its appearance is a good sign that there is some definite activity around the cervix. But it can come out two or three weeks before you actually go into labor and contractions are established, or it may appear when your labor is so far advanced that you may not notice it. So, although you can take it as an encouraging sign, do not rush off to the hospital. Go on with your everyday activities or, if it is night, have a hot milk drink and go back to sleep.

The bag of waters breaks When the membranes surrounding the baby have been pressed down like a wedge in front of its presenting part (usually the head) and pressure has built up, the bag pops. It may do this quite suddenly with a rush of water or, and this is more likely, with a slow trickle of water. In fact, you may not be quite sure whether the bag of waters has burst or you are wetting your pants.

If you are not sure, forget it (if you can) and carry on as usual, unless you are still several weeks away from your EDD, in which case you should call the doctor or midwife. If it is more than three weeks before your baby is due it may actually be best for you to be in a place where special care is ready for the baby at delivery.

You will probably have been told to call the hospital or your doctor or midwife if the waters break and you lose a lot of water at once. This is because, if labor is slow, taking 24 hours or more from the rupture of the membranes, there is a chance of infection. If labor starts within 24 hours, however, there is no increase in infection.*

The other concern is that if the baby's head does not fit neatly into the cervix the waters might sweep the cord down through the cervix (prolapsed cord), which in turn results in blockage of the oxygen supply to the baby. If, therefore, you know that your baby is breech before you go into labor, or that the head is still high, you should be prepared to go to the hospital if the waters break. Although a cord prolapse is rare, prompt arrival at the hospital and quick action, which could include a cesarean, may save the baby's life.

Obstetricians may wish to stimulate the uterus into activity once the membranes have ruptured. If you are sure that your baby's head is well down, it is always a good idea to give nature a chance. There is an 85 percent chance that contractions will start naturally within 24 hours. Many physicians and midwives will allow more than 24 hours if the woman is not a Bela strep carrier. Involve yourself in some gentle everyday activity or have a good night's sleep. Say "no thank you" to vaginal examinations. They increase the risk of infection. Say "no thank you" to any offer of induction before at least 24 hours have passed. Research shows that induction leads to longer labors, greater need for painkilling drugs, more operative vaginal deliveries, and more cesarean sections.*

You do not have to worry about having a "dry" labor, with the baby traveling down an unlubricated birth canal, as there is no such thing. Your amniotic fluid is completely re-formed every three hours. Actually, a "wet" labor is more likely and can be uncomfortable, since a continual leaking throughout labor is cold and unpleasant. If you are leaking, wear a sanitary pad and change it frequently. If you are in a bath or birth pool you will not notice any leaking, and so you will be much more comfortable.

Contractions start They usually feel like a tight elastic belt slung under your bump and round into the small of your back, being drawn tighter, gripping for 15 to 20 seconds, and then being released. This sensation occurs again after ten minutes or even sooner. They might be the Braxton Hicks "rehearsal" contractions, which some women experience in the last three weeks or so of pregnancy. These then tend to be called "false" labor. All this means is that you thought you were in labor, with good reason, but were not. These contractions are probably softening your cervix so that it can open.

Using gravity to help your labor

If you stay more or less upright in early labor, and continue to move around, the downward force of gravity will help push the baby out. Your contractions will be more effective, too, and should prove less painful than if you were lying down. These exercises will help you to do this effectively.

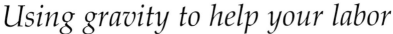

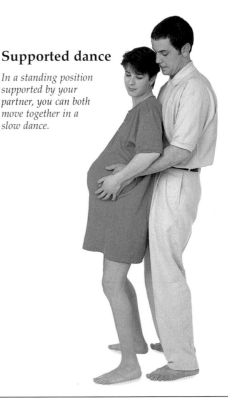

Squatting

If you find squatting comfortable, crouch down between your partner's legs and lean back against him, using his knees for support. Then you can rock or rotate your pelvis.

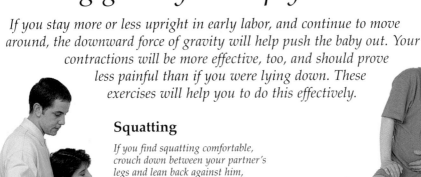

Supported lunge

With firm support from your partner and one foot raised on a chair, stool, or low table, you can move into a supported lunge.

Bending forward

You can lean over a bed or windowsill and rock your pelvis while your partner applies counterpressure to the small of your back.

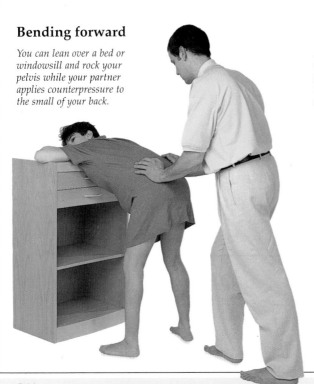

Supported dance

In a standing position supported by your partner, you can both move together in a slow dance.

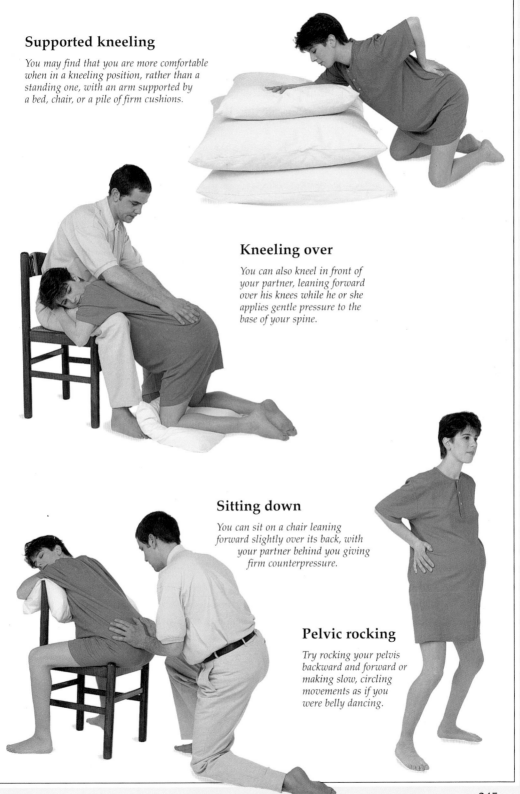

Supported kneeling

You may find that you are more comfortable when in a kneeling position, rather than a standing one, with an arm supported by a bed, chair, or a pile of firm cushions.

Kneeling over

You can also kneel in front of your partner, leaning forward over his knees while he or she applies gentle pressure to the base of your spine.

Sitting down

You can sit on a chair leaning forward slightly over its back, with your partner behind you giving firm counterpressure.

Pelvic rocking

Try rocking your pelvis backward and forward or making slow, circling movements as if you were belly dancing.

If you want to be fairly sure about being in labor, time your contractions over a period of 30 minutes or an hour; make a note of the interval between the start of one and the start of the next, and also note down the length of each contraction. The contractions need to come closer and closer together and to last longer (40 seconds or more) before you can be confident that labor is being established.

During contractions the muscle fibers at the top of the uterus tighten, pressing in and down on the center, and producing an upward pull on the cervix. When the baby's head is pressed down by a contraction, the muscles and fibrous tissues of the cervix are drawn apart. In a straightforward labor most of the physical sensations caused by contractions come from this area in and around the cervix, apart from a hardening and swelling felt at the top of the uterus.

Once contractions are going well, they have a regular rhythm, a wavelike shape, and last longer and longer, while the interval between them is reduced. You may feel your contractions as firm squeezes that make you want to gasp when at their tightest, like hot sunlight pouring through your pelvis, or rushing ocean waves.

THE FIRST STAGE OF LABOR

The hormonal changes that the baby has started now stimulate the beginning of a quite remarkable process. The uterus produces prostaglandins and as a result, contractions like those which you have been having in late pregnancy get bigger and also come closer together. So the contractions of early labor may feel like Braxton Hicks contractions, but heftier and also more regular.

These more efficient contractions press the baby's presenting part down to the base of the lower segment of the uterus and against the cervix. This then becomes progressively more stretched and thinned out as the muscle fibers are pulled up into the upper segment. The effacement and stretching of the cervix trigger the production of oxytocin from the posterior pituitary gland, and this stimulates the uterus into a steady rhythm of contractions. Labor is under way!

MOVING AROUND IN LABOR

Going to bed in the first stage of labor and becoming more or less immobile can slow down labor or interfere with its starting effectively because the presenting part may not be pressed down against your cervix. When you are upright and moving around, you have gravity to help you: everything is being pressed down.

It was not until the end of the 18th century in Europe that women began to lie down in order to give birth. Before that time they had walked around during much of the labor, used labor stools to sit on, or sat up in bed or on a chair. Birth stools were designed like horseshoes, with the open part at the front; were low on the ground so that the woman squatted; and sometimes provided support for her lower back as well as handgrips. As a result, the woman was in a physiologically excellent position for childbirth.

Mauriceau, then the obstetrician to the French court, introduced the lying down position, and it soon caught on because people sought to imitate the manners of the court. When forceps were first introduced, obstetricians found that they were easier to use on a woman who was lying flat. Still later, the lithotomy position, in which the patient lies on her back with her legs fixed to raised stirrups, and which was first devised for surgery on gall stones, was introduced. This highly artificial posture is often very uncomfortable for the woman, pressing her uterus against the big blood vessels in the lower part of the body. This interferes with her circulation, causing hypotension (low blood pressure), and also with the production of urine; it can also sometimes cause distress to the fetus.

Research on the effect of different positions in the first stage of labor* has shown that most women prefer to be up and about, not lying in bed, and that contractions are stronger and labor shorter with the woman in an upright position. The uterus is working nearly twice as efficiently to dilate the cervix.

Keep walking around between contractions. Try pelvic rocking and circling as if you were belly dancing – through contractions, too, if it feels good. If dilatation is taking a long time, soak in a warm bath or squat on a low stool under the shower.

WHEN TO GO TO THE HOSPITAL

Unless you feel strongly that you need to be in the hospital during this time, or your doctor has advised that there is a special reason why you should come in as soon as there are any signs of labor starting, it is best to stay at home and carry on as usual. This is partly because of the psychological effect of going to the hospital, being admitted and prepared, and getting into bed. If you have only just begun labor, all this can stop it entirely. There are many women who have rushed to the hospital with regular contractions that are still more than five minutes apart and who have then gone out of labor and have either had to wait around with their morale dropping steadily or have had an intravenous oxytocin drip inserted in an arm vein to stimulate the uterus into action.

Remember to continue to eat and drink. Labor may last a long time, and both you and whoever is going to be your companion in labor are going to need your strength.

Knowing that your contractions will be coming one every two minutes and will last about one minute or longer just before the baby is born may give you some perspective on your labor when it is just starting. Having contractions every five minutes can be tiring, and some women experience this for 12 hours or more, usually when the baby is in a slightly awkward position, facing the mother's front instead of her back (see page 262); but the baby cannot possibly be born when contractions are coming this far apart, so if you are happier at home, stay there. Keep a careful record of what is happening, time the contractions now and again, and be ready to go to the hospital as soon as the membranes rupture or contractions come more often than every five minutes. Of course you must bear in mind the distance from your home to the hospital and the difficulty of getting there. If you are going in your own car, it is as well to have done a trial run beforehand at the rush hour to see how long it can take and to be sure that you know the way, even in deep snow, hail, or fog, and also any short cuts that may be convenient. Your partner should drive steadily, but not fast, and certainly not brake suddenly at corners or at lights. Decide early what you will need to make the journey comfortable and whether you would prefer to be in the front or backseat of the car. If you are calling an ambulance, find out well in advance how to do this and, if you are relying on getting to the hospital by cab, have a list of numbers pinned up by the telephone in case one is not immediately available.

ADMISSION PROCEDURES

When you arrive at the hospital, a nurse will take you to a little room where you will be "prepped" (prepared) for labor. She will ask you questions about how labor started, if the waters have broken and if so when, how often contractions are coming, and so on. She will do some of the things you are already familiar with, such as requesting a urine sample, checking your blood pressure, feeling the position of the baby through your abdominal wall, and listening to the fetal heart. She or a staff doctor will feel through your vagina and into your cervix, to tell if you have started dilating. If you are already partially dilated, he or she may break the waters (see page 317). This is done routinely in many hospitals at 3–4 cm dilatation, and sometimes before this phase has been reached. If you want your membranes to remain intact until they rupture spontaneously, say so before your internal examination.

It used to be hospital practice to shave a woman's perineum, and in some hospitals every perineum was required to be as bald as a hard-boiled egg. Still today some attendants like the hair surrounding the vagina to be clipped short. Women have spoken out strongly against the unnecessary, uncomfortable, and degrading practice of perineal shaving; research has also shown that it is entirely useless in avoiding infection and, however carefully done, always results in some injury to the skin.

Some hospitals still give an enema to empty the lower bowel, but there is no point in doing this unless a woman is very constipated. In the hours before labor starts, most women have loose motions. In this way the lower bowel is cleared naturally.

After you have been examined you will be asked to don a hospital gown; it is usually done up at the back, but if you hope to have your baby at the breast immediately following delivery you will find it easier to wear the gown with the opening at the front. Many women prefer to wear their own clothes. Select something made of cotton rather than a synthetic fabric, as hospitals are often overheated.

Whatever you wear should be short and loose, so that you can move about freely. An external or internal fetal monitor may be attached to assess your baby's heart rate and response to contractions as well as the strength of the uterine contractions. It is routine practice in many hospitals to do an "admission trace" of the fetal heart sounds for 20 or 30 minutes. There has been no research into the value of this, so it should be your choice whether or not you have it.

In some hospitals your partner may be asked to wait outside while you are prepared, but most take it for granted that a couple will want to stay together. It can seem a very long time to be separated, and if your partner has been helping you cope with contractions up till now, it is good to go on having the same kind of support. It also gives the midwife or nurse a chance to talk with the partner, which means that she is meeting you not as an isolated patient but in your relationship with someone who is important in your life. If you have chosen to have other people there too (a doula, friend, or relative), they should also be able to stay. Labor is not a good time in which to have people coming and going. You will be able to relax knowing that you are with someone who understands you and is giving continuous emotional support.

A doctor may come into the room at intervals to assess progress or to discuss your case. If you have any questions, take this opportunity to ask them. If you are planning a natural birth, want to walk around in labor, or have any other wishes, remind the doctor or midwife of these and ask if they have been or can be noted on your chart.

COUNTDOWN FOR BIRTH AT HOME

If you are having your baby at home, plan ahead and make sure that any major chores do not pile up. When you think you are in labor, start to prepare for the birth. Put a plastic sheet (a shower curtain also works well) on the bed and if the bed is not already at right angles to the wall move it to this position. Put out the things that the midwife has asked you to have ready on a small table or, better still, a cart, arranged on a freshly washed towel or pillowcase, and cover them with another piece of cloth. Arrange the lighting so that the midwife can direct some light onto your perineum for delivery and so that the other lights can be dimmed or turned out when required. Put the baby's clothes out and a change of clothes for yourself. Set aside some water for boiling: this will be used mostly for tea, but is also useful for washing your perineum after delivery.

Then turn your mind to what you are going to eat and drink for the next three days and also what you may want to offer visitors. You will have been wise to have stocked up your food cupboard and freezer well in advance. If you put anything in the oven at this stage, take a timer with you when you go to the bedroom and pin a reminder in a prominent place, or your labor may well be accompanied by the smell of burning food.

Call the midwife to let her know that you may be needing her later, and pin all important phone numbers in easy reach by the phone. The midwife will probably call to check how you are doing and encourage you to contact her whenever you wish.

TRANSITION

Toward the end of the first stage of labor, at the time when you are between 8 and 10 cm dilated, you are in transition.

For most women the very end of the first stage is stormy and challenging. Contractions follow each other relentlessly with hardly a pause between, and they tend to become arrhythmic, with sharp peaks and sometimes with more than one peak to each contraction. The buildup of energy with each may be so sudden and tumultuous that there is no time for slow breathing and you must adapt straight away and breathe much more lightly and quickly if you are to soar over the top of the peaks with your breathing. The very length of the contractions may demand every bit of concentration and determination you are able to summon, and you will need strong emotional support and unfailing encouragement.

At the same time other physiological signs may occur which can be quite unsettling, until you remember that they are indications of progress, and that if you are aware of three or more of them, then you are likely to be 8 cm dilated and hence in transition. Feeling hot then cold, then hot again, your cheeks flushed and your eyes shining bright, suggests that you are in transition. So does a fit of hiccups or belching, or you may even feel nauseous and actually vomit. Perhaps your legs feel icy cold and begin to shake uncontrollably. One of the surest signs is feeling that you have a large grapefruit pressing against your anus or that you want to empty your bowels. You might have a catch in your throat that stops your easy rhythmic breathing or you involuntarily hold your breath or start to grunt. You may suddenly feel that it is all too much hard work and that you really cannot go on and would like to go home and forget all about having a baby. Or you may become irritable with everyone and hypercritical of the help your partner is giving.

Not all women experience these signs, but a sufficient proportion do to make it a good idea for your partner to memorize them, so that at the right moment he can say: "I think you are in transition." You may have forgotten you are having a baby by this time and are simply concentrating on the work of handling each contraction. You are also very likely to feel that you are not making any progress at all and have lost all sense of time. Since in transition you may get an urge to push before you are fully dilated, you may be told to continue breathing and not to hold your breath until you absolutely must.

Pushing powerfully and for a long time against an incompletely dilated cervix can make it puffy and swollen so that the opening actually closes rather than opens wider. This is why you may be asked not to push until you cannot avoid pushing. This is wise advice, because then you can be quite certain that your body is really ready to push, and you will also enjoy the surrender to the great sweeps of energy that come with the contractions in a way you cannot if you are just pushing because someone has told you to do so.

Transition may be very brief – just a few contractions – or it may last an hour or more. It is likely to last longer if the baby is in an occipito-posterior position (see page 262). The cervix has to dilate to 10 cm before the baby can be pressed down through the opening. At full dilatation (10 cm or the width of the palm of a large man's hand including the thumb joint) the cervix is open enough for the baby's head, its largest part, to ease through. There are spaces between the baby's skullbones, the fontanels, which can close up as the baby slides down the birth canal, so shaping its head to make the journey much less arduous, even for a 9 lb (4 kg) baby. This is why, especially in first labors, the baby's head is molded, sometimes into a rather peculiar shape; this gradually disappears in the first week or so after the birth (see page 362). After the cervix has dilated to 10 cm, the second stage of labor starts.

THE SECOND STAGE OF LABOR

The second stage of labor is the most exciting. During the first stage of labor the cervix has thinned out and opened. At the end of the first stage the cervix is open to 10 cm, making the uterus and vagina one birth canal. Contractions ease the baby's head down further and there is often a lull during this phase.

Pushing Women are often told to start pushing as soon as the cervix is fully dilated. This does not shorten the second stage of labor. In fact, if a woman does not have an overwhelming urge to push it may be because the baby's head has not yet fully rotated into the best position for birth. If she starts doing deliberate breathing exercises and straining to push the baby out, or is told when to push, it may not be what her uterus wants to do. Forceful bearing down can push

Dilatation of the cervix
The cervix has to be 10 cm dilated (widened) before the uterus can press the baby out. The time taken to reach full dilatation varies enormously: some women are 3 cm dilated before they realize they are in labor, some take many hours to reach 5 cm.

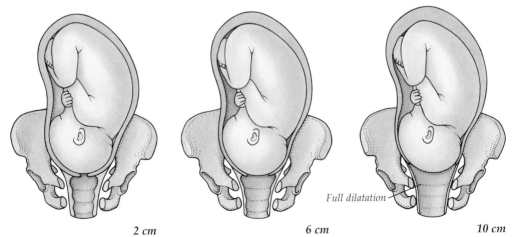

Full dilatation

2 cm   *6 cm*   *10 cm*

the head down too soon and result in deep transverse arrest. That is, the baby actually gets stuck.* The woman has wasted all her energy in this harmful activity and may not be able to push energetically when it is the right time for her to do so. Sometimes she has lost the synchronization between her uterus and her actions and then never gets the desire to start pushing again. Many of the forceps deliveries and vacuum extractions that occur are performed for this reason.

Focus on the idea of *opening up* for the baby to come out. Wait to push until you feel that you cannot avoid doing so, or until the baby's head can be seen on your perineum. If you experience a pause at the onset of the second stage of labor, trust your body and enjoy this "rest and be thankful" phase.

Then follows a wonderful time when you can begin to push. The second stage of labor is often described as if it were sheer, grinding, hard work, but you will want to do it. You will probably have an overpowering urge to bear down and press the baby through the birth canal. This is passionate, intense, thrilling, and often completely irresistible, and for some women it is the nearest thing to overwhelming sexual excitement. Pushing is not something you decide to do with a rational part of your mind, but a force that sweeps through your body and culminates in the delivery of your baby. Let your body take over at this stage.

The journey through the pelvis

About 80 percent of women have good, well-rounded pelvises for childbirth. Problems may be encountered if your pelvis is narrow: an android pelvis, for instance, is shaped like a triangle at the brim, which is hard for the baby to negotiate. Even when the pelvic shape is not ideal, the uterus works to press the baby into a neat package which, given time, can often make the journey easily.

Basically, the baby consists of two balls which move against each other. The ball with the largest diameter is the baby's head. The other ball is the baby's trunk with the limbs well tucked in. The action of a uterus that is contracting well results in the baby being molded into the right shape for the journey down the birth canal.

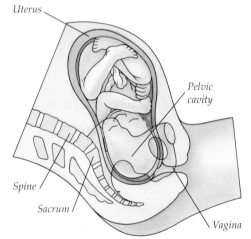

1 *The vagina is almost at right angles to the uterus. The baby has to negotiate an angle similar to a foot putting on a Wellington boot. There are several bones that may hold up the baby's progress. The sacrum is the big bone at the base of the spine that forms part of the pelvic brim. Once the baby's head has traveled below the pelvic brim, it is in the pelvic cavity.*

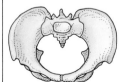

Normal female pelvis

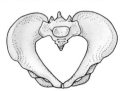

Android pelvis

There are a few women who do not feel much of an urge to bear down during the second stage of labor. Sometimes women who have had other babies do not experience any strong pushing urge. The whole process of labor may be much gentler; the mother seems not to need to do that much bearing down because the baby is going to be born very easily anyway.

There are three to five urges to bear down with each second-stage contraction, though sometimes we talk about these contractions as if they were all push. Frantic pushing results in your becoming desperate, straining to press the baby just that little bit farther. This is not necessary, because surges of desire to bear down come with each contraction, and it is important to go naturally with each as it comes; allow yourself to hold your breath, bear down, and open up with the surge, which usually lasts five or six seconds, no longer. Only you can know when these surges are there. Some people think it is a good idea for a woman to hold her breath for as long as she possibly can in the second stage and only then is she really working hard. However, research suggests that directed pushing, prolonged breath-holding, and sustained bearing down is not only exhausting for the mother, but can also be dangerous for the baby because it reduces the oxygen content of the blood.* So trust your spontaneous feelings and do what comes naturally.

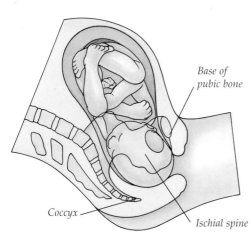

Base of pubic bone

Coccyx

Ischial spine

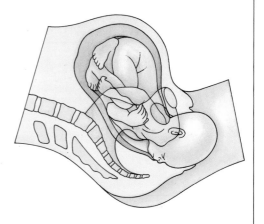

2 Once the baby has negotiated the pelvic brim, it moves onto the pelvic outlet. This is bordered by the coccyx (the tiny bone at the base of the spine) at the back, the bottom of the pubic bone at the front, and the ischial spines, which are the two projecting crests on the side walls of the pelvis. The coccyx slips out of the way as the baby's head comes through the pelvic outlet.

3 It is usually the downward pressure from above that is provided by good and powerful contractions which will ease the baby's head down so that as it comes through the steepest curve at the beginning of the vagina the muscles at the back of the baby's neck extend. This means that the baby is usually facing downward just before and as it is born.

YOUR BABY'S HEAD APPEARS

When the top of your baby's head can be seen for the first time, it looks like a wrinkled walnut in the vagina, not like a baby at all. Your partner will probably see this before you can, and will be able to tell you the color of the baby's hair. With the first baby the second stage make take one or two hours. With the second or subsequent baby it may take only ten minutes.

Then there comes a time when the widest part of the baby's head is at the birth opening and does not go back in between contractions. You feel stretched to your utmost. At this moment of "crowning" it is important not to go on pushing, even though you feel very much like it. Otherwise you might tear the perineal tissue. The doctor or midwife may perform an episiotomy if they think you might tear (see page 320). If you want to avoid having one, just before the head crowns start to breathe the baby out instead of pushing it out (see page 208), and in this way it may slip forward. The midwife or obstetrician checks to see that the cord is free of the neck and may insert a mucus catheter in the baby's mouth and suck any mucus out. A rubber bulb like the top of a turkey baster may also be used.

The baby's head slips under your pubic bone and extends, the chin being automatically lifted off its chest. As the head emerges, damp and sticky with mucus, it is often a violet or purple color. This is nothing to worry about: the child has not yet taken that first great gasp of air that will oxygenate the blood.

The baby may be covered in vernix, a cold-cream-like substance which coats the baby's skin in the uterus and makes it look as if it has been spread with cottage cheese. The head has been molded by the journey down the birth canal, so it may be an odd, pointed, or bumpy asymmetrical shape, and the forehead may recede and the baby be almost chinless. The nose is often flattened like a prize-fighter's and there are little red marks between the eyes and on the eyelids.

At delivery, the baby's head is facing downward but the shoulders are still turned sideways inside you. Once the head is free, it turns to come in line with the shoulders. You may need another push for the shoulders. The doctor or midwife may press the baby's head down so that the shoulder nearer your front slides out first. Then the head is lifted up so that the lower shoulder slides out next. At last the whole body slithers out and your baby is born!

There is often a great gush of water, and the baby may be already breathing and crying, limbs lashing, and face puckered up with what looks like rage. The lower end of the body seems very small in comparison with the head end, apart from the genitals, which often look extraordinarily large. All this is normal. If the baby is not yet breathing, attendants suck out the respiratory tract, hold the child's head downward, and may give oxygen. If you are propped up, you can reach your baby, provided he or she is lying over your thigh or between your legs, or has been delivered up on to your tummy, and you may want to reach down and take your baby in your arms.

THE THIRD STAGE OF LABOR

Though you may not feel the contractions, your uterus continues to contract after the birth of the baby. This makes the placenta separate from its lining, since the placenta cannot contract. As the uterus squeezes down into a firm, hard ball the placental mass is then automatically peeled off. This process has been compared to stretching a piece of rubber on which a postage stamp has been stuck; when the rubber moves, the stamp becomes detached. The sinuses in which the placental blood vessels were rooted are closed by the tight squeezing of the uterus, and these contractions prevent excessive bleeding from the uterine wall.

When the placenta has detached itself, the midwife or doctor may pull on the cord (see page 322). Take a breath, hold it, and bear down at the same time to help this process. You can ask that instead of having cord traction, you can push and do it by yourself.

There is a squelchy, slippery feeling as the placenta slides out. The person who delivered the baby examines the placenta carefully to see that every part is there. Pieces of placenta left inside could cause unnecessary bleeding, pain, and infection in the postpartum period. Though the placenta looks like a large piece of raw liver, it was the tree of life for your baby. You may be interested to examine it yourself and see the difference between the rough side, which was against the wall of the uterus, and the smooth side, which lay toward the baby like a soft, velvety cushion, and to note the network of blood vessels that provided your baby with its life support system.

If you need stitching, it is usually possible to have the baby with you throughout this procedure. Suturing (the technical term for stitching) is done under local anesthetic and may take a long time, sometimes as long as an hour, since careful embroidery has to be done and the underlying layers of muscle must be correctly aligned. So keep your baby in your arms or near enough to touch.

The nurse or midwife will help you put on an ice pack to reduce swelling and a sanitary pad, as there will be some bleeding now and for several days, resembling the height of a heavy period. The length of time during which there is a bloodstained vaginal discharge (lochia) varies greatly among women. Some new mothers bleed for just a few days after the birth, others for as long as five or six weeks.

BEING TOGETHER

In many hospitals the staff tidy up at this point. They wipe and weigh the baby, examine you to see if you need stitches, give you a wash, change your gown, shorten the baby's cord, and reclamp it. But practice is changing fast and many hospital staff now give the parents the opportunity for a quiet time with their baby in the period immediately following the birth, only doing the basic essentials and leaving the couple alone for an hour or so to start to get to know their baby. Being together should always come first. Tidying up can be done later. It is far less important.

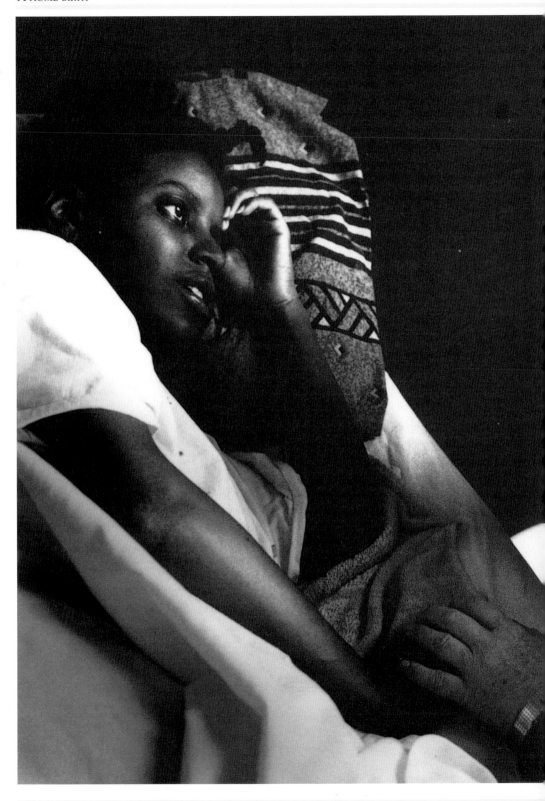

A home birth

Pauline chose a home birth because none of the men she and her husband knew who had recently become fathers and had had hospital births felt totally included, and she believed a home birth would entail less stress for the baby.

She was 7 cm dilated by the time she needed to call her midwife, Nicky. Her husband, Clifton, lay beside her on the bed giving her loving support.

Then she knelt by the bed with a heating pad on her lower back. Nicky told her, "Make as much sound as you want but keep the tones low." Pauline said this really helped. "I felt in control all the time. Being at

home felt safe, and I had my own space, with no restrictions on me or what I did."

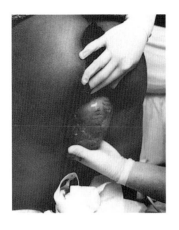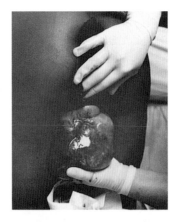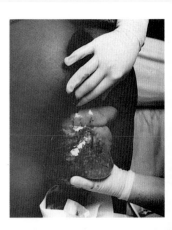

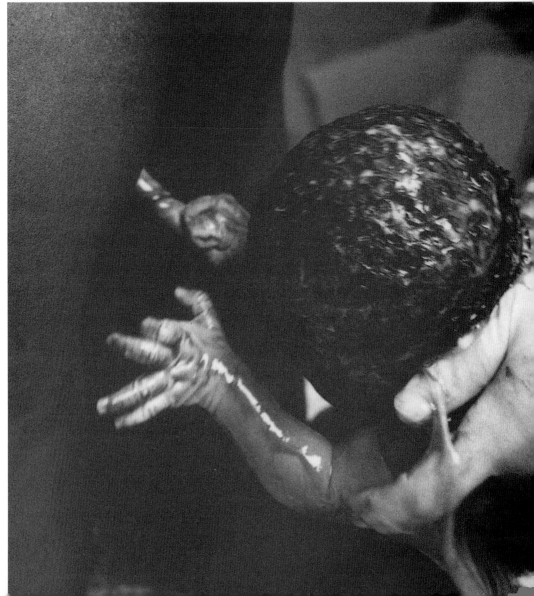

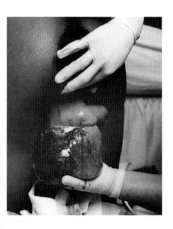
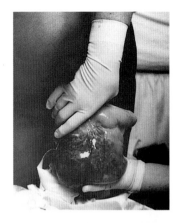
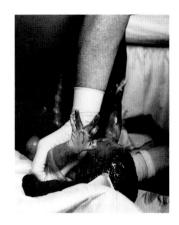

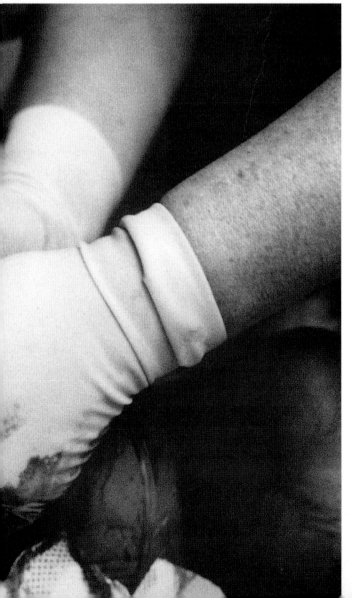

The baby is born still inside the bag of waters. Nicky says, "Pauline was brilliant! Completely focused on the task at hand." She tells her, "It's coming now. It's lovely – well done!" and then she prepares her for not pushing with the next contraction to enable the baby to be born gently.

Then in the space of one contraction, the baby's head advances, inside the membranes; the head slides out facing the mother's back and rotates to align with the shoulders, which are still inside. Next a shoulder and arm slip out, and are followed by the other shoulder; then finally the whole body emerges.

A glistening, transparent veil of membrane envelops the baby. Supporting the baby's back, the midwife takes the membrane off the baby's head so that she can take her first breath. Nicky rests the baby between Pauline's legs and Pauline exclaims, "Oh, it's a girl!"

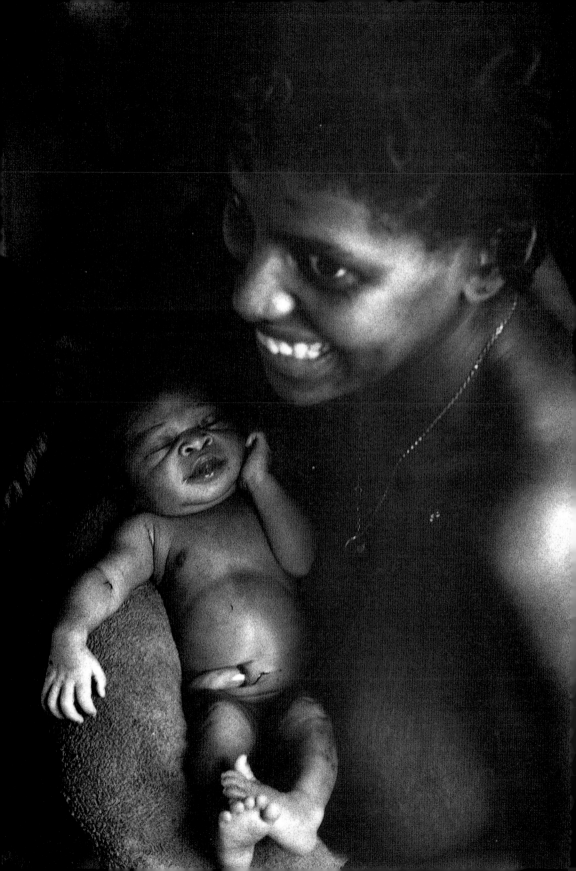

The baby cries and is a perfect color. Pauline picks up her daughter and cradles her in her arms, cord still uncut. After all her striving to bring this child to birth she is radiant.

Everyone is laughing and admiring this beautiful baby. Pauline is still bleeding quite heavily, so Nicky gives her a quick injection of syntocinon in order to stimulate the uterus to contract. Then she clamps and severs the cord.

When the baby's searching mouth indicates that she is ready to suck, her mother offers her the breast, and after nuzzling and licking as she explores this new sensation, she latches on. The parents share together the miracle of birth in an atmosphere of timelessness and peace. These are moments that they will never forget.

Different kinds of birth

However much other people may advise you not to have any preconceptions about your labor, just to be ready for whatever comes, it is difficult not to have some, because it is almost impossible to prepare yourself to cope with a situation that you have not imagined in advance. So it is useful to think ahead to the major variations on the theme of childbirth which you might confront. However, it is still vital to keep in the forefront of your mind the normal, rhythmic, and harmonious pattern of a straightforward labor. Otherwise all the medical technicalities may seem quite bewildering, and you may interpret each uncomfortable physical sign as an indication that something has gone wrong.

This chapter looks at some different types of labor, all of which can throw you unless you understand what is happening.

LABOR WITH A POSTERIOR BABY

When the back of the baby's head presses against your sacrum, the baby is said to be in an occipito-posterior position. Most women have some backache in labor, but women with posterior babies may have it all the time, so that the labor can be described as a "back labor." Few women with posterior babies do not have backache, which can be the most tiring and stressful thing about a labor – especially if, as is often the case when the baby is posterior, it continues *between* contractions as well as during them.

Another characteristic of labor with a posterior baby is that it starts very slowly, often over a period of several days, and contractions are usually felt as one big one followed by a feeble one. Plan for morale-boosting activity during a long first stage. Don't go into the hospital too soon. A walk in the park or the country is probably better. Eat and keep up your strength in early labor and have plenty of fluids, remembering to empty your bladder regularly. Your partner also needs stamina in a back labor, to keep you going by giving you his total attention during difficult contractions.

If the baby is in a posterior position the membranes should not be ruptured artificially. It is much easier for the baby to rotate if it is still floating free. When the membranes are ruptured the baby often drops down into the pelvis in a posterior position and is fixed rather like a cork stuck in a bottle.

The baby will probably rotate at the very end of the first stage or at the onset of the second and things will be plain sailing from then on. About 5 percent of posteriors do not rotate and then the hard work has to be continued in the second stage and you may need obstetric help (see pages 334–340) to deliver the baby. But the chances are that the baby will swivel around by herself and then be able to complete her journey down your birth canal with ease.

Presentations for birth

When the baby is lying head down and curled into a neat ball (occipito anterior), the uterus can usually work well to open the cervix and press the baby down into the birth canal to be born. There are other positions that the baby may adopt and these can sometimes lead to problems during labor and giving birth.

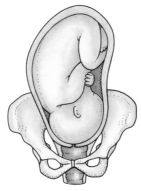

Right occipito anterior
This position is a common presentation for labor.

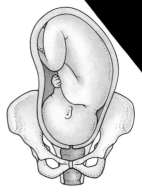

Left occipito anterior
The most usual presentation is with the baby facing to the left.

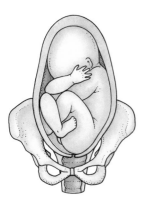

Full breech presentation
With this position the baby's body is able to flex during labor.

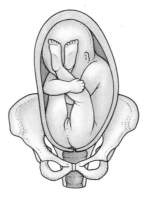

Frank breech presentation
This type of presentation makes flexion difficult.

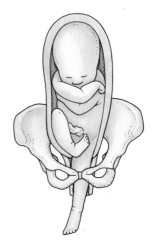

Footling breech
In this type of presentation the baby's foot is born in advance of the rest of the body.

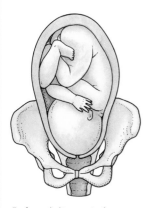

Left occipito posterior
This position can cause backache in labor.

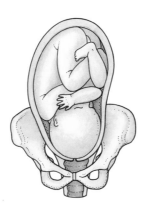

Right occipito posterior
More common than LOP, this also causes backache in labor.

Common abbreviations
Left occipito anterior = LOA
Left occipito posterior = LOP
Right occipito anterior = ROA
Right occipito posterior = ROP

WAYS OF DEALING WITH A BACK LABOR

You may find that some of the things described on the following pages are helpful in the first stage of a back labor.

Heat A hot water bottle wrapped in a towel, or a hot compress (in the form of a facecloth or small towel wrung out in really hot water) applied to where you feel most pain may bring relief. A hot shower with the water pulsing on your back also helps.

Cold Use a bag of frozen peas or corn from the freezer wrapped in a cloth, or crushed ice knotted into an examination glove, to numb pain and relieve muscle spasm.

Changes of position Keep upright and moving around for as long as possible. In this way you tip the baby down to press through the pelvis and birth canal instead of right into the small of your back. Crouching, leaning forward, leaning forward with one foot placed on a chair beside you, kneeling, squatting, getting onto all fours with your lower back arched, and lying on your side with your back well rounded, your head and shoulders curved forward, and a pillow between your legs may all be positions in which pain is eased. They may also encourage the rotation of the baby's head. Research has shown that an all-fours position helps babies rotate from posterior to anterior. It can be combined with pelvic rocking. Seventy-five percent of babies turned when women with posterior babies adopted a hands-and-knees position. No babies turned when women sat upright instead.*

Movement If you want to get a tight ring off your finger you do not just pull it. You wiggle it. In much the same way, you may be able to help your baby's head rotate by rocking your pelvis forward and backward, from side to side, by circling it, doing these movements with one foot up on a stool or chair, going up and down stairs, rocking from foot to foot, walking slowly with big strides, and exploring all the movements which form the intricate steps of a birth dance. Spontaneous movements that are comforting and which feel right not only relieve pain but can help the baby's head rotate.

Pressure Ask your partner to provide firm pressure, either right over the place where your pelvis joins your spine or to the left or right of this if the pain is more to the side. He should use the heel of one hand, with the other resting over it, and press his body weight down through his arm. Or you may prefer the feel of knuckles.

Stimulus on pressure points may help you to handle the pain more effectively. One place where deep pressure of a thumb or finger may feel good is on your bottom, level with the top of the slit between your buttocks and a little more than the width of your palm out toward the leg on each side. Experiment to find the spot: it feels

Relieving your back labor

One of the greatest threats to a woman's morale in childbirth is having constant backache. With the help of your partner you can practice the techniques below. They will help you take the edge off pain in labor and find the energy to cope with it.

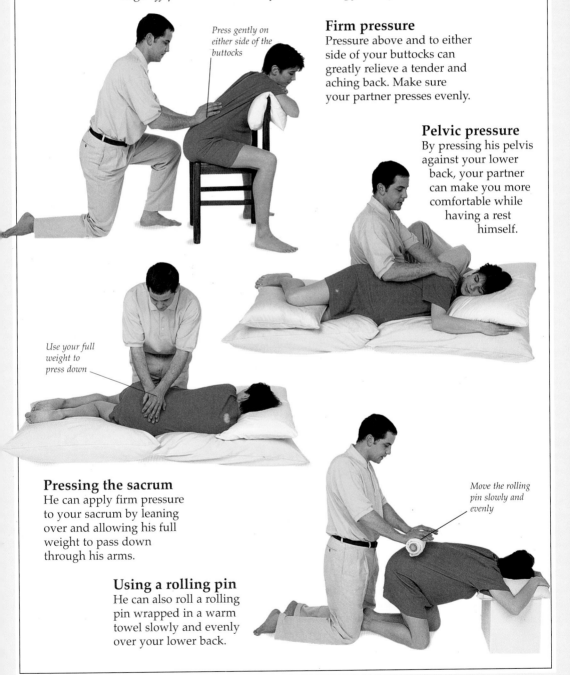

Press gently on either side of the buttocks

Firm pressure
Pressure above and to either side of your buttocks can greatly relieve a tender and aching back. Make sure your partner presses evenly.

Pelvic pressure
By pressing his pelvis against your lower back, your partner can make you more comfortable while having a rest himself.

Use your full weight to press down

Move the rolling pin slowly and evenly

Pressing the sacrum
He can apply firm pressure to your sacrum by leaning over and allowing his full weight to pass down through his arms.

Using a rolling pin
He can also roll a rolling pin wrapped in a warm towel slowly and evenly over your lower back.

tender, but pressure on it is satisfying. If you are in a position in which you are tilted forward, your partner can apply pressure to the spot on both of your buttocks at once.

If you are on your side your partner will be able to reach only one, but even this may help. These areas are called "pain prevention points" in one system of psychoprophylaxis.

Pressure points Your partner can exert pressure on parts of the body far away from where you are feeling pain, but where a really strong stimulus can offer almost miraculous relief. Known as *shiatsu* or acupressure, this can be particularly effective in childbirth when used on the feet. One pressure point is just below the center of the ball of the foot. Another point is between the fleshy pads under the big toe and next toe. Your partner holds one foot firmly, exerting very strong pressure with a finger or thumb on the chosen spot, and providing light counterpressure with the rest of the hand over the top of the foot.

"It was extraordinary how pressure on the balls of my feet relieved the pain during the labor. I wouldn't have believed it to be possible, but it really did. The pain receded into the distance and instead I felt exhilarated and in an odd way could enjoy the contraction."

There are many acupressure points on the buttocks, too. Kneel forward over the seat of a chair or lie three-quarters over on your side so that your partner can "map" the places on your buttocks where it feels good to have strong, steady pressure. Try, for example, pressing up just under the curve of the buttocks, and beneath the bony pelvis at either side of the buttocks. Another place where pressure can be very effective is on the inside wrist, between the tendons. Care should be taken to press only with the fleshy pad of a finger or thumb – but not with the nails. It is surprising how strong the pressure from finger and thumb can be on the right spot, and in all these places continuous pressure will produce a tingling, buzzing sensation. Acupressure for up to 10 seconds at a time followed by a pause, and then repeated, in a steady rhythm, can provide effective pain relief during powerful contractions, whether they are felt on your front or back, and wherever the pain is centered.

Massage Massage may feel better than pressure, or can feel good alternated with pressure. The massage that suits most women best is firm, slow, and steady, moving the flesh and muscle on the bone. You can use powder, cornstarch, or massage oil to avoid skin irritation, and your partner should have some cream to rub into his or her hands if the massage is to be applied for a long time.

Another effective way of giving massage is to use a rolling pin. Knot a face towel or hot compress towel around it to get more grip. Your partner can sit on the bed with his pelvis against your lower spine and lean back against you, too. This provides welcome rest for someone who after several hours of working to relieve backache may develop back pain himself!

Immersion in water A birth pool or really deep bath is enormously helpful in backache labor and may take away the pain entirely. Do not lie back in the water. Try a hands-and-knees or floating squat position instead. Not only is warm water comforting and relaxing, but it will enable you to move smoothly and easily, and if you leave your head loose so that it leads you into different movements, you can change position frequently without any strain, one movement flowing into another as if in a slow, luxurious water dance.

LABOR WITH A BREECH BABY

Labor with a breech sometimes starts with the waters leaking. This is because the baby's bottom does not fit the opening cervix as well as the oval of the crown of the head, and so part of the bag of waters becomes wedged between the baby's bottom and your cervix. It is important that you call the doctor if this happens to you and the baby is not yet engaged. The risk is that the cord might slide down as well and be caught between the baby and the cervix, so that the oxygen supply to the baby is cut off.

If the waters do not break, stand up and keep walking around through the first stage, until they break spontaneously. There is a case to be made for not doing an amniotomy, since if a breech baby is left in its bag of waters there is less chance of pressure on the cord.

After the waters have gone, the best positions are on all fours or on your side. You may have backache and if so your partner could exert pressure with the knuckles over the small of your back.

THE SECOND STAGE OF A BREECH LABOR

You may be moved to an operating room before the second stage starts, in case you should need an emergency cesarean section. Sometimes your partner is shown to the waiting room at this time. If you want to stay together make this clear.

Many doctors prefer to deliver breech babies with the woman in the lithotomy position (see page 247), since they feel that they have most control over the birth this way. But you will probably be more comfortable squatting, on all fours, dangling, standing, or standing and bending your knees during contractions.

It is usually best to let the second stage proceed with no voluntary exertion on your part until the body is born and the head is about to slip out, so that the baby's body is born on contraction waves only. (It may be easiest to do this if you are on all fours.) Concentrate on total release: breathe, rather than push, the baby out.

If you are not having an epidural (see page 309), an injection of local anesthetic is given in your perineum if an episiotomy is to be done (see pages 320–322), before the baby's head is delivered. It takes one or two minutes to be effective. Most obstetricians do a large episiotomy with a breech so that the head can be delivered unimpeded, and some do two cuts, one on each side of the perineum (a bilateral episiotomy). But if you give birth with breathing instead

Foot work
Applying pressure to certain parts of the feet can relieve pain from contractions. One spot is just below the center of the ball of the foot; another is between the fleshy pads under the big toe and next one.

Exploring birth movements in water

Explore different positions for birth, such as squatting and kneeling, with the people who will be helping you at the birth. This will give everyone the opportunity to learn what to expect. Some movements may be more comfortable to do along the width rather than the length of the pool.

Kneeling slide

1 *Kneel forward, grasping the rim of the pool with your arms extended. Slide forward and backward, lifting your head and bending your arms as you pull forward and extending your arms as you slide backward.*

2 *At the height of a contraction it may feel good to drop your head down in the water and blow out.*

3 *Then lift your head as you pull forward and slide back with arms extended.*

Squatting and forward slide

1 *Squat in the water with your arms and shoulders supported by the rim of the pool, feet well apart so that your pelvis is at its widest.*

2 *Slide down in the water with your legs extended, and back up to a squatting position again.*

Squatting and backward slide

1 *Squat in the center of the pool, knees wide apart, arms extended and holding the rim of the pool.*

2 *Drop your body forward, legs extended behind you, and grasp your partner at waist level, while he supports your upper arms.*

269

Forward and backward slide on front

1 *Kneel in the water with your arms supported by the rim of the pool. Keep your knees well apart so that your pelvis is at its widest.*

2 *Slide down in the water with your legs extended, and back up to a kneeling position again.*

Forward and backward slide on back

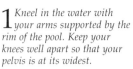

1 *With arms spread wide and supported by the pool rim, sit with your legs across the width of the pool so that your feet are resting on the opposite side. Extra padding behind your head and neck makes this more comfortable.*

2 *Slide forward and backward, using your feet against the side of the pool to propel you.*

Supported kneel

1 *Kneel leaning forward, knees wide apart, with the rim of the pool under your upper arms. In this position the cervix is tilted forward, which is helpful during the second stage of labor.*

2 *Swing back to an upright kneeling position with your legs wide apart.*

Rim support

Lie on your side, your head and arms resting on the rim of the pool.

Head cradling

Lie back in the water with your head cradled in your partner's hands. He should use a light touch, so that you can still move your head quite freely as and when you wish.

271

of pushing, your tissues may fan out well and an episiotomy may not be essential. Since there is unlikely to be an opportunity for discussion at the time, when things will be happening fast, talk about this earlier on in your labor (between contractions). Otherwise the doctor will probably do an episiotomy.

Once the episiotomy is done, the doctor can deliver the head, using hands or forceps to cradle it. You will be asked to push for the head and will probably find that you need to bear down only once.

Sometimes women can help to deliver their own breech babies by leaning forward and lifting the baby's legs up, while the doctor or midwife controls the delivery of the head and supports a shoulder. I first saw this done by mistake when a very helpful midwife told a first-time mother to put her hands down and touch her baby while its head was still inside her. The mother was so excited that she held the baby's legs, lifted them, and as she did so the head slipped out without an episiotomy.

Epidural anesthesia (see page 309) is very often used for breech deliveries and indeed has replaced general anesthesia. It means that you only feel a pulling sensation, and that even if delivery is complicated you are awake and aware and can hold your baby as soon as it is breathing well. Discuss this with your obstetrician. Even if a cesarean section is the safest option for your baby, there is no need to be unconscious if you do not want to be.

Doctors who prefer to do routine cesarean sections for all breech babies explain their practice by saying that vaginal delivery lowers a baby's IQ. In fact, it is doubtful whether there are any long-term benefits for the baby of cesarean section over vaginal birth. Carefully controlled follow-up studies of the health and behavior of 2- and 8-year-olds who were born bottom-first have revealed that the mode of delivery makes no difference at all.* When thinking ahead to the kind of birth you will have for your breech baby, it is important to remember that the pelvis is not a rigid, confined space. During

Standard breech birth
Breech babies can be born vaginally as long as the pelvic outlet is wide enough for the head to pass through it.

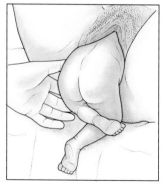

First of all
The buttocks are usually delivered first, and are followed by the baby's legs.

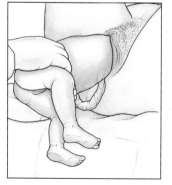

Turning the baby
The baby turns so that the shoulders can emerge as easily as possible.

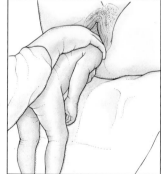

The head appears
The baby's own weight draws the head down and its legs are then lifted to deliver the head.

Breech birth in the squatting position

If you stay more or less upright in early labor, and continue to move around, the downward force of gravity will help push the baby out. Your contractions will be more effective, too, and should prove less painful than if you were lying down.

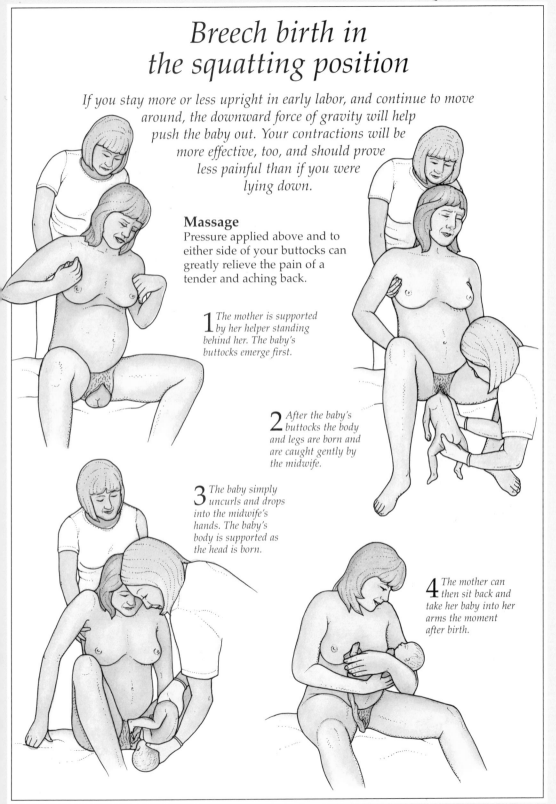

Massage
Pressure applied above and to either side of your buttocks can greatly relieve the pain of a tender and aching back.

1 *The mother is supported by her helper standing behind her. The baby's buttocks emerge first.*

2 *After the baby's buttocks the body and legs are born and are caught gently by the midwife.*

3 *The baby simply uncurls and drops into the midwife's hands. The baby's body is supported as the head is born.*

4 *The mother can then sit back and take her baby into her arms the moment after birth.*

pregnancy the joints relax, bones move more freely on each other, and the pelvis actually expands to make more room for the baby. Moreover, both the width and the size of the opening from front to back are increased in 28 percent of women when they switch from lying down to a squatting position.*

In Dr. Michel Odent's practice most women with breech babies have vaginal births. He likes the woman to be upright: "Our only intervention will be to insist on the supported squatting position for delivery, since it is the most mechanically efficient. It . . . is the best way to minimize the delay between the delivery of the baby's umbilicus and the baby's head . . . We would never risk a breech delivery with the mother in a dorsal or semi-seated position."* If the first stage of labor goes well without any intervention, a woman has every chance of a vaginal birth. But if first stage contractions are inefficient and yet painful, and dilatation does not progress, a cesarean section is decided on.

SHORT SHARP LABOR

It is wrong to assume, as do some obstetric textbooks, that a short labor is bad for the baby. In many apparently short labors the cervix is dilating gently (see page 241) over a period of days before you realize you are in labor. And some short labors can be delightful. But however easy it might be physically, a violent precipitate labor is emotionally demanding and may leave you feeling drained and shocked.

If, from start to finish, your labor lasts less than an hour or two, you may need a great deal of active help from your partner, as well as his or her emotional support: in effect it is like starting straight in at the very end of the first stage. Your partner needs to concentrate with you and to maintain eye contact and breathe with you. A partner who becomes anxious or excited may hyperventilate if everything is happening quickly. So remind each other to keep the breathing butterfly-light over contraction peaks.

When you feel the baby pressing like a grapefruit against your anus it may be easiest to avoid pushing if you turn on your side, with your knees drawn up. But whatever position you choose, push only when you have to and then for as short a time as you can. Open your mouth, drop your jaw, and relax your lips. Then continue breathing in and out through a relaxed mouth and concentrate on releasing all the tissues around your vagina as they fan out and open wide.

If the baby is coming very fast in the second stage you will probably need to blow as well as breathe quickly to stop yourself from pushing. If you feel as if you really must push, blow as if you were extinguishing a candle flame to reduce the intensity of the push (see page 208). You will not stop the push altogether, because the expulsive power of the uterus is there whatever you do, but you can limit it to a certain extent. Some women feel after a labor of this kind that they want the baby inside them again; they wish that they could go back to the beginning, because everything happened so fast that they cannot make sense of it. Some even feel "cheated." If this is so with you, talk through each event of labor with your partner after the birth, fitting the pieces together, and reliving the birth in your thoughts until you can see its shape.

LONG-DRAWN-OUT LABOR

A lengthy labor can be psychologically taxing as well as physically exhausting. You need constant confident emotional support from someone who loves or knows you well and does not leave you. Yet unfortunately a prolonged labor tends to make the partner anxious about what is happening, unsure of his role, and often feeling that he ought to leave it all to the professionals.

A long-drawn-out labor can seem prolonged for two reasons: you may be unable to differentiate clearly between the lead-in to labor proper – sometimes called the "latent" phase – and active labor. Active labor in turn may then be prolonged because contractions are faint and infrequent, or because the contractions are not achieving dilatation of the cervix as they should.

In these cases, psychological support from partner and midwife, accurate information, and an opportunity to rest are vitally important. Even if the contractions seem to be ineffective and dilatation is slow until you reach 4 cm, everything may seem to coordinate suddenly so that from then on labor goes like a bomb. Over 90 percent of women having a lengthy latent phase go on to have a normal labor and delivery if given the chance.* So don't immediately assume that if labor takes several days to start it is going to be like that right through. Have relaxing hot baths, sleep or rest in different beds if possible so that you have a change of scene, and automatically take up different positions. There may be a couch, an easy chair, or even a rug to lie on as a change from your usual bed. Do not go into the hospital until you think you would feel happier there. Even if you have a long first stage, the second stage may be completely normal.

"Throughout the entire labor I was conscious that I could only go with the contractions. I felt it was like running in a marathon."

The progress of your labor is assessed in terms of the rate of dilatation of the cervix (see pages 241–242). Provided the baby is all right and its heart tones are regular, *slow dilatation at the onset of labor does not harm the baby*, however tiring you are finding it. Slow dilatation in the early phase is not the same as complete lack of progress over several hours once active labor has started (that is, after the cervix has dilated about 3 cm); then the baby may be exposed to special risk and the heart rate may slow down.

Do remember that it is difficult for people to be accurate about dilatation: you may be examined by someone who says you are 5 cm dilated, but an hour later someone else says you are only 4 cm or perhaps 5 cm dilated, when by then the first person examining you would have reckoned you to be 6 cm dilated.

WAYS OF DEALING WITH A LONG LABOR

In a hospital it is often difficult to walk about and alternate periods of rest with sessions of activity. But if you can do this, it is the best natural way of helping a uterus which is contracting ineffectually to start working far more efficiently.

Be sure that you are taking enough fluids, as you can forget to drink and become dehydrated. You may be given an intravenous "cocktail" of dextrose solution to keep up your strength and ensure that you do not become dried out. If this is the case, get into an upright position beforehand so that you are not then stuck lying down with an IV in your arm. If you have to stay in bed, take up positions in which the long axis of the uterus is in line with the birth canal. You can do this by kneeling or squatting, and it is one of the most effective non-invasive actions you can take. You can do this *before* taking drugs for pain relief (see page 306–313), having an epidural (see page 309), or accepting hormone acceleration of labor (see page 328).

Sometimes fear or anxiety seems to prevent a uterus from functioning well. If physical difficulties have been ruled out, work together with your partner on facing up to any worries that may be on your mind. Both of you together can create a psychologically positive atmosphere by concentrating on the reality of the baby who is coming to birth and on the visual image of the cervix opening up. In parts of New Guinea, when labor is long drawn out the woman is urged to confess any hidden anger she may feel because it is thought that labor will proceed smoothly and easily once she has got rid of the negative feelings she is bottling up.

The general obstetric term for a long-drawn-out labor is "failure to progress." It is one of the main reasons why cesarean sections are done. In the words of two obstetricians, "In many cases failure to progress is really failure to wait."* However hard the uterus is working it cannot push the baby out unless your cervix is soft and opening up, and in most long-drawn-out labors the cervix simply needs time to soften and open up.

DYSFUNCTIONAL LABOR

One thing that may hold up labor is incoordinate uterine action. Unfortunately it is possible to have massive contractions and yet for the upper segment of the uterus not to be able to draw up and pull open the lower section. It is as if one part of the uterus is working against another part. The result is dysfunctional labor and failure to progress. With this kind of labor, floating or crouching in a birth pool or in a deep bath, with lights dimmed, might help. If there is still no progress, an epidural and augmentation of labor with an oxytocin intravenous drip set up may be the answer. The obstetrician usually decides on augmentation because an epidural itself has the effect of prolonging labor. If you choose an epidural, you will have time for a rest and then, if you wish, the anesthetic can be allowed to wear off a little so that you can push the baby out yourself.

Giving support in labor

It is now accepted that there is a place for fathers in the birth room and that couples often want to be together. There is still some way to go before many hospitals are as welcoming to several companions, or to a woman partner, as they are to the baby's father. They may allow only one person with the woman. Any woman should be able to choose exactly whom she wants with her for this important experience in her life. If the baby's father cannot be with his partner, or if she feels he is not the right person to help her, she may want another person, such as a doula – a woman who is experienced in giving one-to-one support in childbirth – or a woman friend or relation, instead of, or along with, the father. In many cultures it is not acceptable for the husband to be present. In others women appreciate having their partners there simply to know that they can rely on them and that they are loved, and gain strength from this. In the past, women in childbirth have always been supported by other women. A woman should not be deprived of companionship because her male partner cannot offer the support she needs, or she does not want him with her, or because religious or cultural tradition prohibits it. Although this section is addressed mainly to fathers, it is also meant to give guidance to anyone helping at the birth.

Research has shown that the presence of an experienced doula or other woman reduces the need for pain-relieving drugs, shortens labor, makes the birth an easier and happier experience, and results in fewer babies needing intensive care.*

For whomever is going to support a woman in childbirth, it is important to learn in advance exactly how to help most effectively. Childbirth education classes can be useful in teaching how to give emotional and physical support, in exploring emotional aspects of birth, and in understanding the stresses felt by a birth partner. Massage, help with breathing, all the techniques learned in prenatal couples' classes, can be really useful. Or they may not. You may not want your partner to do anything except give quiet encouragement. Though you may want to be held, you may not want to be touched. Some fathers, especially anxious ones, get too busy and do not realize that a woman may need her own space. This becomes intrusive and can have a negative effect on the progress of labor.

THE FATHER AT THE BIRTH

The man who knows what he can do to help is in a much better position than the one who is merely invited into the birth room but has no idea of what is going on. He has every opportunity to be an informed and knowledgeable participant. It is not just a question of holding his partner's hand, although this can be a way of giving emotional support, but of being able to judge where and when she needs guidance and encouragement with relaxation. He has also learned how to breathe "over" the contractions so that he can breathe with his partner at times when she needs extra support. He knows how to rub her back and do gentle, light massage over her lower abdomen when the uterus is opening up, and how to apply firm pressure to her shoulders, arms, and legs.

It can, however, be one thing to learn how to give support in the friendly atmosphere of a small childbirth class where couples are working together, with much discussion interspersed with laughter, and quite another to put that learning to use in a large, impersonal hospital. Confronted in labor with masked figures in white or green whom he has never met before, whose names he does not know, in a strange clinical environment, he can feel out of place, in spite of consent by the hospital to his presence at the birth.

This is why it is a good idea for him, as well as for his partner, to have toured the hospital and especially the birth room beforehand. Women sometimes say that it was when they were approached with some unfamiliar piece of equipment in birth that they began to tense up, and that if they had known what it looked like and how it worked they would have found it much easier to stay relaxed. And men who have been giving good support to their partners before an apparatus of this kind is used sometimes give up, as they feel that the machinery is controlling the labor.

This is understandable, because when an intravenous drip stand or monitoring equipment is brought to the bed it is difficult for the man to get close to his partner, and because a monitoring belt which fits round her abdomen may make it impossible for him to massage that area. In most hospitals, too, once the labor is monitored and speeded up, a nurse will stay with the patient all the time, so the intimacy that the couple had in earlier labor is lost. This can lead to them feeling that experts and machinery have taken over.

The kind of support you can give

The most important thing for a companion helping a woman during the long first stage of labor is to be relaxed. This is difficult in an exciting situation, but any anxiety is immediately communicated to her. If labor is different from what you expected, that awareness can worry you more than the woman, who is enveloped in the force sweeping through her body and who may shut out irrelevant stimuli. You, however, may be made anxious by the doctor's tone of voice, the nurse's remark to a colleague, or by the (quite normal) appearance of blood-stained mucus during a contraction. Ask for information, because if you are in doubt about anything, it is better to find out early rather than late. Speak slowly and quietly. Move slowly and deliberately. Touch your partner without haste, resting a relaxed hand on her body and, when you lift your hand away, do so slowly. If you are massaging her, stroke very slowly.

Opposite
The late first stage, with contractions coming every two minutes, may feel like a whirlwind.

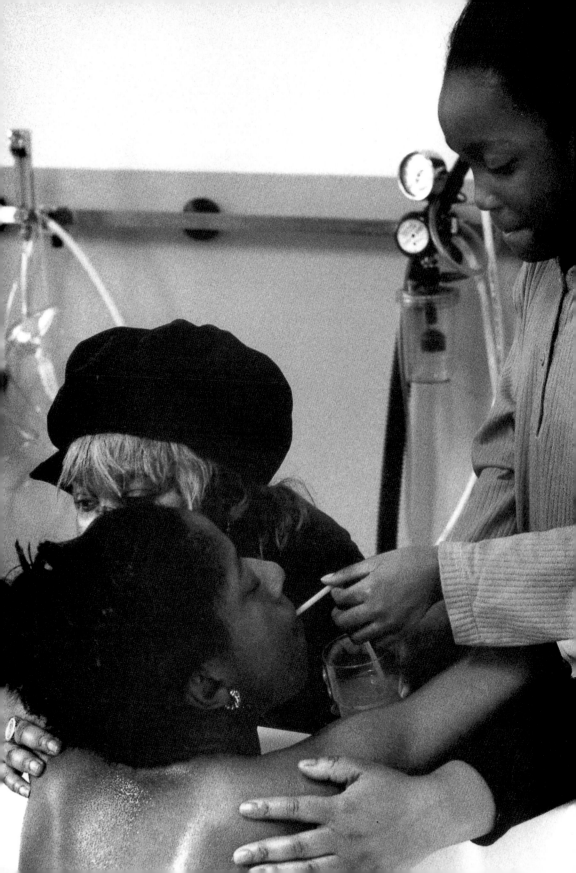

DISTRACTIONS IN THE BIRTH ROOM

When helping her to achieve focused concentration on what is happening in her body during contractions, never break that concentration by chatting to anyone else, watching a machine, or allowing yourself to be distracted by what is going on around you. As well as causing the woman in labor to become anxious and tense up, modern equipment often fascinates her companion, who may become so involved with watching the monitor, for example, that the woman takes second place and feels that emotional support has been withdrawn. You should not forget that, however sophisticated the machinery, it is the woman who is actually having the baby. Once labor is well under way, your attention should be focused entirely on her, and encouragement by word, touch, or look should be given with every single contraction.

On the hospital's side, too, an induced or speeded-up and monitored labor becomes an interesting clinical exercise. Midwives, doctors, and students may come in to watch. Teaching may go on at the bedside. Discussions about the equipment sometimes take place while the woman is busy with a contraction and would appreciate silence so that she can concentrate better. Although you cannot insist that everyone be quiet during contractions, you can indicate politely by your own silence and attention to her that you are not available for conversation, and encourage her to enter a "circle of solitude" with you and the baby coming to birth.

Occasionally machines break down and engineers arrive. This can be very distracting for the woman in labor. Fortunately she is not dependent on the monitor or other pieces of equipment to have her baby. Give her your full and undivided attention during the labor. Be on the same level, not towering over her. Use eye contact to give her emotional support. If she is coping well, she may like to close her eyes and handle contractions without looking at anybody, but if the going gets hard, suggest that she open her eyes and that you go through it together. This is likely to be of special help at the end of the first stage of labor, after her cervix is 6 cm dilated.

POSITIVE SUPPORT DURING CONTRACTIONS

Everything you say should be positive. Avoid saying "You're not relaxed here" or "Your shoulders are tightening." Say "Your feet are beautifully relaxed. Do the same with your hands" or give her positive suggestions such as "Pull your shoulders down and now let them go." When she is doing well, tell her so. This helps most as contractions reach their peak. It can be useful to hold her shoulder firmly during big contractions and if she has practiced relaxation techniques that help her flow out toward your touch (see pages 186–194), these will keep her shoulders loose and so avoid hyperventilating. Between contractions talk to her about where she likes to be held. She may find it helps her to work with her contraction if you describe to her what is happening as the uterus goes into action: "You are opening up wider and wider. Your cervix is being pulled up and open, and the baby's head is pressing right down." Ruth Wilf, an experienced American midwife, suggests that if the woman seems out of touch with her body the support person should quietly discuss with her, between contractions, any negative thoughts she may be having. This gives you something to work on during the next contraction. Create an image for the next one – the baby pressing down, the cervix opening up – and use your hands to suggest gradual opening. After the next contraction ask, "How was that compared to the last one?" The woman may be able to suggest other things you can do to help her focus her concentration.

UNDERSTANDING THE LABOR'S PROGRESS

She also needs information on what is about to be done by her birth attendants. Being in labor can be disorienting. Fear of the unknown is the main reason why women panic, and a request for pain-relieving drugs is usually one for reassurance. A woman may be distressed because she does not realize the progress she is making. She loses all sense of time and each contraction is so enveloping that she cannot see the pattern of her labor. So be clear about the progress of labor and prepare her for what is about to happen. For instance, if the waters have not broken by the time contractions are coming every two minutes, you can be fairly sure that they will break

"I couldn't have done without my partner. I really needed his strength, especially as it took me a long time to push the baby out."

soon. If she does not want to have an amniotomy (see page 317), make this clear to the doctor. If she has one, prepare her for the renewed strength of contractions after it and discuss with her how she might change her breathing to cope with them. In the second stage remind her that the hot, throbbing, tingling feeling is a sign that the baby is about to be born and will soon be in her arms.

Know when to be quiet. This depends very much on your empathy with her. Talk when it helps, but keep quiet when you can give other forms of emotional and physical support. Facial expression, gesture, touch, and massage are all very important. One of the best ways of helping is to rest a hand on her shoulder with the other hand at her wrist as she goes through the contraction. If she has backache, she will welcome firm pressure or massage over the sacrum, or slightly to one side of it (see page 192).

HOW TO HELP WITH BREATHING

Breathe with her through difficult contractions. Do not wait until she is tense to start the breathing. Begin with a relaxed breath out together. Keep closely in rhythm with her own breathing at the beginning of the contraction so that there is a partnership. Do not impose a radically different level or rate of breathing on her, or it will become a fight between her breathing and yours. If she starts to drag through the contraction with heavy gasping breaths, this is the time to try to differentiate your breathing from hers. When you think it is appropriate, try moving your hand in a light butterfly-wing movement in order to stress the lightness of breathing that is necessary when the uterus is at its tightest.

Help her enjoy complete relaxation between contractions. This is especially important in stressful labors, as otherwise the woman carries her tension from one contraction to the next and it is cumulative. When she is relaxed, you can talk together about how to meet the next contraction. Avoid complicated anatomical and physiological terms. When you speak about the uterus or cervix, remember it is "your" uterus and "your" cervix, just as it is also "your" or "our" baby. Words used during contractions should be simple, rhythmic, and repetitive.

COPING WITH PAIN

Labor companions are often unsure whether or not they should mention the word "pain." For some it is taboo. It is imperative to acknowledge pain when it exists and not pretend that it is not there. To do so is to deny a woman the validity of her own experience and to say in effect: "You aren't feeling what you think you are feeling, and if you are, there must be something wrong with you or with your labor." If she tells you it hurts, agree and say, "I understand" or "Yes, I realize that." It might be the moment to add, "Your uterus is working very hard" or "The baby is pressing right down" and also to help her see the pattern of her labor. If she is more than 6 or 7 cm dilated she is now at the most difficult part of labor. Show her with your hand how far she is dilated. Help her to change position, freshen her up with a face wash, brush her hair, and use massage to help her. Give her your total, undivided attention. Emotional support of this kind can often take the place of drugs for pain relief.

"We didn't plan on my husband being there for the birth. But the doctor took it for granted he would come into the room. He was pleased as Punch and afterward could not stop talking about it!"

The most undermining thing that you can possibly do to a woman in labor is to encourage her to feel sorry for herself. The woman who is told by her helper, "I can't bear to see you in such pain," or words to that effect, is actually being deprived of emotional support. Even the expression on a helper's face can give that message, sometimes even more clearly than words could do. We would not think much of someone who leaned over the side of an ocean liner and called to the person in the water, "It looks terrible down there. The waves are so huge and, poor thing, you look as if you are drowning. Do you want an injection?" Yet this is the equivalent of the sympathy and the offer of "something to take away the pain" that some attendants offer to a woman in labor. The woman who has prepared herself for labor often wants help to enable her to cope with the mountainous waves rather than the offer of a drunken stupor or sensation-free childbirth. If she wants drugs for pain relief, this should always be entirely her own decision. If she does ask for narcotics or an epidural, she should do so freely, certainly not because she has been persuaded or coerced.

STAYING TOGETHER

If you feel queasy or that you must have a break, tell your partner you will be back in a moment and stroll out. Women especially need support when they are being examined, when drugs for pain relief are offered, or when there is any intervention, and for you to go out then is the worst time. This is one point in labor when the woman can herself speak up and state her preferences. She could say, "I'd very much like my husband to stay, please. Don't send him away. I really need him," or "I don't think I'll be relaxed if he goes out." She could add, "He's learned about what happens and understands it pretty well. He's being a wonderful support!"

START AND STOP LABOR

Some labors seem to come to a full stop for a time and a woman may be stuck at 4 cm dilatation or more for several hours. This is a sign for a change of activity and a change of scene. Lying flat on one's back is not a good position for labor, from either the woman's or the baby's point of view. You can see that she does not slip down in the bed. When she is lying on her left side or is upright the blood flows freely to the placenta, allowing more oxygen and nutrients to get through to the baby than when she is lying flat on her back, and it is also easier to cope with backache.

It is not a good idea to lie still for long periods, so suggest that she may like to roll over onto the other side occasionally or to sit well up. If she is sitting, supported by four or five pillows, there is not the same problem of decreased blood flow to the placenta. It is also fine if she wants to squat, kneel, stand, or adopt any of the many positions which women spontaneously choose to adopt in labor (see pages 210–215). But the variety of possible positions is obviously very much limited if IVs and machinery are in use.

If labor comes to a stop, encourage her to get up and move around. If she is already walking around, suggest a bath or a shower, perhaps a back massage, and then rest in bed with hot water bottles placed around the areas where she aches. Jamaican folk midwives give the woman a sponge bath and then wrap her in hot towels and offer a drink of hot thyme or mixed-spice tea when labor fails to progress. Perhaps we could learn something from this.

A full bladder can cause unnecessary pain. It used to be thought that it could also hold up labor, but there is no evidence to support this. For her own comfort, remind the woman to empty her bladder every hour and a half, or more frequently if she feels she needs to do so. If progress is slow, help her to feel that her natural pace is the right pace. Each labor is different and having a baby is not a competition to see who can do it fastest or conform to a norm.

A water birth

Jane's third baby was born under water. She decided to give birth at home with a midwife who was experienced with water birth, and to rent a birth pool. When she sank into the water she experienced instant pain relief.

The birth went smoothly and she breathed the baby's head out by herself while the midwife watched and waited. The cord was loosely around the baby's neck, and her midwife unwound it under water and lifted the baby to the surface. They waited for the cord to stop pulsating and then Stewart cut it. She

squatted and pushed out the placenta while still in the pool. Her midwife said, "It was such magic, being there!"

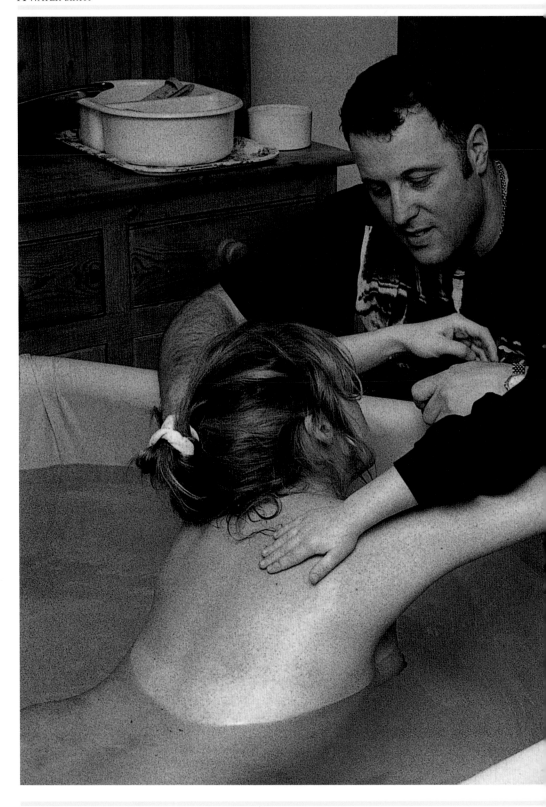

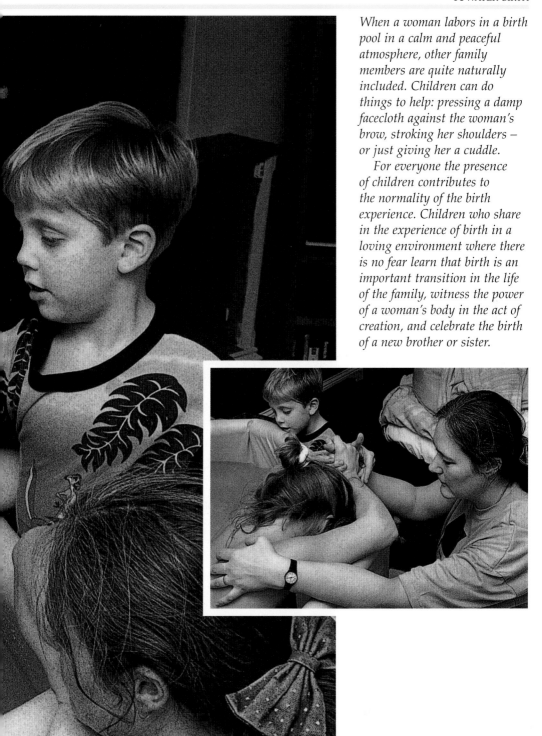

When a woman labors in a birth pool in a calm and peaceful atmosphere, other family members are quite naturally included. Children can do things to help: pressing a damp facecloth against the woman's brow, stroking her shoulders – or just giving her a cuddle.

For everyone the presence of children contributes to the normality of the birth experience. Children who share in the experience of birth in a loving environment where there is no fear learn that birth is an important transition in the life of the family, witness the power of a woman's body in the act of creation, and celebrate the birth of a new brother or sister.

It is easy to move in water and a woman often switches between forward leaning and other upright positions without even thinking about it, because it feels right at the time. This movement helps the rotation and descent of the baby's head.

One position a woman may like to adopt as she pushes the baby down is a supported squat, her upper back against the side of the pool and her partner's arms under her shoulders. It is important that he not press on nerves under her arms and that he hold her securely without gripping her. Her knees are spread wide so that her pelvis is open. She feels her pelvic floor muscles and the tissues of her perineum fanning out as the baby presses through, until at last the top of the head can be seen glistening in her vagina.

Then she has another passionate urge to push and the head begins to slide forward. The midwife watches, leaving the baby to uncurl naturally, her hands poised to support the body as it emerges. Gently, carefully, intermittently pushing and breathing, the mother eases the head out. Only one more push, the shoulders are free, and the whole body slides out.

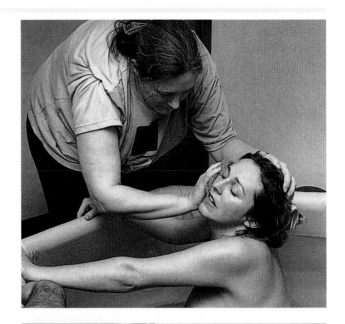

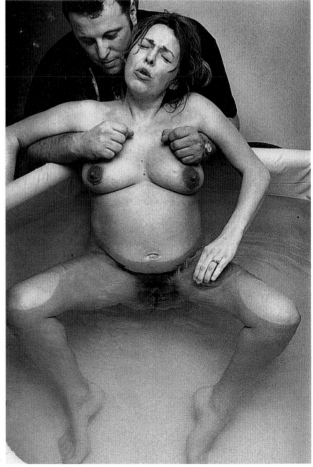

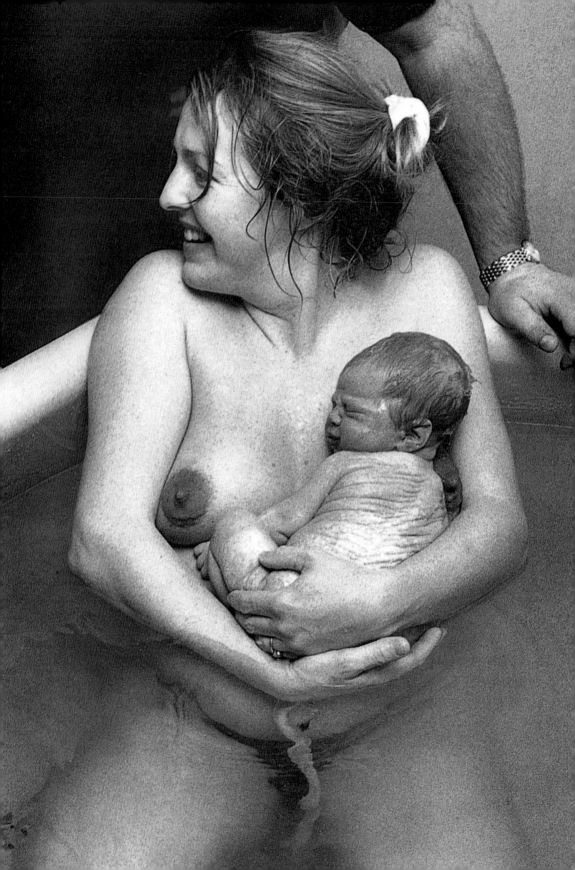

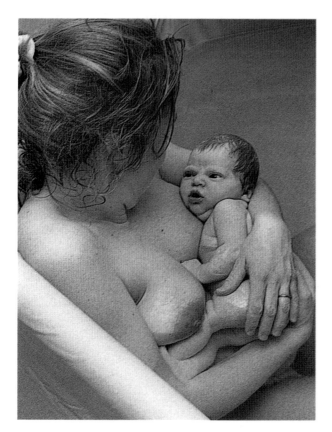

The baby is lifted gently from the water immediately into the mother's arms, either by the midwife or by the mother herself. The cord is not clamped and cut until it has ceased to pulsate, thus enabling the baby to receive the blood which rightfully belongs to her.

With eyes wide open, in the quiet alert state that often follows birth, this baby gazes at her two brothers who welcome her with delight. As her mother cradles her in her arms they start the first of many "conversations" together and join in the dance of interaction which is the basis of all later socialization.

Especially when labor is long, affirm your confidence in her own body rhythms. Between 8 and 10 cm dilatation the woman may feel lost and tossed in the sweep and turmoil of contractions following on each other almost without a break. Keep eye contact and breathe with her through each contraction. Letting her know that you trust her own natural rhythms is nowhere more important than at this point, when many women are made to feel that it is a race to the finishing line. Her legs may feel very cold and begin to shake, and you can help her by firmly massaging the inside of her thighs.

THE LULL

There is often an apparent pause in labor for 20 minutes or more when the woman's cervix is just about fully dilated. She may have no urge to push, and may feel no contractions, yet her attendants are alert for the start of the second stage. They expect action but nothing seems to be happening. They may worry that the uterus is not going to do its job of pushing the baby out, and some try to get the woman to push even though she does not feel like it, so that she gets exhausted. They may also call for oxytocin to stimulate contractions.

If the woman feels rushed and that there are anxious eyes upon her, she becomes tense and anxious herself. Reassure her that there is all the time in the world. This is a normal part of the unfolding birth process – the "rest and be thankful" phase when the baby's head is still not deep in the pelvis. The head usually drops lower naturally if she is able to rest and refresh herself.

So help her stand up, perhaps take a shower, offer her a sponge bath, and put some music on the tape recorder. She may want to walk around, gently rocking and circling her pelvis, perhaps enjoying slow belly dance movements. You can stand cradling her body against yours as she does so, holding her shoulders, elbows, or wrists, and move with her. After half an hour or so – occasionally an hour or more – contractions pick up, and with renewed energy and excitement she enters the expulsive stage. She has had a refreshing interval before the drama of the second stage.

"It is not a question of just being there for her sake, but for your own. You don't know what you're missing if you are not at the birth."

SUPPORT IN THE SECOND STAGE

When the woman begins to push the baby out, she can be in any position which feels comfortable to her: held firmly in your arms, or cradled by your body, or with something solid to grasp or over which she can lean. She needs to be free to round her back, roll her shoulders forward, and rest her chin on her chest during contractions. You can help by providing physical support if she wants it and, perhaps, by reminding her to keep her head forward at the height of each pushing urge (without making any attempt to force it forward). From time to time give her a sip of water or juice through a bendable straw or ice chips to suck.

Do not say "push." Say "open up" instead. Straining wastes valuable energy and results in uncoordinated expulsive efforts. If you suggest she does not push at all unless she feels she has to, she will push in the right way at the right time.

Avoid clock-watching. It can be as disastrous to have one eye on the clock as it would be if you were watching the clock while trying to make love. A birthing woman needs to feel secure in a world without time or standards of performance, simply able to be herself and experience the intensity of what her body is telling her to do. If the pushing urge is strong and difficult to control, and it looks as if everything is happening too fast, help her lie on her side or get down on all fours, as this may reduce the impulse. Encourage her to put her hands down and feel even before any part of the baby's head is oozing through the vagina, then use a mirror for her to see the top of the head as it crowns. If you see that the crown is moving forward, but she is still holding her breath, say quietly, "Breathe." She should breathe out and go on breathing in and out with a dropped jaw.

SHARING IN THE BIRTH
Many women are anxious that they might be too small. Reassure her that there is room, and her feelings of openness and flexibility will help to make room. The power of suggestion is so great that each word and phrase used can affect her ability to work with her body.

When you are with a woman in childbirth, you share with her a journey into the unknown. The helper is like the lookout on a yacht sailing at night, watching for the coastline and helping to steer her through. She needs your constant presence and to be left alone is the most frightening thing of all. Giving support in labor needs vigilance, skill, patience, an understanding of a woman's rhythms, her responses to stress, an awareness of what she is thinking and how she is feeling at each moment, and your complete commitment to this task. Sometimes it demands endurance and courage. It can be hard, exhausting work. But yours, too, is the excitement, the deep satisfaction, and joy when a child is born.

Surprise delivery

If you are alone with a woman who is giving birth the most important thing is to stay calm yourself and give her quiet and confident support. Drop your shoulders and relax! Tell her she is doing well. Hold her in your arms and help her to feel secure.

MAKING HER COMFORTABLE
If the room is cold, heat it. The baby will need a warm environment after birth. If you can, place a pile of newspapers or a plastic sheet or tablecloth under the mother. She may like to sit or kneel on a firm cushion or bean bag. Cover whatever she is on with a sheet if there is one available. Find some big towels, a blanket, or something else

warm to wrap the baby in. Offer her sips of water if her mouth is dry. Put pillows or some sort of firm support behind her back, shoulders, and head to allow her to sit up comfortably or for her to lean over unless she prefers some other position: her own feelings about this are likely to be right. If traces of feces appear at her anus, wipe with cotton or toilet paper down and away from the vagina. Wash your hands and scrub your nails thoroughly.

If she is pushing, gently remind her to "open up" and not to hold her breath or push unless she feels she needs to. Just before the head crowns, suggest that she pant, so that from then on she *breathes* the baby out instead of pushing it out. She can then push gently *between* the contractions if the birth is slow.

If a loop of cord is around the baby's neck as its head slides out, hook a finger around it and lift it carefully over the head. Take care not to pull the baby or the cord, as this may detach the placenta from the wall of the uterus. If a membrane is over the baby's face, lift it off. Either you or she can then catch the baby. Lift the baby up onto the mother's upper thigh or tummy, with the head slightly down so that any mucus can drain away safely.

AFTER THE BIRTH

Cover the mother and baby with a coat or blanket, or better still a quilt, which is both light and warm. Then put a bowl between the mother's legs to receive the placenta as soon as she feels more contractions. There is no need to cut the cord. Enjoy the peace as you together admire the baby and wait for the placenta. Make her comfortable. She may be shivery and appreciate a hot water bottle and a cup of tea. When the baby is ready to suck, lift it to the breast so that the nipple is well back in the mouth.

If you are in a car, away from any help or home comforts, there is no need to do anything about the placenta or cord. However, if you have a plastic bag or some newspaper, you can wrap the placenta in it and keep it at the same level as the baby.

If you are at home, boil shoelaces or soft string for tying the cord, and scissors for cutting it. If the placenta does not come after about 20 minutes, ask the mother to kneel and give long, slow blows out. It may slip out then. Never pull on the cord. Put a bowl under her buttocks and pour warm water between her legs. She can keep her uterus contracting and reduce bleeding from the placental site by massaging it firmly and putting the baby to the breast.

Tie the cord about 4 in (10 cm) from the baby and again about 6 in (15 cm), and cut with a pair of sterilized scissors or a new razor blade between the ties. Check that there is no bleeding from the cord stump. If there is, do another tie nearer the baby.

The greatest heat loss from a newborn baby is from his head, so cover the head. Keep mother and baby cuddled together and cover both of them. When birth comes by surprise it is unlikely that anything will go wrong. This is nature at its most efficient.

Dealing with pain

"I've got a very low pain threshold. I can't stand going to the dentist, so I can't think what labor is going to be like!"

"The idea of the pain really worries me. I've never really experienced severe pain, and I can't imagine what it's like to be in pain for hours and hours and hours."

"What is labor pain like? I mean, is it like breaking your arm or a bad headache or menstrual cramps or indigestion – or what? If I knew more what it was going to be like I could face it better."

These three statements express what many women who are pregnant for the first time feel, but perhaps do not acknowledge or put into words: fear that pain is going to be overpowering, a sense that they have never experienced pain that tested their inner resources, and ignorance of the kind of pain that is likely to be felt.

PUTTING PAIN IN ITS CONTEXT
People often think that pain is just a matter of a "high" or "low" threshold. There are very few women who think that they have a high threshold and can bear pain as well as other women. In fact, the idea of simple thresholds like walls, with some of us possessing high walls and others low ones, is a myth.

It is now known that in all human beings the pain sensation threshold is exactly the same.* In one study in the United States, members of Italian, Jewish, Irish, and Old American ethnic groups were all given electric shocks ranging from mild to fairly strong, and every single person said pain occurred at exactly the same point. Yet obviously people do not *react* to pain in the same way and there are times when a pain which you once bore easily becomes too much to take and you cannot stand it any more. Toothache that you can cope with without difficulty when you are busy and preoccupied can be absolutely shattering when you go to bed, lie down, and try to go to sleep. So you cannot judge the degree of pain by seeing how an individual reacts in a laboratory situation.

People may see a pain-producing stimulus as a test of their power to *endure* pain, and so may not be ready to admit to being hurt. In the Sudan, for instance, a young man who cannot bear pain loses social esteem and is unlikely to find a girl to marry him. As in many cultures, the ability to bear pain stoically is part of a code of values.

In every society there are cultural stress points, situations which are seen as threatening and thus predispose people to feel pain. When we know what makes people anxious, we can begin to understand these stress points. In many societies some painful stimuli may be linked with pleasure. Take lovemaking for example: slightly painful stimulation may be sought because it is sexually exciting. The borderline between pleasure and pain can be indistinct.

The context within which the pain occurs is important. As an experiment,* electric shocks were given to test people first when they were feeling relaxed and cheerful, and then when they had been made to feel anxious. The electric shocks were felt as much less painful when the subjects were feeling cheerful. In another study,* as many as 35 percent of a doctor's patients experienced marked pain relief when given a placebo, an inactive substance which they believed was a painkiller. It has also been found that the degree of pain tolerated bears a direct relation to the rate of increase in pain, rather than to the level of pain reached.* A person experiencing a pain stimulus that gets worse rapidly feels it more than someone experiencing just as strong a stimulus that takes longer to reach the same point. It may help to have time to *adapt* to pain.

This may have particular relevance to very rapid labor, especially an induced labor (see page 324), when the pace is more than a woman can cope with. We sometimes talk about labor as if a long labor were difficult and a short one easy. But speed alone can give no indication at all of how a woman experiences her labor.

Pain perception involves not only a recording of the stimulus by the brain, but a judgment as to its significance, and its place in the scheme of things – the meaning of the total situation in which the stimulus occurs. The experience of pain in labor is profoundly influenced by the values of the society in which the woman grew up and everything that she learned about birth when she was a child.

So labor pain is partly a product of personal and social values about the meaning of childbirth. The way we eat, sleep, empty our bowels, make love, have babies, and die makes these experiences more than simple biological acts. They all express ideas, for the most part shared, about good and evil, beauty and ugliness, the pure and the polluting, what is considered to be healthy and what diseased, and what is normal and what abnormal.

SOME PHYSICAL CAUSES OF BIRTH PAIN

As the first stage of labor progresses, nerve fibers that record pain are stimulated because the muscles of the uterus are squeezed tightly. A similar thing happens if you contract a muscle in your leg or arm very tightly and hold it taut for a minute or so. When you consider that the uterus is the largest muscle in your body, it is not surprising that this squeezing hurts. Pain of this kind is a sign that a woman is having good, strong contractions.

When the uterus contracts firmly the flow of oxygenated blood into the muscle and of deoxygenated blood out of the muscle is slowed down until the contraction is over. For this reason, there is a temporary build-up of waste products, which are released again in the interval between the contractions. Relaxing and taking slow, complete breaths as soon as each contraction is over enables you to provide the necessary fresh oxygen for this hard-working muscle so that it is able to continue to function effectively.

As the cervix is stretched to make space for the baby to pass through localized pain is felt at the place where the cervix is dilating. This pain, at the very bottom of your abdomen, is common in straightforward labors and a good sign that your cervix is opening.

When pelvic ligaments and joints are stretched as the bony pelvis spreads wide and the baby descends, nerve fibers that run through them are stimulated, resulting in pain as your body opens up. This kind of pain from stretched ligaments, though difficult to handle, is a sign that your body is working well.

A baby who is not curled up, head down, in a neat ball with its chin tucked into its chest, may take longer to pass through the cervix and down the birth canal, and the pressure produced by the back of its head sticking into the small of the mother's back, or the unflexed head pushing down through soft tissues, can cause pain. This also happens sometimes if the baby is very big. As contractions become stronger and more frequent they usually have the effect of rolling the baby around and down into a better position. So this kind of pain may disappear entirely once the way is clear and you can push. You can help your baby to rotate into the best position by being upright or on all fours. Upright positions such as standing, kneeling, or squatting enable you to use gravity to your advantage. An all-fours position lets the baby drop away from your spine so that it can turn more easily against your springy abdominal wall.

"The backache was bad, but I kept thinking of what you said, 'The baby is opening the gate,' and suddenly her head turned and from then on it was easy."

PAIN RELIEF IN OTHER CULTURES

There are two myths about the ways in which women in the Third World give birth. One is that labor is always horrific and dangerous, but that women do not cry out because of strong taboos against showing that they are in pain. The other is that the women all have completely painless births, and just squat down in the fields and have their babies before getting back to work again. The truth is probably somewhere in between the two extremes. In many Third World countries healthy women have straightforward labors while other, malnourished women suffer a great deal.

Most cultures have methods of relieving pain in childbirth, so there is obvious recognition that it exists. But the ways in which pain is relieved and labor made more comfortable are radically different in the technological Western countries. We can give complete relief of pain and remove all sensation from the waist down with regional anesthesia. This is what an epidural does (see page 309). We have other forms of pain relief which partially remove pain or which eradicate the memory of it. We rely on pharmacological substances to do this for us. Herbal medicines are used in the Third World and some of them have narcotic or mood-altering properties, just like modern drugs, though it is much more difficult to prepare the right dose when you are using plants. There are also other kinds of help which are much favored in these countries and which used to be employed in the West but tend to be ignored in hospitals today. They include religious and magic rites, counterstimulation, massage, hot and cold compresses, changes in position, and emotional support from others sharing the experience with the woman in labor. These supporters hold her, stroke her, rock her back and forth, and live through the birth *with* her rather than do things *to* her as a patient.

Much of what is done by birth attendants in other cultures provides simple, practical help based on the handed-down experiences of generations of women. It is also intended to have a psychosomatic effect, helping the baby to be born by positively influencing the mind of the woman in labor. This kind of practical help in labor may be forgotten or misunderstood in our modern hospitals. Yet there are advantages in being able to cope without drugs if possible, because all powerful drugs have side effects and they all go through the mother's bloodstream to her baby.

IMAGINING YOUR LABOR IN ADVANCE

In preparing for birth it is a good idea to work out how you might like to be helped to be more comfortable and also how you can use your mind to help your body through relaxation, focused concentration, and ideas and mental images that produce a harmonious pattern between what is going on inside your uterus and the way you think about it. You may find that all this is difficult to conceptualize before you have your first baby.

Trying to master your body or running away from the sensations you are experiencing can actually produce pain, because you are bound to become tense and then chemical messages are sent instantaneously into your bloodstream which affect your whole metabolism. This causes changes in skin, blood pressure and heart rate, breathing, digestion and defecation, as well as changes in muscle tone. Psychosomatic factors can even change the action of the uterus itself in ways we do not yet fully understand. A woman who is very anxious may have a long labor because her uterus does not work efficiently or stops contracting altogether.

"My mind was full of sea images. It was as if I was an island with waves rushing and swirling and opening my body in readiness for birth."

WHAT LABOR FEELS LIKE

In a normal labor any pain experienced is quite different from the pain of breaking a leg, for example, or being injured. The physical feelings produced by a strongly contracting uterus are powerful and challenging. They are likely to involve a combination of sensations – a very tight squeeze, a pulling open of tissues, and the firm downward pressure of the solid ball of the baby's head through a passage which is being slowly stretched wide. In films you sometimes see a pregnant woman suddenly double up, her hands clasped over the top of her abdomen. The director is telling viewers that labor has started. But it never happens like this in reality. Instead there is a sensation of being gripped by tightening muscles low down in your abdomen or in the small of your back. All the sensations are at hip level. Nor is the feeling a sudden one. A contraction has a wavelike shape, building up to a crest and then subsiding and disappearing until the next contraction. There is always a rest period between them, often lasting a minute or more, even in the stormy late first stage. As contractions get stronger, longer, and closer together the tightening may extend right around your body, so that it feels more like a circle of thick, wide elastic across your pelvis which is being steadily drawn in, held firm, and then slowly released again. Or you may be conscious of expansion during contractions and aware of the top of the uterus spreading and rising, tilting forward in your abdomen, while the great muscle squeezes its lower part open and thereby presses the baby down.

"PAIN WITH A PURPOSE"

The feelings that this produces may be painful, but it is pain with a purpose and thus different from the pain of injury. Contractions are not painful in themselves, and in fact the uterus contracts strongly and rhythmically at intervals in the second half of pregnancy, usually without causing any pain. It is the peak of the contraction, when the muscle is working hardest and is making most progress, that is most likely to be perceived as painful, and this may last as long as 30 seconds or as little as 15 seconds.

The idea of a pain that is *qualitatively* different from other kinds of pain is difficult to accept for anyone who has not experienced it. Yet sheer physical effort, like that involved in running a race or climbing a mountain, produces just that kind of "functional" pain, the ache of muscles that are working very hard. If the athlete thought only of pain instead of about winning the race, she would give up. If the mountaineer thought that her aching muscles were the sign of some dreadful physical injury instead of the natural result of working them so hard, she would forget all about her goal and lose the feeling of triumph when she reaches the summit.

Pain in labor is the by-product of the body's creative activity. Contractions are *not* pains. They are tightenings which may be painful, especially when they are being most effective. There is an art in approaching each new contraction, in thinking "Splendid! Here's another one!" and later, as you approach the end of the first stage, when they are at their strongest, "Oh, this is a really good one!"

When you are in the thick of labor, your whole self is involved. It is almost impossible to think about other things or to hold a part of yourself back in any way. The intensity of labor can be frightening, especially for the unprepared woman who does not know what to expect, or for one who wants to keep it all at the level of a learned skill, doing her exercises in much the same way as she might carry out a three-point turn in a driving test. This is why preparation merely for handling contractions is never enough. You also need to prepare yourself mentally and emotionally for the overwhelming nature of the sensations and feelings of labor.

HYPNOSIS

Some women find that hypnosis is an effective method of relieving pain in labor, and it has the great advantage over chemical anesthetics of not reducing the baby's oxygen intake. In fact, about a quarter of women who have had hypnosis in childbirth say that they experienced no pain, but results do vary and most women who have hypnosis need chemical pain relief as well.

The common belief that hypnosis involves some kind of magic trickery and that you can be made to do anything the hypnotist wishes is actually very wide of the mark. Hypnosis is a state of increased suggestibility that is induced by deep relaxation and concentration and you can prepare yourself with a good practitioner so that you can, if you wish, use *auto*hypnosis.

With hypnosis, some women become immune to pain and may have a forceps delivery or be stitched up after an episiotomy without a local anesthetic. It has been calculated that two out of every hundred women can be so deeply hypnotized that they could even have a cesarean section without feeling any pain.*

If you agree to have hypnosis in childbirth you are usually trained in progressive relaxation to remove anxiety and taught to think positively about childbirth. If you want to try autohypnosis, the hypnotist will suggest that you put yourself to sleep and wake up when you wish. After the birth the doctor may suggest that in the future you only be hypnotized by someone for a therapeutic purpose, so that you need not be afraid of being put into a trance by anyone using hypnosis for their own purposes or for fun.

It could be claimed that all good childbirth classes teach an element of autohypnosis. Childbirth educators do not usually like to admit this. Yet in many ways thinking ahead to labor constructively when one is deeply relaxed is equivalent to using the power of suggestion. Whether or not you decide to try hypnosis, you can use autosuggestion and positive fantasies about labor and your beautiful baby in a creative way to prepare yourself for childbirth, in the knowledge that this is completely safe.

ACUPUNCTURE

Acupuncture is another way of reducing pain in childbirth. It derives from a completely different system of beliefs about the human body from that of Western medicine. Hair-fine needles are used to stimulate 12 lines of energy called "channels" flowing beneath the skin. This energy keeps the blood circulating, warms the body, and combats illness. Acupuncture is used prenatally, for example, to relieve nausea and vomiting, cure constipation, encourage a breech baby to turn, and start off labor. Acupuncturists also sometimes use moxibustion, the burning of a small pellet of mugwort at certain parts of the body, to turn the baby. In labor electroacupuncture may be used at points in the ear for analgesia, and with this technique the woman herself can control the degree of stimulation.*

In Peking nowadays acupuncture is performed in preference to epidural anesthesia for 98 percent of cesarean sections.* It is also sometimes combined with small quantities of drugs.

The advantages of acupuncture are that it is non-invasive, easily administered by someone trained in the method, and instantly reversible, and babies are in better condition at birth than after Demerol has been given. Some studies show that acupuncture shortens the first stage of labor for women having their first baby. Women say that they feel more in control of labor and delivery than when they have taken drugs for pain relief.*

TRANSCUTANEOUS ELECTRONIC NERVE STIMULATION

With TENS, a pulsed wave of variable intensity is passed through electrodes attached to the skin surface. This seems to stimulate the production of natural pain-relieving substances in the body (endorphins and enkephalins). The electrodes are attached in the first stage and the woman operates a switch like a push-top pen or two dials as she feels a contraction build up. She feels a tingling sensation when it is switched on. The electrode pads are usually stuck on her back, but can also be used on the abdomen or in the groin. The disadvantage of TENS is that it cannot be used in water. It is increasingly popular in some American hospitals.

"One advantage of the TENS machine was that it gave me something active to do, and that helped me get through a long, tiring first stage."

REFLEXOLOGY

Reflexology is similar to shiatsu, which is a form of acupressure. It consists of manual pressure on reflex points in the feet, hands, and face to stimulate subcutaneous nerve endings. The idea behind it is that it causes the brain to release natural endorphins and other chemicals which reduce pain. In childbirth reflexology involves massage and gentle pressure on the feet.

AROMATHERAPY

At its simplest level aromatherapy is a matter of breathing in pleasant smells that help you feel good about yourself. It can provide you with a positive sensory environment for birth. This is useful if you are having your baby in a hospital, where it can erase any off-putting hospital smells and where doctors and midwives can relax and enjoy it, too. There has not been much research into the benefits and risks of aromatherapy in pregnancy and birth. The essences used are highly concentrated and molecules that can cross into the bloodstream may reach the baby. If we demand rigorous trials of drugs, most of which are derived from plants anyway, we should also be insisting on research into the effects of aromatherapy. Plant essences stimulate sensory cells in the nose which send chemical messages to the limbic area of the brain, which cause neurochemicals to be released into the bloodstream. These essences are energizing – imagine smelling an orange, a lemon, eucalyptus, or a sprig of rosemary – or relaxing – imagine breathing in lavender, sweet geranium, or the scent of an old-fashioned rose. Essential oils also stimulate the production of endorphins, the body's natural analgesics which are similar to morphine, so that you are less likely to need medication for pain relief.

Essential oils can be used in different ways. You can put a few drops on a pillow, handkerchief, or hot, damp wash cloth. They can be mixed with a vegetable or nut oil (soya, jojoba, apricot kernel, wheat germ, sunflower, almond, and avocado are all good) and massaged into the skin. They can be added in concentrated form, or mixed with a dispersal oil, to the water of a bath or birth pool. You can use them in a warm foot bath. Or essential oils can be burned in a porcelain vaporizer over a candle or in an electric vaporizer.

As you inhale essential oils notice how your face becomes softer and your breathing slower and fuller. The breathing of fear, anxiety, or panic is rapid and jerky. When you are relaxed and confident, breathing is rhythmic, and each breath is complete, with a slight pause between the breath in and the breath out, and another between the breath out and the breath in. During pregnancy you can experiment with different essential oils to discover which ones work best for you and enable you to breathe easily, and which refresh and reinvigorate you and help any tensions flow out of your body.

Lavender can be put directly on the skin. It can be mixed with one or two other essences, such as camomile, sweet geranium, cedarwood, frankincense, myrrh, jasmine, neroli, rosewood, rosemary, peppermint (but do not use peppermint if you are also taking homeopathic medication), melissa, or mandarin. Some of the essential oils are overpowering if you use more than one or two drops, so sniff the bottles first before you concoct your recipe to make sure that it is well balanced. Some good combinations – all relaxing – are lavender and orange, lemon grass and orange, geranium and orange, ylang ylang, sandalwood, and jasmine. Rose, neroli (very expensive), and sandalwood in jojoba oil can be massaged into your forehead, face, and neck.

"The obstetrician came into the room and asked, 'What's the wonderful smell? Oh, I like that!' The aromatherapy made a relaxing atmosphere that we all enjoyed."

Clary sage should not be used in pregnancy, as it can stimulate uterine contractions. This is why it may be helpful if the cervix is dilating very slowly in labor, if the introductory phases of labor are lasting a long time, or if you are two weeks or more past your due date and want to give some gentle encouragement to your uterus to start contracting. Some books about aromatherapy and reliable sources of oils and advice are listed at the end of this book (see pages 412–413).

HOMEOPATHY

Homeopathy aims to treat the whole person, including the mental and emotional states that have an adverse effect on physical well-being. There are 2,500 homeopathic remedies, many of them derived from plants, but others from metal (gold, silver), animal products (cow's milk, snake venom), allergens (pollen, house dust), and drug extracts (aspirin). The principle behind the remedies is that like is treated with like, but in minute quantities. The more diluted a remedy, the more effective it is.

A homeopathic labor pack might consist of 7-gram bottles of the following remedies:
•Arnica leopard's bane at 30c. It helps reduce bleeding and bruising.
•Hypericum St. John's wort. This promotes healing of skin after injury.

These two can be taken together, starting when labor begins and continuing for at least 5 days.
•Staphisagria stavesacre at 10 ml. A single dose is said to be a remedy for trauma to the urethra. It is also a treatment for postnatal "blues."
•Hypericum and calendula pot marigold can be combined in a 10-ml tincture, which helps to soothe and heal skin that has been bruised or grazed. Mix ten drops with 20 ml of sterile cooled water and just stroke it in wherever you feel sore.*

When you go to a homeopathic practitioner, the case history will take about an hour, and this readiness to listen may be one element in the success of homoeopathy. On the other hand, there are homeopathic veterinarians, so results cannot all be chalked up to the placebo effect. Some homoeopaths are medically qualified. Others work closely with midwives and family physicians, and all will refer to them when it becomes necessary.

BACH FLOWER REMEDIES

Bach flower remedies are a form of homeopathy designed to treat emotional states, not physical conditions. They can be used in pregnancy and during labor as antidotes to stress, fear, and lack of confidence. Tinctures are available in homeopathic dilutions and the plant essences are preserved in brandy. There are 38 remedies for different emotional states, such as depression, shock, apprehension, and irritability, and because our emotions are often complicated they are often used in combination. The general "rescue remedy" is recommended for those "distressed by startling experiences." You can get further information from the address on page 413.

USING WATER

You probably already know how soaking in a hot bath can relieve pain, whether you have experienced backache, aching muscles from strenuous exercise or a state of physical tension, or menstrual pain. And many women have discovered that being immersed in water can be comforting in labor. Lying in warm water increases venous pressure so that veins can return blood to the heart more efficiently. It also enhances cardiac action and slows the pulse rate. Total relaxation in the warmth and comfort of a bath may help the uterus to contract more effectively. But it does more than this. Water both counteracts the force of gravity and any pressure a woman may feel against her back and buttocks, and also reduces pressure felt from inside the body, so there is a further pain-relieving effect.*

Sometimes pain is so much reduced and dilatation proceeds so fast as a woman surrenders herself to the water that the baby slips out while she is still enjoying the bath. This is quite safe, since the baby only takes a breath when lifted clear of the water, and for a few minutes after delivery blood is still pulsating through the cord, thus providing the baby with oxygen. After the baby has left your body, the midwife will rest a finger on the cord so that she can feel the blood pulsating through it. You may like to do this too.

WATER BIRTH

Below

It is easier to ride the waves of huge contractions if you are immersed in water.

If you would like to use water in labor and birth discuss it with your midwife or doctor and find out more about their particular practice. Most North American hospitals are not happy about births taking place under water, although some encourage it for labor. In most out-of-hospital birth centers and home births, water birth is

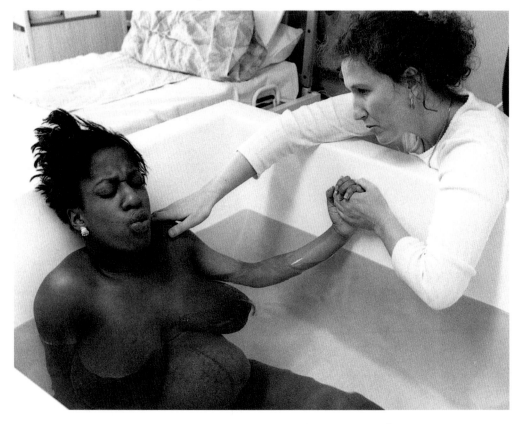

becoming increasingly popular. In some, women who develop high blood pressure, or whose membranes rupture at the start of labor, or who are carrying twins or a breech baby, are not allowed to use water. But you still may be able to stand under a shower and have a powerful jet of water directed against your back. Restrictions on the use of birth pools are currently declining as caregivers gain experience with water and as women ask for them.

Many birth centers and a few hospitals have installed deep pools in which women can float during labor. Others provide specially designed reclining tubs or ordinary bathtubs for use in labor. There are other portable pools on the market which can be used for home births or taken into the hospital with you.

Using a birth pool is now a well-established practice in English hospitals and in home births.* It is no 'longer considered an "alternative," but is a readily available option, and half of all the women who use water in labor go on to give birth in the pool, too. They enjoy the freedom of movement, the way that water relieves pain, and the peaceful atmosphere provided by a birth pool when attendants watch and wait without interfering. They often believe that water provides a more gentle transition to life for the baby, who has been floating in amniotic fluid for 9 months.

In a water birth, the baby should never be left under the water, but should be lifted into the mother's arms. You know yourself how cold you can feel after getting out of a bath. The baby quickly becomes chilled, too, so the room should be warm, and you and the baby should be wrapped in big bath towels so that you do not get cold.

It is probably unwise to decide in advance that you are definitely going to give birth in water. A woman for whom floating in water feels blissful late in the first stage of labor may want to get out of the water and have her feet firmly on the ground once the second stage starts. Do whatever feels right at the time.

THE SAFETY OF WATER BIRTH

A healthy newborn does not breathe under water.* Babies breathe inside the uterus, though it is fluid rather than air that passes in and out of their lungs. Before labor starts the baby stops this breathing, probably because of hormone changes and a rise in prostaglandin E2. This hormonal inhibition of breathing continues while the cord remains untied because blood containing prostaglandins is still flowing through the cord into the baby.

Amniotic fluid is warm. In fact, the baby's temperature is slightly higher than the mother's. If the baby is born into water at approximately blood temperature the baby responds to this warm water as it does to amniotic fluid, and does not breathe it in.

The hard work and all the squeezing of labor cause a normal reduction of oxygen in the baby's blood (hypoxemia). The result is that the baby makes no attempt to inhale water. Only if a baby is very short of oxygen (hypoxia) is gasping stimulated.

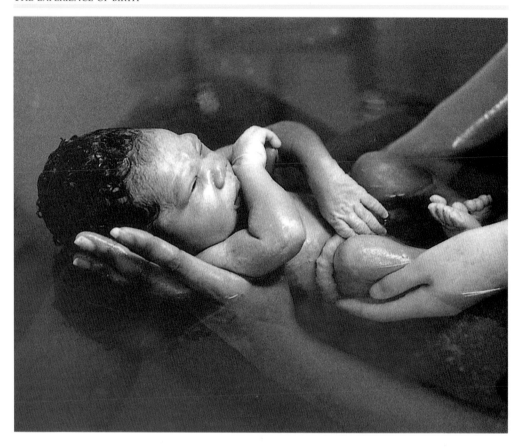

Above
The baby is brought
gently to the surface
with a loving welcome.

There are powerful chemoreceptors at the entrance to the baby's larynx which enable it to taste and discriminate between things that should be breathed and things that should be swallowed. This is how a baby can work out how to breathe and swallow when sucking. A baby born into water is much more likely to *swallow* water than breathe it in. On the other hand, one born into salt water may breathe it in because saline is similar to amniotic fluid. We do not know if this is harmful or beneficial, and research needs to be done.

A baby's head should not be delivered above the level of the water and then dunked. This might happen if there is insufficient water in the pool to cover the mother's pelvis or if she grips the sides of the pool with her arms and pushes her pelvis up. If you are giving birth in water ensure that the water covers your tummy, and keep your shoulders and upper arms relaxed so that you do not tilt your perineum up out of the water.

Drugs for pain relief in labor

There is a variety of pain-relieving drugs available, and different drugs suit different women. It is important to understand what can be used and how each type works so that you can make your own informed decision as to whether you want the help of a drug and, if so, which particular kind. Whether or not you have drugs in childbirth – and how much you have – is up to you. As one obstetric anesthesiologist has stated: "The only arbiter of pain is – or should be – the patient. A stereotyped prescription cannot cope with individual variations in response to pain."*

All drugs for pain relief in labor, whether given by injection or inhaled, pass through the mother's bloodstream to the baby. They all affect the baby – some more than others. None of them does the baby good. When considering whether to accept drugs in labor, bear in mind that some forms of anesthesia and analgesia can interfere with your first meeting with the baby.

TRANQUILIZERS AND ANALGESICS

Tranquilizers are used to relax you if you are anxious and tense and also to lower your blood pressure. Given intramuscularly, tranquilizers take effect in 15 minutes; taken by mouth they are effective in 30 minutes. If taken during labor, tranquilizers tend to make the baby limp and floppy at birth, and probably also slow to suck. They also interfere with the newborn's temperature control.

Tranquilizers are sometimes used in combination with analgesics – Demerol for example (see below) – to increase their effectiveness, though some obstetricians are critical of this practice.

Narcotics The drugs most widely used for analgesia (taking the edge off pain) in labor are narcotics, such as Demerol, Nubain, and Stadol. They are usually given intravenously or by intramuscular injection. They take effect in 2 to 15 minutes and last for 2 to 4 hours. Some women like narcotics and say they helped them cope with difficult contractions by making them feel relaxed and slightly drunk. Others hate the effects of narcotics and call them "stupefying," and say they were woozy and out of control. Some women even hallucinate. Blood pressure may plummet, producing pins and needles, faintness, and disorientation.

A fairly common side effect of narcotics is nausea. One or two women out of every ten vomit when they are given Demerol; fewer with the other narcotic combination drugs. Demerol is sometimes combined with an antihistamine to prevent sickness, but this tends to make you even sleepier. Some narcotics are contraindicated in asthma because they depress respiration, and it is wise to avoid them if you are giving birth to a preterm baby.

Demerol drugs the baby, who may be completely knocked out at birth. Large amounts of Demerol will be present in the baby if it is injected within five hours before delivery, and especially if it is given around three hours before delivery. This is the time when contractions are likely to be strongest, and when a woman may most want drugs for pain relief. If injected within 45 minutes of the birth, however, Demerol is unlikely to have built up in the baby's tissues.

The snag is that you will probably not want Demerol in the second stage of labor as you will then be working hard to get the baby out. Some hospitals provide patient-controlled analgesia by a computerized syringe, allowing you to pump in the drug as you need it. Women tend to use less of the drug when giving it to themselves than when it is injected for them by caregivers.

Some research suggests that when opiate or barbiturate drugs are used in childbirth they can become imprinted on the baby, thereby increasing the risk of addiction when children become adult. Diamorphine, for example, is a form of heroin which is used routinely for pain relief in some hospitals. It is an addictive drug, and passes through the mother's bloodstream to the baby, who may therefore be drugged at birth. Swedish researchers recommend that methods of pain relief which avoid passage of large amounts of drugs across the placenta should be preferred.*

Other narcotic-like drugs Those approved by the Food and Drug Administration for use in labor are nalbuphine (Nubain) and butorphanol (Stadol). Vistaril and Talwin are used in conjunction with one of the above medications to counteract some of their side effects, including nausea, vomiting, and dizziness.

Stadol is 40 times more powerful than Demerol in giving pain relief. Phenergan is a drug given in combination with Demerol so that less Demerol is necessary and nausea is combatted. But it has the disadvantage of impairing blood clotting in the baby with the result that bleeding in the baby's tissues may occur.

Gas anesthetics Inhalant anesthetics such as nitrous oxide (laughing gas) and halothane may be offered for the actual delivery. This leads women to believe that birth must be excruciatingly painful. It is a shame to have gone all the way through labor only to be "put out" for the most rewarding part, the culmination of nine months' waiting. Not only does the mother miss her baby's first cry but she may remain too sleepy and disoriented to hold her baby and to breastfeed right after the birth.

Other possible side effects include respiratory depression, hemorrhage, irregular heart rate, nausea, and vomiting. Babies born under a heavy dose of anesthesia may have difficulty breathing and adjusting to life outside the uterus.

LOCAL ANESTHETICS

Local anesthetics can also cross the placenta but they are least likely to affect the baby when they are injected into the area around the vagina and the perineum. This might be done before an episiotomy (see page 320) and before a forceps delivery (see page 334) if other kinds of anesthesia have not been given. When local anesthetics are used to bathe nerves that cover a large area of the body, they are called *regional* anesthetics.

Paracervical block is a series of injections of local anesthetic around the cervix. It affects the baby immediately, and in three out of ten babies the heartbeat becomes slower (a condition known as bradycardia).* Some babies have died as a result. Paracervical block is rarely used in the United States for this reason.

Spinal anesthesia is given by injection into the cerebrospinal fluid in the lower spine. The effect is to numb the woman from waist to knees. It takes about five minutes to work. If you have a spinal you may have to lie flat for around eight hours after delivery to avoid a postspinal headache and should be careful not to lift your head quickly. Spinals are considered potentially dangerous because blood pressure drops and hence the oxygen supply to the baby is reduced. Labor may slow down, and a forceps delivery is usually necessary. However, they give effective pain relief.

Pudendal block is an injection numbing the nerves in the perineum given at any time after full dilatation, and is often used before an episiotomy or a forceps or vacuum extraction.

Epidural anesthesia is injected into the space just outside the dura, the outer membrane around the spinal cord. Additional injections or a continuous drip of anesthetic can be given through a fine plastic tube which is left in place after the first injection. This is preferable to initiating another injection, as an epidural takes about half an hour to set up. The continuous drip allows anesthesiologists to use a lower concentration of the drug, which reduces undesirable side effects. An epidural may be given with you sitting up and curled forward or lying on your left side curled into a ball.

"I had to look at the machine to see when I was having a contraction . . . I did want to feel him slide out, and not feeling that was terribly disappointing."

An epidural can provide complete relief from pain and can even be used as an anesthetic for a cesarean section. It removes sensation from the waist down, either completely or partially, while allowing you to remain conscious. For a painful, prolonged labor it seems the perfect answer. Many women say how marvelous the epidural was, but it should be your own choice – no one should be put under pressure to have one. Some hospitals give epidurals to all first-time mothers, unless there is no time to give one.

An epidural should not be given if there has been bleeding from the placenta, if a woman has low blood pressure or is taking anti-coagulants such as Warfarin to avoid blood clots, or if she has a skin infection at the site where the needle is to be introduced. In practice, in the United States virtually anyone who wants it can have an epidural. It depends on the availability of an anesthesiologist, and on the agency paying for it. An epidural tends to prolong labor, so stimulation of the uterus with an oxytocin intravenous drip is often necessary. It is also important to remember that epidurals do not always work. It may be difficult to inject into the right place, or the anesthetic may take on one side only, so that you get the odd feeling of contractions occurring in only half your body. The usual practice is for the anesthesiologist to make some necessary adjustments in the placement of the epidural so that finally you can get good pain relief.

The anesthetic is similar to that used by dentists, and you feel it like liquid ice numbing your tummy, bottom, and legs. Even though it anesthetizes only part of you, it must be given by a skilled anesthesiologist and under sterile conditions. If by mistake the needle punctures the dura, you end up getting a complete spinal: you are more heavily anesthetized and may have a bad headache which can last a week or more after the birth.

An epidural lowers blood pressure, sometimes drastically, so that other drugs may have to be given to raise your blood pressure again. Because of this, an epidural is sometimes offered to a woman whose blood pressure is already high, even though she may not be having a painful labor. In one study 39 percent of women having epidurals experienced hypotension and low blood pressure, though it did not last longer than one hour. The proportion went up to 47 percent when women were also receiving an oxytocin intravenous drip (see page 325).* When your blood pressure suddenly drops, you feel sick and faint and may vomit. This sudden lowering of blood pressure affects the baby too, since the oxygen-bearing blood supply is pumping more weakly and slowly through the placenta. If your blood pressure drops and causes fetal distress, you will wear an oxygen mask to get more oxygen to the baby.

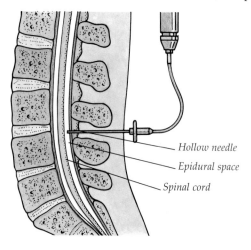

— Hollow needle
— Epidural space
— Spinal cord

Epidural
An epidural is the most effective pharmacological pain relief. The needle does not enter the spinal cord. It stays short of it in the epidural space.

Epidural techniques and drug dosages vary in different countries. In the US a continuous infusion pump is almost always used and bupivacaine is usually kept low with the aim of reducing side effects. But because drug cocktails are often given, there are new side effects from these other drugs. To reduce the risk of a sudden drop in blood pressure, IV fluids are given very fast before the epidural. This increases the woman's blood volume. In the UK, however, if blood pressure drops significantly another drug is given to raise the blood pressure. Excessive IV fluids cause water intoxication. This means that the body becomes overloaded with fluids. One result is that women often have swollen legs and feet for some days after an epidural.

Having an epidural may start a whole train of other procedures which you did not bargain for. You may receive oxytocin to augment labor and have continuous fetal monitoring. There is also an increased risk of finishing up with a cesarean section.* This appears to be greatest if a woman is given the epidural before she has reached 5 cm dilatation. Because you have no feeling in your bladder, it will need to be emptied by catheter. And because you may not feel any urge to push, the obstetrician may rotate the fetal head with forceps or manually.*

Since there is an increased chance of a forceps delivery once an epidural has been given, you may want to refuse a top-off and let the anesthetic wear off as you reach the very end of the first stage. If you have not actually felt the first-stage contractions at all and then suddenly have to cope with the long, hefty ones as you approach full dilatation, the experience can be overpowering.

Do not push just because you are fully dilated. Breathe your way through each of the contractions, which you can feel as waves of pressure, until the baby's head is well down on your perineum. If you push because you think that you *ought* to be pushing, you are more likely to have deep transverse arrest of the baby's head, because with an epidural the natural tone of the pelvic floor muscles is lost, and it is these pelvic floor muscles which help the baby's head to rotate as it descends against them. If you have deep transverse arrest you will need a forceps or vacuum extractor delivery. An epidural multiplies the chance that your baby will get stuck in an occipito-posterior (see page 263) or transverse position.* Obstetricians often tackle this problem by setting up an oxytocin intravenous drip to make the uterus work harder, in order to avoid the possible need for an assisted delivery. But you can do something yourself about this, and will reduce the risk of deep transverse arrest by more than half by waiting to push until the baby's head can be seen. That may take two hours or longer.*

One side effect of having an epidural is that your temperature rises. This in turn can have an adverse effect on the baby during labor. Moreover, when a woman has a fever in labor, investigations are made to find out if she and the newborn baby are suffering from an infection, and the baby is treated for infection "just in case." This may entail a "septic-workup" which is traumatic for the baby, and often isolation, antibiotics by IV, and observation in the special care nursery for at least two days – the time it takes for a culture to come back from the laboratory.

Epidurals may have long-term side effects, too. A small proportion of women have problems with backache, migraine, neckache, or numb areas of skin after an epidural.*

An epidural anesthetic passes into the baby within ten minutes, and studies are still being carried out on the possible effects of an epidural on the newborn.* Some suggest that the baby becomes nervous and jittery while others show that the baby is very drowsy after delivery,* but this may vary according to what drug and dosage are used, how long the epidural is in place, and the condition of the fetus before the epidural is given. If you decide to have an epidural, be sure to bear in mind that some of the difficulty you might have in coping with the baby in the week or so after the birth may be connected with the effect of the anesthetic on the baby, and does not mean that you are an incompetent mother. You will soon be over this difficult period and the interaction between you and the baby will rapidly become much easier.

Mobile or "walking" epidurals To achieve an epidural so that the woman retains some feeling in her legs and can move a little, the drug bupivacaine is given in smaller doses than when full anesthesia is required. There are three ways of doing this.

1. The first dose of anesthetic – half as much as usual – is injected into the subarachnoid space where cerebrospinal fluid circulates. A very fine spinal needle is used. This reduces the risk of the mother's suffering a post-dural puncture headache but the problem is that this space is more difficult to find than the epidural space, and if mistakes are made the mother might get meningitis.

2. Opioids and local anesthetics are injected into both the subarachnoid and epidural spaces. Again, when a drug cocktail that includes opioids is given the bupivacaine can be cut by almost half.

3. Epidural top-offs are injected when needed, or the drug is given by continuous infusion pump. Having top-offs reduces the drug dose by 35 percent compared with an epidural infusion.

Advantages of lower drug doses are that a woman can move around in bed, and possibly walk. But spinal opiates can make a woman dizzy and she may not feel able to walk about. She should have someone with her all the time and should not leave the labor room. There is less need to catheterize her bladder. And a mobile epidural may reduce the risks of long-term backache and the need for a forceps delivery, though many women find their legs feel rubbery.*

WHAT WOMEN THINK ABOUT EPIDURALS

My own research into epidurals reveals that women are sharply divided in their opinions about them. In one study of women's experiences many were very happy with their epidurals and said things like "It was a miracle!" and "It was pure magic." However, 18 percent of women very much regretted having had the epidural and said, in effect, "Never again!"* *Women praise epidurals when:* it was their own decision, and theirs alone, to have one; they felt that they were among friends; the epidural provided effective pain relief; there was minimal other intervention; and the mother managed to push the baby out herself. *Women are highly critical of epidurals when:* they felt that they were not able to make a free choice about having

"If I had known what I do now about epidurals I wouldn't have agreed to it, but it was presented as entirely risk-free and without side effects."

one; they did not feel that they were in an emotionally supportive environment; the epidural was not effective; delivery was by forceps; and there were side effects – they felt sick and giddy, suffered headaches, or had long-term problems such as pain or numbness which they attributed to the epidural.

Caudal A caudal is like an epidural, except that it is injected into the epidural space around the sacrum and blocks only that area, rather than the larger area that is blocked by an epidural. A greater dose of anesthetic is necessary for a caudal than with an epidural, and a caudal is not of much use in the first stage of labor. A caudal is usually given for short-term pain relief to a woman having a very difficult second stage of labor.

THE FUTURE OF DRUGS IN CHILDBIRTH

Hospitals should provide an environment and the kind of personal care in which each woman is free to accept or reject pain-relieving drugs as and when she wishes to do so. Whatever drugs are given to you in labor, their effects and their possible side effects on you and the baby should certainly be fully explained and your consent should always be obtained beforehand.

Unfortunately, drugs are often used in place of loving emotional support and encouragement and one-to-one care. Fear, anxiety, loneliness, and the feeling that you are part of a factory for producing babies all increase the experience of pain. Understanding what is happening inside you and what is being done to help you and your baby, being able to move freely, having non-pharmacological ways of handling pain, knowing what you can do to help yourself, feeling you are among friends, and having someone you love with you all make pain much more easy to bear.

Pain-relieving drugs almost invariably have an effect on the progress of labor, and often prolong it or make an operative delivery more likely. This may be a price worth paying. It is up to you to decide. Nobody else should make the decision for you. Modern obstetric anesthesia, used only when necessary, is fairly safe for the baby, but little is really known about the subtle effects, short- and long-term, on the child. One consultant anesthesiologist warns that "numerous questions about the effects of drugs given to the mother on mother–baby interaction and future child development require an answer,"* and stresses that long-term studies should be carried out to assess exactly what risks are being taken. For the present this still remains a largely unexplored field of research.

Toward the medical control of birth

You have the right to decide what happens to your body before, during, and after childbirth. You are not bound, either in law or out of politeness, to agree to procedures and investigations to which you object. If things are done without your consent, it is a form of assault on your body. But your consent is implied when you are forewarned about an obstetric intervention and concur by remaining silent.

You are also entitled to full information about anything that is being done to you and your baby, and can reasonably expect to be able to ask questions about it and to be given straightforward and honest answers. You may also want time to think through any of the alternatives that are available to you, and should not be rushed into agreeing to any treatment that is proposed. If you do not ask questions, then the professionals may well take it for granted that you do not want to know any more, and even that to offer further information might make you uncomfortable.

If birth is to be a fulfilling and satisfying experience the important thing is to feel in control of what happens to you and your baby before, during, and after the birth. Once you are secure in that knowledge, you can then "let go" and allow your body to work freely. You are not fighting it or trying to rein in the power that is released from your uterus. Women are sometimes blamed for approaching birth with expectations that are "too high." But research into psychological outcomes of birth reveals that feeling cheated or let down has nothing to do with having had rosy expectations of birth which are destroyed by the grim reality of labor. In fact, women are more likely to be disappointed in their birth experiences when they did not expect much anyway. How you feel about the birth afterward has to do with human relationships. You are much more likely to have a positive birth experience if you are able to get the information you want, discuss everything fully, and share in all the decisions that are made.*

"I was made to lie flat on my back for hours. I felt like a lump of meat being poked and prodded as if my body didn't belong to me."

YOUR RIGHT TO CHOOSE

In all medical procedures it is a question of carefully balancing the relative risks of a policy of intervention on the one hand and a policy of "wait and see" on the other. To be able to make an informed choice you may value the counsel of skilled professionals, but ultimately you make the decision. This applies to both *where* and *how* you have your baby. If you want natural childbirth, go all out to get it. Plan for it, prepare yourself for it, and do everything you can to create the right setting for it to take place. But also be flexible, so that if something in your physical condition, or that of your baby, indicates that modern technology can be used with advantage, you will not miss out on its undoubted benefits, even if this means that the birth of your baby is less "natural."

A woman having a baby has responsibilities as well as rights. One of the most important of these is the responsibility to give the baby the best possible start in life. Some obstetricians believe that whenever a machine or a procedure is available which permits greater medical control of childbirth, it ought to be used. An equally valid view is that one should be selective in the use of technology, employing it where necessary, but bearing in mind that birth is also a psychological experience which affects the relationship between mother, father, and baby – perhaps for a long time after.

THE BEST ENVIRONMENT FOR BIRTH

The highest-quality childbirth and the best welcome into life for the baby must address emotional as well as medical aspects of birth. If you accept medical help, it does not automatically follow that you relinquish concern about the psychological dimensions of the experience. Technology need not, and should not be permitted to, ruin a woman's personal experience of childbirth.

When machines are used they may seem to preclude warm and friendly human relations. But when they take second place to emotional support and encouragement, and you feel free to reach your own decisions about how much aid to accept, they can be a useful adjunct to good care, especially when the risk to a baby is considered to be higher than usual.

Many couples can bear witness to ways in which sophisticated modern apparatus made them feel more secure in childbirth and helped rather than hindered. But for this to happen the environment provided for birth has to be a very special one, and all those coming into contact with the expectant parents need to be able to give of themselves in addition to lending their technical skills. For it is only in such a setting that there can be trust, honesty, and self-confidence.

THE GROWING USE OF TECHNOLOGY

Obstetricians are discovering new ways of controlling a process which in the past was left to nature. Many now say, "Why stand by watching and intervene only when something goes wrong?" and believe that, instead, labor should be regulated from start to finish. To do this effectively they need to be able to monitor exactly what is happening in the uterus, and to the fetus, at every second, and to intervene at any point to ensure that cervical dilatation, the strength of contractions, and the biochemical state of mother and fetus conform to a predetermined norm. This is called *active management of labor.**

Many inventions are appearing on the market which obstetricians, eager to reduce the perinatal mortality rate, want to buy for their units. Some women hate this intrusion of machinery into what they feel should be a natural process, and question its benefits for labor and for the baby. Others find security in knowing that labor is controlled by the obstetrician with all his machinery; they like knowing exactly when the birthday will be, and are relieved to know that the labor will not last longer than 12 hours at the most. In some hospitals the love affair with technology is gradually giving way to a new concern about the quality of human relations during the process of giving birth. But there is no standard recipe that will suit all women. The vital element is *personal* care.

Common procedures in labor

The usual way to assess the progress of labor is by vaginal examinations. Dilatation of the cervix is estimated by inserting two gloved fingers through the vagina into the os, the mouth of the cervix. The examining fingers can also detect how soft the tissues of the cervix are, whether the baby is head down, how far the head has descended, and which part of the head is presenting. The problem is that vaginal examinations disturb the laboring woman's concentration, may be painful, can feel threatening, and also introduce the risk of infection. However, some women like to be told that the cervix is dilating well and ask for an examination. Especially when a woman is in an undrugged state, an experienced midwife who has remained with her should be able to assess the progress of labor by observing the whole woman – her facial expression, her movements, her breathing, and any other sounds she is making, rather than relying on frequent vaginal examinations.*

When you arrive at the hospital, you may be given an amniotomy, linked to a fetal monitor, and hooked up to an intravenous drip. During the second stage, an episiotomy may be performed to hasten delivery. Some women experience many kinds of intervention

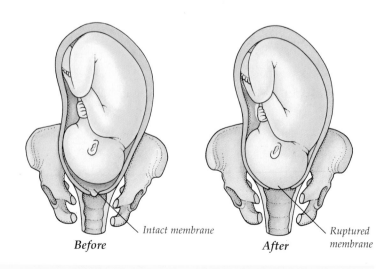

Rupture of the membranes
When membranes are intact, they act as a cushion in front of the baby's head. When the membranes have ruptured, the baby's head is pressed against the cervix.

Intact membrane

Before

Ruptured membrane

After

during the course of their labor, and unless you specifically tell the obstetrician or midwife that you do not want your labor controlled in this way, there is a chance that you will have at least one of them.

ARTIFICIAL RUPTURE OF THE MEMBRANES

Artificial rupture of the membranes (ARM for short), or amniotomy, has come to be accepted as a normal routine in most hospitals and is frequently performed as part of the "prepping" done after you are admitted. It should not be done until you are in active labor (more than 4 cm dilated). The membranes surrounding the fetus are punctured with a small tool like a crochet hook, which is introduced through the open cervix. Routine amniotomy is now open to question, however (see below).

When the membranes are allowed to rupture spontaneously, they tend to do so toward the end of the first stage of labor.* In 12 percent of women the membranes remain intact right through to delivery. Some membranes rupture spontaneously when the midwife or doctor touches them during a vaginal examination. Since there are no nerve endings in the membranes, their rupture is not painful. All you feel is a gush of warm liquid. Be prepared for contractions to increase in intensity after this has happened. ARM can shorten labor by 30–45 minutes if the membranes have still not ruptured spontaneously by the end of the first stage, since the baby's head is pressing harder against the cervix once the cushion of fluid is gone, and this produces a rush of oxytocin in your system which triggers the start of strong contractions.

REASONS FOR AMNIOTOMY

Besides being necessary for induction, rupturing the membranes also allows the obstetrician to assess the state of the amniotic fluid. When a fetus is in distress it passes meconium, the first contents of the bowels, into the amniotic fluid, which is easily seen when the fluid is released. Many obstetricians believe that amniotomy is important in assessing the condition of the baby. Once it has been done, it is possible to insert an electrode in the baby's scalp so that its heartbeat can be recorded throughout labor (see pages 329–333).

In some countries obstetricians prefer to use an *amnioscope* in order to examine the amniotic fluid while still keeping the membrane intact. A cone-shaped instrument with a fiber-optic light positioned inside it is introduced through the vagina and cervix. This technique is less invasive than ARM. Obstetricians in the United States, however, do not use this technique.

THE RISKS OF ROUTINE AMNIOTOMY

Pressure on the cord Intact membranes protect the baby's head. The amniotic fluid equalizes pressure on the head, and amniotomy takes away the cushion of water in which the fetus lies, thus exposing its head to the direct effect of contractions. Rupture of the membranes also gives rise to the possibility of pressure on the cord, which may hinder the flow of blood through it. It is not rare for a baby to have the cord around its neck, and without the cushion provided by the amniotic fluid, such babies are particularly vulnerable to pressure on the cord. It has also been suggested that once the amniotic fluid is gone, the fetal surface of the placenta is compressed, which may reduce the flow of blood to and from the baby.*

Pelvic infection Amniotomy increases the possibility of pelvic infection.* Infection is more likely if labor continues for more than 24 hours after amniotomy, especially if there is no restriction on vaginal exams, and operative delivery may be necessary if the baby has not been delivered naturally by that time.

Sometimes, when the membranes are ruptured before labor is going strong, later contractions become weak or stop altogether, and it turns out that the woman was in "false" labor. Because of the risk of ascending infection if labor takes a long time following rupture of the membranes, it is often decided to stimulate the uterus with an oxytocin intravenous drip.

Deceleration of the baby's heartbeat Certain studies have clearly demonstrated that after amniotomy there are more early decelerations of the baby's heartbeat. These early decelerations occur at the start of a contraction, and the heart is back to normal by the end of the contraction. The slowing down is slight, by less than 40 beats a minute. Many obstetricians consider this innocuous and quite normal.* Because babies who are born after amniotomy are generally in good condition, with high Apgar scores (see page 356), some doctors have concluded that the procedure does not subject the fetus to any special stress during labor.

Head molding A number of obstetricians are concerned about head molding and disalignment of the cranial bones, which may be increased after amniotomy. There is some disagreement about this, but, in any case, the molding of the baby's head gradually disappears during the first week or two of life.

So amniotomy raises many questions which have yet to be adequately answered. It is a subject that you may want to discuss with your obstetrician. You have a right to be fully informed. You can, if you wish, request that amniotomy be done not as a routine but only if the baby is showing signs of distress.

THE INTRAVENOUS DRIP

In almost all American hospitals, an intravenous drip (IV) is set up for every woman in labor. A fine catheter (hollow tube) is introduced into a vein in your arm or hand and fixed with adhesive tape so that fluids can be infused straight into your bloodstream. The argument for setting up an IV is that once a vein is open, emergency action can be

A typical hospital partogram

This is how the events of birth may be recorded by your caregivers. It is a kind of map of your physiological processes during labor and delivery. The partogram consists of a series of graphs filled in over a timescale of 12 hours.

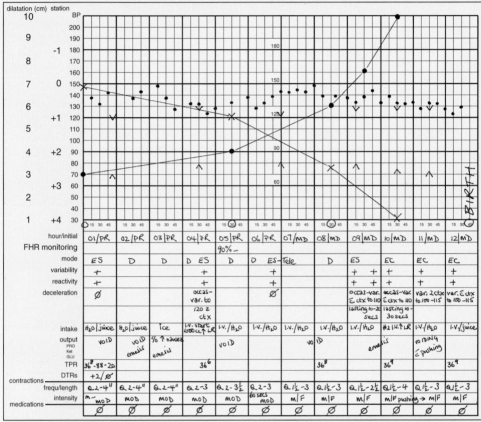

hour/initial	01/PR	02/PR	03 PR	04/PR	05/PR	06/PR	07/MD	08 MD	09 MD	10 MD	11/MD	12 MD
FHR monitoring					90% –							
mode	ES	D	D	D ES	D	D ES–Tele		D	ES	EC	EC	EC
variability	+			+		+			+	+ + +	+	+
reactivity	+			+		+			+	+ +	+	+
deceleration	∅			occas–var. to 120 2 ctx		∅			occas–var c̄ ctx to 110 lasting 10–20 secs	occas–var c̄ ctx to 110 lasting 10–30 secs	var. 2 ctx to 100–115	var. c̄ ctx to 100–115
intake	H₂O/juice	H₂O/juice	Ice	I.V./start 1000cc↑LR	I.V./H₂O	I.V./H₂O	I.V./H₂O	I.V./H₂O	I.V./H₂O	H₂ I.V.↑LR	I.V./H₂O	I.V./juice
output PRO Ket GLU	VOID	VOID emesis	% ↑ nausea emesis		VOID			voID	emesis	voIDiNG c̄ pushing		
TPR	36⁸-88-20			36⁶			36⁸		36⁹		36⁹	
DTRs	+2/∅											
contractions frequ/length	Q2-4"	Q2-4"	Q2-4"	Q2-3	Q2-3½	Q2-3 60 secs	Q1½-3	Q1½-3	Q1½-2½	Q1½-4	Q1½-3	Q1½-3
intensity	m~ MOD	MOD	MOD	MOD	MOD	60 secs MOD	m/F	m/F	m/F	m/F pushing→	m/F	m/F
medications	∅	∅	∅	∅	∅	∅	∅	∅	∅	∅	∅	∅

FHR *The fetal heart rate is charted in beats per minute, with 120–160 beats considered normal. FHR may be taken by ultrasound stethoscope (doppler), external EFM (electronic fetal monitoring), and continuously, intermittently (strip), or internally (scalp lead). Other FHR information (variability, reactivity, and decelerations) are also recorded.*

Blood pressure *The mother's blood pressure is recorded about every 20 minutes. The upper level is the systolic pressure, the lower one the diastolic pressure.*

Cervical dilatation *The degree of cervical dilatation is noted every 3 or 4 hours and a curve is drawn.*

Station *This refers to the baby's presenting part (usually the head, sometimes the buttocks) within the pelvis. As the head descends the station changes from "minus" 2 or 1 to "plus" 4 (the birth).*

TPR *This refers to the mother's temperature, pulse, and respirations.*

KEY

FHR MONITORING

	Mode			**Reactivity**	
FHR (Fetal Heart Rate) ●	doppler	= D		present	= +
	ext EFM	= E		absent	= –
	strip	= S		no fetal activity	= N/A
BP (Blood Pressure) ∨∧	continuous	= C			
	scalp lead	= I		**Decelerations**	
Dilatation ●	**Variability**			Usually described in notes at bottom of the chart (not shown here)	
	present	= +			
	absent	= –			
Station ✗	decreased	= ↓			

DTRs *This refers to the mother's deep tendon reflexes, or nervous system: 2 is normal.*

Contractions *The frequency of contractions is recorded in minutes, the length in seconds, and the intensity as mild, moderate, or strong.*

Medications *Any drugs given are noted.*

Intake and output *Fluids drunk or given intravenously are recorded as "intake," urinary volume as "output."*

taken rapidly and your strength can be kept up without your needing to eat or, sometimes, even drink anything. This means that if a cesarean section is necessary (see pages 336–338) and a general anesthetic is used, your stomach is likely to be almost empty already and there is not a great deal of risk that you will regurgitate or inhale its contents. If needs be, to lower the risk even further, you can have an antacid drink to reduce the acid of your stomach contents.

Forcing women to go through labor without food and drink is bad policy.* It medicalizes the birth experience and is unnecessary. Labor is hard work. In the early phases especially, you may get hungry, and should be allowed to eat whatever you fancy. And you will certainly be thirsty and should feel free to drink.

Dextrose, a glucose solution, or "Ringer's lactate" solution, containing electrolytes and water, may be given through an IV to act as a "pick-me-up" in labor. Since it bypasses the stomach, you do not have to digest it. Dextrose may be useful if labor is long and you are becoming dehydrated, or if lactic acid builds up in the course of a difficult labor, causing acetone to appear in the urine – an indication that your body is short of glucose. But a dextrose IV can lead to hypoglycemia (low blood sugar) in your baby after birth.

If you have an IV set up, it is especially important to remember to empty your bladder regularly: every hour is not too frequent. You will be accumulating fluid, and should urinate frequently to prevent urine from building up in your bladder.

Once an IV is in place, other substances can be introduced by the same route. This may be done without your consenting to or being aware of the administration of drugs. If you have an intravenous infusion and the bag or bottle is changed, ask why. Your partner will be able to get close enough to read the label. Oxytocin is introduced by this means. The label will probably read "Pitocin." You can find more information about this in the section on induced labor on pages 324–329. Other medicines and narcotics are also given via the IV.

You need not consent to an intravenous drip unless you are confident that there are good reasons for it. It is yet another way in which women are sometimes made needlessly uncomfortable in labor. The IV can be very helpful when needed, but used routinely it merely makes it difficult for you to move. In most hospitals where intravenous drips are administered as a matter of course, it is taken for granted that the woman in labor stays in bed.

EPISIOTOMY

An episiotomy is a surgical cut made to enlarge the birth opening. It is done with scissors, under local anesthetic, just before the baby is born. It can be midline (down from the bottom of the vagina toward the anus) or mediolateral (sloping out to the side, away from the anus, or down and then out again in the shape of a hockey stick). Mediolaterals are virtually never done in the United States and very rarely in Canada, though they are commonplace in the UK.

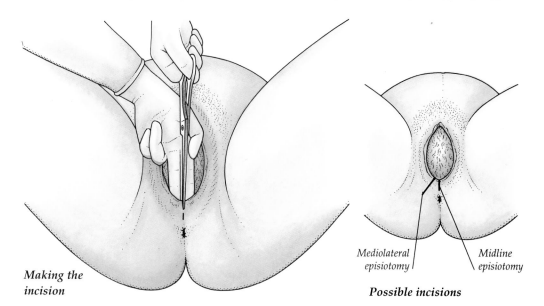

Making the incision

Mediolateral episiotomy

Midline episiotomy

Possible incisions

Since the incision is made through both skin and muscle, careful repair of the wound must be made afterward. The local anesthetic given before the episiotomy is usually enough for the repair. If not, more can be given. This requires a few minutes to take effect, and the doctor or midwife should wait until the area is fully anesthetized before stitching the wound. The suturing is done with a curved needle and it may take as long as an hour to sew up a mediolateral episiotomy or one which has been extended by tearing. Stitching a midline episiotomy is usually quicker, because there is a natural dividing line between muscles in the midline, which makes the repair much simpler to carry out.

The stitches can be left in if they are the kind that dissolve, but have a look at the area in a mirror every couple of days to make sure they have disappeared, since sometimes they do not drop out and become embedded in tissue. You may feel as if you are sitting on thorns. When this happens, the stitches should be snipped out by a midwife or doctor on or before the tenth day after the birth.

After an episiotomy your perineum is likely to be very tender, swollen, and sore for days, or even weeks. Ask for a local anesthetic spray to apply to the area. This really helps.*

Having an episiotomy
An episiotomy is done as the baby's head crowns and between contractions. The local anesthetic, combined with the numbing effect of the baby's head pressing against the perineum, means that the cut is rarely felt.

REASONS FOR EPISIOTOMY

Some obstetricians believe that all first-time mothers should have an episiotomy to relieve strain on their tissues and get the baby delivered quickly. When there are signs of fetal distress, an episiotomy can speed delivery and make birth easier for the baby. You may be told that it is a good idea to have an episiotomy because a straight, clean cut is better than a nasty, jagged tear, which is more difficult for the obstetrician to sew up. Sometimes episiotomy is done in an attempt to prevent damage to tissues inside the vagina when there is evidence of "buttonhole" tearing (that is, a series of very tiny lacerations deep inside the perineum).

The practice of routine episiotomy is still favored by many North American obstetricians and those on the European continent, but is declining in British hospitals. In the seventies, almost 100 percent of women had episiotomies in certain hospitals in Britain. Now the proportion is generally below 40 percent. As soon as a research project investigating episiotomy was begun in any hospital – that is, as soon as questions were raised about its necessity – the rate dropped by about a third, even before any results were obtained.

PROBLEMS WITH EPISIOTOMY

Trials conducted in Dublin, Montreal,* and Argentina* have revealed that women with an intact perineum, or only a superficial tear, experienced less pain after childbirth than those who had undergone an episiotomy. The pain after an episiotomy is about the same as that experienced from a second-degree tear (one that affects the underlying muscle). Women are also more likely to suffer severe tears into the anus when they have had an episiotomy than when they have not had one.* Another trial, in England, as well as the Montreal trial, showed that there is no advantage to episiotomy over a natural first- or second-degree tear.*

Many women say they feel terribly uncomfortable when making love for several months after an episiotomy, and they tend to resume intercourse later than women who have had a tear.

There are other problems with episiotomy which should be borne in mind: if done too early – before the perineum has thinned out – it can cause unnecessary bleeding; sometimes the cut is much larger than a tear would have been; and quite often the stitches get infected and antibiotics are then necessary.*

With skilled guidance at delivery and a gentle birth (see pages 343–353), more and more women are now having no injury to the perineum – and this makes an enormous difference in how they feel in the days and weeks after the baby is born.

MANAGING THE THIRD STAGE

A now widely accepted method of controlling the third stage of labor, the expulsion of the placenta, is to give an intramuscular injection of oxytocin after the delivery of the shoulder nearest your front (the anterior shoulder). The placenta then usually separates from the lining of the uterus with the next contraction and is expelled within five minutes of the birth.

However, if the placenta does *not* separate completely after the injection, it can be trapped by the powerfully contracting uterus. So attendants clamp and cut the cord as soon as the baby is born and then press a hand on the top of the uterus, pulling on the cord at the same time in order to get the placenta out.

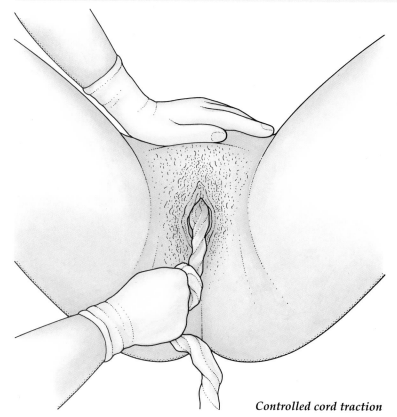

A healthy placenta

Cord traction
After the birth of your baby, your uterus continues to contract strongly to expel the placenta. You may be asked to push the placenta out, once it has peeled off the wall of the uterus, by pushing against the doctor's or midwife's hand placed against your lower abdomen, while he or she gently pulls on the cord with the other hand.

Controlled cord traction

If the placenta is left to separate naturally, it may take half an hour or longer. Clamping of the cord immediately at delivery may make a retained placenta more likely. If the cord is not clamped until after it has stopped pulsating there is much less chance of a retained placenta. This is because when the cord is clamped, blood cannot flow out of it, which would encourage the now defunct placenta to peel away from the uterine wall. A blood-packed placenta stays firm and full and is less likely to separate.

If the third stage is allowed to proceed naturally, your first physical contact with your baby produces a rush of emotion that is accompanied by the release of oxytocin. This *natural* oxytocin rush keeps the uterus firm and causes further contractions. Once the placenta has separated, the doctor or midwife gently places one flat hand over your lower tummy, just above the pubic bone, and you push against the hand, in order to deliver the placenta and membranes. It often helps to have a hand to push against like this. The alternative is to squat over a bowl or pail and to deliver the placenta with the help of gravity.

There is no reason for a cord to be clamped before the placenta has been delivered except for convenience, although sometimes the cord is so short that it is impossible for the mother to hold her baby unless it is cut first; or the cord may be twisted in a succession of loops around the baby's neck and is cut so that the baby can slide out. If a woman is Rhesus negative with a Rhesus positive baby (see page 113), there is a case for *delayed* cord clamping. If the cord is clamped while still pulsating, fetal blood is retained in the placenta, blood vessels rupture as the uterus contracts, and the chances of Rhesus positive blood being pushed back into the mother's blood stream are greatly increased.

Induced labor

Induction is the obstetric way of starting off labor. When labor begins naturally, the uterus becomes sensitive to hormones present in your bloodstream at the end of pregnancy. When labor is induced the doctor tries to obtain a similar result by flooding your system with hormones, until they reach a level much higher than that which occurs naturally. This can be done by introducing synthetic hormones into your bloodstream, through a continuous intravenous drip or by inserting prostaglandin suppositories into your vagina. Both methods are usually combined with artificial rupture of the membranes.

INDUCTION PROCEDURES

Remember that you have the right to receive full details of exactly what is going to be done and why *before* being admitted to the hospital for induction, and you can then choose to accept or refuse the treatment once you know all the facts.

Stripping the membranes Some doctors strip the membranes to stimulate labor. This is done by pushing the membranes away from the cervix by hand, while leaving them intact. This is a rather uncomfortable procedure, but may successfully start things off.

Artificial rupture of the membranes (see page 317) This may be performed as the only means of induction if your cervix is already starting to dilate. Most obstetricians believe that once the membranes are ruptured the baby ought to be born within 24 hours, because there is some risk of infection if labor is long and drawn out. So you need to be aware that if your labor is started by ARM but is slow to get going, it may then have to be accelerated with hormones.

Prostaglandin gel One commonly employed way of inducing labor is to introduce prostaglandin gel into and around the cervix. While prostaglandin gel may not start labor, it helps to ripen and efface a firm, thick cervix, making it more likely to dilate when oxytocin is given. If the gel is inserted in the evening, by the following morning the cervix may have ripened significantly. Or it may take several doses of gel over a day or two to achieve this result. Then an oxytocin drip, often with amniotomy, will be started. You can go home between gel applications after being observed for an hour or two.

Oxytocin drip If induction involves being connected to an oxytocin (pitocin) drip, ask that the IV be placed in the arm or hand you use less. If the connecting tube is short, you cannot easily move your arm or change position without dislodging it, but there is no need for it to be short, and you can ask for it to be securely fixed so that you can still change position. Many women have discovered that when they are in labor they get a backache simply from lying in one position for too long, quite apart from the backache that is frequently a result of contractions. A glucose solution may be passed through the IV first. The IV oxytocin may sometimes be removed once the contractions are effective and the cervix is 5 cm dilated. You can ask the obstetrician to do this. But an IV is usually kept in until after the end of the third stage, since it can control bleeding from the uterus by keeping it contracting hard.

> *"I found it so much easier to be upright and moving that I got out of the bed and walked around attached to the IV stand."*

WHEN INDUCTION MAY HELP

Induction is a useful obstetric technique when a baby must be born without delay. Many doctors believe that between 15 and 25 percent of women and their babies benefit from either induction or acceleration of labor. Some believe that these figures are too high, while others contend that 60 percent or more of labors ought to be induced. Symptoms of preeclampsia (see page 139), including high blood pressure, albumin in the urine, sudden excessive weight gain, and edema (puffiness resulting from fluid retention), are a good reason for induction, since the baby may not continue to be well nourished inside your uterus if the pregnancy is allowed to go on.

INDUCTION BEFORE THE EDD

Some babies stop growing because the placenta, through which they receive nourishment and oxygen, is not working well at the end of the pregnancy, even before there is any question of being "overdue," and even though the mother may be feeling fit and healthy. Such babies may fare better outside the uterus.

INDUCTION AFTER THE EDD

Between 10 and 12 percent of women go two weeks or more "overdue" (known as "post-dates"), but in only 1 percent of these babies is there any real evidence of post-maturity. What has frequently happened is that the date of the start of pregnancy has been miscalculated. In only 3 percent of women is the term of pregnancy actually unusually long.

If you are 43 weeks pregnant, there is a chance of the placenta not functioning so well because it is aging. However, *premature babies are most at risk*, so the obstetrician needs to be sure that the baby really is overdue before inducing labor. Some doctors make it a rule to induce if you are more than one or two weeks overdue. Others like all their patients to deliver at about term, and bring you into the hospital if you are just a few days past your date. Ultrasound can be used to check the flow of blood to the baby and the volume of amniotic fluid – which is reduced once a baby really is postterm – and to discover whether induction is necessary (see pages 223–226).

THE LENGTH OF INDUCED LABORS

Although you may have a rapid labor with induction, this cannot be guaranteed. Some obstetricians prefer labors not to last longer than ten, eight, or even five hours and deliver with forceps or by cesarean section if labor is prolonged beyond that fixed point. When a policy of routine induction is introduced in a hospital, there is a large increase in the number of instrumental deliveries and cesarean sections performed, and the proportion of babies with low Apgar scores (see page 356) goes up – evidence that a policy of routine induction is bad for babies as well as mothers.* Since

"I declined the offer of induction at 42 weeks and asked for some tests to be done instead. The baby was fine, and I went into labor the next day."

there is so much variation in obstetric policy, it may be a good idea when discussing the possibility of induction with the doctor to ask what his or her practice is. Depending on whether or not you want a short, sharp labor, this may affect your decision about whether to agree to induction if it is not urgently necessary for your baby's sake.

Induction is a form of intervention which, while useful when necessary, is not without risks, and the relative risks of leaving the baby inside your uterus and of inducing labor have to be assessed.

Unripe cervix It has been stated that "the major factor governing the success of induction is the state of the cervix."* When the cervix feels soft – like your lips when you hold your mouth slack – then it is ripe and ready for labor. Unfortunately, induction is often done before the cervix is ripe, and in consequence the uterus may not respond to the hormones. If the membranes have been ruptured, then the only way to get the baby born is by cesarean section. In cases where an induction is necessary and the cervix is unripe, prostaglandin gel over a period of several days may be used before oxytocin.

Powerful contractions If the uterus is triggered to work harder, labor is more violent than it would be if it started naturally. In an induced labor there are often two "peaks" to each contraction, and each may last one minute or longer. Women who have had babies before, and whose previous labors were not induced, say that contractions start more powerfully and that there is not much lead-up to each contraction, but instead a sudden "explosion." There may be only a short interval between contractions; just time to let out one relaxing breath, and then you are into the next one! You may find you need to go straight into the breathing techniques you will have learned about for half-dilatation (see pages 201–208).

Interrupted blood flow Extremely powerful contractions are likely to interfere with the blood flow through the uterus. In one study it was discovered that fetal distress was significantly more common in women taking oxytocin, that the babies were more likely to have low Apgar scores (see page 356), and that far more of these babies than usual went to the nursery for special care.*

So it is important to have expert assistance, and the obstetrician will order continuous monitoring of the baby's heart. If you experience a contraction that lasts longer than 90 seconds, let the obstetrician know immediately. Even with a small dose of oxytocin, some women have a prolonged contraction in which the uterus clamps down on itself – and on the baby. There is no test by which the sensitivity of your uterus to oxytocin can be known beforehand, so it is best to start with a small dose and gradually build up until good contractions result. The aim should be to simulate normal labor.

MEASURING CONTRACTIONS

During an induced labor, an intrauterine pressure catheter may be used to monitor the pressure of uterine contractions, and the flow of oxytocin will be slowed down when the uterus is contracting too hard for too long. The intrauterine pressure catheter means that the woman does not have to be strapped into a tight belt to record the contractions. These techniques aim to solve the problem of too strong, harsh labor contractions, which result when more oxytocin is put into a woman's bloodstream than her particular uterus needs.

INDUCTION WITH EPIDURAL ANESTHESIA

In some hospitals you may be offered a "package deal" of induction combined with epidural anesthesia. (For more about epidurals see pages 309–313.) Women who accept the package deal know that labor will take place on a certain day, and that complete pain relief will be available. This new style of childbirth is attractive to many obstetricians and to many women, too.

As with any intravenous drip, if you are receiving a large quantity of fluid, it is important that you remember to empty your bladder regularly. If you cannot urinate (and you often cannot if you have had an epidural), the nurse will insert a catheter and draw off the urine for you. A full bladder makes contractions painful (sometimes even with an epidural) by acting as a barrier between the baby's head and the base that forms the front of your pelvic arch.

ELECTIVE INDUCTION

Elective induction, also called induction for convenience, is induction with no medical indication. Some doctors believe that most women should be induced. Some think it is the only way in which all labors can be efficiently managed. They say it is important for women to be in labor when staff are on duty, that hospital organization is easier when it is known how many women will be in labor each day, and that it is better if women are not in labor at night. There will always be those women who go into labor spontaneously at inconvenient times, but the earlier they are induced the less this is likely to happen. So some obstetricians believe that induction any time after 38 or 39 weeks is right for most women. The logical development of this approach to obstetrics is that all spontaneous labors will come to be considered as "emergencies" and "normal" labors will all be induced.

The U.S. Food and Drug Administration, after considering the findings of research, has withdrawn approval for the use of oxytocin for the elective induction of labor, asserting that it can expose both mother and baby to unnecessary danger.

COPING WITH INDUCTION

While there are basic questions that women need to ask about induction and acceleration of labor in terms of our increasingly technological style of childbirth in the West, these may not seem very relevant if your doctor advises you that your labor should be induced. It may come as a shock. You may even feel that all your careful preparation for the birth of your baby is pointless now.

Many women have enjoyed induced labors and coped with them well. But unfortunately many whose labors were induced say that they did not have any choice and that they were given inadequate information. Yet the British Department of Health and Social Security has stated: "A mother should have learned about induction at antenatal classes and if later it appears that induction would be the safer course of action for her, she should have every opportunity of discussing it with professional advisers. Knowing what is likely to be involved, she can make a fully informed decision about it."*

The important thing is to ask questions at the hospital. Do not wait and hope that the obstetrician will explain things to you. Discuss it all fully, learn about what might happen, and share in the decision-making rather than feeling it is all being decided for you. When you have the facts and your obstetrician's advice, take time to weigh them and choose what seems to be the best path, always leaving your mind open to new evidence which may later point to a different course of action. It is your baby and your body and the experts are there to help you, not to take over.

ACCELERATED LABOR

Labor is said to be augmented or accelerated when it has already started and then been speeded up by the use of an oxytocin drip. If a drip is used *before* the cervix has started to dilate progressively, even though you have felt contractions and have had a "false labor" or many Braxton Hicks contractions, your labor is being induced, not augmented. Labor may be augmented when there is uterine inertia or incoordination – that is, when the uterus is not working effectively (see page 276). Some of the most difficult labors are long ones, and if you are getting tired out with the stress of experiencing continued back pain, for example, augmentation may help you cope because it stimulates uterine action.

If it looks as if labor ought to be induced or accelerated, there are breathing skills you can use in order to help you deal with the challenge (see pages 201–208). You need not give up when this occurs, feeling that the doctors have now taken over.

ACTIVE MANAGEMENT OF LABOR

This is a system of controlling and hastening labors, and ensuring rapid and efficient uterine action, by introducing the hormone oxytocin into each woman's bloodstream. It is claimed that it cuts the cesarean section rate. It was devised by obstetricians in the National Maternity Hospital in Dublin, where 40 percent of women have their labors stimulated in this way, and is increasingly popular with obstetricians all over the world. A woman is told that under no circumstances will her labor be allowed to last longer than 12 hours, and if her cervix does not dilate by at least one centimeter every hour, the uterus is stimulated artificially to work harder and faster.

In Dublin, uterine stimulation is restricted to women giving birth for the first time. Its use is considered potentially dangerous for women who have already had babies – multigravidae.* In addition, an important part of management is one-to-one care from a personal midwife who usually stays with each woman until the baby is born. Her duties primarily involve continuous presence, eye contact, and encouragement throughout every contraction, along with some clinical responsibilities. Obstetricians elsewhere often use active management indiscriminately. They favor it for multigravidae, too. And they neglect or forget that one-to-one care is part of the method, because it is administratively difficult. There is evidence, however, that it is not active management, but continuous one-to-one care, that reduces the need for cesarean section.* It is having someone with you who has experience and who gives emotional support which is the single effective element in this method of labor management. With this in mind, the decision to have a birth partner with you is probably one of the best ways of keeping your labor normal and reducing the chances of having a cesarean delivery, and you may want to ensure that you have the same midwife, or a doula, present with you throughout the birth.

"The birth was turned into a race against time, for no reason except that the obstetrician believed the best labors were the fastest."

Electronic fetal monitoring

The electronic fetal monitor (EFM) is used to track the fetal heartbeat and to record the pressure of the uterus during contractions. Either a transducer is placed over your abdomen near the baby's heart (external monitoring), or a spiral wire electrode is inserted through

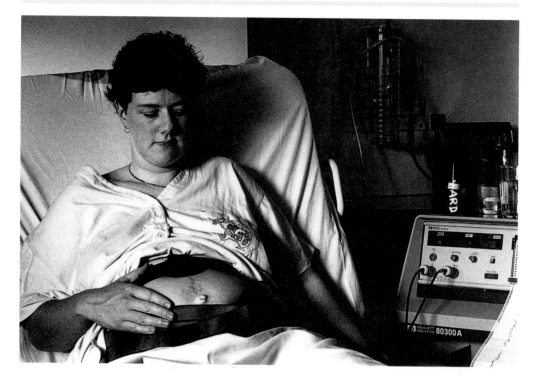

Electronic fetal monitoring

The monitor is near the bed so you can see when the next contraction is starting even before you feel it, and can get ready to meet it with your breathing. Before you are attached to a monitor, get into an upright position so that you do not get stuck lying down.

the open cervix and fastened to the baby's scalp (internal monitoring). A printout, usually in the form of a continuous graph on a long spool of tape rather like ticker tape, shows the baby's heart rate in relation to the work being done by the uterus. The monitor is a compact box which can amplify the baby's heartbeat so that it becomes clearly audible. It incorporates a flashing light which also registers the beating of the baby's heart and the contraction intensity, but this can be turned off. If anything goes wrong, the monitor sounds an alarm. This often indicates something wrong with the machine rather than with the baby.

MAKING A DECISION ABOUT ELECTRONIC FETAL MONITORING
When EFM was invented in the 1970s, it was believed that it would make birth safer for babies. But nine randomized controlled trials have shown that it does not. Babies are just as safe when someone listens to the fetal heart just after a contraction has finished and in the interval between contractions with a Pinard's stethoscope or a hand-held Doppler machine. Babies who are intermittently monitored are not more likely to have low Apgar scores or go to the special care unit.* In fact, more babies suffer from cerebral palsy after EFM labors than when they are monitored intermittently.*

Continuous monitoring reduces the rate of neonatal seizures (fits). Some people have concluded from the findings of this research that the value of continuous monitoring has been affirmed. Then it was revealed that this kind of neonatal seizure was not the type that produced long-term health problems, and that it occurred only in babies whose mothers had received oxytocin in labor. A major disadvantage of EFM is that it increases the cesarean section rate by 160 percent, without any benefit to the baby.* This rate is reduced if fetal blood sampling is done before the decision to proceed to operative delivery, but there is still a 30 percent increase in the cesarean section rate, again without any benefit to the baby.*

Continuous monitoring also has a profound effect on the way that labor is conducted. With the monitoring set-up, the woman is unable to move freely. She is more likely to be left alone at times during the labor, because the caregivers believe that the electronic equipment is doing the job of monitoring for them. She cannot use a birth pool or have transcutaneous electronic nerve stimulation for pain relief. For many women the process of electronic monitoring makes the labor much more stressful than it need be.

THE EXTERNAL MONITOR

An external monitor has two straps which are attached to your abdomen. One strap holds the tocodynamometer (the pressure gauge that records contractions). The other holds the ultrasound transducer which registers the baby's heartbeats.

THE INTERNAL MONITOR

The internal monitor, which is more accurate, is inserted through your vagina and cervix, and fixed to the skin of the baby's head. It is connected to a wire leading to the machine and another device, and an intrauterine pressure catheter is inserted into the uterus to record electronically the pressure of contractions; or you may wear a single strap around your abdomen in order to hold the tocodynamometer. An internal monitor cannot be used until the membranes have ruptured spontaneously or have been ruptured artificially, and until the cervix is dilated at least 2 cm.

ADVANTAGES OF MONITORING

The monitor is particularly useful in high-risk pregnancies and also when the labor is induced or augmented with an oxytocin drip, since the length, power, and frequency of the contractions produced by the drip and their effect on the baby must be carefully observed lest they prove to be too stressful for the baby to cope with. Until recently induction was often done "blind," and enormous, turbulent contractions were produced as a result which sometimes cut off the fetal blood supply. This is much less likely nowadays since, by monitoring these artificially aided births, it has been discovered that small amounts of oxytocin are effective.

Another undoubted advantage of monitoring during labor is that the monitor indicates when the next contraction is beginning, so that however drowsy you are feeling during labor you can breathe out and relax, and get ready to breathe over it.

PROBLEMS OF MONITORING

Many women say that the abdominal strapping of the external monitor is very uncomfortable during labor. Some even say that the pressure of the transducer on their tummies was the most painful thing about labor. Sometimes the internal electrode slips off the baby's head or, if an external monitor is being used, the baby moves and its heartbeat is then lost on the monitor. Some new external monitors have transducers which track the position of the baby's heart so that they do not lose it in this way.

As with an intravenous drip, an external monitor requires you to remain more or less in one position lest the transducer slip off. As we have seen, this immobility means discomfort for you (page 320) and possibly problems for the baby. So monitoring may sometimes produce the failing fetal heart rate which it then records. If you are being monitored, do not allow this to keep you from moving around within the range of the wires to which you are attached. The nurse or midwife can adjust the monitor when you move, if necessary.

Some women in labor are wired to the monitor only to find that nothing is being recorded at all because the machine is not operating. It is very irritating to be immobilized and connected to a machine when it cannot possibly be doing anything to help. Yet staff sometimes appear shocked at a woman's request for the transducer to be detached so that she can move about and get on with her labor unhindered. If this happens to you, you are entirely justified in insisting that the monitor be disconnected. But when the monitor is working well some women are reassured to know that every heartbeat of the baby is being recorded.

TELEMETRY

Monitoring by telemetry (radio waves) is an advance on the older method and allows you to be up and about in labor unattached to wires but continuously monitored at the same time. The equipment is less cumbersome and the machinery can be placed at some distance from you. Telemetry is not yet widely available in the US; in the UK most women prefer it, labors seem to go faster, and babies do better. Because you are able to stay upright, you may feel less pain, and the uterus can work more efficiently.

But even monitoring by telemetry is often invasive, since internal monitoring methods are sometimes used with telemetry, though a method of sticking the monitor onto the baby's scalp with epoxy resin is now available. Any invasive technique (one which entails entering your body) introduces added risk of infection. This is a risk worth taking when there is reason to suspect the baby is encountering difficulties, but not, many people would think, when everything seems to be straightforward.

A scalp electrode probably causes the baby some pain. It involves breaking the skin of the baby's scalp. (It is uncomfortable to prick your finger on one.) It remains on the baby's head until after delivery, when it should be removed gently and deftly, not merely yanked. In 85 percent of newborn babies a rash appears at the site of the electrode and in 20 percent a small abscess develops.* Sometimes the child is left with a permanent bald patch.

INTERPRETING THE DATA

It is only too easy to interpret normal variations in the fetal heart rate as pathological, sometimes because of the design of the machine, or to miss out on clinical signs that something is wrong, because the monitor indicates that everything is normal. Obstetricians and midwives experienced in auscultating the fetal heart and assessing clinical conditions have a valuable skill which is being revived today as we come to recognize the limited value of electronic monitors in supplying accurate findings during labor. Interpretation of electronic monitoring data sometimes causes more harm than good.

Half of all babies show some irregularities of heartbeat during labor. Usually this is of no significance. We don't know how they manage it, but babies actually sleep during labor. They change from rapid eye movement (REM) or dreaming sleep to deep, quiet sleep for a period of up to 40 minutes, and then back again. As the sleep state varies, so the heart rate changes; in deep sleep, the heartbeat stays steady, and the printout of the heart rate tends to be flat. Until the deep sleep was understood, this kind of trace made doctors anxious; but it has now been discovered that the baby only has to be roused a little for the heartbeat to pick up. One way of doing this is to touch the top of the baby's head. Mothers have their own ways of achieving the same result – changing position, for example, or even talking to the baby – and this may reassure the doctors.

The baby's heart rate is usually between 120 and 160 beats per minute. A quicker rate than this is termed tachycardia, and a slower rate, bradycardia. Incomplete understanding of the normal range of variation in the fetal heart rate during and between contractions leads to a great deal of intervention. Emergency cesarean sections are often performed because of changes in the fetal heart rate which are judged to be signs of asphyxia. Yet more than 50 percent of babies delivered by cesarean section turn out to be in good condition, so operating was unnecessary.
What has actually occurred is a series of complex changes in the baby's heartbeat as a result of a normal catecholamine (stress hormone) surge, and these alterations have been misinterpreted as signs of fetal distress.

"There was some concern about the baby's heart rate because it was abnormally slow. Then they found they were picking up my heartbeat, not the baby's."

In Spain and West Germany, when abnormal fetal heart patterns are recorded, obstetricians stop the uterus from contracting by introducing drugs into the mother's bloodstream. In all countries, electronic fetal monitoring has led to more forceps deliveries and cesarean sections, and the introduction of a monitor in any hospital is always associated with a sharp increase in the rate of operative deliveries – though this often drops after a while as they become more comfortable with the normal variations in fetal heart rate. Both the American College of Obstetricians and Gynecologists (ACOG) and the Society of Obstetricians and Gynecologists of Canada (SOGC) now recognize and support a policy of regular, frequent listening with an ultrasound stethoscope (auscultation) as equal or superior to electronic fetal heart monitoring. Despite this reversal of support for electronic fetal heart monitoring by the leaders in obstetrics, most nurses and physicians have not been trained in auscultation, and thus continue to rely on EFM.

TESTING THE BABY'S BLOOD

If the fetal monitor suggests that the baby is under stress, the baby's blood should be tested in order to check the findings, since if the baby is having any difficulties this always shows up in the blood chemistry. But this testing is not always done. A biochemical test carried out in order to assess the pH level of the baby's blood cuts down the number of unnecessary cesarean deliveries. One kind of electrode both records the baby's heart rate and also tests its blood.

It has usually been accepted that if a blood test reveals high levels of lactic acid, which builds up if the baby is short of oxygen in the second stage of labor, the baby's brain will be damaged. But it is now known that if it does become short of oxygen, a healthy baby can switch to another kind of metabolism which allows it to draw on energy reserves that have been built up over the previous weeks; in this way the baby can survive on less oxygen with no ill effects whatsoever. Indeed, babies whose blood is acid at birth often have high Apgar scores (see page 356). And neurological studies on four-year-olds whose blood was acid at birth due to oxygen shortage show that this had no harmful effects.*

Helping the baby out

In most American hospitals nowadays about one baby in every four or five is delivered by forceps. The rate is higher in some hospitals.

FORCEPS DELIVERY

Forceps look like metal salad servers and dovetail into each other so that they cannot press too far in on the baby's head. If the woman has not already had an epidural, an injection to numb the birth outlet is given first. The curved blades are inserted one at a time and cradled around the baby's head, one at each temple. Forceps are of different shapes for different situations: most bring the baby down the birth canal, though some are simply used to lift the baby out. If the baby's head is occipito transverse or occipito posterior (see page 263), the obstetrician may first turn the head manually, or may use curved Kiellands forceps for the delivery to rotate the head from the transverse or posterior to the anterior.

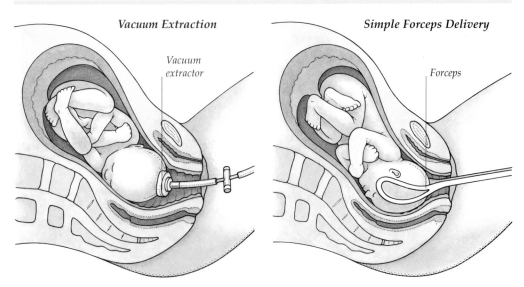

Vacuum Extraction   *Simple Forceps Delivery*

Vacuum extractor

Forceps

VACUUM EXTRACTION

Increasingly a vacuum extractor is used instead of forceps. There is a certain amount of evidence that vacuum extraction is better for both mother and baby than forceps extraction. But, of course, it is a skill that needs to be learned.* A vacuum extractor works like a miniature vacuum cleaner to suck the baby out. A vacuum cup is attached to the baby's head. It may take between 10 and 20 minutes to be applied. During this time if you want to push, push. Once the cup is on, it helps if you can bear down, so that the baby is pressed down from above as well as being pulled down the birth canal by the suction that is being applied from below.

REASONS FOR FORCEPS DELIVERY OR VACUUM EXTRACTION

Forceps or vacuum extraction is used only during the second stage when delivery needs to be hastened because your blood pressure has risen dramatically, for example, or because there are signs of fetal distress, or when the baby is in an unusual position, making its journey through the pelvic outlet more difficult. The obstetrician has to use clinical judgment to decide whether your baby will pop out like a cork from a bottle given a firm, long pull, or whether it is so firmly wedged that it might harm both you and the baby to deliver vaginally. Sometimes after forceps or vacuum have failed a cesarean section is performed (see pages 336–340).

Forceps or vacuum extraction may also be used if you have had an epidural (see pages 309–313), as in this case you may well feel too numb to be able to work with contractions.

A forceps delivery or vacuum extraction is frequently advised if you are having a prolonged second stage. Different obstetricians have different ideas of what a prolonged second stage is. Some would say that it is any second stage longer than half an hour in

Help with delivery
The forceps (right) are the kind used simply for lifting the baby's head out of the birth canal. Vacuum extraction (left) can sometimes avoid a difficult forceps delivery, and the suction cup may be attached to the baby before it has started to descend the birth canal.

which there are no signs of progress. Many set a definite time limit on the second stage and instruct nurses to call them when it looks as if this stage is extending. Some believe that this is rather doctrinaire and that the important thing is to observe whether or not the baby is coming down the birth canal progressively, while checking its condition carefully and regularly.

Some women seem to be able to cope with long second stages without tiring, whereas others quickly become exhausted. If you have already had a long labor and then a slow second stage, it is difficult to retain enthusiasm and, unless given a great deal of encouragement, you might hope that someone would just come and take the baby out of your body one way or another.

Sometimes a woman may be given encouragement to push or be persuaded to hold her breath too long, when she does not feel any spontaneous urge to bear down. This is because the nurse knows that the delivery will be by forceps unless the baby is born within the time decreed by the obstetrician, so she tries to avoid the intervention by getting the mother to push more strenuously in the hope that this will help the baby to be born before the deadline comes.

AVOIDING A FORCEPS DELIVERY OR VACUUM EXTRACTION

If you have been struggling to push the baby out and it is suggested that forceps may be necessary because the second stage is taking too long, you are becoming too tired, or the fetal heart rate is slow, explore the effect of *not pushing*. You may find that you do not need to push at all for several contractions – a welcome rest for both you and the baby – and then there is an unmistakable and irresistible pushing sensation which is much more effective than pushing just because you are following instructions. It is a good idea to stand, squat, or kneel so that gravity can help the baby out.

Cesarean section

If the obstetrician tells you that you need to give birth by cesarean section, this means that you will be anesthetized and your baby will then be delivered abdominally rather than vaginally.

The most common reason for cesarean section is the failure of your labor to progress, due to malposition of the baby or to cephalopelvic disproportion, when the baby's head is too large to pass through the pelvis. Some obstetricians prefer to deliver all breech babies abdominally, or all breech babies of first-time mothers, because they believe it is safer for the baby. But the size of the baby in relation to the maternal pelvis and the way the baby is lying are factors to take into account. If fetal distress is picked up by an electronic monitor and the obstetrician becomes anxious about the state of the baby, he or she may decide to perform an emergency cesarean section. A biochemical test of the baby's scalp blood should be done first to check whether the baby is finding birth hard going.

Abdominal delivery may also be performed for twins, when amniocentesis has revealed that a baby is damaged, for very low-weight babies, and also for women suffering from active herpes or diseases such as diabetes, renal disease, and severe hypertension. Research has been carried out on the outcomes of automatic cesarean sections for multiple births and when women have diabetes, and it has been shown that this practice is unlikely to be of benefit.* Delivering all twins by cesarean section does not save babies' lives or produce babies in better condition. A study compared birth outcomes in two parts of Denmark, one where the rate of cesarean section was about twice as high as the other, and found no differences in perinatal mortality or morbidity.*

THE RISE IN CESAREAN BIRTHS

Cesarean rates vary. In Britain, they make up about 15 percent of all births. In some cities in Latin America, a staggering 85 percent of babies are delivered abdominally, whereas in the Netherlands the overall rate is less than 10 percent. In South Africa the rate varies from 14 to 17 percent in state teaching hospitals to 33 percent in private hospitals. Private obstetricians there, as in other countries, are much more likely to opt for cesarean sections than those in a national health service. South African obstetricians themselves report that they do cesarean section for convenience in 75 percent of cases.* The cesarean rate in the United States is approximately 24 percent. In some hospitals it is 50 percent or more. But there has not been a corresponding rise in the fetal survival rate. And cesarean section imposes on women extra risk, as well as unnecessary pain and, often, postoperative infection. The World Health Organization recommends that cesarean section rates should never be allowed to go higher than 10 to 12 percent.

"It was a shock to have a cesarean section, as I'd looked forward to a natural birth. I felt cheated and as if I weren't a normal woman."

In the past the obstetrician would have corrected a breech baby's position by external version through the mother's abdominal wall (see page 234). This practice declined for a generation and it became the tendency to deliver by section rather than attempting to turn the baby first. As a result, doctors no longer knew *how* to perform external version. When the cesarean section rate rose to shocking heights, the technique of external version was revived and is used again by increasing numbers of physicians.

More and more women are now included in the category of "high risk." The age at which a woman is considered obstetrically high risk went down from 40 to 35, then to 30. If you are over 35 and it seems likely that there may be problems with your labor, you may find that you are advised to deliver by cesarean section. Some obstetricians like to do a cesarean section just because a baby looks as if it is going to be big. This is not an adequate reason for abdominal delivery.* Throughout North America it is also the practice to do *repeat* cesarean sections, even when the conditions which resulted in the first section are not present: "Once a cesarean, always a cesarean." Many repeat cesareans are unnecessary. Only about one woman in four who had a cesarean with one birth even tries for a VBAC (vaginal birth after cesarean) with her next. Women often ask to have a cesarean in order to avoid the pain of labor and because they can be conveniently scheduled. American doctors argue that the uterine scar might possibly break open during VBAC, but British obstetricians differ. They normally prefer the labor to proceed naturally but are ready to do a cesarean if this becomes necessary. One professor of obstetrics says that problems of scar separation are "much less than the one percent that is often quoted" and that even if the scar is pulled open by strong contractions, "careful monitoring of the fetus and mother usually means that any harm to either is rare."* VBAC is advised whenever possible by the American College of Obstetricians and Gynecologists.

PLANNED CESAREAN SECTION

The decision to perform a cesarean section is often made days or weeks in advance. As one woman said, "I got out my diary and wrote 'BABY' in a square several months ahead."A section will usually be planned if it is known that the baby is in a difficult position to be delivered vaginally. You may also be advised to have a cesarean if there is clear evidence of cephalopelvic disproportion – although you can be certain that there is genuine CPD only when you are actually in labor. The baby must be delivered abdominally if the placenta is lying at the bottom of the uterus and over the os (the mouth of the cervix), in front of the baby's presenting part (placenta previa). You usually have a scan at 32 weeks to confirm that the placenta is still in this position. If your placenta is low lying, surgery is arranged either for the 39th week or as soon as the baby's lungs are known to be mature, which can be tested by amniocentesis.

UNPLANNED (JUST-IN-CASE) CESAREAN SECTION

During a long labor in which there is little progress, the obstetrician may make the decision to perform a cesarean section for no other reason than that dilatation is slow. It is important that you share in the decision-making about this. It is up to you.

EMERGENCY CESAREAN SECTION

Some of the different reasons for a planned cesarean section (such as cephalopelvic disproportion) may also apply to an emergency section, when they have not been obvious until labor. An emergency section may also be decided on during a long labor in which the baby is in obvious difficulties and is short of oxygen; if the placenta is failing to service the baby sufficiently or is becoming detached from the lining of the uterus, causing the mother to hemorrhage; or if there is a prolapsed umbilical cord.

Anesthesia for cesarean section

Cesarean section in the past was always performed with the patient under a general anesthesia, but now epidural or spinal anesthesia (see below) is preferred for this operation. Though general anesthesia still has to be used when a very quick decision is made to do a section, those women who have epidural or spinal anesthesia have usually liked being awake, aware of what is going on, and ready to welcome the baby as soon as he is lifted out.

General anesthesia If general anesthesia is used, you are typically given as small a dose as possible for the baby's sake, and you may be unconscious for only a few minutes. All the preparation for the operation is done while you are awake and you are often given pure oxygen to breathe in during this time. It should also be possible to arrange for the baby who is in good condition to be held by the father while you are still unconscious.

Epidural anesthesia You are given the epidural after being taken to the operating room or an existing epidural will be increased – the dosage is larger for this surgery than it would be if an epidural were being given just for pain relief. An anesthesiologist checks carefully to see that the anesthesia is sufficient for the operation and is ready with general anesthesia should the epidural not take effectively. You may possibly have postoperative nausea and vomiting, as there often is with general anesthesia. An epidural is safer for you because you cannot inhale your stomach contents, and safer for the baby, who does not receive a knock-out dose of anesthesia. Another advantage is that you can hold your baby and put it to the breast immediately after the operation.

Spinal anethesia If you have had no anesthetic prior to the decision to do a cesarean, a spinal anesthetic may be preferred over an epidural because it can be done more quickly and achieves good anesthesia more simply than an epidural.

Horizontal or vertical uterine incision

Incisions for cesarean section are either horizontal or vertical. The classical incision is vertical but this is rarely done now unless there is no time to spare. The main advantages of the horizontal incision are that it is made low down near the line of the pubic hair, in the area which would be covered by a bikini, and that a horizontal scar is less likely to break down than a vertical scar.

What happens during a cesarean section

Before you have a cesarean section, you should be given antibiotics because one very frequent problem is pelvic infection afterward.* A midwife will shave off your pubic hair and slip a catheter into your bladder so that it is kept empty. In the operating room sterile drapes

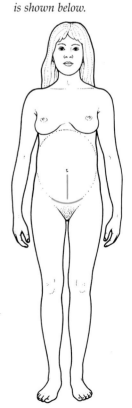

Cesarean incisions
The classic cesarean incision is vertical. Though this is still used in emergencies, horizontal incision is now more common, and there is much reduced risk of rupture in another pregnancy. The positioning of a vertical and a horizontal incision is shown below.

are put around your tummy, and if you are going to be awake, a screen is erected at about chest level so that you do not see the surgery. Your tummy is washed in antiseptic solution. If there is anything you want to know, ask.

You will be given an epidural, spinal, or, rarely, a general anesthetic. When your whole tummy is numb or you have become unconscious, a series of small cuts is made through the layers in your lower abdominal wall until the lower uterine segment is revealed. Packs of surgical gauze are pressed in to keep other organs out of the way. A horizontal slit is made through the uterus and the bag of waters then bulges through it. The obstetrician pops the bag and sucks out the amniotic fluid – if you have had an epidural or spinal, you may hear the glug-glug-swoosh sound – and uses one blade of the forceps or a hand under the baby's presenting part to ease it out of the small opening, at the same time pushing with one hand on the upper part of the uterus so that the baby is pressed down through the incision.

"They asked me what music I would like during my cesarean section. I didn't have to listen to the extraordinary sounds of being cut open and sucked out."

If you have had an epidural or spinal, it may be possible for you to watch the birth at this stage. Ask the doctor to put the screen down for a few moments. You will see your baby emerging and, from your horizontal position, will not see anything gruesome. In fact you will have eyes only for your baby and will not think about the surgery that has been done. The baby is lifted out, suctioned with a mucus catheter, and, once he is breathing well, can be handed to you or your partner. The process from the beginning of surgery to the birth need take only about four minutes in an emergency, but usually takes approximately 10 to 15 minutes.

As the baby is being delivered, you may be given an injection of oxytocin to make the placenta peel away from the wall of the uterus. It will then be lifted out through the abdominal opening that has been made. The obstetrician stitches the cut in the uterus, layer by layer, with absorbable sutures. Suction instruments are used to draw out blood and amniotic fluid, and then the obstetrician repairs the abdominal wall. This takes much longer than the birth – up to an hour – and entails repairing the skin with non-absorbable sutures, steritapes, staples, or metal clips, which are removed the next day.

HAVING YOUR PARTNER WITH YOU

Not all couples want to be together during surgery. You may worry that perhaps it will be too much for your partner to cope with, or he may expect to find the experience so distressing that he feels he will be unable to give you any support. Those couples who do want to be together feel that the birth of a baby, by whatever route, is something they want to share, that it should be family-centered, and that, if the mother is not able to cuddle the newborn baby, the father should certainly be there to do so.

AFTER THE DELIVERY

After the operation, say that you want to hold your baby if he or she is not already beside you. An intravenous drip is left in for some hours so that you can be given plenty of fluids straight into your bloodstream if this is necessary. If you had general anesthesia, you may feel sick and weak for the first day or so. As soon as you feel you can move about in bed a little, do so. Even small actions such as wiggling your toes and rotating your ankles are good for you and prevents pooling of blood in your legs.

Whatever anesthesia you have had, the nurses will help you get up later the same day. Though it hurts, moving around is important in order to avoid thrombosis. To move off the bed, first work your way to the side of it, roll onto your side, and push yourself to sitting with your hands. As you get up you may have a lot of bleeding from the vagina. This also tends to happen after a vaginal delivery and is simply the blood that has pooled in your pelvic region while you were lying still. Stroll around the room to encourage good circulation and, as you do so, use the slow, complete breathing that you learned in childbirth classes.

If you feel you need drugs for pain relief, ask for them. Though you probably want to be awake to enjoy your baby, you cannot do this if you are in severe discomfort. The more your partner can be with you, even while you doze, the more you can relax, feeling that the baby is being looked after by someone who loves her.

You will probably go home 48 or 72 hours after the surgery, with instructions on self-care. Feel free to call the hospital or your doctor if you have problems or questions.

Dressings will probably be removed by you or your partner three or four days later. Because the obstetrician has had to cut through muscle, your tummy will look very big and soggy. Once the dressings are off, you will then be able to have a bath. The stitches inside your body dissolve naturally, but the external stitches or staples will be removed before you leave the hospital. Do not worry about them bursting open – with every layer stitched separately there is little chance of any such damage.

After general anesthesia, fluid collects in the lungs and then has to be coughed up. A nurse will teach you how to do this so that it causes least discomfort. The breathing techniques you learned in pregnancy can help in this process, too.

It is natural to feel a flood of conflicting emotions after cesarean birth. Some women say that they are grateful to have the baby, but at the same time they feel "cheated."

A cesarean birth is a surgical operation and you need time to recover from it as from any abdominal surgery. For the first six weeks after the birth you should avoid any heavy lifting. If it is possible to arrange for extra help at home, especially if you already have a toddler who expects to be lifted, it is an enormous benefit to have someone else to do the more strenuous work.

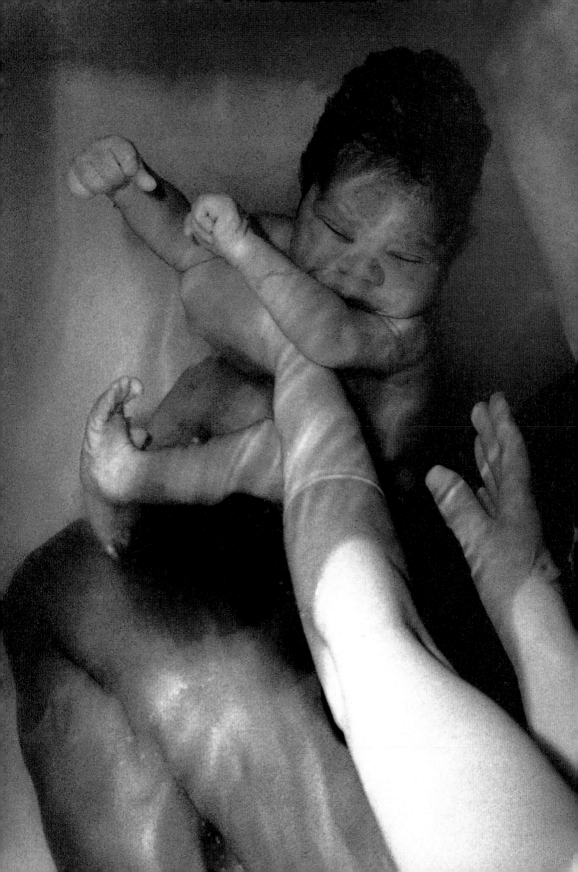

Gentle birth

At birth eyes open for the first time on a new world. Your baby's life outside your body begins. Yet your baby already has nine months' experience of life inside the uterus. The ancient Chinese dated life from conception rather than from delivery and perhaps this corresponds more nearly to reality. The baby started off as the chance collision of a ripe egg and a sperm. Forces which have their origin far back in time poured energy into the cells, nourishing and multiplying them to make an embryo budding on a stalk and drawing sustenance from your uterus. Gradually as the days passed a fully formed being developed, albeit in miniature, and there was already at the third month a fetus whose main task was one of growth and maturation. As week followed week its senses became sharper so that it was increasingly aware of its surroundings, responding to your movements and to bright light, loud sounds, and music. This long-drawn-out period of preparation culminates in the dramatic journey into the brilliance and bustle of our own world.

What is it like to be born?

Birth is an intense experience not only for you: for the baby, too, it is the climax of a time of growing and waiting. The new human being is caught up in a rush of powerful uterine activity, which squeezes it out from the confines of the tight muscle enveloping it and the cradle of bone in which it has been rocked, into a separate existence.

Traveling from the depths of the uterus, under the arch of bone and out through the soft, opening folds of the vagina, the baby passes through a barrage of different kinds of sensory stimulation. It is the original magical mystery tour and must be rather more astonishing and full of surprises than any tunnel traveled through in search of excitement in a fairground.

THE BABY'S EXPERIENCE OF LABOR

Pressure builds up over the crown of the baby's head where it is directed through the dilating cervix, which is pulled up over the head like a turtleneck sweater. Pressure is also directed over the baby's buttocks as the uterus contracts down on them and propels the baby forward. So the baby is fixed between the uterus gripping her bottom and the cervix being progressively drawn over her head. This pressure causes the baby to roll into a ball, head tucked in and knees bent up, arms folded over her chest. The upper part of the head, not yet hard bone all over, is molded so that the brow is pressed backward.

As the baby is forced downward the crown of the head also confronts resistance from the pelvic floor muscles, which are springy and firm and which are also little by little eased over her head.

Opposite
Birth need not be violent for a baby. Instead, there is welcome from loving arms and a gentle transition to life.

343

The passage is narrow but yielding and the baby's body is massaged vigorously with each contraction as she gradually descends.

Beneath the stretched abdominal skin and the thinned translucent wall of the uterus itself the baby in the last weeks of pregnancy has been aware of glowing light whenever bright sun or artificial light shone on your body. It must be rather like firelight or the light cast by a red-shaded lamp. When the journey to birth begins the baby is pressed deeper into the cavity of the pelvis, under arches of bone and a canopy of thick supportive ligaments and muscles. Perhaps it is a sensation rather like traveling through a long, dark avenue of overhanging trees.

The baby is not just a hunk of flesh or a life-sized doll. She is a human being fully equipped to feel pain and pleasure, a person coming to birth. The baby cannot remember or anticipate in the same way that we can, but nevertheless feels keenly and is a fully sentient being. The uterus holds and presses tightly in on the child not yet born, with steadily escalating power. By the end of the first stage of labor it is embracing the baby tightly for one or two minutes at a time. Each hug begins gently and grows tighter and tighter until at the height of the contractions the baby is being gripped fast for 20 to 30 seconds. Then the wave of pressure recedes again and the baby floats once more in her inner sea: she is in labor along with you.

NEWBORN REFLEXES IN LABOR

In some obstetric textbooks the baby is described simply as "a passenger," and purely in mechanical terms as two ovoids, the head and the trunk, the long axes of which are at right angles to each other and which can take the curve of the pelvic axis independently. While this is accurate as a description of the mechanics of fetal descent, it omits any mention of what the baby might be doing during this process and how the reflexes with which he is born are also already functioning during labor.

The baby changes position in response to the power unleashed in your body, and does this not only because of mechanical forces which act on him but probably also because he is making active movements.

"I expected a baby, of course, something I would hold. But he was born with eyes wide open, and as he looked at me I realized, 'this is a person!'"

Your baby is working *with* you toward birth, a partner in the struggle, not just a passenger, and can do this because of built-in reflexes (see page 357). A newborn baby turns his head in the direction of a touch, moves his head up and down against a firm surface, curls his toes down when pressure is applied to the ball of the foot, lifts his foot up and puts it down at a higher level when pressure is applied over the top of the foot, and makes forward stepping movements when tilted forward with his feet against a firm surface. Two of these actions probably operate to help the baby onward in its journey. One is the reflex to move his head up and down against firm resistance, which means that he actually wriggles his way forward through the cervix and the fanned-out tissues of the vagina with much the same action that we make when putting on a new sweater with a rather tight neck. The other is the stepping movement when resistance is offered to the feet, so that in effect the baby pushes away from the solid wall of the uterus as it tightens around him.

THE IMPACT OF THE OUTSIDE WORLD

In the second stage the head has to take a nearly right-angled bend. The pressure builds up until it swivels the neck around so that the baby is facing downward and ready to slide out. You can imagine that this provides a very sharp stimulus to the baby, a message which says unmistakably, "Things are changing. Wake up! It's all systems go!" At last the crown of the head oozes through the vagina and remains there. Perhaps you reach down with eager hands to stroke the damp, warm top of your baby's head. This is the first greeting.

The head slips out and suddenly the baby encounters space and air. The shoulders and chest slide forward, followed by the whole body. There is a gasp and air rushes into the lungs, inflating them for the first time. The damp inner surfaces of the lungs, previously clinging together like wet plastic bags, open up with the first cry with which the baby meets life.

Air, space, the baby's own limbs moving in an unfamiliar medium, weight, strange sounds, glaring lights, cold hands picking the baby up, turning him over – all at once myriad new sensations assail the newborn. Not only must lungs fill with air and start to function rhythmically, but the circulation must find new pathways.

LABOR AS A STIMULUS

In his book *Birth Without Violence,** Dr. Frederick Leboyer called the mother "a monster" because of the pain he believes she cannot help but inflict on the baby as he passes through the throes of birth. But the process of being born can also be seen to involve stimulation and awakening for which the baby is ready and which prepares him for life. Looked at from this point of view, muscles hold and embrace the baby, triggering powerful sensations, then soften again in a rhythmic pattern. The space between contractions is like the trough between two waves. Inevitably the next wave comes and again the muscles tighten firmly around the child.

Though labor is undoubtedly traumatic for some babies, others look extraordinarily peaceful and contented after their journey. It may feel to you as if you are swimming in a stormy sea when you reach the end of the first stage of labor. You may be anxious that these massive squeezings of the great muscle of the uterus are causing your baby suffering. Yet in spite of the relentless onslaught of contractions as full dilatation approaches, the baby who is pressed through the cervix and down the 9-inch (23-cm) birth canal responds more vigorously to life than do most babies who are merely lifted out through an abdominal incision. The baby born vaginally has less mucus in her respiratory tract than one delivered by cesarean section (especially an elective cesarean) and is better prepared for the great new activity of breathing. The baby can also maintain her own body temperature better after a vaginal birth than after a cesarean with little or no labor.

CATECHOLAMINES: THE AMAZING "STRESS" HORMONES

Stress is often talked about as if it were invariably harmful. But stress is part of active living. Labor is exciting, challenging – and stressful, for both you and the baby. As a result, hormones pour into your bloodstream and give you a "buzz." They are the same hormones that come with the triumph and satisfaction of at last climbing to the top of a mountain, or of drawing on all your reserves of strength and persistence in a race, the same hormones that flood through you when the curtain rises and you stand floodlit in front of an audience. There is striving, longing, concern to give your utmost, and the thrill of the unknown. It is like that, too, when labor begins. These hormones are produced by the baby as well as by you, and the baby produces them in vast quantities.

"My labor was long and hard and I felt sorry for the baby. But he came out alert, peaceful, and soon started to search for my breast."

All hormones are chemical messengers. Catecholamines give the baby the message of life. A surge of the stress hormones – adrenaline and noradrenaline – course through the baby's bloodstream before labor starts. They protect the baby from shortage of oxygen, shunt blood away from nonessential organs – the skin, for example – ensure a rich supply of blood to the heart, brain, and muscles, slow the heart rate so that the heart does not have to work so hard or need so much oxygen, prepare the lungs for breathing by dilating the bronchioles, cause fat and glycogen to be broken down and available for quick energy, and in all these ways prepare the baby for the demands of life outside the uterus.

A scientist who researches the function of catecholamines at birth writes, "Nearly every newborn has an oxygen debt akin to that of a sprinter after a run."* This catecholamine surge is the reason why babies can cope so well with oxygen deprivation at birth. They handle it much better than adults, who develop heart rate irregularities after just a few minutes.

Catecholamine levels in the baby build up even in early labor, when the cervix is still only two or three centimeters dilated, and are about five times the concentration of those in a resting adult. They surge still higher in the second stage, and after the birth are double or triple the level of the early first stage, dropping to a resting level after about two hours.

Pressure on the head of the fetus causes increased secretion of catecholamines. Babies who have not experienced labor and been delivered by elective cesarean section have much lower levels. This is why whenever possible the mother should experience some labor.

A baby who is simply removed through an abdominal incision is likely to have breathing difficulties because liquid in the lungs has not been absorbed during the process of birth and because the lungs have not produced much surfactant – the substance like soap bubbles which prevents the lungs' surfaces from sticking together. Both absorption of lung liquid and release of surfactant are dependent on catecholamines in the hours immediately before the baby is born. Some drugs used to treat hypertension in the mother also interfere with the action of catecholamines.

A newborn baby loses heat rapidly because of her high surface-to-volume ratio. If a baby gets cold after birth, catecholamines also activate special heat-producing tissue called "brown fat." Another effect of catecholamines is to dilate the pupils of the baby's eyes and increase alertness. Mother and baby fix their gaze on each other. Each is for the other the most interesting person in the world. The baby is not only cuddly and warm, but alert and responsive. In this way catecholamines are an element in the process of bonding between mother and baby.

WELCOMING YOUR BABY

Have you thought about how you want to welcome your baby into the world? This is not just a matter of safe or speedy delivery, of making sure that the baby has enough oxygen or is not traumatized by delivery, but one of greeting the baby with gentleness.

Most babies cry at the shock of birth and this first cry ensures that a rush of air enters the lungs. But if they *go on* crying there is something wrong. The crying of abandonment and distress is quite different from the healthy crying of the newborn. Yet people often take persistent crying for granted and even smile indulgently and say, "She's got a fine pair of lungs!" The newborn baby continues to scream because of insensitivity to her needs and the lack of a sufficiently caring environment. If the setting for birth is changed and, above all, if the attitudes of those assisting are different, so that the baby is treated with respect, the child will become quiet, open her eyes, reach out her hands, and start to discover herself. But if this is to happen the birth room must be calm and hushed, the lights dimmed, and those handling the baby must do so slowly, carefully, and lovingly. This is *gentle birth*.

Creating a caring environment

Gentle birth need not start only as the baby is born. In the way that labor is conducted, and in the whole atmosphere of the birth room, an environment of peace and serenity can be created. A mother and baby are so close and in such a subtle and yet intense relationship that everything done to you during labor must affect the way in which you are able to respond to your newborn baby. If you are treated as if your body is merely the container from which a baby is removed, or as an irresponsible child who has to be given orders, you will find it very difficult to be in harmony with the forces which are bringing the baby to birth, with your own body in its work of creation, and also with the baby. The caring environment for the newborn starts with a caring environment for you, a respect for your rhythms, patience to wait and watch, and loving support.

DIMMING THE LIGHTS

It is irritating for you to labor under bright lights, just as it is for the baby to confront brilliant fluorescent light at delivery. For a gentle birth all unnecessary lighting is switched off so that the room is softly illuminated, with a clear light only on the perineum. Instead of lying flat on your back or with your legs suspended in lithotomy stirrups you need to be in a position you find comfortable and in which you can be an active birthgiver. Many women like to be sitting up, crouching, or kneeling so that they can catch the first glimpse of the baby's head and can put their fingers down to touch it even before it has started to emerge through the vagina. We have already seen (on page 246) that an upright position has many advantages for the mother in terms of mechanical function. If you are well raised you are also in a splendid position for greeting your baby.

When the head crowns some women put their hands down to caress the top of the baby's head. The head feels warm and firm and as it eases forward you touch more and more warm, damp, silky hair. This very first contact between mother and child is beyond excitement; it is a moment of awe.

Then the head slides out and turns to align with the shoulders still inside and you can see your baby's profile; with a rush the shoulders and whole body are born. As the baby slips out and starts to breathe the lights can be dimmed further so that the baby can take his time to open his eyes in the half-light. Many years ago Maria Montessori, the educationalist, stressed that babies are assaulted by bright light. She said that they should be able to begin the gradual exploration of the world with their senses in a soft glow and shadows, similar to the uterine environment they have just left. Yet we have subjected newborns to harsh hospital lights and acted as if they were unable to see or hear.

REDUCING THE NOISE LEVEL

In nonviolent birth there is no unnecessary conversation and those attendants who speak do so in hushed voices. Frederick Leboyer believed that the mother should be quiet, too, and that excited voices can startle the baby. When he wrote his book, it was not known that the intrauterine environment was full of sound, particularly the mother's heartbeat and voice and the voices of others. He and Dr. Michel Odent think that there is too much emphasis nowadays on the father's presence in childbirth and that fathers sometimes get too emotional. Couples who value sharing birth together would not

Opposite
In a tranquil setting, the midwife lifts the baby into the mother's arms, with her finger resting on the baby's chest to feel the baby's heartbeat.

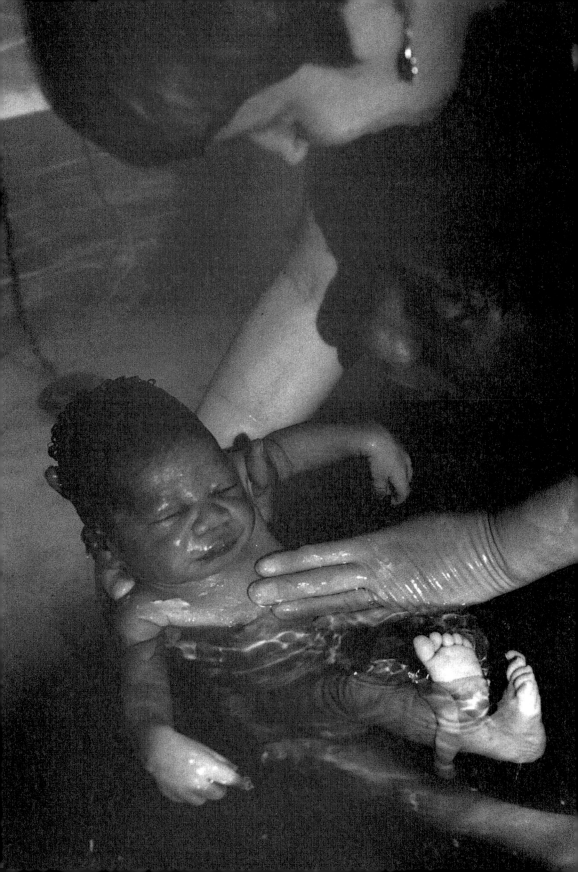

agree. I feel myself and know many women who also feel that it would not have been possible to go through labor and birth without the child's father there. In fact, couples often do cry out with astonishment and wonder when they see their baby leap into life and this is a spontaneous outpouring of emotion, of joy, an integral part of childbirth, which *in itself* is a life-enhancing experience for both parents. We don't carefully work out exactly what we are going to do when we are caught up in other sorts of peak experience; we don't weigh the different factors and come up with a formula. To do so would diminish the experience. Life is exultant and we are borne along with it. Birth is that kind of climactic process. It is also an act of love, the culmination of the passion which first started the development of that baby.

PHYSICAL CONTACT

It is because birth is a peak experience that arms reach out to take and hold the baby and draw him close. It is not just that this small, wrinkled, vulnerable baby is yours and that therefore you decide to take him in your arms (though unfortunately this is just how it is for some women in a loveless, uncaring environment); if the right atmosphere exists you are totally enveloped in a rush of intense feeling. This does not mean that the baby is neglected in an orgy of self-indulgent emotion. The baby is drawn into the warm circle of love between the parents and becomes part of it. This is what it means for not only a baby to be born but also a *family*.

"I lifted her out and up onto my tummy and held and stroked her. It suddenly burst on me that this incredible little creature had come out of my body! She had been a part of me. Now we were separate but we needed each other."

In nonviolent birth the baby is handled gently and slowly, without haste. There are no rough, quick movements. He or she is delivered up onto your tummy or over your thigh. If you ask beforehand it is often possible to do this yourself and the midwife or doctor will remind you to reach out and draw the baby onto your body.

Leboyer believed that the baby should be lovingly and gently massaged until he or she stops crying and becomes calm. Only then does he think the baby is ready to go to the mother's arms. In his own obstetric practice he used to do this massaging. But many women think that this is yet one more way in which professionals, however caring, attempt to take over childbirth and to intrude on the mother's natural role.

Where gentle birth is practiced today it is usually the mother who holds and caresses her baby. You do not have to learn how to massage your newborn. The way you explore and stroke him is spontaneous and right. But this is only possible if the baby is naked and in skin contact with you. Babies are often bundled up in wrappings in case they lose heat. It is true that new babies quickly become chilled unless they are in a warm atmosphere and are held close. Research has shown that the baby, even the low-birthweight baby, keeps warmer when in flesh-to-flesh contact with his mother and nestling against her breast than when wrapped up and put in a bassinet. So ask a helper to slip your gown down over your shoulders or to take it right off before delivery.

A blanket can easily be thrown over you and your baby or a heater can be placed over you both. Mothers often feel chilled and shaky after birth and appreciate the warmth. Putting a hat on the baby's head also helps to avoid heat loss.

If your baby is handed to you bundled up in a cloth, unwrap the covers and cuddle him close. Do not be afraid to talk to your baby. He or she will respond to the sound of your voice and be especially sensitive to the higher-pitched tone of a woman's voice. The baby is also getting to know your unique scent and by the time she is a few days old will already prefer a cloth which has been against your body to one which has been close to another new mother's body.

DELAYING THE CLAMPING OF THE CORD

Ask your midwife or doctor to wait to clamp the cord until it has stopped pulsating. Midwives always used to wait, but nowadays the whole birth is often so rushed that the cord is sometimes clamped and cut immediately while blood is still flowing back and forth between placenta and baby. Even though this blood is not particularly well oxygenated – because the placenta begins to peel off the wall of the uterus as soon as delivery takes place – it is important that the correct balance between blood supply in baby and placenta be reached. The way to ensure that is to hold the baby at approximately the same level as the placenta and wait for the cord to become flaccid, indicating no further flow of blood in either direction (to or from the baby). There are occasionally reasons for early cord clamping such as a Rhesus negative mother who has already produced antibodies against her Rhesus positive baby (see pages 113–114) or a cord wrapped tightly around the baby's neck. Otherwise there is no reason why the cord has to be cut until after the placenta is delivered; it is separated only for convenience.

You can rest your fingers on the cord and feel the blood throbbing through it and wait for the moment when it stops completely. Cutting the cord between two clamps is a very simple procedure and something which a father may enjoy doing. If you would like him to do this, ask in advance.

Some obstetricians are concerned that blood could drain back into the placenta if the baby is placed above the placenta with the cord still unclamped. This is not a sufficient reason for early clamping or not placing the baby against your body. The baby can be rested over your thigh at the level of the placenta, where you can hold him. Mucus usually drains out naturally and there is therefore no need to use a mucus extractor, though the baby should be carefully observed and a mucus extractor used if his or her airways are blocked, followed by a few puffs of oxygen.

WAITING FOR THE ROOTING REFLEX

Your baby may emerge from your body already wanting to suck. But many babies are not quite ready and need time to feel secure before they reach out to find the nipple. The rooting reflex (see page 357) is a sure sign that the baby is ready to be put to the breast. Wait until the baby shows interest rather than stuffing your breast into her mouth.

Women often try to nurse before the baby is ready. Then even nursing can be another assault on the newborn. Many women today are anxious to nurse immediately after delivery and perhaps their anxiety to do this in an alien environment, and one which they may even feel is hostile, makes them rush things. Be patient if you can. Let the baby rest against your bare breast and in his own time he will start to explore with mouth, hands, and eyes. This time is precious for you and your baby. It cannot be speeded up without interfering with spontaneous, natural rhythms. The baby will begin to lick your nipple and then will seek it and, with a little help as you lift your breast into his searching mouth, will latch on and begin to suck.

BATHING THE BABY

An important part of the Leboyer style of birth was the warm water bath in which the baby is supported shortly after delivery, and in his film illustrating gentle birth the bath is given even before the mother holds her baby. Leboyer believed that the baby needs time to feel safe again in the medium which he has just left in the uterus – water – and that suspended in a bath the baby becomes peaceful and sometimes positively beatific, discovers himself and starts to open his eyes and explore the world around him. It is true that some babies seem to enjoy the bath very much, but only if it is given slowly and calmly and if the water is deep enough for the baby to float. The ideal way to give a bath is in a container with a thermal lining and an air heater over the bath, or, alternatively, the mother may prefer to give birth in a tub of warm water in the first place.

You may find that the hospital where you are having your baby does not allow a bath because of the risk of hypothermia (chilling). Unfortunately, cold air ventilation ducts have been incorporated into the design of many modern maternity units and the baby in water or exposed to this air is likely to get chilled. Many hospital pediatricians are concerned that the baby can lose a great deal of body heat while wet through evaporation or in a bath that is too cool; they say that if a bath is given at all it should be done speedily, which defeats its purpose. You obviously cannot add hot water to a bath when the baby is in it, and you know yourself how shivery you feel when you get out of a hot bath into a relatively cold atmosphere. It is much harder for a newborn baby, who cannot shiver yet and whose largest area of heat loss is her big head, to keep warm. The baby can maintain heat by using brown fat to create warmth, just

"She looked at me very critically at first as if to say, 'Do you know what you are doing?' Then she relaxed and it was like watching a flower open in water."

like a bear or any cold-adapted hibernating animal, although a low-birthweight baby does not have enough brown fat to do this. Muscular activity and crying also help the baby to keep warm; a baby in a cool room will hyperventilate, though one with respiratory depression cannot do this. Another way heat loss is reduced is that blood vessels near the surface of the skin tighten up. But babies who have received drugs from their mothers' bloodstreams, including narcotics, are not only sedated but also unable to prevent heat loss efficiently. So if you want the bath to be given, bear in mind that you should not have had narcotics in the last five hours; that your baby should be full term, weigh more than 5 lb (2.5 kg), and not have had breathing difficulties at delivery; and that the room should be warm.

Parents are sometimes very doubtful about the advantages of the bath, preferring to be in skin contact with their baby and to let him or her suck at the breast indefinitely instead. If a baby is happy lying against his mother and ready to go to the breast after a little while, it seems purely ritualistic to insist on putting him in a bath because of preconceived ideas about how babies *ought* to behave.

Dr. Michel Odent* uses the bath in a different way. The baby goes first to the mother's arms and sucks if he is rooting; only then is he immersed in a bath, and instead of the doctor bathing the baby the father takes over this responsibility, but close enough to the mother so that she can see and touch, too. It can be moving to watch a father doing this first service for his newborn child.

A midwife described what happened in one case when a father bathed his baby in this way: "The baby, who had been resting quietly with its mother, gradually opening its eyes, now seemed to wake to its surroundings and gaze serenely around. It is this serenity which is so remarkable and such a joy to watch. The baby's body was totally immersed in the water, which kept it warm, and gave it total relaxation. After five to ten minutes a midwife took over and gently lifted the baby onto the warmed towel below the overhead heater. Not one cry and all handling was done with an awareness that the baby had never been handled before and that its skin was acutely sensitive. There were no sudden jerks, movements, or pulling while the baby was being dressed. I now realize that the crying which so often accompanies these tasks is the result of sheer fright."*

AFTER THE DELIVERY

Gentle birth does not end with the minutes after delivery. It is part of a continuum, a flow of interaction between you and your baby beginning in pregnancy and going on following childbirth. It is a question not just of how the delivery is conducted or even whether you are able to hold your baby right away, but of creating an environment in which throughout the 24 hours you have access to your baby, feel she is yours and can act spontaneously. You need to know that everyone around you understands what you are feeling, and to be confident of emotional support as you learn to be parents.

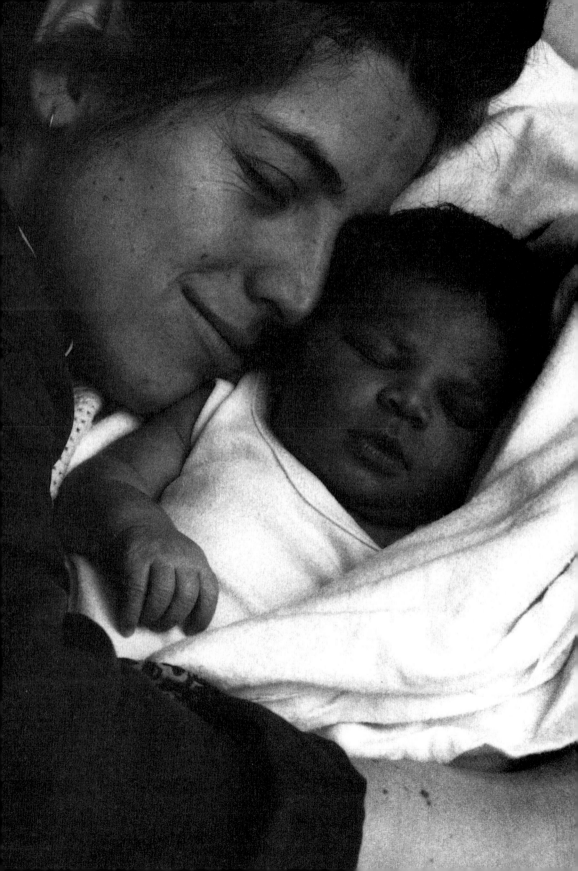

You and your newborn

The first hours of life

The hours immediately following birth are for many women some of the most intense of their lives. A peak experience like that of giving birth does not suddenly subside after you have spent half an hour holding the baby or end when the lights are turned out. After such a dramatic time it is not surprising that some women cannot sleep, and that many remain in a party spirit for hours or even days after.

Unfortunately, many hospitals treat the period after birth as a time for quiet rest, once you are clean and tidy; if you are too excited to sleep you may be offered some sleeping pills or tranquilizers. Most hospitals do not make provision for the continuity of passionate feeling which ensures that motherhood become part of you as a person and is not just something which you are straining to learn. These overpowering emotions propel you through the interim phase between knowing nothing about your baby, who is like a stranger, and realizing you know everything about her and have become centered in this tiny new existence as much as you are in yourself.

YOUR FIRST MEETING WITH YOUR NEWBORN

You look down at this new little person, and feel the weight of the body as he or she begins to relax after the struggle to birth. The head is the biggest part, the hair silken and perhaps still wet and curled in damp fronds or streaked back as if after a swim. The ears are tiny and carved like convoluted shells and the fingernails, too, are like

THE APGAR SCALE

Immediately after birth your baby's vitality is tested; she is tested again after about five minutes. Babies who get low marks the first time usually score nine or ten when tested the second time; but a baby does not have to cry to be vigorous and healthy.

What is Tested	0 Points	1 Point	2 Points
Heart rate	Absent	Below 100 beats per minute	100 beats per minute or more
Breathing	Absent	Slow or irregular	Regular
Skin color	Blue	Body pink, extremities blue	Pink all over
Muscle tone	Limp	Some movements	Active movements
Reflex response	Absent	Grimace only	Cry

Newborn reflexes

Babies are born with reflexes to help them adjust to life outside the uterus. The most important are the reflexes to breathe, suck, and swallow. Some others are illustrated below.

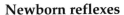

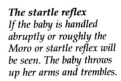

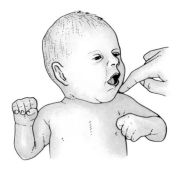

Rooting
The baby opens her mouth, often screws up one eye, and turns her head. This is known as "rooting" for the nipple.

The startle reflex
If the baby is handled abruptly or roughly the Moro or startle reflex will be seen. The baby throws up her arms and trembles.

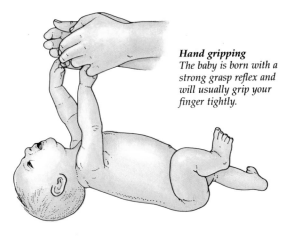

Hand gripping
The baby is born with a strong grasp reflex and will usually grip your finger tightly.

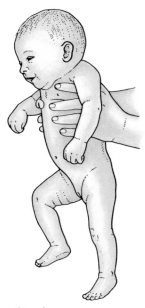

About to crawl
When you place a newborn baby on her stomach she will automatically assume what appears to be a crawling position.

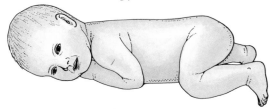

Stepping
When you stand a newborn baby up she will make "stepping" movements.

the little pink shells you picked up from the sand when you were a child. If the baby is still crying the mouth looks huge, a most efficient organ capable of reaching out to and grasping the breast for essential nourishment. And the cry itself, a high-pitched, almost animal wail, is well adapted to summon immediate attention, to drive you to find out what is wrong and how you can answer the baby's needs, and to be intensely anxious until you have stilled the crying. It is a biological mechanism of vital importance for survival.

As you hold the baby, the hands start to scan the air, encountering space, meeting the face, perhaps brushing against your body or hand. The fingers move and undulate like sea anemones, embarking on the important task of finding out about this new world.

If lights have been dimmed the baby will open wide eyes and look straight at you sometime during this process of unfolding. It has been discovered that newborn babies find the human face the most attractive thing to look at, far more so than woolly bunnies or painted ducks – and the moving, speaking human face is best of all.

THE EXPERIENCE OF BONDING

The environment into which the baby is born and the attitude of all those handling the baby are important not only for the baby's sake but for yours, too, and for the relationship between you. It is far more difficult for a mother to feel her baby belongs to her and she to him – to bond – if she does not have time immediately following birth to begin to get to know her baby.* An important element in this is naked skin contact. The baby should not be wrapped up and turned into a solid little package which you are allowed to hold but not to explore. He should be delivered onto your body and you should be able to put the baby to the breast as soon as he is ready to suck.

Marshall Klaus and John Kennell,* working at a hospital in Cleveland, recommended that mothers be able to hold their babies naked on the delivery bed and have undisturbed time to get to know them, and then be encouraged to look after them themselves, with help available if they need it. They should have their babies with them and be responsible for them at least five hours a day and be given ample emotional support from hospital staff. They found that when mothers and infants remained together undisturbed for the first hour after birth, and had extended contact with their babies in the first 48 hours, the attachment between mother and baby was stronger than when minimal contact (for feeds only) was allowed.*

Still, in many hospitals the hours after birth are used mainly for medically processing you and your baby; and you must pass tests of fitness before being pronounced not "at risk" and discharged.

WHAT TESTS ARE CARRIED OUT?

As soon as the baby is born the midwife or doctor assesses the baby's condition and rates it at one and five minutes of age, according to the Apgar scale. This is done by simple observation of

Testing the newborn

*These are some of the standard tests which are given
routinely to all new babies. You can ask that they be done right beside
you so that you can discuss the results.*

The baby's mouth is checked for cleft palate ...

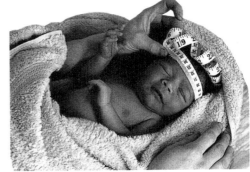

... the diameter of his head is measured ...

... his weight recorded ...

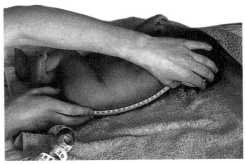

... jaw and hips tested for dislocation ...

... length measured from head to foot.

the baby's breathing, skin color, muscle tone, heart rate, and reflexes. The important measurement is the one done at five minutes when a baby has had time to adjust to life and has received any help necessary, such as a whiff of oxygen. The highest score is ten and most babies get seven or higher. Once you have had a cuddle a further check is made on the baby. Many women say they like this check-up to be done close beside them so that they can see what is happening and can discuss with the pediatrician anything that they find worrying. If the baby stays by your side and never leaves you this will happen as a matter of course.

The baby's weight and the length of the body are recorded. Then the depth of breathing is noted, whether the extremities are still blue, and whether he or she responds vigorously to stimuli and seems to be strong and healthy.

Certain specific things are looked for, too. These include the size of the head, the genitals, and – in a boy – whether both testes are descended. If the baby has not already passed meconium the anus is checked to ensure that it is formed normally. And the baby's heart is listened to (auscultated). The upper part of the mouth is examined to ensure that the palate is complete, and the legs are gently bent up and circled outward to make sure that there is no dislocation of the hips. Gentle feeling of the baby's tummy discloses whether the liver and spleen are the right size, and feeling around the top of the baby's head reveals the state of the skull bones. In all states and provinces in the United States and Canada, it is required by law that prophylactic eye treatment be introduced into the baby's eyes to prevent blindness from gonorrheal infection. This is usually an antibiotic solution or ointment which does not cause pain. The baby will also get an injection or oral dose of vitamin K.

"I never thought I could create something so beautiful. He is perfect, and I just lie and stare at him in wonder. And when he opens his eyes and looks at me, I am bowled over."

RELATING TO YOUR BABY

Unfortunately, the adjustment of mother and baby to each other is sometimes treated as of secondary importance to this process of medical screening. As a result many new mothers lack confidence in handling and relating to their babies. Much of what is called postnatal depression" is connected with a mother's inability to relate to her baby; it feels to her as if the baby belongs not to her, but to the hospital. It can be even more difficult for a man to feel that his baby belongs to him than it is for a woman. In one Stockholm maternity hospital, men were shown how to handle, change, bathe, and weigh their babies and were helped to understand the emotional and physical stresses of pregnancy and birth on their partners. This was done on two separate occasions while the women were in the postpartum ward. It was discovered that these fathers became more involved in baby care later on and it seemed that they were more understanding than another group of fathers who had not been given the chance to become involved with their babies in this way. Research shows that *both* parents need an unhurried and peaceful time with their baby in the hour following birth.

How your baby may look

Your new baby may have a low, sloping forehead, a receding chin, hair in sideburns (low on the brow, in the nape of the neck, and sometimes down the back as well), an odd, bumpy head which has been molded like a ripe grapefruit in its passage down the birth canal, a squashed boxer's nose, and blotchy skin. Yet to most new parents their baby looks beautiful! You respond in a protective, caring way to the wonder of this new human being who has come out of the inner depths of your body, having been pressed and kneaded and squeezed out of the uterus and down the vagina to the outside world and into your waiting arms.

Even if you are unaware of feeling anything particularly remarkable at the time, you will probably look back at those moments as being special, as you piece together the fragments of the birth experience and place it in its setting of life lived. This kind of reflection and thinking back is especially important after a long and difficult labor. It probably comes spontaneously to the majority of women if they allow themselves time and do not try to forget about what happened to them.

HOW THE BABY HAS HAD TO ADJUST

Enormous changes occur as the baby adjusts to the challenges of an extrauterine existence. One of the most dramatic things that happens, though unseen, is the change from fetal to newborn circulation, with the blood flowing along different pathways. When the baby is inside you all the blood flows in and out through the umbilical cord and bypasses the lungs, which do not need to function (see page 70–71). Since the placenta is doing much of the work that will later be performed by the baby's liver and kidneys, little blood needs to be carried to these organs in the intrauterine state.

At birth the first great gasp of air causes pressure changes in the whole circulatory system so that the baby's blood enters the lungs, liver, and kidneys. The increased pressure in these organs brings about the collapse of the umbilical blood vessels and of the bypasses around lungs, liver, and kidneys. Once these pressure changes have taken place the system is all set to work for a lifetime and the blood vessels which are no longer used waste away.

WHY YOUR BABY MAY LOOK STRANGE

Many things you notice about your baby may worry you. It helps to understand the wide range of the normal and to realize that the baby may look very different once she has uncrumpled after a few days.

Lanugo The dark hair which may cover large parts of the newborn's body, especially if it is premature, is called lanugo and drops out over the next week or so. The hair on the head is often a different shade from that which will grow in a few weeks' time to replace the original hair. One of my babies was born with almost black hair and in a few months was a flaxen blond.

Vernix The creamy substance which may coat the baby's skin, sometimes quite thickly, is vernix. It is produced by skin cells as they drop off into the amniotic fluid and forms a protective coating. Vernix is gradually absorbed, so it is not necessary to wipe it off, except on the head, where it tends to stick to the hair, and in the folds and creases under the arms, in the neck, and in the groin.

Caput Some babies are born with a peculiar bump like a large blister on their heads, often just off center. This is where the head was pressing down through the inadequately dilated cervix before the second stage of labor; the swelling does not affect the baby's brain, and will gradually go away. The bump is known as a caput.

Molding Usually the brow is sloped back and rather low in a newborn baby, but some babies who were in a posterior position during labor have, when they are born, high, domed heads like figures in an Egyptian hieroglyph.

A baby who was presenting by the face is usually very swollen, bruised, and puffy, but, again, this gradually goes away.

Mongolian spots Some babies have patches of slate-blue skin on their tummies or backs. These are called "Mongolian spots." They have nothing to do with mental handicap or Down's syndrome, and are completely harmless. They occur most often in families of African, Asian, Mediterranean, or Native American and Canadian origin.

Sexual characteristics A newborn baby's genitals can look very large, especially if the baby is premature. Sometimes there is milk in the breasts of both girl and boy babies. It is harmless and disappears without treatment. This is a result of the withdrawal of estrogen received from the mother's bloodstream and the action of prolactin released by the baby's pituitary. Some baby girls even have a kind of period – pseudo-menstruation – as the result of the withdrawal of maternal estrogen. Again, it is nothing to worry about, and stops within a few days.

Opposite
Meeting a new brother or sister, encountering the amazing reality of a newborn person, is a very important event in a child's life.

BONDING AS A GRADUAL PROCESS

Some of the reactions that you have to your newborn baby are instinctive. You respond to the sight of the baby's plumpness, the rounded head, the large forehead, the smell of the skin, the bright gaze of her eyes (which look as if they say "So that is who you are!"),

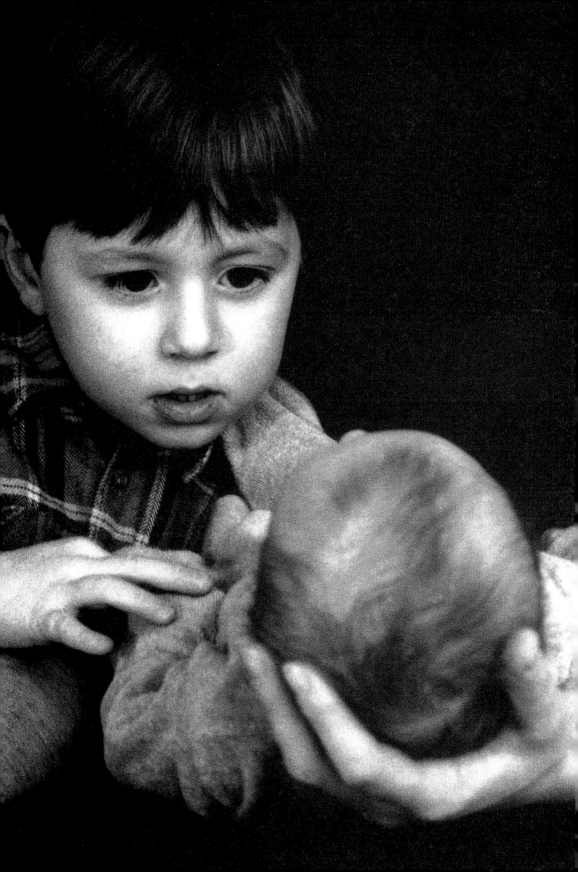

your baby's cry, her exploring hands and mouth, her vigorous movement, and the extraordinary compactness of her neat little body. But even instinctive behavior needs the right setting if it is to be triggered and to unfold into appropriate nurturing. Then you can go on to learn from the baby how to respond to her signals.

Bonding is often talked about as if it were instant glue which sticks a mother and baby together the minute after delivery, and some women who do not spend the time immediately after the birth with their babies worry that they have failed a test in motherhood and are anxious that this will have lasting effects. In fact, bonding is a gradually unfolding process which only *starts* then and develops each hour you and your baby are together. During all this time you are learning about each other, and further physical changes in you are set off by stimuli provided by the baby. The most obvious of these is the milk ejection reflex (let-down response), which is stimulated by the baby's crying and searching for the nipple, the touch of his mouth against the breast, and his sucking.

One aspect of hospital care which Klaus and Kennel stress is the way in which doctors and nurses can support the family – not just the mother, father, and baby, but also other children. Older brothers and sisters should be allowed to have close contact with the baby, too, and be made welcome in the hospital. In practice, some hospitals are restrictive about sibling visits.*

THE IMPORTANCE OF THE TIME AFTER BIRTH

Wherever you are having a baby, and even if you are "high risk" and need obstetric help, provision should be made for a quiet, intimate time together after birth. This can be done in a big teaching hospital just as it can in a small birth center, *and it is part of the job of the hospital to create that environment for each mother, each father, and each baby*. Discuss it with your doctor. It is only when doctors, nurses, and midwives know what women want that they will be sufficiently enlightened to offer the loving environment which is every baby's birthright.

The minutes, hours, and days after birth are a time for emotional "work" which may be no less significant in the lives of the newborn baby and of both parents than the sheer physical work of labor. The hospital should provide an environment which supports these unfolding emotional processes. New parents do not need to be shown how to develop a relationship with their babies. They do need, however, to feel that they are among friends, to be handed the baby at birth, and to be left in peace and privacy together.

The question of circumcision

The United States is the only country in the world that surgically removes the foreskin of most male babies for non-religious reasons. Circumcision is an unnecessary operation. It can be dangerous, too.

It may result in excessive bleeding or infection. Sometimes the penis is damaged irreparably. Some babies have to be rushed to a hospital's intensive care unit because of complications following circumcision. Occasionally a baby dies.

Newborn babies feel pain. In fact, they may feel it more acutely than adults. At least an adult knows that the pain of an operation will end. A baby cannot know this. If you are considering circumcising your son, bear in mind that amputation of the foreskin, even when a local anesthetic is injected into the penis, is a painful procedure. It is true that some unanesthetized babies do not cry during circumcision. They are too shocked to do so; instead, they withdraw. Whether a baby cries or is overwhelmed by shock, he has a raw and painful scar afterwards. There may be feeding problems, and a woman who longed to breastfeed may be unable to do so. Sometimes a mother observes that her baby's personality seems to have changed. The rhythms of love and intimacy between a mother and her newborn are disrupted. We can only guess the possible long-term emotional effects of this mutilating surgery.

"We were under pressure from our parents to circumcise him. We did research and decided that we could not do this to our child."

Though few doctors still defend circumcision as medically necessary, they are often slow to criticize the practice because they believe that babies cannot really feel much, and perhaps also because they are concerned that any challenging of circumcision may appear to be anti-Semitic. Men who were circumcised themselves may affirm that it never did them any harm. Some want a son circumcised so that he can be the same as "everyone else" – an argument that is also used to support the practice of female clitoridectomy and infibulation in Egypt and Somalia.

The foreskin protects the tip – the glans – of a baby's penis. You do not need to retract it or work it loose. Trying to do so may tear delicate structures and hurt the baby. By the time a boy reaches adolescence it will have become more flexible.

If you are Jewish, circumcision may be important to you, or you may want to welcome your baby into Judaism in a ceremony of blessing that does not entail circumcision. An organization which will give further information on this subject is listed on page 413.

The baby who needs special care

About 6 percent of all babies weigh 5 lb (2.25 kg) or less (the internationally agreed definition of a low-birthweight baby). Such babies can be divided into two categories – preterm and small-for-dates – and they will probably require special care.

Half or more of low-birthweight babies are born too soon – preterm or premature babies. There seems to be no obvious reason why such babies should be expelled from the uterus so early, and research is still being carried out into the causes of preterm delivery. Maternal illness, smoking, poor nutrition, a high-stress lifestyle, and poverty are all associated with preterm delivery, but sometimes none of these factors is present in preterm births.

Small-for-dates babies are born at the right time but have not flourished in the uterus in the last months of pregnancy for a variety of reasons. Sometimes this happens because of malnutrition in the mother, because of her smoking, high blood pressure or preeclampsia, because the placenta has not been working well (placental insufficiency), or because she was carrying twins or more. These undernourished babies often have difficulty during labor, are short of oxygen, and have problems with breathing after delivery. They may suffer from hypoglycemia (low blood sugar) or have convulsions. A few small-for-dates babies, however, are small right through pregnancy for genetic, chromosomal, or other reasons.

THE BABY WITH POOR TEMPERATURE CONTROL

Low-birthweight babies may have problems during labor and are also more likely to have poor temperature control, because there is very little fat under the skin. They may be jaundiced, difficult to feed, and susceptible to infection. Their skin is usually red because the blood vessels are visible through the thin layer of fat. Such babies are kept in a nursery that is warmer than the wards and may be cared for in incubators. A thermostat may be strapped to a baby's tummy so that the temperature can be regulated according to his or her needs. Sometimes a baby is placed under a plastic heat shield and wears a hat. Tiny babies who are kept warm grow faster.*

THE BABY WITH BREATHING DIFFICULTIES

Premature and low-birthweight babies may have interrupted breathing (apnea) in the early days after the birth. This is why a very tiny baby is kept on a special mattress which sets off an alarm should breathing stop. All that is usually needed to start the baby's breathing is a little stimulation of the baby by touch. One in every ten premature babies has insufficient surfactant in its lungs.

Surfactant reduces the surface tension in the lungs, allowing them to expand and stopping them from deflating entirely with each breath out; it normally develops before the baby is ready to be born.

A baby usually inflates its lungs with the first breath after delivery, when they pop open like parachutes. With the first breath out, half the air is retained, so that breathing after this is much easier. The baby who has not enough surfactant has to work hard to breathe and may become exhausted in the struggle to get enough air. She breathes very quickly, the chest collapses with each breath out, and she looks blue and grunts as she breathes. This condition is called respiratory distress or hyaline membrane disease. It is obviously important in these cases to give the baby oxygen to help with breathing.

Other babies who may suffer from respiratory distress are those born to diabetic mothers (even though they are large babies), those who have not had sufficient oxygen during labor, those who have been delivered by cesarean section, and those who develop pneumonia as a result of infection.

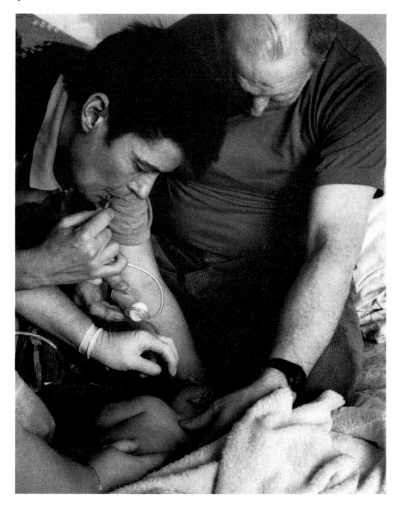

Left
If a baby has inhaled meconium at birth, the midwife or doctor will suck it out from the airways so that he does not breathe it into his lungs, where it can cause pneumonia.

If the pediatrician decides to give the baby oxygen, a small catheter is inserted through the cord stump into an artery so that blood samples can be taken about every three hours to test the amount of oxygen present in the baby's blood.

Oxygen can be administered with continuous positive pressure so that the baby's lungs are kept open. A tiny catheter is inserted through the nostrils, or a face mask or headbox is used.

THE BABY WITH LOW BLOOD SUGAR

A baby may have low blood sugar (hypoglycemia) if he has a low birthweight or is premature, if the mother received large amounts of dextrose in an IV during labor, if she is diabetic, or if she had a difficult delivery. The hypoglycemic baby may have breathing difficulties and be jittery or lie limp and apathetic.

Treatment involves giving the baby ample nourishment, so the pediatrician may decide to set up an intravenous glucose drip. It is because of the risk of hypoglycemia that a very tiny baby may be given additional feedings, even though there are no obvious symptoms of low blood sugar.

For babies who are of 30 weeks gestation or more, cup feeding may be successful. The babies lap the milk from a cup with their tongues, like kittens do. When they are over 34 weeks gestation they can often sip it. The transition to breastfeeding is often easier than after tube feeding, perhaps because the baby has already had a satisfying oral experience, and has learned to work to get milk.*

NEONATAL JAUNDICE

If your baby looks beautifully suntanned as if just back from a cruise in the Bahamas, he or she has jaundice. A newborn baby has a surplus of red blood cells which are broken down after birth. During this process a yellowish substance called bilirubin is produced, which has to be excreted by the baby's liver. Sometimes the liver is unable to cope rapidly enough with the large amount of bilirubin, so it builds up in the blood, giving the skin a yellowish tinge. Bilirubin levels peak between the third and fifth day and then drop.

Physiological jaundice About half of all babies develop jaundice. It is usually harmless and is then called physiological jaundice. Jaundice is most likely to develop after the second day of life and to disappear after a week. In premature babies jaundice tends to be most marked on about the fifth or sixth day of life and to go on longer – often for ten days or more.

A jaundiced baby needs sunlight and frequent feeding. If you have the chance, put your baby beside a window and, if it is warm enough, uncover the baby so that light can reach her limbs and trunk.

Jaundiced babies tend to get very sleepy and do not readily awaken. Yet they should have plenty of fluids to cope with the bilirubin, so need to be roused for feedings – perhaps every two hours.

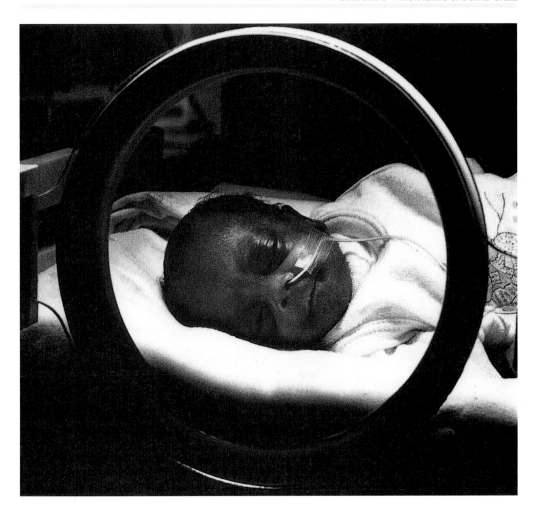

If the bilirubin level is high, the pediatrician may decide to use phototherapy on a baby to bring the level down. This light treatment produces a photochemical breakdown of bilirubin into substances which are then passed out in the urine. The baby is blindfolded so that the light cannot possibly harm her eyesight. This can be especially distressing for a mother who feels out of touch with her baby when she cannot make eye contact with her. When you lift your baby away from the light for her feeding, take off the eye covering.

Another form of phototherapy is a blanket filled with fiber-optic wands that emit light. The blanket is wrapped around the baby and turned on. The blanket glows while the baby is held or nursed by his mother. This type of phototherapy as well as the standard photo-therapy unit can be used in the home, supervised by a visiting nurse.

Hemolytic jaundice Pediatricians always watch the jaundiced baby carefully because, although neonatal jaundice is a common and not very serious complaint, the baby may be jaundiced as a result of a

Above
Nowadays mothers and fathers are usually encouraged to spend time in the special care nursery with their babies, touching and cuddling them through the portholes in the incubator.

blood group incompatibility with the mother. This is called hemolytic jaundice and can damage the baby's nervous system and brain cells. Sometimes, too, the jaundice is associated with infection or with a metabolic condition such as low blood sugar, or is the result of drugs administered to the mother in pregnancy.

FEEDING THE BABY IN SPECIAL CARE

It has been shown that very small babies do best if they are fed soon after delivery,* so a low-birthweight baby may be given a milk feeding within two hours of birth. The best food is his mother's breast milk, but it will take a few days to be produced in quantity. The baby can be put to the breast if strong enough to suck, to derive benefit from the protein and antibodies in the colostrum that is already there. Supplements of vitamins D and K are often given, and if phosphate in the bloodstream falls, supplementary phosphates, too.

A baby who cannot suck is usually fed through a small, soft catheter, a nasogastric tube, which is passed through a nostril down into the stomach. Feedings should be small and frequent – about every half hour – but a slow, continuous drip is often best for a sick baby. If your baby is being fed in this way it is usually possible for you to help with the feedings once you can express your own breast milk. Breast milk is an important protection against the disease of necrotizing encolitis, when the baby's intestines become damaged, and formula-fed preterm babies are at risk of developing this illness, which can be fatal. If you have any difficulties, contact one of the breastfeeding organizations listed on page 413.

RELATING TO THE BABY IN SPECIAL CARE

It is distressing for parents to see their baby in intensive care, attached to tubes and wires, isolated in an incubator. They may feel that the baby is being treated as just another interesting specimen. Very low-birthweight babies look so fragile and weird that it can be difficult to see them as real people: your baby may look to you like an odd, misshapen doll or a little animal and not like your child at all. On the other hand, you may feel passionately that the baby belongs to you and want to grab him away from all the machines and other contraptions to hold him close. The obvious skills of those working with sophisticated technology can make parents feel clumsy and awkward so that they lack confidence to handle their baby. Yet it is important to do this. *All* babies need touching and talking to and, if they are well enough to be taken in your arms, they like being cuddled. If your baby is in an incubator, you can stroke her through the portholes. Tender, loving care may be just as important for the health of your baby as modern medical technology.

Many hospitals now have rooms where mothers of babies in special care can stay to be close to them, help look after them, and breastfeed. It is better for both mother and baby and makes it easier to build close links between them if the mother stays in the special care unit rather than merely visiting. When a woman can start to look after her baby herself, she begins to feel that her baby belongs to her. One model intensive care unit has rooms where babies are cared for by their mothers, with a glass wall at the side of the babies' cubicles so that nurses can keep a constant eye on them. A nurse in this unit said: "One thing the nurses must not do is to take away responsibility for the baby. We always try to make a mother feel it is her baby, even when it is very small and sick."

THE BABY WITH A DISABILITY

The moment when someone tells you, or when you yourself recognize, that your baby is not "normal" is engraved on your mind forever. This happens to 3 in every 100 women. The most common handicaps are cerebral palsy, which can affect both brain and body, and Down's syndrome, which has a genetic cause. For many disabilities no cause is known. It used to be thought that cerebral palsy was always caused by lack of oxygen during labor and birth, but it is now known that it is more likely to be a result of oxygen deprivation during pregnancy. There is no way a mother could have known about this or taken steps to avoid it.

Your first reaction to being told that an abnormality is suspected may be simple denial. It cannot possibly be, or if there really is something wrong they will discover that it is minor. As tests are done and information trickles in, you may start to feel cheated. You see other mothers with their perfect babies and ask, "Why me?" Having a baby with a disability sets you apart from other mothers and may make you feel not only different but stigmatized. There may be an overwhelming sense of guilt: "What did I do wrong?" Though you are assured that nothing you did or did not do brought about this outcome, you probably continue to blame yourself even when your rational mind acknowledges that bad things

"We couldn't believe it. We hoped that they'd say, 'There has been a mistake. The baby is going to be fine.'"

happen in life which you cannot possibly control. Other peoples' attitudes are often very difficult to cope with, whether it be their careful avoidance of the topic, their pity, or the ways in which they try to be positive and reassuring. Feelings of shame and resentment jostle with anger. You want to blame someone but there is no one to blame and, of course, you feel a realistic anxiety about the future. Since one of the most painful things about having a child who is different is the isolation that often results, it is a good idea to contact one of the organizations that enable you to meet other parents who have children with the same disibility, in order to learn more, share experiences, and develop coping strategies. Addresses of these organizations are given on page 413.

Losing a baby

Many women know what it is like to have an interrupted pregnancy, although the distress caused by even an early miscarriage is often underestimated. Stillbirth, on the other hand, is now rare. But still today, for a small number of women, the birth is also a death.

Women who make the painful decision to have an abortion, because of fetal handicap or for any other reason, may grieve deeply, too. This is so even though they know they have made the best possible choice under the circumstances and have behaved sensibly. Abortion should never be dismissed as a simple expedient to get rid of an unwanted pregnancy. Yet it is still largely a taboo subject, and women often have to go through the experience alone, without help, socially isolated, and deprived of the emotional support they need.

It might seem easier for most people to sympathize with a woman whose baby dies at birth. Yet often they do not know how to help and they withdraw from her grief in embarrassment. After all the preparations and happy expectations the woman has made, she goes through a labor which culminates in the delivery of a stillborn baby, or of a frail or handicapped baby who dies a week or so after birth. Her arms are empty and she is left alone. The more medical advances reduce perinatal mortality, the more isolated is the woman whose baby dies.

Miscarriage

A miscarriage usually comes as a terrible shock, and yet one in every five pregnancies probably ends in miscarriage or "spontaneous abortion." In three out of four cases this occurs before the tenth week and sometimes even before the woman realizes she is pregnant.

THREATENED MISCARRIAGE
In the first three months of pregnancy, you may notice a heavy feeling around your pelvis and in the pit of your tummy and have periodlike twinges and aches.

Sometimes you may have bleeding that is really a suppressed period. This happens when there is insufficient pregnancy hormone to stop your period, even though it will be scanty. Such bleeding is not a miscarriage and the blood comes from the endometrium, not from the placenta or the baby. Sometimes this also occurs at the time when each period would have been due, and right through the early months of pregnancy each would-be period is marked by slight bleeding. Your doctor may advise you to have injections of progesterone to stop this bleeding. Bleeding in pregnancy is not the baby's blood but yours, and comes from the maternal side of the placenta where it is not adhering to the uterus, or from around the cervix. It used to be thought that the best thing was to go to bed and stay there until the bleeding stopped. But there is no evidence that this is of any help at all. So do whatever you feel like.*

INEVITABLE ABORTION

An "inevitable abortion" is a miscarriage that occurs because the baby is no longer alive and, whatever you do, the bleeding is bound to continue. If the fetal heart cannot be detected by ultrasound (see pages 223–226), the abortion is inevitable and you might just as well be up and about and let it run its course. If ultrasound picks up the baby's heartbeat, there is only a 10 percent chance that you will miscarry, even though you may go on bleeding for a while.

POSSIBLE CAUSES OF EARLY MISCARRIAGE

The cause of early miscarriage is often not known. Defective embryos with abnormalities that would not allow them to survive after birth are usually miscarried, and a large proportion of miscarriages are probably the natural way of getting rid of imperfect babies. Sometimes there has been no development beyond the very early stages of segmentation and what is termed a blighted ovum is passed. It is estimated that one in six miscarriages may result from fertilized eggs that do not develop properly.

After it had been noted that more women than usual miscarry in early pregnancy during influenza epidemics it was discovered that a high fever can result in miscarriage. There is more about this on page 111. Sometimes the presence of uterine fibroids (common in older mothers) or an oddly formed uterus means that there is not enough space for the pregnancy to develop.

Cleaning out the uterus Some doctors take it for granted that a woman who has had a miscarriage should go to hospital for a D & C (dilatation and curettage) to scrape out surgically any remaining contents of the uterus, in order to avoid infection. This is a traumatic experience. Research using ultrasound shows that it is rarely necessary.*

There may be a hormonal factor in some miscarriages since one third of women who have repeated miscarriages have also found it difficult to get pregnant. (Insulin-dependent diabetic women with poor glucose control have up to three times more miscarriages than other women.) Occasionally, recurrent miscarriage is a sign of an autoimmune condition. The mother produces antibodies that cause blood clots in the placenta. Low doses of aspirin throughout pregnancy may help these women.

LATE MISCARRIAGE

Miscarriage after the 12th week of pregnancy is approximately three times less common than early miscarriage. Miscarriage is more likely as you grow older (over 35), if you have had difficulty in conceiving (if it has taken longer than six months), and if you have had two or more previous miscarriages. If you have had only one miscarriage before, there is no obvious reason why the next pregnancy should not be straightforward. After three miscarriages there is a 50/50 chance of miscarrying again, so talk to your doctor *before* you become pregnant again and plan your time to include extra rest from the first days after possible conception.

"Incompetent" cervix Late miscarriage is often the result of a weak or "incompetent" cervix which starts to dilate long before it should. The bag of waters is wedged between the baby and the cervix and ruptures as the cervix starts to dilate, so the first sign may be the breaking of the waters. This type of miscarriage is particularly likely if a woman has already miscarried repeatedly in mid-pregnancy. An incompetent cervix may be the result of a previous abortion if it was done after the 12th week, or of a previous difficult labor. There is more information about incompetent cervix on page 115.

Placental insufficiency Miscarriage after the 20th week may mean that the placenta has failed to function in servicing the baby. (After 21 weeks the loss of the baby is termed a stillbirth.) If there is evidence of poor placental function and inadequate growth of the baby in the uterus, bedrest will allow a better flow of blood through the placenta to the baby. One way you can improve the efficiency of the placenta is by making sure that you have a good diet during pregnancy. If you have had a miscarriage, it is recommended that you start a high-standard diet before you become pregnant again (see pages 93–100). If you have had a series of miscarriages, keep any large blood clots from the latest one (a vacuum-sealed jar is suitable) for the doctor to see and perhaps have tested in a laboratory.

GUILT ABOUT A MISCARRIAGE

Every woman who has had a miscarriage wonders if anything she did or failed to do caused it. A miscarriage can happen at any time, so most women will be able to think of some event that might have triggered it. You had a fight with someone in the office, your mother-in-law came to stay, you slipped in the street, had just had intercourse, or were overtired from a party the night before.

"I miscarried late in pregnancy, so I started to lactate. It felt as if my breasts were weeping milk for my lost baby, and it was all being wasted."

Whatever your guilty suspicions, none of these things has been shown to cause miscarriage. However, it can be difficult to convince yourself that you are in no way responsible.

GRIEVING FOR THE LOST BABY

Miscarriage, however early it occurs, is for most women equivalent to the loss of a baby. If it was to be your first child it is also the loss of yourself as a mother, and when you have had repeated miscarriages you have experienced this loss over and over again. It may be the loss of your partner as a father, too, and of your parents as grandparents. It may be a child's loss of an expected brother or sister. So it is a time for grieving. But women often feel ashamed about this and fear that they are being "over-emotional" or "silly."

Talk with your partner about what you are feeling. Even if you have not yet felt fetal movements, the loss of your baby is sometimes emotionally shattering. If you have had miscarriage after miscarriage or are slow to conceive, you may experience every single period as the loss of a baby and may grieve as a result. This grieving is necessary for you to be able to look forward to the future with confidence in yourself as a "real woman." Suppressed grief always causes trouble later.

Your partner, however, may not have accepted the reality of the pregnancy by the time you miscarry and so it can be difficult for him to understand why you need to mourn, but it will help you if he can take time to listen. Or you may find you can talk more easily with another woman who has been through a miscarriage herself.

After it is all over, the longing to start another pregnancy can interfere with relaxed and spontaneous sex. If you feel that you are getting anxious and that this is spoiling your sexual relationship, try having a vacation from each other and coming together again at the time when you expect to be ovulating (see pages 62 and 405).

Stillbirth

"I'm so sorry. Your baby has died." Almost every expectant mother has thought at some time that someone might say these words to her. For some women it is a nagging fear which haunts them as they punish themselves for negative feelings they have about the baby and about becoming a mother or for daring to expect too much of the birth and the baby. Sometimes, not as often as in the past, but nevertheless in about eight out of every thousand births, it really happens and the baby dies before, during, or shortly after birth.

THE EXPERIENCE OF LOSS
Despite everything that anyone can do you are suddenly confronted with the experience of loss. This is a loss not only of the baby, but of all the expectations of yourselves as parents and the new images of the self and the family that have been built up through pregnancy.

Nothing can take away the suffering that accompanies stillbirth. This is so even when the care that is given to you is loving and sympathetic, though such emotional support can help you gradually deal with the experience and eventually come to terms with it. Unfortunately some members of hospital staff cannot cope with their own feelings of guilt and distress when a baby dies, and you may be left alone in your room, avoided as much as possible by nurses and doctors who do not want to "upset" you by referring to what has happened. When they do talk to you, they may urge you to put it behind you, say that you will forget when you have another baby, or tell you to think of your partner. The more such advice is given the longer it may take to live through the experience.

You will be offered bereavement counseling, and though you may not feel like it at the time, it helps to have someone to talk to who is not a friend or relation. The task of grieving is a personal and intimate one. It consists of slowly and painfully – and sometimes you may feel that you will never succeed – integrating the experience into the total pattern of your life and finding a place for it in which it has meaning. Once you have done this you will be able to stand back from it a little and will no longer be overwhelmed by it. This process cannot be hurried and if an attempt is made to force the pace grieving will be delayed and you may be overpowered by grief at a later stage of your life.

STILLBIRTH IN THIRD WORLD SOCIETIES

A hundred years ago everyone expected a certain proportion of babies to die. A woman bore ten and reared six if she was lucky. In many Third World countries even today, babies are not named or spoken of publicly for the first few weeks because the chances are that they will not survive. It has been suggested that the mothers themselves are able to remain slightly emotionally detached from a new baby whose life may be transitory.*

In these societies death is incorporated into the web of life and there are supportive rituals to deal with it, whereas we are ill-prepared in Western society for facing death. We each struggle to find our own way and often feel that we are the only people who have ever faced such emotional upheavals. Death is a shocking intrusion into the normality of existence.

FACING UP TO THE LOSS

If professional helpers know that something is going wrong with your birth, you have a right to expect them to give you clear information, discuss the difficulties openly and honestly, and stand by you as you try to cope emotionally with what is happening. Women who have been through this ordeal say that it helped to be told the truth and to be fully involved rather than shielded from the event by the mystique of medical practice. If your baby dies while still inside the uterus, you know that you are carrying a dead baby. It is then as if your uterus, a place of life, has become a grave. The obstetrician may advise that it is safer to wait to go into labor naturally, which often happens within a couple of weeks, but may offer you induction if you wish. Many women feel an urgent need to "get it over with"; others feel that they want to spend the last remaining days possible with the baby inside them.

When something so distressing happens, there is no easy "solution," no one course of action that can wipe out the anguish. Sometimes a man asks what he can say or do to help his partner and to make the suffering less, or other family members or friends want to help but do not know how. People are so different in their responses to loss that the most helpers can do is make themselves available, reach out, and be ready to receive whatever the bereaved person wants to tell them, without holding back for fear of intruding or feeling embarrassment at her grief. The most valuable thing they can offer is a *waiting silence*, without tension or unnecessary words, so that the sufferer's pain can flow into them.

MOURNING FOR THE BABY

This may sound simple, but it can be very difficult, because grieving is a matter not just of tears and sadness, but also of numb shock and guilt and anger, all of which are felt at different phases of the experience. It is not easy to acknowledge destructive guilt, and even harder to cope with anger which involves hostility toward people, including doctors, nurses, and midwives who tried to help.

For you the time immediately following the death of a baby may be a time of frozen half-awareness of what has happened, and frequently it is not until at least three weeks afterward that you begin to live through these other phases of grieving.

It is sometimes difficult for a mother to mourn her stillborn baby because she never really knew this person for whom she is grieving. It can be still more difficult if you have not *seen* the dead baby and realized that your bulging tummy held a living creature that has since died. This is why some grief counselors and pediatricians think it is a good idea for a mother to touch her stillborn child, and encourage her to do so. You can ask to hold your baby and to be left alone to say goodbye to her. Take as long as you need.

"I needed to be held and cuddled, but it was hard for my husband to do this, as he was trying to be strong and hide his emotions."

THE BABY'S BURIAL

You and your partner may wish to discuss together arrangements for the baby's burial. Some women do not wish to know where the baby is buried, but others do. It is up to you to learn as much or as little as you wish to know. Some women feel afterward that perhaps the baby was a figment of their imagination and never actually existed at all. It was removed from them like a tooth which was causing trouble and then extracted. You may think of your baby's body being handled with indifference and lie awake wondering what "they" did with it.

THE EFFECT ON YOUR RELATIONSHIPS

Being depressed affects all our relationships with other people, including those we love and need the most. Though the death of a baby may draw you and your partner closer together, it introduces stresses into the relationship which may be too severe for you to be able to cope with effectively. You both may need help from other people. Your partner has to grieve, too, and yet may feel that it is "unmanly" for him to show any emotional weakness and that he must be strong to support you. The result may be that he simulates a matter-of-fact acceptance of the inevitable and leaves you feeling isolated because he seems not to understand.

If the baby lived for a time and went to the special care nursery, your partner probably had a chance to go there and see and touch the baby while you may have stayed on the maternity floor. So you rely on his descriptions and the details he can give you to be able to build up a complete picture. Yet a man who is himself depressed and grieving may find it difficult to talk about such things without showing his own distress and may resist it, thus giving you the impression that he is holding back on vital information.

Losing a baby almost invariably causes a deterioration in the couple's sexual relationship. It is difficult to feel sexually excited when you are depressed. And even as time goes on, when you are beginning to "function" again, feelings of pleasure can be followed by a rush of grief. When you start to enjoy life again, even when you start to feel sexually aroused, you may both feel at times that you are betraying your dead child.* So both of you need to give understanding to each other.

If you have lost your baby and want to be in touch with other people who have undergone this experience, contact one of the organizations that are listed on page 413.

The next pregnancy

If you have had an abortion or have lost a previous baby as a result of miscarriage or stillbirth, or if your baby died after birth, the previous experience tends to cast its shadow forward. Strangely, this tends to happen even if you really did not want that particular pregnancy to continue.

A woman who has lost a baby through accident, who has had miscarriages, for example, or a crib death, may feel angry that the emotions of one who has had an abortion should be discussed in the same context as her own ordeal and even that the woman who got rid of a baby deserves whatever happens to her. Yet the experience of loss may be equally haunting and the sense of guilt even greater.

We tend to compare and contrast the progress of the present pregnancy with past pregnancies. If a previous pregnancy had an unhappy outcome, it colors our view of the whole experience and it is natural to become acutely conscious of risks and dangers. We do not always realize that this is what we are doing, since a common way of trying to deal with fear and anxiety about repeating a traumatic experience is to attempt to shut out thoughts of it, to protect ourselves from the pain of yet another failure.

A woman who feels guilty about aborting a previous baby or who feels somehow responsible for a miscarriage may transfer this guilt to the present pregnancy and be anxious that she is going to have a terrible labor, bear an abnormal baby, or lose the baby as a kind of retribution or punishment. This is not a rational or even necessarily a conscious thinking-through of the risks, but a kind of primitive expectation that automatic punishment comes from the gods.

If you try to forget what happened or to put it to the back of your mind, you will be unprepared for the emotions that may assail you in situations of stress, such as when you have a vaginal examination or when you go into the hospital. And when labor starts you may find that you cannot help thinking back to the loss of the other baby.

You may tell yourself to be sensible and not to dwell on negative thoughts. Though understandable, this is rarely successful. You are right to acknowledge your feelings and also justified in getting those who care for you to take them seriously. But do not leave this process until the end of pregnancy and certainly not until you go into labor. Try to find the kind of preparation for birth and parenthood that includes frank and open acceptance of any previous unhappy experience.

"It was as if I were betraying my dead baby when I became pregnant again. I couldn't help feeling guilty."

In a pregnancy following the loss of the baby, women often experience painful, disturbing dreams about bearing a damaged child or losing the baby and feel that in some awful way this is their own fault. The dreams may be clearly about birth and babies or may be heavily disguised. The baby is often represented in such dreams as a doll or small animal or one's own tooth or limb, and death as the irretrievable loss of anything that is treasured.

You may feel that you are carrying a baby of the same sex as the previous one or even that you are pregnant with the child you lost before. That is one way of trying to cope with the painful experience. In fact, some people even say, "Have another baby and you'll forget about it." But of course you cannot really substitute one baby for another or replace a lost baby by getting pregnant again. It is vital for both you and the baby you are bearing that you work toward an acknowledgment that this baby is its own unique self.

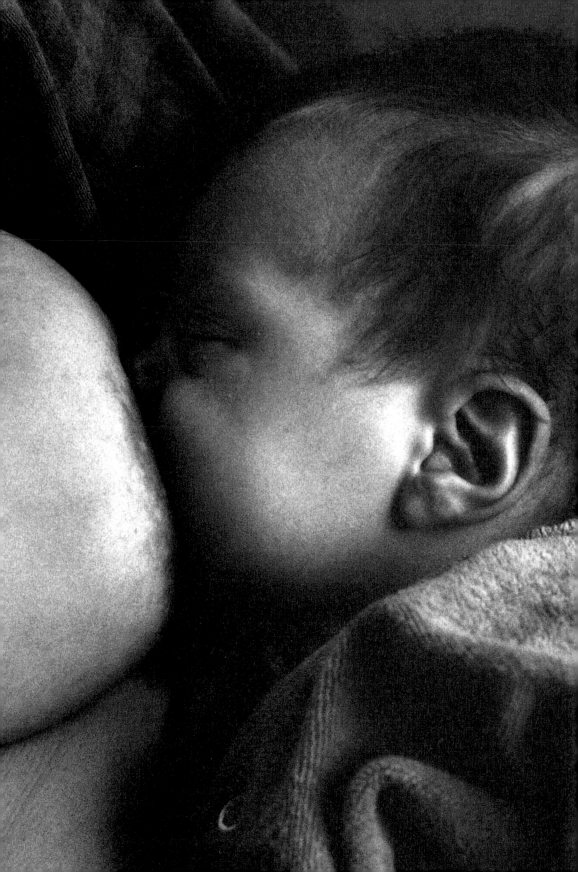

The first ten days

It is recognized that a woman with a child who is handicapped or ill, or who has a baby who dies, needs to pass through a period of grieving. It is less well understood that for *any* woman the time immediately after birth may be experienced as a loss which she needs to grieve over, however perfect the baby. As a new mother you are on the threshold of a new beginning which entails the death of some aspects of your self and, with the birth of a first baby, also the relinquishing of the self as child and adolescent.

Emotions after birth

UNSUSPECTED EMOTIONS

Many women need time to part with the fantasy baby they carried inside them before they can come to terms with the real baby who has been born. The real baby is often astonishingly different from the one they imagined they were bearing. The death of a fantasy which has been cherished can be painful. It is especially threatening if the baby is premature and needs to have special care, or if he suffers from any form of handicap. But even a healthy, mature baby may be so unlike what you expected that you cannot come to terms with the reality or with the fact that you have been turned into a mother with different responsibilities from those you had before, who is emotionally committed to that baby for every minute of every day.

CHANGES IN MOOD

All the intense feelings you have during the hours and days after having given birth have a biological survival value for the baby. Without them you would be just a caretaker. Sometimes your emotions are mind-altering and if you had not just had a baby would rightly be thought pathological. But during the first week after birth they are perfectly normal and experienced by many more women than ever openly admit to them.

It is not just a matter of depression. In fact, you may feel on a permanent high. But it is likely that at some time during the first five days after the birth you will experience an abrupt drop in mood and a sudden feeling of depression. Your stitches are uncomfortable, the first days at home are like a thick fog, you start to worry about the baby or whether you will be a good mother, or you simply feel flat because the party is over and it is now "the morning after the night before." Then again, you may experience violent mood swings and feel you are on an emotional roller coaster in the days immediately after the birth. You are more likely to feel like this if you usually have pronounced mood swings anyway. Our society often has a very romanticized stereotype of the new mother in a frothy pink negligée

Opposite
A mother gives her newborn her first taste of one of the great pleasures of the first year of life.

381

with a cherubic baby in her arms. The violent mood swings of the postpartum period can come as a shock because they are so different from the way you think you *ought* to feel.

NEEDING TO BEHAVE SPONTANEOUSLY

You do not become a different person once you have had a baby: it is just that all the colors of your personality may become more vivid. This is why you may want to cry and then a short while later laugh helplessly at something which is not really very funny. And this is why indignation you may feel about something or someone in the hospital – and, above all, longing for your baby if he or she is in a nursery – seems to have a physical impact, knotting your stomach, drying your throat, burning you up.

Some women who have their babies in the hospital are emotionally unstable until they get home. For them an institutional setting for the postpartum experience is unsettling and confusing. They seem to have a great need to be *in their own place*. On the other hand, if you are sent home within 24 or 48 hours of the birth, you may not feel ready. You may not have successfully breastfed your baby; you may have painful stitches; there may be no one there to help you. You may feel quite frightened and helpless at the prospect of taking on all that responsibility so soon. There is nothing at all abnormal about you if you feel like this. The most important thing is to acknowledge the kind of person you are and for your partner to accept it, too. Then you can make arrangements as decisively and speedily as possible.

"I was very depressed but told no one, as no one asked and I felt too terrible about it to bring up the problem."

If all seems to be well with you and the baby, and you have help at home, it works well to leave the hospital as soon as possible. Ask to see the pediatrician and let him or her know how you feel. A visiting nurse can visit you at home. Consider having a postpartum doula who can help not only with breastfeeding and newborn care, but also cooking, cleaning, shopping, and care of older children.

COMPLICATED EMOTIONS

Your partner may be experiencing violent emotions himself at this time; he too may be torn between laughter and tears after the birth. Our society tends to stress that men ought to be strong and offer broad shoulders for the new mother to lean on, but in fact some men are so deeply touched by the experience of birth that they undergo much the same emotional turmoil as the new mother. A new father may suffer acutely on leaving the hospital, because he is surrendering you and his newborn baby to the care of strangers. In spite of the rejoicing and excitement, there may be a strange undercurrent of grief. The intimate bond linking him to the woman who has borne his child is cut by an enforced separation. When he returns to the hospital it is as a visitor.

Your changed body

After you have had a baby you encounter your body in a dramatically changed state. Whereas before you enjoyed your smooth body heavy with fruit, the curve of your abdomen like an enormous melon still awaiting the harvest of birth, after birth you may feel astonishingly alone, bereft, and empty. If you are in the hospital without people you love near you, in the care of people who treat you as just another "mom" or, worse still, as an involuting uterus, a sutured perineum, and a couple of lactating breasts, you need time to come to terms with your changed body and to rediscover yourself as a person.

For many women the euphoria of having given birth and of having produced a real baby, which comes as a delightful surprise at first, gives way to this confrontation with the body. Changes in the breasts associated with breastfeeding can be an ordeal for some women. Many set their sights on the birth, seeing labor and delivery as the challenge, and are ill-prepared for the new challenges that follow immediately after. One mother who felt a revulsion at her much-changed body exclaimed: "But it was all supposed to be *over!*" Once the baby had arrived she wanted her self back again.

WEIGHT LOSS

Immediately following delivery you probably feel beautifully slim and lightweight. You have lost the combined weight of the baby, the placenta, the amniotic fluid, and the membranes. It is only when you first put your hand down on your tummy that you become aware of the folds of skin, like a soft and soggy cream puff. When you first catch sight of yourself naked in a full-length mirror you may be horrified at the amount of weight you have put on: the thickened waist, the heavy thighs, and (if you are breastfeeding) the ballooning breasts – which you and your partner may enjoy if you were small and flat before, but which can be too much of a good thing if you were top-heavy anyway.

Water loss During the week after childbirth most women sweat out the excess fluid they no longer need, and any puffiness you may have noticed in your legs and ankles will disappear; so will the plumped-out facial features and the fluid which might have been retained in your fingers, making them fatter than usual.

Restoring muscle tone If you use your abdominal muscles your tummy will flatten after a few weeks, but you cannot achieve this if you go without exercise. Some exercises suitable for the early postpartum period are illustrated on pages 398–401. Brisk walking is good for abdominal muscles: if the weather is suitable, put the baby in a carrier against your body and walk, in the country if possible. At first your pelvic floor muscles may feel as if they are sagging like a heavy hammock, but their tone will be gradually restored over the next three months, and, if you use them regularly, without straining them, rehabilitation will be complete.

Breasts and breastfeeding

The sooner you put your baby to the breast the sooner her stomach will be lined with colostrum, a substance which forms a protective "paint" and a barrier to invading bacteria. Colostrum also provides the baby with antibodies to diseases to which you yourself are resistant. Ready in your breasts at the end of pregnancy, it is the earliest form of milk, rich in protein, and an ideal first concentrated food for your baby. Do not wash your nipples before breastfeeding. Babies are attracted to the breast partly by their sense of smell, and prefer an unwashed to a washed breast.*

THE MILK EJECTION REFLEX
When your baby sucks, the action stimulates an area in your brain (the hypothalamus), which in turn stimulates the pituitary gland at the base of your brain to release oxytocin into your bloodstream. Oxytocin flows into the blood vessels in your breasts and causes specific cells around the milk glands deep inside your breasts to contract. This has the effect of squeezing the milk out through the tiny holes in your nipples.

Below
The shape of the baby's face is perfectly adapted to sucking at the breast: a snubnose, a receding chin, and a mouth that opens wide and latches on.

Oxytocin also makes your uterus contract, so you can have the odd feeling of milk being pushed down into your baby's mouth at the same time as your uterus is squeezing tight. After about a week you can no longer feel uterine contractions when you breastfeed. You will probably feel the warm, tingling glow of the milk ejection reflex immediately preceding the flow of milk. This occurs as the

oxytocin-carrying blood rushes into the breasts and you feel them getting warmer. Infrared photographs of lactating breasts show that they really do grow hotter in response to the baby's cry.

The first feedings Notice what happens when you put the baby to the breast. She should have the nipple deep in her mouth and as much of the areola as will make a good mouthful. Cuddle the baby close and wait. Drop your shoulders: if they feel really stiff *pull* them down and then let them go. It may take a few minutes for the sensation to come and then suddenly it is there: deep inside both breasts, not just the one the baby is sucking, there is a prickling, buzzing feeling as if champagne were flowing through your veins, while a wave of heat flows toward your nipples. And then you see the baby's jaws beginning to work, and the strong, steady movement of the bone at the top of the baby's jawbone, just by her ear, as she begins to swallow as well as suck.

The milk ejection reflex can happen spontaneously when you just think about feeding the baby or when you hear her crying. If she is not in your arms you can press the palm of a hand firmly against your breast and the milk flow – a slow but steady dripping from the nipple – will then come to a stop.

THE DIFFERENCE BETWEEN SUCKING AND FEEDING

Having milk in your breasts is just the beginning. Obviously the important thing is to *release* it so that it flows into your baby. For nutritional purposes it is not enough to have a baby sucking at your breasts, though he will enjoy this anyway. He needs to *swallow,* and until this happens he is not feeding.

Hospitals are more relaxed than they used to be about the time babies spend at the breast, but if you are in one where feeding time is still restricted, you should count the time from the moment the baby is actually feeding, not from when he is just sucking.

Even before the reflex occurs the baby gets some milk, because it collects in the ducts just behind the nipple. This is called "foremilk" and is rich in protein. It usually keeps the baby happy until the rush of milk comes with the reflex. But if you give a baby foremilk only, because he is not sucking long enough to stimulate the reflex, your milk supply will dwindle or never build up.

If you feel embarrassed or self-conscious or experience strong emotions of anxiety, fear, or anger, the milk ejection reflex will probably be slower in coming, and sometimes may not occur at all. This is why the setting for breastfeeding in the first days after birth is so important and why emotional support from your partner or someone who understands how you feel is helpful. Even though you may think you have emptied a breast, a fresh reflex can occur when you put the baby back to it again. A breast is not like a pitcher of milk, but produces a constant supply, provided that the baby gives the right stimulus.

LITTLE AND OFTEN

If you can, keep your baby with you all 24 hours of the day, and feed whenever the baby wants. If you are concerned that the baby is taking too little milk, bear in mind that the frequency of feedings is more important than their length. Look at your baby's little clenched fist: that is about the size of her stomach. Though some babies, especially in the first four to six weeks of life, enjoy sucking more or less continuously at certain times of the day, the main nutritional content of the milk is obtained during the first five to seven minutes. This is why many short feedings, with the baby dropping off to sleep in between, is for many mothers and babies the perfect style of feeding in these first weeks. You may be able to unplug the baby's mouth gently from your nipple by depressing the breast with a finger, or by slipping a finger just inside the baby's mouth to break the vacuum – but don't, whatever you do, just pull the nipple out.

BABIES LIKE SUCKING FOR COMFORT

You may feel very "drained" when nursing is long and drawn out: if you are tired and the baby is constantly demanding to be fed, it is easy to think that you cannot be providing enough milk. Though this is sometimes the case, many babies want to go on feeding nonstop because they like it so much, not because they are starving. So after about ten minutes' sucking it is sensible to put the baby down or hand him or her over to a friend or your partner for a cuddle. Relax a bit; offer some more breast milk on whichever side feels more generously supplied; then have another break, and so on.

EACH BABY'S FEEDING PATTERN IS DIFFERENT

Breastfed babies do not suck continuously through a feeding. They enjoy bursts of sucking, stopping for a while, then starting again. This is normal. If you think about meals you enjoy you will realize that you do not chomp away nonstop, either. Nor do you want an equal quantity of food at each meal. Babies are the same.

Think of each feeding as divided into different courses. Some will be seven- or eight-course banquets, but others will be only two courses. You will gradually be able to work out when the baby likes the banquets, and then you may be able to cater for them by arranging your day to fit this pattern. Somehow, anticipating and preparing for feeding sessions of this kind make them much easier to cope with, and you are less likely to feel exhausted by them.

IS BREAST MILK ENOUGH?

You may wonder if and when your baby needs any food other than your breast milk, especially if you secretly feel that your baby is not getting enough milk from you.

Water Many hospitals still give water or sugar water. The baby needs milk, not water. If your baby is producing six or more wet diapers in the course of 24 hours and frequent bowel movements and is having no other fluid, and if the urine is pale amber or colorless, this is an indication that she is indeed getting enough milk from you. You will probably find that *you* are thirstier than usual. Drink as much as you like, though there is no point in having more than you want, since it will not produce more milk. Giving a newborn baby any fluid other than breast milk may be harmful.

Supplementary bottles If you think your baby is not getting enough milk and you start to give bottle feedings, the amount of milk you are producing will diminish, since demand stimulates supply.

Solid foods When you introduce solid foods, be prepared for your milk supply to be reduced. This is one reason why introducing solid foods early is counterproductive. It replaces food the baby needs, human milk, with food she does not need until she is about six months old. A baby's appetite cannot cope with human milk *plus* all the other foods which are on the market. Manufacturers of so-called "baby foods" are often responsible for breastfeeding difficulties which start at three to four months, a common time for mothers to discover that they are failing to produce enough milk.

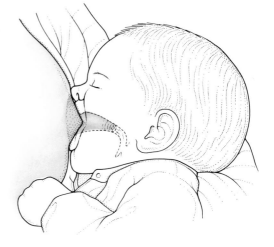

Test weighing Weighing the baby before and after a feeding (test weighing) is a method of finding out exactly how much breast milk he or she has taken. It is pointless unless done over 24 hours, since the baby takes different quantities at different times; even then it tends to increase your anxiety and make you feel inadequate. A much better guide to a baby's wellbeing is good muscle tone and alert responses.

Breastfeeding
For the breastfeeding to go well the baby needs to suck at the breast, not just the nipple. The nipple is drawn back into the baby's mouth and the jaws press on the areola to pump the milk.

More frequent breastfeeding When you want to increase the quantity of milk you are making, put the baby to the breast more often. If the baby has not gained weight, or has lost weight, nurse him every time he stirs over a 24-hour period. If the baby is very sleepy, rouse him every two and a half hours if you can, except at night. Unwrap him, talk to him, and "woo" him with the breast. I call this my *"Twenty-Four-Hour Peak Production Plan."* It works in the first weeks after birth and is also useful at about six weeks.

BREASTFEEDING DIFFICULTIES
Engorged breasts Many new mothers find that they are engorged on the third or fourth day after birth, when the milk really floods in. The longer you go between feedings the more likely you are to be painfully

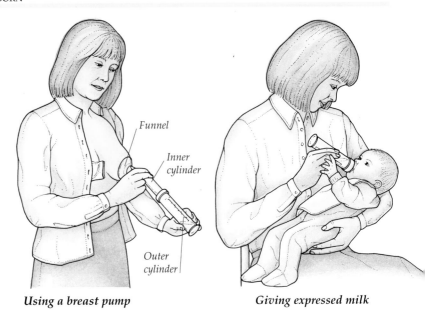

Funnel

Inner cylinder

Outer cylinder

Using a breast pump

Giving expressed milk

Expressing milk
A small breast pump is a useful accessory. Sometimes breasts become so full of milk that the baby cannot latch on. You can either hand express or express a little with a breast pump.

engorged. A cold compress, such as a cloth with some ice inside, resting against your breast will ease the pain of engorgement, and the baby's frequent sucking will help you through this difficult transitional phase. The hospital will have a breast pump that you can use if it is important to draw off some milk and if you find it difficult to express by hand, but make sure to draw off only enough for comfort.

Sore nipples Nipple soreness, especially when the baby is a vigorous sucker, is common in the first few weeks after the birth and does not mean that you will necessarily fail at breastfeeding. Studies show that those mothers who go on to enjoy breastfeeding include many women who have had initial trouble with sores and cracks, and that the only difference between these and others who give up is that they persevere. Ensure that your baby is well latched on the breast and has a good mouthful.

Go topless whenever you can; avoid using soap on your nipples or using breast pads against them; and let them dry off after a nursing, exposed to warm air. It is best not to use a towel and to avoid cotton wool, which tends to disintegrate and stick to your skin.

Cracked nipples Sometimes a crack appears at the point where the nipple joins the areola. This is almost invariably because the baby has not fixed well on the surrounding tissue and has not obtained a really good mouthful. If a baby drags on the nipple stem and does not draw the nipple into the back of the mouth, not only will you have problems with sores and cracks but also the baby will not be able to take enough milk after the first spurts at the beginning of a feeding. A soft, flexible nipple shield made of rubber with a wide brim like a Mexican sombrero can sometimes help to relieve the soreness that is caused by cracks and make nursing tolerable until the nipple has had time in which to heal. Avoid using plastic-lined breast pads, since if there is any leaking your nipples will be sitting in dampness.

Breast tenderness If you develop a red area on a breast, nursing more frequently can help. Ensure that the baby is well latched on. Exercise your arms to increase the circulation to your breasts (see page 401). If an infection develops and you run a temperature while you have a red area, cold compresses and oral antibiotics prescribed by the doctor will quickly treat it. Continue nursing the baby, as this makes it far less likely that you will develop an abscess.

Excitable babies Some babies nurse with great bluster and excitement, spluttering and coughing and really making a meal out of it. In the first weeks they suddenly draw back as they start to choke, pulling on the nipple at the same time. Or they may let go for a second and then grab on again, but because they have jerked their heads back they now have only the nipple stem in their mouths so that they are dragging on the place where the stem joins the areola. These babies need a calm environment in which to nurse. Talk to yours soothingly and reassuringly, and reposition her firmly and securely. If your milk comes with a sudden rush after the ejection reflex has occurred, see if a little boiled water or mint tea, which can be given by spoon or in a bottle, encourages her to be more relaxed at the breast. If your milk streams out fast you may need to express a little before each feeding.

Sore abdomen After a cesarean section breastfeeding may be difficult because you find it almost impossible to settle with the baby in a position where she is not pressing on the wound. Try placing a pillow on the wound and lie on your side, or sit up and prop the baby's legs under the arm on the same side as the breast you are using.

GIVING BREAST MILK IN A BOTTLE
When you desperately need sleep and your partner wants to give the baby some feedings, it can be a good idea to express some breast milk after each feeding and store it in the refrigerator (perfectly safe for 2 or 3 days). Use a sterile plastic container. If you want to keep your milk longer than that, freeze it. Express the milk after each feeding, either immediately or about 30 minutes later. If you find that milk shoots out of one breast when you put the baby to the other, you can collect this milk, too. If you do not find it easy to express milk by hand, you can buy a small breast pump. There are several different varieties on the market.

A woman who meets obstacles to breastfeeding – who discovers, perhaps, that her husband does not like her feeding in front of other men, or who sees disgust. on peoples' faces when she is breastfeeding in a public place – is coming up against a social system in which breasts are considered exclusively as playthings for sexually aroused men, and in which the life-giving milk with which she sustains her baby is treated like an unclean physical discharge. Breastfeeding is an intimate personal experience and a way of loving. Once it is going well it often brings sensual feelings of closeness to and pleasure in your baby. When women fail to breastfeed it may have less to do with failing to get the techniques right than with the fact that breastfeeding can be a lonely struggle in a culture that disapproves of its being visible.

It helps to get together with other women who are breastfeeding so that you can discuss your experiences, including any problems and the strategies you have worked out to deal with them. Organizations that can put you in touch with other breastfeeding mothers are listed on page 413.

Bottlefeeding

If you decide to bottlefeed, avoid taking lactation suppressants. Bromocriptine, the generic name of the drug that was once used widely to suppress breast milk, has not been proved safe. Some women who took it have had a stroke or seizure. If you want to bottlefeed or to give occasional bottles because it is more convenient, the formula you choose for your baby should be as much like your own milk as possible.

No manufacturer has yet been able to invent anything better than an *approximation* of human milk, because your own milk adapts to your baby's individual needs. Substitute milks are a great improvement over unmodified cow's milk, however, and those which are "humanized" have the proportions of fats, sugars, and trace elements changed to be more like the real thing.

DIFFERENT KINDS OF FORMULA

If there are allergies in your or your partner's family, breastfeeding is the easiest way to help protect your baby against eczema, asthma, and other allergies, although it is no guarantee that a child will never develop such conditions. Some babies are allergic to the protein in cow's milk. With this in mind, formula companies promote milk containing hydrolyzed protein, though it does not always solve the problem and there are reports of babies becoming ill from it. Another alternative is to use soya milk, but this may not be a good idea. Babies fed on soya milk receive the equivalent of up to five contraceptive pills a day, because soya milk contains 100 times more estrogen than breast milk. Such an estrogen overdose may have toxic effects.

Human milk also contains long-chain fatty acids which help brain development.* Some formula companies are now adding long-chain lipids derived from egg yolk or bioengineered yeasts. This makes sense, but some babies are allergic to these lipids. Discuss with your doctor or midwife the choices available.

MAKING UP BOTTLE FEEDS

You do need to be scrupulously hygienic when preparing formula. It is vital that your kitchen and all utensils be clean and that you sterilize both bottles and nipples carefully, and follow the instructions on the can of formula. You can make up enough feedings for 24 hours, put caps on the bottles, and store them in the refrigerator. It is then easy to feed your baby whenever he or she shows signs of hunger, just as you would if you were breastfeeding.

Never leave warm formula out for more than a few minutes, as bacteria will multiply. After the feeding, always throw away any leftover milk, clean out the bottle immediately, and sterilize it. Keep nipples in sterilized, covered containers. When you go out, do not take warm milk with you. Take it cold, straight from the refrigerator, and reheat it in a pan of hot water or an electric bottle warmer. It is tempting to tuck the bottle under the bassinet covers to keep it snug and ready as soon as the baby wants it. But if you do this you are running the risk of harboring bacteria capable of causing your baby gastrointestinal illness.

Though it seems pleasanter for a baby to have warm milk, this is not strictly necessary; if the baby is impatient for a feeding and you are in a hurry, it is quite all right to give her a cold bottle. Powdered formula must be thoroughly mixed. Some brands dissolve more easily than others. Even the tiniest lumps can block the hole in the

Below
When giving milk in a bottle, hold the baby close. Never feed a baby who is lying in a crib or leave a baby with a propped-up bottle.

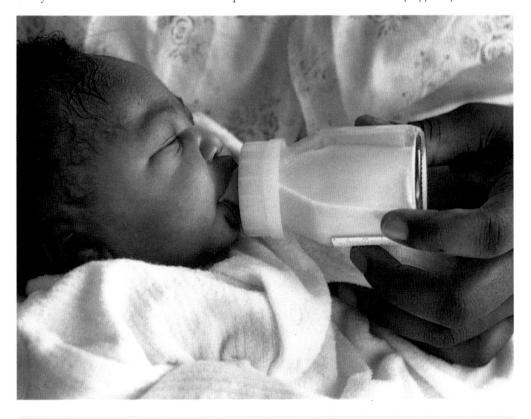

nipple and, if your baby splutters or vomits, can be inhaled and cause trouble with breathing. When you are making up dried milk, measure it very carefully and never be tempted to put in an extra scoop to make it richer, as this overloads the baby with minerals which his system can absorb only with difficulty.

The baby who is fed on formula may go longer between feedings since the milk takes longer to digest. Avoid trying to make the baby finish the bottle just because there is milk in it. In hot weather give drinks of water, too, and introduce sips of fruit juice, since the bottlefed baby will need an extra amount of vitamin C. But formulas do contain some extra vitamins, so do not give vitamin supplements unless advised to do so by your doctor, and then take care that you do not exceed the prescribed dose.

FEEDING FOR PLEASURE

When bottlefeeding, remember to hold the baby close, cheek against your breast, just as if you were breastfeeding. Though it may produce a less comfortable cushion for the baby's head, a man can also do this. The baby may sometimes like to lie nestled against your partner's bare skin, and fathers who give a feeding like this in the middle of the night say how much they enjoy it.

Never prop a baby up to feed on its own in a crib, however rushed you are. It can be dangerous, and it means that the baby misses out on one of the most important experiences of early life.

Sleep and crying

After being awake and alert, eyes wide open, for an hour or so after birth, the baby often sinks into a deep sleep for about 24 hours, waking only to suck and then dropping off to sleep again while still at the breast. This period is often followed by another lasting about 24 hours, in which the baby may be sucking almost continuously. This is a normal pattern. It is the frequent sucking that stimulates your milk supply. Some babies suck in short bursts, get drowsy, then suck again. Others sleep for two to three hours between prolonged sucking sessions. Some babies start a pattern of evening fussing when they are one or two weeks old, which may then continue for as long as three months. Though this behavior is tiring for you, it is completely normal. It may be a sign that the baby is over-stimulated and therefore needs to discharge tension.

SLEEP PATTERNS OF NEWBORN BABIES

When your baby is asleep you will sometimes notice that the eyelids flicker and the eyeballs are moving behind them. This is rapid eye movement (REM) sleep similar to that which adults have – the dreaming time. It has been discovered that REM sleep is essential for mental wellbeing and to prevent exhaustion.* These little eye movements also stimulate the flow of blood to the brain. Even if the baby seems to be stirring and is making little jerking movements or fussing noises, this is not a time to wake her. This kind of sleep is probably just as important for babies as it is for adults.

THE MEANING OF YOUR BABY'S CRY

Another innate biological mechanism is your baby's cry on waking, which alerts you to care for her. The baby may also cry whenever you undress her and seem to hate being without clothes. This is nerve-wracking for the new mother and father, especially if they are about to bathe her. But remember that the baby was held firmly inside your uterus, hugged by its tightly enclosing walls. If your baby startles and cries when you change a diaper or when you start taking off her clothes, keep your movements slow and firm. With one hand hold the baby's arms over her chest, as they would have been folded inside the uterus at the end of pregnancy, and speak soothingly.

You will soon discover that the baby has different cries to express different needs. But in the first weeks the cry nearly always means hunger and the right thing to do is to let the baby suck. At this age a wet or dirty diaper does not really concern most babies.

Practical care

There is a great gap between studying something in a book and doing it in practice. Experiment and see what works best for you.

BATHING YOUR BABY

It does not matter how you bathe your baby, so long as he is head-above-water, keeps warm, and has a chance to enjoy it. Many babies hate being undressed and abhor being bathed in the first weeks of life, and make you feel that you must be a tyrant for ever doing either of these things to them. And because they cry you are convinced that you must be utterly incompetent and hopeless as a mother. The single most important thing to remember is to talk to your baby while dressing, undressing, and bathing him.

If you do not want a very hot bath yourself, you can take the baby with you into your own bath. This provides the baby with a personal swimming pool. Start by placing him facing you on your knee and have a conversation. Then you will discover that you can work out little games together and the baby will find out what fun it is to splash. Have ready the biggest bath towel you can find and make the patting-dry fun, too, so that the whole process is enjoyable.

DIAPERS

The main choice is between cloth diapers and disposables. Cloth diapers really are more ecologically sound, and many women find that with a bit of extra organization washing becomes routine and they do not mind the extra laundry. Although they entail high initial expense, you can often get them secondhand, and they do work out

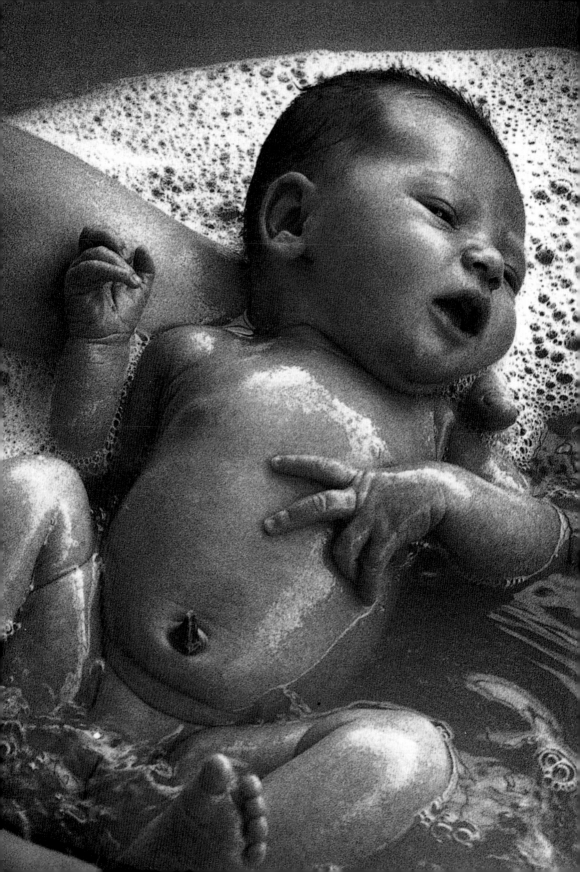

more cheaply in the long run if you have a washing machine. Even so, you would be wise to buy a packet of disposables before the baby is born. You are bound to resort to them occasionally when you go out for the day. Babies often soil or wet their diapers before, during, and after a feed. Since many like to suck every two or three hours at first, you may need as many as 24 diapers to see you through the 24 hours, especially if you do not have an efficient tumble dryer. You can save some washing by buying disposable diaper liners and plastic pants. A diaper service may solve all the problems.

On the other hand you will be busy with a baby, and disposable diapers save time and work. There will be no pails of dirty diapers soaking, no frantic hunt for clean diapers on days when you have not been able to catch up with yourself, and no waiting for diapers to dry. Mothers tend to change their babies more often when it is simply a matter of taking another diaper out of a packet, rather than estimating how many clean ones are left, and that must be more comfortable for their babies. But disposables end up being more expensive, and there are none which are completely biodegradable.

MOTHERS WITH DISABILITIES
If you have a disability which makes caring for your baby difficult, you will want special equipment to help you. A woman in a wheelchair, for example, welcomes a crib and a bath on a stand the height of which can be adjusted, and with space underneath so that she can get up close to the baby. If you have back pain you will want equipment which reduces the need to bend and lift. (For organizations, see page 413.)

THE BABY'S CLOTHING
Newborn babies lose heat rapidly, so they need to be warm and cozy. You can do this in any way you like, but several fine layers are usually warmer than one thick one. Choose things which do not have to be pulled over the head, as most babies hate narrow neck holes. In cold weather the baby's head ought to be covered outdoors.

Avoid strings and ribbons near the baby's mouth and hands, and lacy knitted jackets and shawls in which the baby will catch fingers and toes. You are bound to be given bootees and mittens; these can be wriggled off or lost, get dirty and germ-ridden. Stretchy one-piece suits are better for keeping feet covered; babies should be able to get at their hands and explore with them when they are awake.

A baby carrier is not strictly clothing but is important for your mobility. And the most useful item of clothing in cold weather is something for you, not the baby. It is a big wrap-around overcoat, cape, or other voluminous top garment. Then you can tuck the baby underneath it in a baby carrier against your body with just her face peeping out; your own body heat will provide warmth and the outer garment will hold the warmth around the baby. The baby carrier you use to begin with should be one of those where the baby is held in front of you and the head is supported.

Opposite
Even if they do not take to it the first few times, most babies love to be bathed, when handled gently and reassuringly.

The challenge of new parenthood

Though most women look forward to the time after the birth when they will have their new baby under their own roof, taking an important part in family life, the first days at home alone with a new baby can be filled with unexpected worry and even a sense of panic. You may suddenly feel like a stranger in your own home as you try to both understand and cope with the various needs of this demanding new person. However, you will soon learn to be able to interpret the different cries of your baby and understand exactly what it is that he or she is trying to tell you.

POSTNATAL CHECKUP

Your postnatal checkup will be arranged for between five and seven weeks after the birth, and is important in ensuring that you have complete physical rehabilitation after childbirth. The obstetrician will give you an internal examination to see if your pelvic floor muscles are well toned and that the uterus and bladder are correctly positioned, and will also check on the state of any scar tissue. If you have been finding that sexual intercourse is difficult and uncomfortable or you are feeling depressed and unhappy, it is a good idea to tell the doctor at this visit. If you are dissatisfied with any aspect of the care you have received or seek further explanation of things that happened to you in labor, take the opportunity to discuss these things with the doctor.

Sex after childbirth

For many women the full flood of passion is slow to return after childbirth. This is not really surprising, considering that so much has happened in your body and to your emotions; you may need time to find yourself again and to get in touch with your feelings. If your labor was unpleasant or the delivery traumatic then you may need additional time, too, in order to like yourself again and to gain back trust in your body.

If you have had stitches after the birth you may feel at first as if you will never want to make love again. If you are one of the minority of women who do not have stitches then you may not be able to wait to make love. So there is a great difference in attitude to making love after giving birth, depending very much on the state of your perineum. The initial healing of the tear or episiotomy wound (and it is a wound) often takes two weeks or sometimes longer, and even then you may be very conscious of having scar tissue at the lower end of your vagina.

REDISCOVERING EACH OTHERS' BODIES

Make sure that your partner knows which areas are likely to feel sore and help him discover what feels good and where. Do not attempt to have intercourse at first and certainly do not try to prove anything to yourselves. Choose a quiet time when you need not be rushed, perhaps after a feeding when you know the baby is most likely to settle and sleep soundly. Squeeze a little lubricant jelly onto your partner's fingers and, taking his hands in yours, guide him, showing him where you like to be touched. Many couples need two or three exploratory sessions like this before they feel sufficiently confident and passionate to have complete intercourse. If you rush it, you may have unexpected discomfort and will then tense up in anticipation of pain next time, and because your pelvic floor muscles have contracted you will experience more pain.

"I was sore, and a bit scared. The baby had an uncanny knack of knowing when we were making love and wanting a feed."

When you feel you are ready for intercourse, adopt a position in which your partner's weight is not going to pull and drag on the lower part of your vagina or, if you are breastfeeding, on your breasts. For example, if you lie or sit with your legs over the side of a low bed, feet on the floor, your partner will be able to penetrate you gently without pressing against or pulling on any tender areas. You will probably feel extraordinarily full up. Release your *throat* and this will help to release muscles around your vagina. It is best if you do not aim for simultaneous orgasm. It is usually very much more comfortable and pleasurable for you in the weeks immediately after birth if your partner comes to orgasm first and then stays still inside until you have an orgasm too.

ADJUSTING TO YOUR CHANGED BODY

You and your partner will learn a lot about each other after the birth and, as a result, sex will sometimes be funny, sometimes tender, and occasionally passionate. Even if you do not feel that you are making a wild success of your sex life in the first few months after birth, lovemaking helps both you and your baby by releasing oxytocin into your bloodstream. This helps the uterus contract so that it returns to its previous size and shape and it also encourages the flow of breast milk. When you do have an orgasm, milk may actually shoot out of your nipples.

You will probably find that the shape of your body has changed after giving birth to a first baby. The labia, like the outside petals of a flower, are now softer and fleshier, and away from the site of the episiotomy you may find the entrance to the vagina also more yielding. If your uterus is still involuting, you will also feel after-contractions following lovemaking. This is a good sign. If they are uncomfortable, then it is a good idea to use a hot water bottle against your lower tummy or against your back. Even if you thoroughly enjoyed lovemaking, you may feel slightly sore

Postnatal exercises

Many of the exercises recommended during pregnancy are also good for getting your figure back after delivery. It is important to remember, though, that postnatal exercises should be progressive. Do only the gentlest exercises for the first day or two. Then move on to the more strenuous ones. Never do an exercise that hurts.

Pelvic rock

Lie on your back on the floor, knees bent, soles of feet flat, and your baby lying between your legs and along your tummy. Breathe out, and push against the floor with your feet. Allow your pelvis to roll and your lower back to press against the floor. Then release your feet and rock your pelvis so that the pressure of your lower back is lifted away from the floor. Notice the movement all along your spine to your head, and how your back flattens as your chin rolls up from your chest and arches as it rolls down on to your chest.

The leg slide

1 *Lie on your back, knees bent, feet flat on the floor. Place one hand under the small of your back. Release your chest, press against the floor with your feet, and notice how your back also presses against your hand.*

Feel how your back pushes against your hand.

2 *Keeping up this pressure against your hand, slowly allow both feet to slide forward so that you extend your legs and feel the pull of your abdominal muscles. Let your toes come up off the floor. Continue to breathe.*

Unfolding

1 *Sit on the floor, knees bent and together, soles flat, with your hands crossed on your chest. Relax your chest and let your back drop slowly backward with your legs sliding forward. Feel how vertebrae in your lower back press on the floor one after the other like a string of pearls unfolding.*

Fold and unfold yourself in a rhythmical way.

2 *Then fold yourself together by moving your knees and nose toward each other, and lean back and unfold again, continuing this folding and unfolding movement rhythmically.*

Sideways curl-up

1 *Lie on your back on the floor, knees bent, with your left hand tucked behind your head. Breathe in, breathe out, let your chest become soft, lift your head and shoulders, and lift your left knee.*

2 *Continue to lift your knee until it touches the elbow. Stay in the position for a few seconds, breathing gently. Then slowly return to the starting position. Continue the movement on your right side, then repeat the left side again and so on.*

The twist

1 *Sit on the floor, legs crossed, holding your baby in your lap. Extend one arm behind you at shoulder level, allowing your body to turn with it and turning your head to look at your hand.*

2 *Lower your hands to the floor behind you and continue to look over your shoulder. Hold this position for ten seconds. Return to the starting position. Repeat the movement with the other arm.*

Make sure you are holding the baby firmly with the other hand.

The hammock

Lie on your back on the floor, knees bent, feet flat, holding your baby sitting on your tummy. Soften your chest and press your feet and head against the floor, allowing your bottom to lift up off it. Rock your baby by swinging from side to side in this position. Then relax your body and let your bottom drop back to the floor.

Rocking the baby

Lie on your back, knees bent, feet up off the floor so that your lower legs are parallel with it and your baby is resting on your lower legs, face down, and supported under the arms. Tuck your chin in and, slowly lifting your head and shoulders, rock forward and back, alternately lifting and lowering to and from the floor.

Complete rock

1 *Lie on your back, knees bent, feet lifted off the floor, your hands behind your knees. Rock backward and forward, keeping your back rounded and an equal distance between your nose and your knees.*

2 *You may find that you rock completely until you sit upright, but do not force it.*

Roll up

Lie on your back, knees bent, your hands holding your lower legs, elbows forward. Let your head and knees roll toward each other, then apart, then together again, and continue this rocking movement. You may find that you roll right up until you are sitting. Do not force this. You can also do this movement with your hands behind your head.

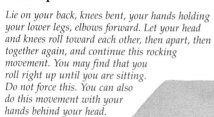

Up, up, and away

Lie on your back, knees bent, feet flat on the floor, your baby lying on your chest, and your hands supporting her under the arms. Gently lift the baby up above your face, noticing the pressure of your lower back against the floor as you do so. Hold the baby in this position for a few seconds. Then slowly lower her onto your chest and rock her gently.

afterward, once the sexual intensity has faded. Again, this is quite normal. A cold witch-hazel compress held against the area may feel soothing and help to bring relief.

PAINFUL INTERCOURSE

For some women intercourse is acutely painful after childbirth and no amount of trying to relax does away with the pain. This is called "dyspareunia." It can occur when stitches have been inserted too tightly and the surrounding flesh has become puffy and swollen (edematous) and is perhaps infected. Ask your doctor or midwife to look at the sore area as soon as possible. Sometimes it is just a question of nicking a few stitches, sometimes a matter of taking antibiotics. If you have pain up near your cervix, it may be that the transverse cervical ligaments have been torn and it takes time for them to repair themselves. Make sure that your doctor knows that you are having this sort of pain.

Many women worry that they have become "frigid" after childbirth. Often a lack of interest in sex is directly caused by tiredness. Try to rest regularly with your feet up and, if it is possible, sleep at some time during the day when your baby sleeps. Even the most active baby sleeps sometimes, and you could try to discover your baby's pattern and then take advantage of it yourself. This is more difficult if you also have a toddler, but many toddlers enjoy a cuddle in bed or on the sofa.

Although you may not feel like making love for some time after childbirth, it is sensible to have explored sensations and had intercourse before your postnatal checkup. Most women with new babies are so busy that it is not easy to fit in another appointment in order to discuss sexual difficulties, and they may hope that if they take no notice then the problems will disappear gradually of their own accord. Make a note of where and when you feel pain during intercourse and let the doctor know that you are experiencing dyspareunia and that you want help.

Sex after childbirth takes you on a new journey with your partner. It involves discovery, change, for many women a fresh awareness of the depth and drama of their own sexual feelings, and for both of you a new kind of closeness and tenderness as parents of the baby who has been born of your love.

Contraception after childbirth

There is no easy answer to contraception and what pleases one couple may be completely unsuitable for another. Many couples consider the matter in advance so that they can have intercourse safely whenever they feel ready. Barrier methods also protect against sexually transmitted diseases which the IUD and hormonal contraceptives cannot do. You may find that a combination of methods works best for you but, whatever kind(s) you select, study

Opposite
To be a parent is all about learning. A child with a younger sibling has new opportunities for development, too.

them carefully and never deviate from the correct routine. It is not worth being worried about another pregnancy when you are only just beginning to enjoy the results of the last!*

BREASTFEEDING

If you are breastfeeding, your periods may not come back until you wean the baby or introduce some form of solid food. Ovulation, and hence the possibility of conception, can occur a couple of weeks or so *before* you have this first period. Breastfeeding tends to reduce fertility but is not an effective contraceptive unless you are suckling the baby intermittently right through the 24 hours and are giving her no other food or fluid at all. A fully breastfeeding woman may not have a period for a year. In many Third World cultures lactating women rarely conceive. Since children are breastfed for three years or longer, this is an effective method of family planning. But bear in mind that in these societies intercourse is often prohibited during lactation, too.

COITUS INTERRUPTUS

Hoping that your partner will withdraw before ejaculation, and deposit semen outside your vagina, is not a reliable method, though it is very common throughout the world. In spite of working well for some couples, it demands great control on the man's part and may lead to dissatisfaction for you both. Sperm can flow from the penis *before* ejaculation and if you have intercourse again within a short time live sperm may already be present in your partner's urethra and be introduced into your vagina before ejaculation. Sperm do not have to be deposited right inside your vagina for you to become pregnant, and even a drop or two of semen leaking against the labia may contain a million sperm or more.

NATURAL FAMILY PLANNING

Natural methods of birth control entail identifying the period of ovulation, the phase of the menstrual cycle at which you are most fertile, and abstaining from intercourse during that time. It is impossible to calculate ovulation accurately using a calendar alone. The only methods of birth control officially approved by the Roman Catholic Church are the rhythm method and the symptothermal method. They both require that you keep an accurate record of your menstrual cycle and also a daily chart of body temperature, using a special thermometer. By doing this you can identify when ovulation occurs and avoid intercourse at that time. With the symptothermal method you also observe changes in the cervical mucus, which gets thinner during your fertile period. There are drawbacks, however: in the first year or so after childbirth a woman may not have a regular menstrual cycle, and it can be difficult to work out the significance of the changes she observes; natural methods require instruction from someone who is really skilled in using them, and a firm commitment from both partners.

Ovulation prediction There are kits on the market that can tell you if and when you are ovulating, though they are expensive. They work in a way similar to chemical pregnancy tests (see page 19), and they signal, by a color change, the presence of luteinizing hormone in your urine, which increases a couple of days before ovulation. You start testing the urine several days after the beginning of a period and go on testing, at the same time each day, noting exactly when the equipment records a surge in luteinizing hormone. You should not empty your bladder for four hours beforehand. Two to three days after you have observed a color change you are at your most fertile.

THE CONDOM

The condom (rubber), made of latex or polyurethane (for those allergic to latex), is the most widely used of the barrier methods and, employed carefully, is effective (12 percent failure rate without spermicide, 1 percent with). It has no harmful side effects. The one big disadvantage of using condoms during intercourse after childbirth is that your vagina may not be well lubricated and may be tender following an episiotomy. Unless you use a lubricant cream the latex rubber sticks and drags, interfering with pleasure and reducing confidence. So have some artificial lubrication ready – preferably a spermicidal cream or jelly, or mineral oil, but avoid Vaseline, as this causes rubber to disintegrate. Do not use old condoms; their shelf life is about two years.

THE DIAPHRAGM

If you used a diaphragm before you became pregnant you will probably need to use a larger size after you have had a baby, and it must be fitted by a doctor or midwife, who cannot do it accurately until about six weeks after childbirth. The diaphragm should then be left in place for at least six hours after intercourse; do not, however, leave it for longer than eight hours if you have had any kind of bladder infection during pregnancy or following the birth, since the pressure of the rubber rim on your bladder can sometimes cause irritation and perhaps exacerbate an infection. Use one teaspoonful of spermicidal cream on the diaphragm; never use Vaseline. It is probably best not to dust with powder as some manufacturers advise, since some kinds of powder can contain carcinogenic substances. Corn starch is a better substitute. Using a diaphragm does not affect your breastfeeding and the spermicidal cream or jelly cannot harm your unborn baby if you should conceive accidentally. The failure rate ranges from only 4 percent (4 pregnancies per 100 women per year) to as high as 29 percent, but the efficiency of the diaphragm depends very much on the motivation and care of the user.

"After the baby came, I switched to a barrier method – a condom or a diaphragm, depending on how we were feeling at the time – I didn't want to introduce chemicals into my body while breastfeeding in case it would harm her."

Sometimes ligaments running across the cervix are slack after childbirth and the diaphragm cannot be wedged snugly up under the pubic bone but slips, especially when you bear down.

THE CERVICAL CAP

This is a rigid, thimble-shaped rubber dome, into which you have placed some spermicide, which fits by suction right over the cervix itself, and which you have to place in position very carefully. It can remain in place for two to three days. It is about as safe as the diaphragm. The cervical cap is not always easy to find, and some doctors have not been trained to fit it. Contact a women's health group to learn where to get a cervical cap. The failure rate in women who have given birth is about 26 percent. The cap is more effective (18 percent failure rate) in women who have never given birth (about as effective as a diaphragm).

SPERMICIDES

Foaming spermicides are more effective than creams or gels because they effervesce into every crevice. But you may find that this in itself interferes with your pleasure in intercourse. Spermicides in the form of foaming tablets or suppositories are not so reliable, because women often do not place them sufficiently high up in the vagina. You must give the tablets sufficient time to thoroughly dissolve in your vagina before ejaculation.

If you notice any vaginal irritation with a particular brand of spermicide, try changing to another one. Some spermicides come in prefilled applicators; others have to be measured out into an applicator. One problem with using spermicides is that you are supposed to lie on your back so that the spermicide does not drip out before you have finished intercourse, and this may not be the position that you would necessarily choose.

Spermicides are safest when they are used in combination with other contraceptives, for instance, a diaphragm, cap, or condom. The failure rate when used alone is anything between 5 and 30 pregnancies per 100 women per year (5 to 30 percent). Most spermicides contain nonoxynol-9, which also protects against some sexually transmitted diseases.

THE INTRAUTERINE DEVICE

It is usually easier for an intrauterine device (IUD) to be inserted and retained without excessive cramping once you have had a baby. So it may be that the IUD will suit you. The failure rate is less than 1 percent, depending on the skill of the doctor who inserts it. Copper IUDs need to be replaced every few years, and after each insertion you may feel faint and sick. Progesterone-releasing IUDs are also available and must be replaced yearly. Avoid intercourse for the first few days. You may notice some bleeding after intercourse for the first month or so. Plastic IUDs can be left in longer; some need to be

Types of contraception

There is now a widespread range of birth control choices on the market, from spermicides to pills. It is a good idea to explore your options and discover which might be the best for you and your partner. It need not necessarily be the same method as you used before you became pregnant.

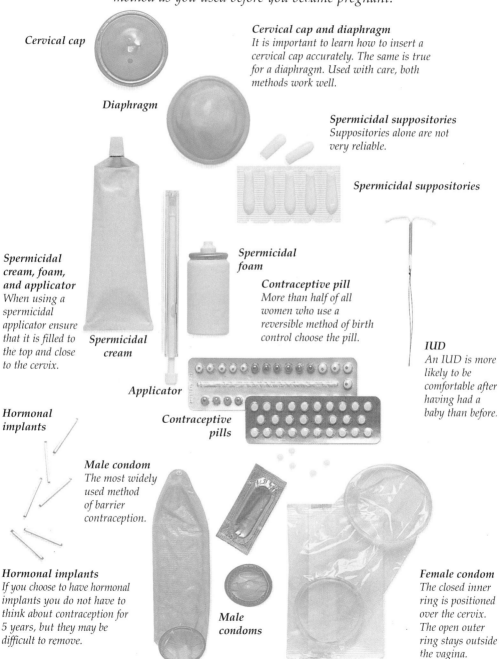

Cervical cap

Diaphragm

Cervical cap and diaphragm
It is important to learn how to insert a cervical cap accurately. The same is true for a diaphragm. Used with care, both methods work well.

Spermicidal suppositories
Suppositories alone are not very reliable.

Spermicidal suppositories

Spermicidal cream, foam, and applicator
When using a spermicidal applicator ensure that it is filled to the top and close to the cervix.

Spermicidal cream

Applicator

Spermicidal foam

Contraceptive pill
More than half of all women who use a reversible method of birth control choose the pill.

IUD
An IUD is more likely to be comfortable after having had a baby than before.

Contraceptive pills

Hormonal implants

Male condom
The most widely used method of barrier contraception.

Male condoms

Hormonal implants
If you choose to have hormonal implants you do not have to think about contraception for 5 years, but they may be difficult to remove.

Female condom
The closed inner ring is positioned over the cervix. The open outer ring stays outside the vagina.

changed only every seven years. Many problems associated with IUDs are related to the way they are inserted, so the longer you can go without changing your IUD, the safer it will be.

Pelvic infection within three weeks to three months after insertion is common, but after that is unlikely in a woman who has only one partner. Infection should be treated with antibiotics, all of which pass through into your milk, though the only obvious effect on the baby may be that his or her stools become loose. In some way the thread is reassuring: occasionally an IUD is expelled or buries itself in the uterine lining and many women like to have some means of knowing whether or not their IUD is still there.

Rarely an IUD actually perforates the uterus, and this is more likely to happen if it is inserted within a short time after delivery when the uterine wall is thin and soft. An IUD with a rounded rather than a spiky edge is less apt to do this.

There is also an IUD which works by releasing 20 micrograms of levenorgestrel, the hormone used in the progestogen pill. It is an effective contraceptive and has fewer side effects than many other kinds of IUD that are commonly available.

ORAL CONTRACEPTIVES

Though the pill is the most reliable method of contraception so far invented, there are certain conditions, some of which are not evident until pregnancy, that indicate that you should not choose the pill as your postnatal contraceptive. If you have high blood pressure which continues after the birth or if it has been discovered during pregnancy that you have diabetes, you should *probably* not go on the pill. If you are suffering from severe postnatal depression, it may also be wiser to avoid taking the pill. If you developed varicose veins during your pregnancy, you should watch for any pain that appears in your legs which could be a sign of a blood clot. If you have had a blood clot in a vein (thrombo-phlebitis), you should *not* take the pill. Progestogen changes the bacterial flora of the vagina and some women develop thrush (yeast infection) for the first time when they are taking the minipill (see below). If you have already had thrush this may not be the contraceptive you should choose.

"I went on to the progestogen-only pill and it certainly did affect my milk supply at first, but I fed whenever the baby wanted to and it soon adjusted."

The pill also needs reassessment as you get older. If you are over 35 the risk of cardiovascular disorder is increased. If you smoke you should not take the pill, as you are running grave risks.

The combined estrogen-progestogen pill This is almost 100 percent effective in preventing pregnancy, but is definitely *out* if you are breastfeeding. It affects your metabolism and therefore indirectly the baby's. It may alter both the quantity and the quality of milk, and there may possibly be long-term effects on the child.

The progestogen-only pill Many women who breastfeed are prescribed the progestogen-only pill, the "minipill." Since it contains no estrogen, it probably does not prevent ovulation but works by thickening the cervical mucus, making it difficult for sperm to travel beyond the cervix, and by preventing the normal cyclical changes in the endometrium (the lining of the uterus) which allow a fertilized egg to implant. It is a less effective contraceptive than the combined pill, but has fewer side effects. There is a 1 to 4 percent failure rate. It has to be taken at about the same time every day without a break in order to be effective.

Many women say that though their milk supply was diminished for a few days after they started taking the minipill, feeding on demand, more or less continuously, for a day or two brought the supply back up to normal. On the other hand, we do not really know what effects these powerful synthetic hormones may have on the baby.

The morning-after pill (emergency contraception) A series of high-strength contraceptive pills is taken within three days of unprotected intercourse. Two pills should be taken as soon as possible after intercourse, and another two twelve hours later. This morning-after pill is useful in an emergency but, because of the strength of the hormones taken, it is not a wise form of contraception and often makes a woman feel nauseated. The contraceptive used is available by prescription. A women's health clinic or your doctor can help you with this emergency contraception.

THE CONTRACEPTIVE IMPLANT
Norplant consists of six rods, the size of paper matches, which are inserted under local anesthetic under the skin of an arm, and which release progestogen into the bloodstream for five years. As with its predecessor, Depo-Provera, approximately half of all women using this contraceptive method stop ovulating. The other half ovulate, but the hormone makes the cervix and uterus a hostile environment for sperm and discourages the implantation of a fertilized ovum. Up to 80 percent of users have longer periods, irregular bleeding, or no periods at all. The rods can be surgically removed, but sometimes there are problems with this because they have not been inserted correctly or a woman may be left with scar tissue afterward. After successful removal fertility returns in just two or three days. The failure rate is a tiny 0.04 percent.

Gaining confidence as parents

Many women in our society have no experience of babies and some have never held a newborn baby in their arms before. They are anxious that they will not know when the baby is hungry, that they will drop or drown her in the bath, that they will never be able to stop her from crying or that the baby who is not crying has stopped

breathing. New mothers are often too ashamed to talk about such feelings and may even repress recognition of them. Talk with other mothers and you will find that you are not alone with anxieties such as these. Talk about good feelings, too – when the baby falls asleep and lies in your arms in perfect contentment, the soft, downy head resting against your skin, when he opens his eyes wide and gazes at you with excited attention, or when you watch and feel him contentedly sucking at your breast.

You are not just a caretaker of the baby but a partner in a unique and evolving relationship. You learn more about each other every day, synchronizing with each other as dancers do. You respond to facial expression, eye movement, muscle tension – even breathing – quite spontaneously. When you act on these impulses *you are invariably doing the right thing*. When you are self-conscious you miss steps in the dance and confidence drains away.

The developing relationship between a mother and her baby is a process that needs time to unfold and blossom, patterned, just as a hyacinth bulb or a crocus is patterned, by the laws of its own inner energy. Yet this is only part of the dance. The baby's father has his own special kind of interaction with his child, as well as with you. When a man is fully involved with his baby, enjoying her, responding to her needs, and getting to know her as intimately as you do, the pattern becomes even more intricate and exciting.

SHARING IN PARENTHOOD

Parenthood is a shared task. In the past fathers missed out on the baby's early months and were supposed to be interested in their children only when they started to play games and talk. But babies have astonishingly strong personalities and are different from each other even in the early weeks. It is worth getting to know the person who is your child from the outset. The man who turns his back on this opportunity to establish a relationship with the newborn baby may be denying a whole aspect of himself.

Being a parent is not just an endless series of repetitive tasks or a heavy responsibility, though all parents see it like that at times. It is a journey of discovery – discovery of the baby's personality, of who you are, who your partner is, and who you are *becoming* together.

Opposite
You need time to fall
in love with your
baby, being together in a
relaxed, peaceful atmosphere.

Useful reading

Arms, S.
Immaculate Deception II: A Fresh Look at Childbirth.
Berkeley: Celestial Arts. 1994.

Balaskas, J.
Active Birth., rev. ed.
Boston: Harvard Common Press. 1992.

Baldwin, R.
Special Delivery: The Complete Guide to Informed Birth.
Berkeley: Celestial Arts. 1986.

Cohen, N. W., and L. J. Estner.
Silent Knife: Cesarean Prevention and Vaginal Birth After Cesarean.
South Hadley, Mass.:
Bergin and Garvey. 1983.

Davis, E.
Heart and Hands: A Midwife's Guide to Pregnancy and Birth, 2nd ed.
Berkeley: Celestial Arts. 1987.

De Crespigny, L., and R. Dredge.
Which Tests for Your Unborn Baby?
New York: Oxford University Press. 1991.

Flamm, B.
Birth After Cesarean: The Medical Facts.
New York: Fireside. 1992.

Harper, B.
Gentle Birth Choices.
Rochester, Vt.: Inner Traditions International. 1994.

Johnson, J., and M. Odent.
We Are All Water Babies.
Berkeley: Celestial Arts. 1995.

Kitzinger, S.
Birth Over Thirty-Five.
New York: Penguin. 1985.

Kitzinger, S.
Woman's Experience of Sex.
New York: Penguin. 1985.

Kitzinger, S.
The Experience of Breastfeeding.
New York: Penguin. 1987.

Kitzinger, S.
Some Women's Experiences of Epidurals.
London: National Childbirth Trust. 1987.

Kitzinger, S.
Your Baby, Your Way: Making Pregnancy Decisions and Birth Plans.
New York: Pantheon. 1987.

Kitzinger, S.
Breastfeeding Your Baby.
New York: Knopf. 1989.

Kitzinger, S.
Giving Birth: How It Really Feels.
New York: Farrar, Straus & Giroux. 1989.

Kitzinger, S.
The Experience of Childbirth.
New York: Penguin. 1990.

Kitzinger, S.
Pregnancy Day by Day.
New York: Random House. 1990.

Kitzinger, S.
Home Birth.
New York: Dorling Kindersley Inc. 1991.

Kitzinger, S.
The Year After Childbirth.
New York: Scribner. 1994.

Kitzinger, S.
Ourselves As Mothers.
Reading, Mass.: Addison Wesley. 1995.

Kitzinger, S., and L. Nilsson.
Being Born.
New York: Dorling Kindersley Inc. 1989.

Kitzinger, S., and P. Simkin.
Episiotomy and the Second Stage of Labor, 2nd ed.
Seattle: Pennypress. 1986.

Klaus, M. H., and P. H. Klaus.
The Amazing Newborn.
Reading, Mass.: Addison Wesley. 1985.

Klaus, M. H., J. Kennel, and P. H. Klaus.
Bonding.
Reading, Mass.: Addison Wesley. 1985.

Klaus, M. H., J. Kennel, and P. H. Klaus.
Mothering the Mother: How a Doula Can Help You Have a Shorter, Easier, Healthier Birth.
Reading, Mass.: Addison Wesley. 1985.

Korte, D., and R. Scaer.
A Good Birth: A Safe Birth, rev. ed.
Boston: Harvard Common Press. 1992.

Lubic, R.W., and G. R. Hawes.
Childbearing: A Book of Alternatives.
New York: Maternity Center Association. 1987.

Maxwell-Hudson, Clare.
Aromatherapy Massage.
New York: Dorling Kindersley Inc. 1994.

Moen L., and J Laik.
Around the Circle Gently.
Berkeley: Celestial Arts. 1995.

Odent, M.
Birth Reborn, rev. ed.
Modford, N.J.: Birth Works. 1994.

Olkin, S. K.
Positive Pregnancy Fitness: A Guide to a More Comfortable Pregnancy and Easier Birth Through Exercise and Relaxation.
New York: Avery Publishing. 1987.

Panuthos, C.
Transformation Through Birth: A Woman's Guide.
South Hadley, Mass.:
Bergin and Garvey. 1987.

Rothman, B. K.
In Labor: Women and Power in the Birthplace.
New York: Norton. 1991.

Simkin, P.
The Birth Partner.
Boston: Harvard Common Press. 1989.

Simkin, P., J. Whalley, and A. Keppler.
Pregnancy, Childbirth and the Newborn.
Deephaven, Minn.:
Meadowbrook. 1991.

Useful addresses

**American Academy of
Husband-Coached Childbirth
(AAHCC)
(Bradley Method)**
P.O. Box 5224
Sherman Oaks, CA 91413
(800) 4ABIRTH or (818) 788-6662

**American College of Nurse
Midwives (ACNM)**
818 Connecticut Ave., N.W.
Suite 900
Washington, D.C. 20006
(202) 728-9860; fax (202) 728-9897

**American College of Obstetricans
and Gynecologists (ACOG)**
409 12th Street, S.W.
Washington, D.C. 20004-2188
(202) 638-5577

**American Foundation for
Maternal/Child Health**
439 East 51st Street
New York, NY 10022
(212) 759-5510

**American Society for
Psychoprophylaxis in
Obstetrics (ASPO)**
1200 19th Street, N.W.
Suite 300
Washington, D.C. 20036-2422
(800) 368-4494 or (202) 857-1128

**Bach flower remedies:
information available from**
Judy Howard or John Ramsell
Mount Vernon
Sotwell
Nr. Wallingford
Oxon
(01491) 834-678

**Be Healthy Inc.
Positive Pregnancy
and Parenting Fitness**
R.R. #1, Box 172
Waitsfield VT 05673
(800) 433-5523

Bereavement Services RTS
1910 South Ave.
LaCrosse, WI 54601
(800) 362-9567 ext. 4747
or (608) 791-4747

Birth & Life Bookstore
Cascade Health Care Products
141 Commercial Street N.E.
Salem, OR 97301
(503) 371-4445

**The Compassionate
Friends (for perinatal
bereavement)**
P.O. Box 3696
Oak Brook, IL 60522-3696
(312) 990-0010

**Depression After
Delivery (DAD)**
P.O. Box 1282
Morrisville, PA 19067
(215) 295-3994

**Doulas of North America
(DONA)**
1100 23rd Ave. E.
Seattle, WA 98112
(206) 324-5440

**Global Maternal/Child Health
Association, Inc.**
P.O. Box 1400
Wilsonville, OR 97070
(503) 682-3600

Informed Home Birth
P.O. Box 3675
Ann Arbor,
MI 48106
(313) 662-6857

**International Childbirth
Education Association
(ICEA)**
P.O. Box 20048
Minneapolis, MN 55420-0048
(612) 854-8660; (800) 624-4939
for book orders

**International Lactation
Consultant Associations**
200 N. Michigan Ave.
Suite 300
Chicago, IL 60601
(312) 541-1710

**National Association of
Childbearing Centers**
3123 Gottschall Road
Perkiomenville, PA 18074
(215) 234-8068

**National Organization of
Circumcision Information
Resource Centers**
731 Sir Francis Drake Boulevard
San Anselmo, CA 94960
(415) 454-5669

**National Organization of
Mothers of Twins Clubs, Inc.**
P.O. Box 23188
Alberquerque, NM 87192
(800) 234-2276 or (505) 275-0955

**National Women's
Health Network**
514 10th Street, N.W.
Suite 400
Washington, D.C. 20004
(202) 347-1140

Pregnancy and Infant Loss Center
1421 E. Wayzata Blvd.
Suite 30
Wayzata, MN 55391
(612) 473-9372

**Sudden Infant Death
Syndrome Alliance**
1314 Bedford Ave.
Suite 210
Baltimore, MD 21208
(800) 638-SIDS

**TTT Helpline
The Toxoplasmosis Trust**
61–71 Collier Street
London N1 9BE
(0171) 713-0599

Appendix 1

It is important to be aware of the laws concerning pregnancy and childbirth and the help available if you are unable to afford care.

Health and hospitalization insurance

By federal law it is mandatory for all employers with fifteen or more workers to provide equal benefits for male and female employees. This means that if you receive a health insurance benefit, it must cover pregnancy and birth in the same way as a medical condition. This does not mean that the employer is required to provide health insurance, but if provided it must not discriminate against a pregnant woman, whether married or not. Contact your insurance carrier for the precise details of your policy.

Most policies, however, do not cover the full cost of the obstetrician and may not cover any part of the cost of a midwife. In addition, you may be asked to pay a standby fee for an anesthesiologist and a fee for a pediatrician. Some insurance policies do not cover prenatal classes. The conditions of coverage for well baby care also vary with the policy. It is worthwhile for women to group together to put pressure on the company to cover these costs.

You should be aware that the majority of policies do not pay anything until after the baby is born. Therefore it is important to make financial arrangements with your birth attendant regarding a schedule of payment, so that if possible you can pay when it is most convenient for you.

Childcare leave

The federal Family and Medical Leave Act requires many employers to allow up to 12 weeks of unpaid maternity or paternity leave without loss of benefits or seniority. Many states may have even more generous laws.

Disability benefits

You may be entitled to these benefits, which are determined by company policy. For further information, contact your state Department of Labor.

Union benefits

You should contact your shop steward for information regarding union benefits since these vary widely.

Public assistance

As this book goes to press, the Welfare Reform Act of 1996 is poised to restructure the nation's public assistance programs in many ways. Contact your local Bureau of Public Assistance or Department of Social Services for information about any benefits for which you may be eligible.

Medicaid

If you cannot afford prenatal care, contact your local Bureau of Medical Assistance or the Department of Social Services office at your local hospital or clinic. If your medical bills are excessive, you may qualify for Medicaid even though your income is otherwise adequate.

Free clinics

Contact your state or local Board of Health and local Women's Health Center for information about free or low-cost clinics.

Women, Infants, and Children's Supplementary Food Program (WIC)

This program supplies supplementary foods to women, infants, and children at nutritional risk. Each state determines the standards for nutritional risk but two of the common criteria are inadequate weight gain and anemia. Women should apply through the appropriate state agency; in most instances this is either the Department of Health or the Department of Social Services. The income regulations are standard throughout the 48 contiguous states. In 1996 a family of four may gross $28,860 a year and still be eligible.

Prohibition against discrimination

Keep in mind that the federal Pregnancy Discrimination Act prohibits an employer with fifteen or more workers from discriminating against an employee because of pregnancy.

Appendix 2

These research references relate to the asterisks in the text. Where there is more than one asterisk on a page, the references appear in order. A bold dot indicates where a new reference begins.

p.22 Quoted by Pamela Nowicka, Independent, November 23, 1987.

p.24 *Pregnancy and Childbirth*, Cochrane Database, Cochrane Institute, Oxford, *available from* BMJ Publishing Group, P.O. Box 295, London WC1H 9TE.

p.36 R. Melzack, E. Bélanger, and R. Lacroix, "Labor pain: effect of maternal position on front and back pain," *Journal of Pain Symptom Management*, 6, 8, 476–480, 1991.
S-Z. Chen, K. Aisaka, H. Mori, et al., "Effects of sitting position on uterine activity during labor," *Obstetrics and Gynecology*, 69, 1, 67–73, 1987.
• *Pregnancy and Childbirth*, Cochrane Database, op. cit.

p.37 U. Waldenström and K. Gottvall, "A randomized trial of birthing stool or conventional semirecumbent position for second-stage labor," *Birth*, 18, 1, 5–10, 1991.

p.43 M. Enkin and I. Chalmers (eds.), *Effectiveness and Satisfaction in Antenatal Care*, Spastics International Medical Publications, London, 1982.
Ann Oakley, *The Captured Womb*, Blackwell, Oxford, 1984.

p.45 "Routine iron supplements in pregnancy are unnecessary," *Drug and Therapeutics Bulletin*, 32, 4, 30–31, 1994.
• Jon F. R. Barrett et al., "Absorption of non-hem iron from food during normal pregnancy," *British Medical Journal*, 309, 79–81, 1994.

p.47 Sheila Kitzinger, *The New Good Birth Guide*, Penguin, London, 1983.
• Sheila Kitzinger, *Homebirth and Other Alternatives to the Hospital*, Dorling Kindersley, New York, 1991. Sheila Kitzinger, *Some Women's Experience of Induced Labour*, National Childbirth Trust, London, 1978.

p.52 J. G. Thornton and R. J. Lilford, "Active management of labour: current knowledge and research issues," *British Medical Journal*, 309, 366–369, 1994.

p.74 Marion H. Hall et al., "Is routine antenatal care worthwhile?," *Lancet*, 2, 78–80, 1980.

p.75 A. Saari-Kemppainen, O. Karjalainen, P. Ylöstalo, et al., "Ultrasound screening and perinatal mortality: controlled trial of systematic one-stage screening in pregnancy: the Helsinki ultrasound trial," *Lancet*, 336, 8712, 387–391, 1990. J. P. Newnham, S. F. Evans, C. A. Michael, et al., "Effects of frequent ultrasound during pregnancy: a randomized controlled trial," *Lancet*, 342, 8876, 887–891, 1993.

p.88 *Pregnancy and Childbirth*, Cochrane Database, op. cit.

p.93 Sir Dugald Baird, *Journal of Biosocial Science*, 1, 113, 1974.
• R. W. Smithells et al., "Maternal nutrition in early pregnancy," *British Journal of Nutrition*, 38, 3, 497–506, 1977. *Nutrition and Fetal Development* (ed. M. Winick), John Wiley & Sons, 1974. H. A. Kaminetzky and H. Baker, "Micronutrients in pregnancy," *Clinical Obstetrics and Gynecology*, 20, 2, 363–380, 1977. R. M. Pitkin, "Nutritional support in obstetrics and gynecology," *Clinical Obstetrics and Gynecology*, 19, 3, 489–513, 1976.
• P. J. Illingworth, R. T. Jung, P. W. Howie, and T. E. Isles, "Reduction in postprandial energy expenditure during pregnancy," *British Medical Journal*, 294, 1573–1576, 1987.

p.94 Gary K. Oakes and Ronald A. Chez, "Nutrition in pregnancy," *Contemporary Obstetrics and Gynecology*, 4, 147–150, 1974.
• M. D. G. Gillmer, "Obesity in pregnancy – physical and metabolic effects," in *Nutrition in Pregnancy: Proceedings of the Tenth Study Group of the Royal College of Obstetricians and Gynaecologists*, 213–230, RCOG, London, 1983.

p.95 Anni Somerville, *Field of Greens*, Bantam, New York, 1993.

p.97 The MRC Vitamin Study Group, "Prevention of neural tube defects: results of the Medical Research Council vitamin study," *Lancet*, 238, 131–137, 1991. Nicholas J. Wald and Carol Bower, "Folic acid and the prevention of neural tube defects," *British Medical Journal*, 310, 1019–1020, 1995.

p.98 A. Malhotri and R. S. Sawers, *British Medical Journal*, 293, 465–466, 1986.
• M. Puig-Abuli et al., "Zinc and uterine muscle contractivity," Paper given at European Congress of Perinatal Medicine, Dublin, 1984.

p.99 M. Robinson, "Salt in pregnancy," *Lancet*, 1, 178–181, 1958.
• B. S. Worthington, J. Vermeersch, and S. R. Williams, *Nutrition in Pregnancy and Lactation*, Mosby, 1977.
• Ibid.

p.100 Peter C. Rubin, "Prescribing in pregnancy: general principles," *British Medical Journal*, 293, 1415–1417, 1986. Martin J. Whittle and Kevin P. Hanretty, "Identifying abnormalities," *British Medical Journal*, 293, 1485–1486, 1986.
• Jonathan Scher and Carol Dix, *Pregnancy*, Penguin, London, 1983.

p.101 G. M. Stirrat, *Obstetrics*, Grant McIntyre Ltd., 1981.

p.102 *Federal Register*, 43, 114, U.S. Department of Health, Education and Welfare, 1978.

p.103 *Perinatal Problems* (eds. N. R. Butler and E. D. Alberman), Livingstone, 1969.
• M. B. Meyer, "How does maternal smoking affect birth weight and maternal weight gain?" *American Journal of Obstetrics and Gynecology*, 131, 888–893, 1978.

• F. D. Martinez et al., "The effect of paternal smoking on the birth weight of newborns whose mothers did not smoke," *American Journal of Public Health*, 84, 9, 1489–1491, 1994.

• J. Kline et al., "Smoking: a risk factor for spontaneous abortion," *New England Journal of Medicine*, 297, 793–795, 1977. R. L. Naeye, "Relationship of cigarette smoking to congenital anomalies and perinatal death," *American Journal of Pathology*, 90, 289–297, 1978. M. B. Meyer and J. A. Tonascia, "Maternal smoking, pregnancy complications and perinatal mortality," *American Journal of Obstetrics and Gynecology*, 128, 494–502, 1977.

p.105 I. J. Chasnoff et al., "Cocaine use in pregnancy," *New England Journal of Medicine*, 313, 666–669, 1985.

p.106 Cree et al., *British Medical Journal*, 4, 251, 1973.

p.107 Peter Parish, *Medicines: a Guide for Everybody*, Penguin, London, 1976.

p.108 *Federal Register*, 41, 115, 1976.
• J. Moore-Gillon, "Asthma in pregnancy," *British Journal of Obstetrics and Gynaecology*, 1018, 658–660, 1994.

p.110 Roger Hoag, "Perinatal psychology," *Birth and the Family Journal*, 113, 1974.
• Parish, op. cit.
• Studies of babies born in England and Wales between 1943 and 1965 revealed that the children of mothers who had had pelvic X-rays in pregnancy were almost twice as likely to develop leukemia before they were 10 years old as those whose mothers had had no X-rays. The greatest risk is in the earliest weeks, when the mother may not know she is pregnant. The risk of cancer was increased 15 times when X-rays were done in the first three months of pregnancy. *See* A. Stewart and G. W. Kneale, "Radiation dose effects in relation to obstetric X-rays and childhood cancers," *Lancet*, 1, 1495, 1970.

p.111 David W. Smith, Sterling K. Clarren, and Mary Ann Sedgwick Harvey, "Hyperthermia as a possible teratogenic agent," *Journal of Pediatrics*, 92, 6, 878–883, June 1978. Peter Miller, David W. Smith, and Thomas H. Shepard, "Maternal hyperthermia as a possible cause of anencephaly," *Lancet*, 1, 8063, 519–521, 1978.

p.115 *British Journal of Obstetrics and Gynaecology*, 91, 724–730, 1984.
• *Pregnancy and Childbirth*, Cochrane Database, op. cit.
• Ibid.

p.119 Sarah Key, *Body in Action*, Penguin, London, 1995. I am grateful to Sarah Key for the information and imagery about the spine included in this section.

p.127 Aidan MacFarlane, *The Psychology of Childbirth*, Fontana, London, 1977.

p.130 E. Noble, *Essential Exercises for the Childbearing Year*, 3rd ed., Houghton Mifflin, Boston, 1988.

p.132 *Pregnancy and Childbirth*, Cochrane Database, op. cit.

p.135 Ibid.

p.137 Fraser R. Watson, "Bleeding during the later half of pregnancy," in I. Chalmers, M. Enkin, and M. J. N. C. Keirse (eds.), *Effective Care in Pregnancy and Childbirth, Vol. 1*, Oxford University Press, Oxford, 594–611, 1989.

p.139 Baha M. Sibai et al., "Prevention of preeclampsia with low-dose aspirin in healthy, nulliparous pregnant women," *New England Journal of Medicine*, 329, 17, 1213–1218, 1993.

p.140 Christopher Redman, "Old-fashioned alertness is the key," *General Practitioner*, 1979.
• *Pregnancy and Childbirth*, Cochrane Database, op. cit.

p.143 Henci Goer, *Obstetric Myths versus Research Realities: A Guide to the Medical Literature*, Bergin and Garvey, Westport Connecticut, 1995, 157–178. R. J. Jarrett, "Gestational diabetes: a non-entity?," *British Medical Journal*, 306, 37–38, 1993.
• P. Steer, M. A. Alam, J. Wadsworth, et al., "Relation between maternal hemoglobin concentration and birth weight in different ethnic groups," *British Medical Journal*, 310, 489–491, 1995.
• Pregnant women often have "physiological" anemia. There is a greater volume of blood circulating in their bodies; hence the red blood cells are dilated. This is normal – they are not suffering from anemia. Unnecessary iron supplements may do more harm than good; excess iron makes the red blood cells too big to pass through some of the capillaries in the mother's and the baby's circulatory systems (macrocytosis). This deprives the baby of essential nutrients and can cause its growth to be retarded. *See* T. Lind, *British Journal of Obstetrics and Gynaecology*, 83, 760, 1976.

p.172 Sherry L. Jimenez, Linda C. Jones, and Ruth G. Jungman, "Prenatal classes for repeat parents," *MCN*, 4, 305–308, Sept./Oct, 1979.

p.173 Sheila Kitzinger and Lennart Nilsson, *Being Born*, Dorling Kindersley, New York, 1989.

p.176 Penny Simkin, "Just another day in a woman's life? Part I: Women's long-term preconceptions of their first birth experiences," *Birth*, 18, 4, 203–210, 1991. Penny Simkin, "Just another day in a woman's life? Part II: Nature and consistency of women's long-term memories of their first birth experiences," *Birth*, 19, 2, 64–81, 1992.

p.179 Grantly Dick-Read, *Childbirth Without Fear*, Pan, London, 1969.
• Erna Wright, *The New Childbirth*, Tandem, London, 1969.

p.180 Janet Balaskas, *Active Birth*, Harvard Common Press, Harvard and Boston, 1992

p.184 Marshall H. Klaus, John H. Kennel, and Phyllis H. Klaus, *Mothering the Mother – How a Doula Can Help You Have a Shorter, Easier and Healthier Birth*, Addison Wesley, New York, 1993.
• *Pregnancy and Childbirth*, Cochrane Database, op. cit.

p.200 Both poems quoted in Rosemary Palmeira (ed.), in *The Gold of Flesh: Poems of Birth and*

Motherhood, The Women's Press, London, 1990.

p.202 Sheila Kitzinger, *Ourselves As Mothers*, Addison Wesley, New York, 1995.

p.220 Christine Gosden, Kypros Nicolaides, and Vanessa Whitting, *Is My Baby All Right?: A Guide for Expectant Parents*, Oxford University Press, Oxford, 1994.

p.225 CMO's Update 4: A communication to all doctors from the Chief Medical Officer, Department of Health, London, November 1994.

p.227 *Pregnancy and Childbirth*, Cochrane Database, op. cit.

p.229 Medical Research Council Working Party on the evaluation of chorionic villus sampling, Medical Research Council European trial of chorionic villus sampling, *Lancet*, 3, 37, 1491–1499, 1991.
• G. Kolata, "Fetuses treated through umbilical cords," *The New York Times*, March 29, 1988.

p.234 F. Chenia, Ch. B., and C. A. Crowther, "Does advice to assume knee-chest position reduce the incidence of breech presentation at delivery? A randomized clinical trial," *Birth*, 14, 2, 75–78, June 1987.
• *Pregnancy and Childbirth*, Cochrane Database, op. cit.
• J. P. VanDorsten, B. S. Schifrin, and R. L. Wallace, "Randomized controlled trial of external cephalic version with tocolysis in late pregnancy," *American Journal of Obstetrics and Gynecology*, 141, 417, 1981.

p.236 *Pregnancy and Childbirth*, Cochrane Database, op. cit.

p.243 S. L. B. Duncan and S. Beckley, "Prelabour rupture of membranes – why hurry?," *British Journal of Obstetrics and Gynaecology*, 99, 543–545, 1992.
• J. Grant and M. J. N. C. Keirse, "Prelabour rupture of membranes at term," in I. Chalmers, M. Enkin, and M. J. N. C. Keirse (eds.), *Effective Care in Pregnancy and Childbirth*, Oxford University Press, Oxford, 1112–1117, 1989.

p.247 Professor Mendez-Bauer discovered that dilatation of the cervix and the efficiency of

contractions is much greater when a woman is standing up than when she is lying on her back. The uterus works nearly twice as well. [1]

Professor Caldeyro-Barcia found that contractions were just as frequent when a woman was standing as when she was lying on her back, but that the contractions were stronger when she stood. He concluded that for the uterus to work really effectively, the woman should be standing. [2, 3]

Eleven hospitals in seven Latin-American countries joined in a study of the effects of the mother's position in labor. At each hospital half the mothers were told to lie in bed during the first stage and the other half were encouraged to get up or sit or lie in bed as they liked. Some 95 percent of the women did not want to lie down. First-time mothers who stayed upright had shorter first stages than those who were lying down. The majority of the women were more comfortable when upright.

To find out whether an upright position could produce traumatic pressure on the baby's head the researchers looked at the incidence of caput and also at the effect on the baby's heart rate and discovered that, when the membranes had not ruptured, there was no increased rate of caput if the mother was standing, nor was there an increase in deceleration of the fetal heart as recorded by an electronic monitor. They concluded that in normal labor an upright position is fine for the baby, shortens labor, and reduces pain. [4]

Further research at the Queen Elizabeth Hospital, Birmingham, England, came up with the same results. [5]

See 1 Peter M. Dunn, "Obstetric delivery today," *Lancet*, 1, 7963, 790–793, 1976.
2 R. Caldeyro-Barcia et al., "Effects of position changes on the intensity and frequency of uterine contractions during labor," *American Journal of Obstetric Gynecology*, 80, 284, 1960.
3 Yuen Chou-liu, "Effects of an upright position during labor,"

American Journal of Nursing, December 1974.
4 R. L. Schwarcz et al., "Fetal heart rate patterns in labors with intact and with ruptured membranes," *Journal of Perinatal Medicine*, 1, 153, 1973.
5 A. M. Flynn, J. Kelly, G. Hollins, and P. F. Lynch, "Ambulation in labour," *British Medical Journal*, 11, 591–593, 26 August 1978.

p.252 *Pregnancy and Childbirth*, Cochrane Database, op. cit.

p.253 Ibid.

p.264 C. M. Andrews and E. C. Andrews, "Nursing, maternal postures, and foetal position," *Nursing Research*, 32, 336–341, 1983.

p.272 S. A. Huchcroft, M. P. Wearing, and C. W. Buck, "Late results of cesarean and vaginal deliveries in cases of breech presentation," *Canadian Medical Association Journal*, 125, 726, 1982.

p.274 J. G. B. Russell, "Moulding of the pelvic outlet," *Journal of Obstetrics and Gynaecology, British Commonwealth*, 76, 817, 1967.
• Michel Odent, *Birth Reborn*, Fontana, London, 1986.

p.275 Emanuel A. Friedman, *Labor: Clinical Evaluation and Management*, Meredith Publishing Co., 1967.

p.276 K. S. Olah and J. P. Neilson, "Failure to progress in the management of labour," *British Journal of Obstetrics and Gynaecology*, 101.1, 1–3, 1994.

p.277 Marshall H. Klaus, John H. Kennel, Steven S. Robertson, and Roberto Sosa, "Effects of social support during parturition and infant morbidity," *British Medical Journal*, 293, 585–587, 1986.

p.295 Ronald Melzack, *The Puzzle of Pain*, Penguin, London, 1973.

p.296 Melzack, op. cit.
• Ibid.
• Ibid.

p.300 Josephine A. Williamson, "Hypnosis in obstetrics," *Nursing Mirror*, November 27, 1975.

p.301 Sharon Yellard, "Using acupuncture in midwifery care," *Modern Midwife*, 5, 1, 8–11, 1995.
• Song Meiyu, "Acupuncture anaesthesia for caesarean section," *Midwives' Chronicle*, April 1985.
• I. F. Skelton, "Acupuncture

in labor," *Society of Bio-physical Medicine*, June 1985.

p.303 Peter Webb, *Homoeopathy for Midwives*, British Homoeopathic Association, London, 1992, 30–31.

p.304 Christine Brown, "Therapeutic effects of bathing during labor," *Journal of Nurse-Midwifery*, 27, 1, 1982.

p.305 F. Alderdice et al., "Labour and birth in water in England and Wales," *British Medical Journal*, 310, 837, 1995.
• Paul Johnson, "Birth under water: to breathe or not to breathe," *British Journal of Obstetrics and Gynaecology*, 103, 3, 202–208, 1995.

p.307 M. Rosen, "Patient controlled analgesia," *British Medical Journal*, 289, 640–641, 1984.

p.308 Bertil Jacobson et al., "Opiate addiction in adult offspring through possible imprinting after obstetric treatment," *British Medical Journal*, 301, 1067–1070, 1990.

p.309 Michael Rosen, "Pain and its relief," in T. Chard and M. Richards (eds.), *Benefits and Hazards of the New Obstetrics*, William Heinemann, 1977.

p.310 M. B. Wingate, "Effects of epidural analgesia on fetal and neonatal status," *American Journal of Obstetrics and Gynecology*, 119, 1101–1106, 1974. B. S. Schiffrin, "Fetal heart rate patterns following epidural anaesthesia and oxytocin infusion during labour," *Journal of Obstetrics and Gynaecology, British Commonwealth*, 79, 332, 1972.
• *Pregnancy and Childbirth*, Cochrane Database, op. cit.

p.311 Andrew Doughty, *Journal of Royal Society of Medicine*, December 1978.
• J. A. Thorp et al., "The effect of intrapartum epidural analgesia on nulliparous labor: a randomized controlled prospective trial," *American Journal of Obstetrics and Gynecology*, 169, 851–858, 1993.
• M. Maresh, K. H. Choong, and R. W. Beard, "Delayed pushing with lumbar epidural analgesia in labour," *British Journal of Obstetrics and Gynaecology*, 90, 623–627, 1983.

• C. MacArthur, M. Lewis, E. G. Knox, and J. S. Crawford, "Epidural anaesthesia and long-term backache after childbirth," *British Medical Journal*, 301, 9–12, 1990. C. MacArthur, M. Lewis, and E. G. Knox, *Health After Childbirth: An Investigation of Long-term Health Problems Beginning After Childbirth in 11701 Women*, HMSO, London, 1991.
• A. D. Noble et al., "Continuous lumbar epidural using bupivicaine," *Journal of Obstetrics and Gynaecology, British Commonwealth*, 78, 559, 1971.
• Kay Standley et al., "Local-regional anesthesia during childbirth: effect on newborn behaviors," *Science*, 186, November 15, 1974.

p.312 Barbara Morgan, *Journal of Obstetric Anaesthesia*, forthcoming.
• Sheila Kitzinger, *Some Women's Experiences of Epidurals*, National Childbirth Trust, London, 1987.

p.313 Michael Rosen, op. cit.

p.314 Josephine M. Green, Vanessa A. Coupland, and Jenny V. Kitzinger, "Expectations, experiences, and psychological outcomes of childbirth: a prospective study of 825 women," *Birth*, 17, 1, 15–23, 1990.

p.315 Kieran O'Driscoll and Declan Meagher, *Active Management of Labour*, 3rd ed., Mosby Yearbook, Times/Mirror, London, 1993.

p.316 *Pregnancy and Childbirth*, Cochrane Database, op. cit.

p.317 R. Caldeyro-Barcia et al., "Adverse perinatal effects of early amniotomy during labor," in L. Gluck (ed.), *Modern Perinatal Medicine*, 431–439, Yearbook Medical Publishers, Chicago, 1974.

p.318 A. Huch et. al., "Continuous transcutaneous monitoring of fetal oxygen tension during labour," *British Journal of Obstetrics and Gynaecology*, 84, Suppl. 1, 1977.
• G. C. Gunn et al., "Premature rupture of the fetal membranes," *American Journal of Obstetrics and Gynecology*, 106, 469–477, 1970.
• P. J. Steer et al., "The effect of membrane rupture on fetal heart in induced labour," *British*

Journal of Obstetrics and Gynaecology, 83, 454–459, June 1976.

p.320 *Pregnancy and Childbirth*, Cochrane Database, op. cit.

p.321 Ibid.

p.322 M. S. Klein, R. C. Gaultier, J. Robbins, et al., "Relation of episiotomy to perineal trauma and morbidity, sexual dysfunction, and pelvic floor relaxation," *American Journal of Obstetrics and Gynecology*, 1, 71, 3, 3, 591–598, 1994.
• Argentine Episiotomy Trial Collaborative Group, "Routine vs. selective episiotomy: a randomised controlled trial," *Lancet*, 342, 1, 517–518, 1993.
• R. F. Harrison et al., "Is routine episiotomy necessary?," *British Medical Journal*, 288, 1971–1975, 1984.
• J. Sleep et al., "West Berkshire perineal management trial," *British Medical Journal*, 289, 587–590, 1984.
• S. Kitzinger and R. Walters, *Some Women's Experiences of Episiotomy*, 2nd ed., National Childbirth Trust, London, 1993, *available from* Sheila Kitzinger, The Manor, Standlake, Nr. Witney, Oxon OX8 7RH, UK. S. Kitzinger and P. Simkin (eds.), *Episiotomy and the Second Stage of Labor*, ICEA, Minneapolis, 1984.

p.326 Linda Cardozo, "Is routine induction of labour at term ever justified?," *British Medical Journal*, 306, 840–841, 1993.
• "Caesarean Childbirth," Summary of a National Institute of Health statement, *British Medical Journal*, 1981.

p.327 A. W. Linston and A. J. Campbell, "Danger of oxytocin-induced labour to fetuses," *British Medical Journal*, 3, 606–607, 1974.

p.328 *Reducing the Risk*, Department of Health and Social Security, London, 1977.

p.329 Kieran O'Driscoll and Declan Meagher, op. cit.
• J. G. Thornton and R. J. Lilford, "Active management of labour: current knowledge and research issues," *British Medical Journal*, 309, 6951, 366–369, 1994.

p.330 D. A. Luthy, K. K. Shy, G. van Belle, et al., "A randomized trial of electronic fetal monitoring in preterm labor," *Obstetrics and Gynecology*, 69, 5, 687–695, 1987. D. MacDonald, A. Grant, M. Sheridan Pereira, et al., "The Dublin randomised controlled trial of intrapartum fetal heart rate monitoring," *American Journal of Obstetrics and Gynecology*, 152, 5, 524–539, 1985.
• K. J. Leveno, F. G. Cunningham, S. Nelson, et al., "A prospective comparison of selective and universal electronic fetal monitoring in 34,995 pregnancies," *New England Journal of Medicine*, 315, 10, 615–619, 1986.

p.331 A. D. Haverkamp, M. Orleans, S. Langendoerfer, et al., "A controlled trial of the differential effects of intrapartum fetal monitoring," *American Journal of Obstetrics and Gynecology*, 134, 4, 399–412, 1979. I. M. Kelso, R. J. Parson, G. F. Lawrence, et al., "An assessment of continuous fetal heart rate monitoring in labor: a randomised trial," *American Journal of Obstetrics and Gynecology*, 131, 5, 526–532, 1978.
• S. Neldam, M. Osler, P. K. Hanse, et al., "Intrapartum fetal heart rate monitoring in a combined low- and high-risk population: a controlled risk trial," *European Journal of Obstetrics, Gynaecology and Reproductive Biology*, 23, 1–11, 1986.

p.333 D. M. Okada and A. W. Chow, "Neonatal scalp abscess following intrapartum fetal monitoring," *American Journal of Obstetrics and Gynecology*, 127, 875, 1977.

p.334 G. S. Sykes et al., "Fetal distress and the condition of newborn infants," *British Medical Journal*, 287, 943–945, October 1983. P. W. Howe, "Fetal monitoring in labour," *British Medical Journal*, 292, 6518, 427–428, February 1986.

p.335 *Pregnancy and Childbirth*, Cochrane Database, op. cit.

p.337 Ibid.
• T. Henriksen et al., "Caesarean section in twin pregnancies in two Danish counties and different section rates," *Acta Obstetrica Gynaecologica Scandinavica*, 73, 123–128, 1994.
• B. E. Chalmers, J. A. McIntyre, and D. Meyer, *South African Medical Journal*, 82, 161–163, 1992.
• *Pregnancy and Childbirth*, Cochrane Database, op. cit.

p.338 Stuart Campbell, *Sharing*, Maternal Health Committee of Social Planning and Review Council of British Columbia, Summer 1979.

p.339 *Pregnancy and Childbirth*, Cochrane Database, op. cit.

p.345 Frederick Leboyer, *Birth Without Violence*, Fontana, 1977.

p.346 Hugo Lagercrantz and Theodore A. Slotkin, "The 'stress' of being born," *Scientific American*, 4, 86, 100–107, 1986.

p.353 Michel Odent, *Birth Reborn*, Fontana, London, 1986, and *Entering the World: The Demedicalization of Childbirth*, Penguin, London, 1985.
• Johnson's Baby Newsline, Autumn 1978.

p.358 Robert Hinde discovered that rhesus monkey babies separated from their mothers shortly after birth became very distressed and withdrawn. He suggested that separation from the mother might also be bad for a newborn human baby. [1]

Other research has indicated that mothers who had greater contact with their babies, and continued this contact through early childhood, produced children whose IQ, when tested at the age of five, was significantly higher than average. [2]

Those concerned about bonding between mother and baby at birth also advocate skin-to-skin contact between mother and child. It was suggested that the baby could become chilled, but a study of heat loss in warmed cots as compared with that in the mother's arms showed no significant difference between the temperature of babies lying in heated cribs and others left with their mothers. [3]

See 1 Robert Hinde, *Proceedings of the Royal Society*, 196, 29, 1977.
2 F. S. W. Brimblecombe, *Separation and Special Care Baby Units*, Heinemann, London, 1978.
3 C. N. Phillips, "Neonatal heat loss in heated cribs vs. mother's arms," *Journal of Obstetrical, Gynecological and Neonatal Nursing*, 6, 11–15, 1974.
• Marshall Klaus and John Kennel, *Maternal-Infant Bonding*, Mosby, 1977.

p.364 Marshall Klaus and John Kennel, op. cit.

p.366 L. Silverman, W. A. Silverman, and J. C. Sinclair, *Pediatrics*, 41, 1033, 1969.

p.368 E. Jones, "Breastfeeding in the premature infant," *Modern Midwife*, 4, 1, 22–26, 1994.

p.370 P. A. and J. P. Davies, *Lancet*, 2, 1216, 1970.

p.373 *Pregnancy and Childbirth*, Cochrane Database, op. cit.
• Kevin Forbes, "Management of first trimester spontaneous abortions," *British Medical Journal*, 310, 1426, 1995.

p.376 Cicely Williams and Derrick B. Jelliffe, *Mother and Child Health*, Oxford University Press, Oxford, 1972.

p.378 Harriet Sarnoff Schiff, *The Bereaved Parent*, G. K. Hall, 1977.

p.384 H. Varendi et al., "Does the newborn baby find the nipple by smell?," *Lancet*, 344, 8, 989–990, 1994.

p.390 F. Cockburn et al., "Effect of diet on the fatty acid composition of the major phospholipids of the infant cerebral cortex," *Archives of Disease in Childhood*, 72, 198–203, 1995.

p.392 Rudolph Schaffer, *Mothering*, Fontana, London, 1977.

p.404 If a woman has never had rubella, the obstetrician may advise her to have a vaccination after delivery. This vaccine could affect a baby conceived within the next three months. Therefore it is vital that she not conceive during this time. Women who are unsure about what kind of contraceptive to use may be offered an injection of a long-acting contraceptive called Depo Provera. Women who intend to breastfeed may be reluctant to have this injection, as it introduces hormones into the bloodstream.

Glossary

Abdomen The part of the body containing the intestines, stomach, bowels, and uterus.

Abortion (Miscarriage) Either spontaneous or induced delivery of the fetus before the 28th week of development.

Abruption placentae (Accidental hemorrhage) The peeling away of part of the placenta from the wall of the uterus in late pregnancy, which may result in bleeding.

Accelerated labor The artificial augmentation of contractions, after the cervix has started to dilate, by the injection of oxytocin through an intravenous drip. Often used to speed up a long labor.

Active birth An approach to childbirth that entails practicing stretching positions and movements and being in "open" and upright positions in labor.

Active management of labor The constant monitoring and technical control of labor.

ALB See *Albumin.*

Albumin A protein present in all animal tissues. Albumin in the urine of a pregnant woman can be a sign of preeclampsia.

Alphafetoprotein (AFP) A substance produced by the embryonic yolk sac, and later by the fetal liver, which enters the mother's bloodstream during pregnancy.

Alveoli Milk glands in the breasts, which produce a flow of milk when they are stimulated by prolactin and the baby's sucking.

Amenorrhea The absence of menstrual periods.

Amino acids The main organic chemical constituents of proteins found in all foods produced from animals, but only in limited and varying combinations in vegetables.

Ammonium chloride See *Diuretics.*

Amnesia Loss of memory, usually short term, which can be a side effect of certain drugs, especially Valium.

Amniocentesis The surgical extraction of a small amount of amniotic fluid through the pregnant woman's abdomen. Usually carried out as a test for fetal defects or maturity.

Amnion The layer of membrane immediately enveloping the fetus and the amniotic fluid inside the uterus; it is also referred to as the amniotic sac, or bag of waters.

Amniotic fluid The fluid surrounding the fetus in the uterus.

Amniotic sac See *Amnion.*

Amniotomy The surgical rupture of the amniotic sac, often done to speed up labor. Referred to as ARM (artificial rupture of the membranes).

Amytal See *Barbiturates.*

Analgesics Painkilling agents not inducing unconsciousness.

Anemia A condition in which there is an abnormally low proportion of red corpuscles in the blood, treated by iron (Fe) supplements.

Anencephaly The congenital absence of the brain.

Anesthetic Medication that produces partial or complete insensibility to pain.

Anesthetic, general Anesthetic that affects the whole body, with loss of consciousness.

Anesthetic, local Anesthetic that affects a limited part of the body. See also *Caudal; Epidural; Paracervical block.*

Antepartum cardiotography Test to check fetal heartbeat.

Anterior position See *Occipito anterior.*

Antibacterials Chemical agents that limit the growth of, or destroy, bacteria. See also *Sulfonamides.*

Antibiotics Substances capable of destroying or limiting the growth of microorganisms, especially bacteria.

Antibodies Protein produced naturally by the body to combat any foreign bodies, germs, or bacteria.

Anticholinergic drugs Used in the treatment of nausea and vomiting, partly by limiting the impulses through the nervous system and partly by restricting the secretion of stomach acids.

Anticoagulants Drugs that prevent the blood from clotting.

Anticonvulsants Drugs that combat convulsions, especially epilepsy.

Antihistamines Tranquilizers used in the treatment of nausea, vomiting, and certain allergies.

Apgar scale A general test of the baby's wellbeing given immediately after birth to ascertain the heart rate and tone, respiration, blood circulation, and nerve responses.

Apnea Interrupted breathing that may occur in preterm and low-birthweight babies.

Areola The pigmented circle of skin surrounding the nipple.

Arrhythmic contractions Irregular contractions.

ARM See *Amniotomy.*

Aspirin (Salicylate) A mild analgesic.

Bag of waters See *Amnion.*

Barbiturates Powerful and highly addictive tranquilizers.

Bearing down The pushing movement made by the uterus in the second stage of labor.

Bile pigment See *Bilirubin.*

Bilirubin Broken-down red blood cells, normally converted to nontoxic substances by the liver. Some newborn babies have levels of bilirubin too high for their livers to cope with. See also *Jaundice, neonatal.*

Birth canal See *Vagina.*

Blastocyst An early stage of the developing egg when it has segmented into a group of cells.

Blighted ovum An abnormal development of the egg in which the cells do not develop in the usual way to form a baby. It results in miscarriage.

Bradycardia A slow heart rate in the fetus and newborn baby. This is a rate of less than 120 beats a minute.

Braxton Hicks contractions (Rehearsal) Contractions of the uterus that occur throughout pregnancy, but which may not be noticed until toward the end.

Breast pump Apparatus for drawing milk from the breasts.

Breech presentation The position of a baby who is bottom down rather than head down in the uterus.

Brow presentation The position of a baby who is head down in the uterus, but with chin up, so that the brow comes through the cervix first.

Candida See *Thrush.*

Caput A small, temporary swelling on the crown of the baby's head caused by the head being pressed against an incompletely dilated cervix.

Carpal tunnel syndrome Numbness and tingling of the hands arising from pressure on the nerves of the wrist. In pregnancy it is caused by the body's accumulation of fluids.

Catheter A thin plastic tube inserted into the body through a natural channel to draw off urine from the bladder, or into a vein to maintain a constant input of fluids, or into the epidural space to introduce anesthetic.

Caudal (Caudal epidural block) An anesthetic injected into the base of the spine. See also *Epidural.*

Cephalhematoma A temporary swelling on the side of the baby's head caused by pressure during labor.

Cephalic presentation The position of a baby who is head down in the uterus. The most common presentation.

Cephalopelvic disproportion A state in which the head of the fetus is larger than the cavity of the mother's pelvis. Delivery must therefore be by cesarean section.

Certified Nurse Midwife A graduate of an approved program who has passed National Boards and is licensed to practice by her state.

Cervical dilatation See *Dilatation.*

Cervical erosion Superficial inflammation of the cervix.

Cervical incompetence A disorder of the cervix, usually arising after a previous mid-pregnancy termination or damage to the cervix during a previous labor, in which the cervix opens up too soon, resulting in repeated mid-pregnancy miscarriages. It is sometimes treated by suturing to hold the cervix closed.

Cervix The lower entrance to the uterus, or neck of the womb.

Cesarean section Delivery of the baby through a cut in the abdominal and uterine walls.

Chloasma Skin discoloration during pregnancy, often facial.

Chloral drugs Non-barbiturate hypnotic tranquilizers.

Chlorpromazine (Thorazine) A powerful sedative often used in conjunction with hypnotics, analgesics, and anesthetics.

Chorion The outer membranous tissue enveloping the developing fetus and placenta.

Chorionic gonadotrophin See *Human chorionic gonadotrophin (HCG).*

Chorionic villi The tiny fronds around the fertile ovum that enable it to become embedded in the uterine wall.

Chorionic villus sampling A method of screening for genetic handicap by analysis of tissue from the small protrusions on the outer membrane enveloping the embryo that later form the placenta.

Chromosomes Rodlike structures containing genes occurring in pairs within the nucleus of every cell. Human cells each contain 23 pairs. See also *Gene.*

Circumcision An operation to cut the foreskin from the penis.

Cleft palate A congenital abnormality of the roof of the mouth.

Clitoris Exquisitely sensitive small organ at the upper end of a woman's genitals, just under the pubic bone and between the folded external labia.

Club foot A congenital abnormality in which the foot is twisted out of shape.

Codeine An addictive painkilling agent derived from opium.

Colostrum A kind of milk, rich in proteins, formed and secreted by the breasts in late pregnancy and gradually changing to mature milk some days after delivery.

Conception The fertilization of the egg by the sperm and its implantation in the uterine wall.

Congenital abnormality An abnormality or deformity existing from birth, usually arising from a damaged gene, the adverse effect of certain drugs, or the effect of some diseases during pregnancy.

Contractions The regular tightening of the uterine muscles as they work to dilate the cervix in labor and press the baby down the birth canal.

Cordocentesis See *Umbilical vein sampling.*

Corpuscles Constituents of blood, divided into red and white varieties.

Corpus luteum A glandular mass that forms in the ovary after fertilization. It produces progesterone, which helps to form the placenta, and is active for the first 14 weeks of pregnancy.

Cortisone A steroid produced by the adrenal gland that appears in the amniotic fluid immediately before labor.

Crowning The moment when the baby's head appears in the vagina and does not slip back again.

CVS See *Chorionic villus sampling.*

Cystitis An inflammation of the bladder and urinary tract, producing a painful stinging sensation when urine is passed.

D and C The surgical dilatation (opening) of the cervix, and curettage (removal of the contents) of the uterus.

Dehydration An excessive loss of body water.

Demerol See *Analgesics.*

Depression, respiratory Breathing difficulties in the newborn baby.

Dextrose A solution of glucose used to supplement the level of blood sugar, usually introduced by intravenous drip.

Dextrostix A test to assess the level of sugar in the urine.

Diabetes Failure of the system to metabolize glucose, traced by excess sugar in the blood and urine.

Diastolic pressure The blood pressure between the heartbeats. See also *Systolic pressure.*

Diazepam (Valium) See *Tranquilizers.*

Dilatation The progressive opening of the cervix, caused by uterine contractions during labor.

Distocia, shoulder A state in which the baby's shoulders get stuck during delivery.

Distress See *Fetal distress.*

Diuretics Drugs that increase the amount of urine excreted.

Dizygotic See *Twins.*

Doppler A method of using ultrasound vibrations to listen to the fetal heart.

Down's syndrome A severe congenital abnormality producing subnormal mentality.

Drip See *Intravenous drip.*

Dura The outer membrane protecting the spinal cord.

Eclampsia The severe form of preeclampsia, which is characterized by extremely high blood pressure, headaches, visual distortion, flashes, convulsions, and, in the worst cases, coma and death. The condition is now rare since the symptoms of preeclampsia are treated immediately.

Ectopic pregnancy A pregnancy that develops outside the uterus, usually in the fallopian tube. The mother has severe pain low down at one side of the abdomen at any time from the 6th to 12th week of pregnancy. The pregnancy must be surgically terminated.

EDD The estimated date of delivery.

Edema Fluid retention, which causes the body tissues to be puffed out.

Elective induction Induction done for convenience rather than for medical reasons. See also *Induction.*

Electrode A small electrical conductor used obstetrically for monitoring the fetal heartbeat.

Electronic fetal monitoring The continuous monitoring of the fetal heart by a transducer placed on the mother's abdomen over the area of the fetal heart, or by an electrode inserted through the cervix and clipped to the baby's scalp.

Embryo The developing organism in pregnancy, from about the 10th day after fertilization until about the 12th week of pregnancy, when it is termed a fetus.

Endocrinological changes Changes in the secretion of the endocrine glands that occur in pregnancy or the four weeks after delivery (the puerperium).

Endometrium The inner lining of the uterus.

Enema The injection of fluids through the rectum to expel its contents.

Engaged (Eng/E) The baby is engaged when it has settled with its presenting part deep in the pelvic cavity. This often happens in the last month of pregnancy.

Engorgement The overcongestion of the breasts with milk. If long periods are left between feedings, painful engorgement can occur. This can be relieved by putting the baby to the breast or expressing the excess milk.

Epidural (Lumbar epidural block) Regional anesthesia, used during labor and for cesarean sections, in which an anesthetic is injected through a catheter into the epidural space in the lower spine.

Episiotomy A surgical cut in the perineum to enlarge the vagina.

Estriol A form of estrogen. Its level in the urine or blood may be tested in late pregnancy to find out if the placenta is working well.

Estrogen A hormone produced by the ovary.

External version (External cephalic version, or ECV) The manipulation by gentle pressure of the fetus into the cephalic position. This may be done by an obstetrician sometime between the 32nd and 34th weeks of pregnancy if the baby is breech.

Face presentation The position of a baby whose face is coming through the cervix first.

Fallopian tube (Oviduct) The tube into which a ripe egg is wafted after its expulsion from the ovary, along which it travels on its way to the uterus.

False labor Braxton Hicks (rehearsal) contractions, which are so strong and regular that they are mistaken for the contractions of the first stage of labor.

Fertilization The meeting of the sperm with the ovum to form a new life.

Fetal distress A shortage in the flow of oxygen to the fetus that can arise from numerous causes.

Fetus The developing child in the uterus, from the end of the embryonic stage, at about the 12th week of pregnancy, until birth.

FH Fetal heart

Fiber optics The transmission of light along flexible bundles of glass. Sometimes inserted into the uterus to give a view of the fetus inside.

Fluid retention See *Edema.*

FMF Fetal movement felt.

Folic acid A form of vitamin B essential for the production of blood cells and hemoglobin, shortage of which may produce handicaps in the fetus.

Fontanels The soft spots between the unjoined sections of the skull of the fetus.

Foremilk Milk that accumulates naturally in the ducts behind the nipple and precedes the main release of milk.

Fraternal twins See *Twins.*

Fundal palpation Feeling through the abdominal wall for the top of the uterus to assess its height.

Fundus The upper part of the uterus.

Gamma globulin A protein-based antibody.

Gene The part of every cell that stores genetic characteristics.

Genetic counseling Advice on the probability of recurrent hereditary abnormalities or diseases.

Gentle birth One term used for a method of delivery proposed by Frederick Leboyer in which the shock of birth upon the baby is minimized and the baby is welcomed by loving hands, skin contact, and soft lights and is able to discover itself in a warm bath.

German measles See *Rubella.*

Gestation The length of time between conception and delivery.

Glucose A natural sugar found in certain organic materials and in the blood: the main source of energy.

Glycogen The natural source of glucose; glycogen stores carbohydrate materials and is formed by the liver and muscles.

Gynecologist A doctor who specializes in female medicine.

Hb See *Hemoglobin.*

HCG See *Human chorionic gonadotrophin.*

Hegar's sign The softening of the lower part of the uterus that gradually occurs during the first six weeks of pregnancy.

Hemoglobin (Hb) A constituent of the red blood cells that contains iron (Fe) and stores oxygen.

Hemorrhage Excessive bleeding.

Hemorrhoids (Piles) Swelling of the veins around the rectum.

Hormone A chemical messenger in the blood that stimulates various organs to action.

Hormone accelerated labor See *Induction.*

Human chorionic gonadotrophin (HCG) A hormone released into the woman's bloodstream by the developing placenta from about six days after the last period was due. Its presence in the urine means that she is pregnant.

Hyaline membrane disease Respiratory distress affecting some preterm babies, resulting from a lack of surfactant that holds the lungs open.

Hydatidiform mole A rare abnormality in which the egg fails to develop after becoming implanted in the uterine wall, so there is no baby, although the placenta and chorionic villi go on developing. If the woman does not miscarry, the growth must be removed.

Hydrocephalus A congenital abnormality in which the baby's head is swollen with fluid.

Hyperemesis gravidarum Almost continuous vomiting during pregnancy.

Hypertension High blood pressure. In pregnancy this can reduce the fetal blood supply.

Hyperventilation Abnormally heavy breathing that flushes carbon dioxide out of the bloodstream, so that the normal chemical balance of the blood is lost.

Hypnosis A state of mental passivity with a special susceptibility to suggestion. This can be used as an anesthetic, and can be self-induced.

Hypnotics See *Tranquilizers.*

Hypoglycemia Low blood sugar is sometimes apparent in babies who have suffered a difficult delivery, preterm babies, or those of diabetic mothers. It can be artificially produced by giving the mother intravenous glucose in labor, since this increases the release of insulin, which breaks the sugar down. The baby may have to be given extra sugar.

Hypotension Low blood pressure.

Hypothermia A very low body temperature.

ICEA International Childbirth Education Association.

Identical twins See *Twins.*

Implantation The embedding of the fertilized ovum within the wall of the uterus.

Incoordinate uterine action See *Uterine action, incoordinate.*

Induction The process of artificially starting off labor and keeping it going.

Insulin A hormone produced by the pancreas that regulates the level of carbohydrates and amino acids in the system. It may be used as a means of controlling the effects of diabetes. See also *Diabetes.*

Internal monitoring See *Electronic fetal monitoring.*

Intramuscular injection An injection into a muscle.

Intravenous drip The infusion of fluids directly into the bloodstream by means of a fine catheter introduced into a vein.

Intravenous injection An injection into a vein.

Invasive techniques Any medical technique that intrudes into the body.

Involution of the uterus The process by which the uterus returns to its normal state after pregnancy.

Jaundice, neonatal A common complaint in newborn babies, caused by inability of the liver to break down successfully an excess of red blood cells. See also *Bilirubin.*

Ketosis The accumulation of lactic acid in various body tissues and fluids, often indicated by acetone in the urine.

Labia The folds (or lips) of skin at the mouth of the vagina.

Lanugo The fine soft body hair of the fetus.

Lateral position Transverse lie of horizontal positition of a fetus in the uterus (sometimes occurring if the mother has a large pelvis), where the presenting part is either a shoulder or the side of the head.

Laxatives Purgative drugs.

Leboyer approach See *Gentle birth.*

Let-down reflex See *Milk ejection reflex.*

Lie The position of the fetus in the uterus.

Ligament A fibrous tissue binding and connecting bones.

Lightening The engagement of the fetus in the pelvis, with its presenting part fitting securely in the pelvic inlet like an egg in an egg cup.

Linea nigra A line of dark skin that appears down the center of the abdomen over the rectus muscle in some women during pregnancy.

Lithotomy position The position for delivery, in which the mother lies flat on her back, with her legs wide apart and raised, fixed in stirrups.

Lochia Postnatal vaginal discharge.

Longitudinal lie The position of the fetus in the uterus in which the spines of the fetus and the mother are parallel.

Long l See *Longitudinal lie.*

Low-birthweight baby A baby who at birth is below the weight of $5\frac{1}{2}$ lb (2.5 kg).

Meconium The first contents of the bowel, present in the fetus before birth and passed during the first few days after birth. The presence of meconium in the fluid before delivery is usually taken as a sign of fetal distress.

Milk ejection reflex The flow of milk into the nipple.

Miscarriage See *Abortion.*

Molding The shaping of the bones of the baby's skull as it passes through the birth canal.

Mongolism See *Down's syndrome.*

Monilia See *Thrush.*

Monitoring See *Electronic fetal monitoring.*

Monozygotic See *Twins.*

Montgomery's tubercles Small bumps on the areola surrounding the nipple.

Morphine A narcotic opium derivative used as an analgesic.

Morula A stage in the growth of the fertilized egg when it has developed into 32 cells.

Mucus A sticky secretion.

Multigravida A woman in her second or subsequent pregnancy.

Multiple pregnancy The development of two or more babies. See also *Twins.*

Mutation A damaged genetic cell. This can occur naturally or, more commonly, as an effect of outside agents, such as radiation.

Narcotic A drug that induces a state of stupor.

Nasogastric tube A pliable catheter passed into the stomach through the nose.

Nembutal See *Barbiturates.*

Neural tube defects Abnormalities of the central nervous system. See also *Anencephaly; Hydrocephalus; Spina bifida.*

Nicotine A highly poisonous substance present in tobacco. During pregnancy it enters the bloodstream of a woman who smokes and affects the efficiency of the placenta, often resulting in a low-birthweight baby.

Notochord The cells that form the primitive nervous system.

Nucleus The central part or core of a cell, containing genetic information.

Occipito anterior The position of the baby in the uterus when the back of its head (the crown or occiput) is toward the mother's front (anterior).

Occipito posterior The position of the baby in the uterus when the back of its head (the crown or occiput) is toward the mother's back (posterior).

Os The mouth of the cervix.

Ovary One of the two female glands, set at the entrance of the fallopian tubes, which regularly produce eggs.

Oviduct See *Fallopian tube.*

Ovulation The production of the ripe egg by the ovary.

Oxygenate To saturate with oxygen.

Oxytocin A hormone secreted by the pituitary gland that stimulates uterine contractions and the milk glands in the breasts to produce milk.

Oxytocin challenge test A way of assessing the condition of the fetus and of the placenta, by which oxytocin is introduced into the mother's bloodstream and the reactions of the fetal heart to uterine contractions are recorded.

Palpation Feeling the parts of the baby through the mother's abdominal wall.

Paracervical block Regional anesthesia sometimes used during labor, involving a series of local anesthetic injections around the cervix.

Pelvic floor The muscular structure set within the pelvis that supports the bladder and the uterus.

Pelvis The bones forming a girdle about the hips.

Perinatal The period from the 28th week of gestation to one week following delivery.

Perineum The area surrounding the vagina and between the vagina and the rectum.

PET See *Preeclampsia.*

Phenobarbital See *Barbiturates.*

Phenothiazine Strong tranquilizers used in the treatment of nausea and vomiting. See also *Tranquilizers.*

Phototherapy Treatment by exposure to light, used in the treatment of jaundice.

Pitocin A synthetic form of oxytocin, used to induce or accelerate labor.

Pituitary gland A gland set just below the brain that, among other functions, secretes various hormones controlling the menstrual cycle. In late pregnancy it releases a hormone, oxytocin, into the bloodstream, which stimulates the milk glands.

Placenta The organ that develops on the inner wall of the uterus and supplies the fetus with all its life-supporting requirements and carries waste products to the mother's system.

Placental function tests Tests to assess the condition and efficiency of the placenta. See also *Estriol; Oxytocin challenge test.*

Placental insufficiency A condition in which the placenta provides inadequate life support for the fetus, resulting in a baby at special risk.

Placental previa A condition in which the placenta lies over the cervix. This part of the uterus stretches in the last few weeks of pregnancy, but the placenta cannot stretch, so it may separate; the result is antepartum hemorrhage. A woman with a complete placenta previa is delivered by cesarean section.

Polyhydramnios An excess of amniotic fluid in the uterus.

Posterior See *Occipito posterior.*

Postmaturity The state of the fetus in an overdue pregnancy. The skin may be dry and peeling, and the fingernails may need cutting immediately after birth.

Postnatal After the birth.

Postpartum After delivery.

PP See *Presenting part.*

Preeclampsia (Preeclamptic toxemia) An illness in which a woman has high blood pressure, edema, albumin in the urine, and often excessive weight gain. See also *Eclampsia.*

Premature See *Preterm.*

Prenatal Before delivery.

"Prepping" Procedures carried out to prepare the woman for delivery.

Presentation The position of the fetus in the uterus before and during labor.

Presenting part The part of the fetus that is lying directly over the cervix.

Preterm A baby born before the 37th week of pregnancy and weighing less than 5½ lb (2.5 kg).

Primigravida A woman having her first pregnancy.

Progesterone A hormone produced by the corpus luteum and then by the placenta.

Progestogen A synthetic variety of the hormone progesterone used in oral contraceptives.

Prostaglandins Natural substances that stimulate the onset of labor contractions. Prostaglandin gel may be used to soften the cervix and induce labor.

Psychoprophylaxis The Lamaze method of preparation for childbirth, which is centered on techniques of breathing.

Pubis The bones forming the front of the lower pelvis.

Pudendal block Injection to numb the nerves in the perineum.

Puerperium The four weeks following delivery.

Purse-string (Shirodkar) suture Stitches passed through and around the cervix, and then drawn tight to support the uterus when the cervix is "incompetent."

Pyelitis An infection of the kidneys. It is treated by a course of antibiotics.

Pyridoxine Vitamin B6.

Quickening The first noticeable movements of the fetus.

Rectus muscle The muscles running up the center of the abdomen.

REM Rapid eye movement in sleep, indicating mental activity.

Respiratory depression See *Depression, respiratory.*

Rhesus factor A distinguishing characteristic of the red blood corpuscles. All human beings have either Rhesus positive or Rhesus negative blood. If the mother is Rhesus negative and the fetus Rhesus positive, severe complications and Rhesus disease (the destruction of the red corpuscles by antibodies) may occur, unless prevented by anti-D gamma globulin.

Rooting The baby's instinctive searching for the breast.

Rubella (German measles) A mild virus that may cause congenital abnormalities in the fetus if it is contracted by a woman during the first 12 weeks of pregnancy.

Sacrum The big bone at the base of the spine, forming the back of the pelvis.

Salicylate See *Aspirin.*

Scan (Screen) A way of building up a picture of an object by bouncing high-frequency soundwaves off it. The sonar or ultrasound scan is used during pregnancy to show the development of the fetus in the uterus. See also *Transducer.*

Senna Derivatives of the cassia plant, components of many laxatives.

Shirodkar See *Purse-string suture.*

Shoulder distocia See *Distocia, shoulder.*

Show A vaginal discharge of bloodstained mucus occurring before labor, resulting from the onset of cervical dilatation. A sign that labor is starting.

Small-for-dates Babies who are born at the right time but for some reason have not flourished in the uterus. See also *Placental insufficiency.*

Sonogram See *Doppler.*

Sperm (Spermatozoon) The male reproductive cell that fertilizes the egg.

Spina bifida A congenital neural tube defect in which the fetal spinal cord forms incorrectly, outside the spinal column.

Spinal anesthesia An injection of local anesthetic into the spinal cord.

Spontaneous abortion See *Abortion.*

Stanislavsky technique Acting exercises that increase body awareness.

Stasis of milk A reduction in the flow of breast milk.

Steroids Drugs used in the treatment of skin disorders, asthma, hay fever, rheumatism, and arthritis. Because they alter the chemical balance of the metabolism they may cause fetal abnormalities if used extensively during pregnancy.

Stethoscope, fetal A trumpet-shaped instrument placed against the pregnant woman's abdomen for the fetal heart to be heard.

Stillbirth The delivery of a dead baby after the 28th week of pregnancy.

Stool bulk producers Drugs to treat constipation.

Streptomycin A broad-spectrum antibiotic that should not be taken in pregnancy.
See also *Antibiotics*.

Stress tests Tests during pregnancy that cause stress to the fetus.

Stretch marks See *Striae*.

Striae Silvery lines that sometimes appear on the skin after it has been stretched during pregnancy.

Sulfa drugs See *Sulfonamides*.

Sulfonamides Chemicals sometimes used to combat infections.
See also *Antibacterials*.

Supplementary feeding Additional bottles given to a breastfed baby.

Surfactant A creamy fluid that reduces the surface tension of the lungs so that they do not stick together when deflated. Preterm babies may have breathing difficulties if surfactant has not developed sufficiently.

Suture The stitching together of a tear or a surgical incision.

Syntocinon A synthetic form of oxytocin, which is used to induce or accelerate labor.

Systolic pressure The blood pressure built up in the arteries when the heart beats. The upper figure on any record.
See also *Diastolic pressure*.

Telemetry A method of monitoring, using radio waves.
See also *Electronic fetal monitoring*.

Teratogenic A general term for drugs that cause physical defects in the embryo.

Term The end of pregnancy: 40 weeks from the last menstrual period.

Termination An artificially induced abortion before the end of the 28th week of pregnancy.

Test weighing A method of assessing how much breast milk the baby is taking by weighing the baby immediately before and after a feeding.

Tetracycline A wide-spectrum antibiotic that should be avoided during pregnancy, as it can affect the development of the fetal teeth and bones.
See also *Antibiotics*.

Thrombosis A blood clot in the heart or blood vessels.

Thrush A yeast infection that can form in the mucous membranes of the mouth, genitals, or outer nipples.

Thyroid gland A gland in the throat that produces hormones to control the metabolic rate.

Tochodynamometer A pressure gauge attached by a belt to the mother's abdomen in order to record her contractions.

Touch relaxation A means of stimulating release of muscular tension by resting the hands on tense areas and gently drawing out the tension.

Toxemia See *Preeclampsia; Eclampsia*.

Toxoplasmosis, congenital Toxoplasmosis is a parasitic disease spread by cat feces. If it crosses the placenta during the first 12 weeks of pregnancy, it can cause blindness in the baby.

Tranquilizers Drugs used to calm a state of anxiety or tension without inducing unconsciousness. Mild tranquilizers, such as Valium, may be prescribed during pregnancy, but should be avoided during labor as they can cause fetal respiratory depression. Powerful tranquilizers (along with antihistamines and hypnotics, which are sometimes used for their tranquilizing properties) should be avoided during pregnancy.
See also *Barbiturates*.

Transducer An instrument that is sensitive to the echoes of very high-frequency soundwaves bounced off the developing fetus in the uterus, and that translates the information to build up an image on a television screen. This form of scan is known as ultrasound.
See also *Scan*.

Transition A phase between the first and second stages of labor when the cervix is dilating to between seven and ten centimeters.

Trial of labor A situation in which, although a cesarean section may be necessary, the mother labors in order to see if a natural delivery is possible.

Twins The simultaneous development of two babies in the uterus, either as a result of the production of two eggs that are fertilized independently by two sperm – dizygotic or fraternal twins – or, more rarely, as a result of one fertilized egg dividing to produce monozygotic or identical twins.

Ultrasound See *Scan; Transducer*.

Umbilical cord The cord connecting the fetus to the placenta.

Umbilical vein sampling (Cordocentesis) A fine needle is passed through the mother's abdomen into the fetal vein in the umbilical cord. The technique allows fetal blood to be tested, facilitates intra-urine blood transfusions, and enables drugs to be injected directly into the baby.

Undescended testicle A testicle that has failed to drop naturally from the lower abdomen into the scrotum.

Uterine action, incoordinate Irregular uterine contractions.

Uterine inertia Weak and ineffective uterine contractions.

Uterus (Womb) The hollow muscular organ in which the fertilized egg becomes embedded, where it develops into the embryo and then the fetus.

Vacuum extractor An instrument, used as an alternative to forceps, which adheres to the baby's scalp by suction and, with the help of the mother's bearing down efforts, can be used to suck the baby out of the vagina.

Vagina The canal between the uterus and the external genitals. It receives the penis during intercourse and is the passage through which the baby is delivered.

VE Vaginal examination.

Vernix A creamy substance that often covers the fetus in the uterus.

Vertex presentation (VX)
See *Cephalic presentation*.

Vulva The external part of the female reproductive organs, including the labia and clitoris.

Water birth Birth of the baby under water.

XX/XY chromosomes The chromosomes that genetically distinguish the female and male, respectively.

Yolk sac The sac that stores the nutrients for the developing fertile egg.

Index

Acknowledgments

Additional editorial assistance
Colette Connolly, Samantha Gray,
Sasha Heseltine, Annabel Morgan,
Joanna Warwick, Anna Youle

Additional design assistance
Stephen Croucher, Ellen Harris, Darren Hill,
Philip Ormerod, Karl Thurston-Brown

Additional illustrations
Vanessa Luff

DTP Operator
Jason Little

Assistant for additional photography
Pauline Naylor

Black-and-white prints
Debbie Sears

Index
Debbi Scholes

Picture research
Alison McKittrick, Damian Smith

Picture credits
CNRI: 220b; Antonia Deutsch: 407;
Sally Greenhill: 323t; National Medical Slide
Bank: 62bl; Science Photo Library, Andy
Walker, Midlands Fertility Service: 135br;
Debi Treloar: 135, 407cr.

Dorling Kindersley Limited would like to
thank all the parents and the parents-to-be who
allowed themselves and their children to be
photographed for this book. Marcia May would
especially like to thank those who so generously
agreed to share the experience of the birth of
their babies with her.

The publisher and photographer are also
deeply grateful to the nurses, doctors, and
midwives involved for their warm cooperation
and advice. Special thanks go to all the staff
of the maternity ward at King's College
Hospital, London. Thanks also to Blooming
Marvellous Ltd., who kindly supplied props
for studio photography.

Parents, children, and midwives
Abigail Akinola, Jane and Steve Bassett,
Amanda Browning, Stephanie Chocieszynska,
John Clarke, Rosaline Cole, Michelle
Davidson, Luke and Rufus Dye-Montefiore,
Jane Evans, Claire Farman, Jeronima Garcia,
Louise Gardner, Jayne Heaton-Harris,
Nathalie Hennequin, Sue Holt, Shoonagh
Hubble, Angela Hutcheson, Deborah Jones,
Carmel Lacy, Dave Lambert, Nicky Leap,
Rachel Lewis, Anne Magee, Stephanie
and George Marden, Pauline and Clifton
McDonald, Linda Miller, Lucinda Montefiore,
Julia Morrissy-Swan, Damilola Mercy
Oye-Akinola, Susan Ray, Becky Reed,
Alison Retout, Adrian Richardson, Simone
and Ricardo Roberts, Hugo Robins, Imogen
Poppy Robins, Lisa Scott, John Stewart,
Polly and Lucy Stewart, Julia Terrila and
Isaac Acheampong and their baby Una,
Max and Sophie Toocaram, Mr. and Mrs.
Trew, and Patsy Tummings.